CW01090796

"I don't speak Greek"
Dimitri Jordan

'I don't Speak Greek'
For the world to read free at:
http://ds.dial.pipex.com/town/way/px38/

Sacred Seal Publications ©

All rights reserved.

Published by Sacred Seal Publications.

Copyright exists 1999.

All rights reserved.
First print April 1999.

Sacred Seal Publications
United Kingdom.
© copyright 1999.
ISBN 0 9535673 0 3

Cyprus

The birthplace of Aphrodite
The Ancient Greek Goddess of Love
The third largest island in the Mediterranean.

Dedicated to the Spirit of Freedom.

Preface:

I am not a writer but you are holding my destiny, this book and the message it gives. I've been on a personal passage this last year or so, in search of a part of me that I always knew existed, but ignored for so long. My father's British, English to be more precise, his family originated from the West Country. I used to take some pride in that. Land of King Arthur, and no, he wasn't just a legend, the bear was real. He ruled a kingdom in a land that would see its share of invaders and I took some pride, in that, he held out for what and who he was. I was talking to a friend recently who's known about my book, and the direction it was taking. He told me he felt ashamed to be English, I told him not to be and I understood what he was feeling, as I remembered what it felt like to be English. I only remember though, he's just a memory now, the Englishman and England's woods and green meadows will never feel the same again. I tried to summon him up again recently, the Anglophile, I thought of pleasant nights on loved beaches, my days of riding horses through the English countryside and of churches and of one church in particular, but even that was Saxon, I couldn't find him. I tried, I really tried, I looked to Stonehenge and our ancients, but they got lost and so would I have been.

There was a time only recently I would have told you I was glad to be English but proud to be British and it's how I felt, then something happened. It had been slowly building up in me. Unknowingly pulling me through a love that I'd long forgotten, the Cypriot, Cyprus called. It felt like she'd been calling me for a long time, but last summer she called me in a different way, she called me with Love. I've told many people that I know how to love, and I do, so I returned that love I felt, and found myself in trauma. That's Cyprus at this moment, in trauma. I found myself writing a book the final direction of which, I had no idea of and could never comprehend until now. I thought I must have been writing about myself to show how the Cyprus problem had affected me. The more I wrote, the more I felt my life an epitome of Cyprus. Then I discovered the real reason why I was writing about myself, and my destiny I must now accept. I was given a book and it changed my life. It changed my life in some terrible ways. I am no one as a person, but my voice is this book and the voice you are going to hear is going to tell many Cypriots a terrible truth about their present crisis, at the same time as the world will hear. But at the same time as I found myself informing a nation, I found myself answering for a nation and responding in honesty for a nation, as I love that same nation, Cyprus. We watch conflicts on T.V. and we know they exist. They're beamed straight into our living rooms and homes via this media and the world watches and condemns those that are deemed to be responsible. But what about when a country's at war, only fighting with its heart and soul, a people psychologically tearing themselves apart, for what they know is right.

I've never quite known how to describe this book, either as an autobiography or a startling insight into recent Cypriot history and a revealing in-depth guide to the heart and soul of the Cyprus problem. Or and then, finally, but most importantly, a wakeup call for mankind and a prophecy fulfilled, I'll let you decide for yourself.

The late Sir Winston Churchill to the Legislative Council in Cyprus 1907:
"I think it is only natural that the Cypriot people who are of Greek descent should regard their incorporation with what may be called their mother country as an ideal to be earnestly, devoutly and fervently cherished. Such a feeling is an example of the patriotic devotion, which so nobly characterises the Greek nation."

Introduction;

More than once have I questioned myself on whether there was even any point to writing this book. But every time I asked the question something happens to give me the answer, the latest answer after giving it some consideration, came from my own brother. But funny enough it's a common one to hear, he told me of a Cypriot restaurant that he's found near where he lives. Both my brother and I have that Mediterranean look, and looks account for a lot, but it's simple conversations like this that tell me it is worth the work, and even the heartache;

Rest. Owner: "Hi, where you from?"
Brother: "Cyprus, and you?"
Rest. Owner: "Cyprus"
Brother: "Greek or Turkish"
Rest. Owner: "Does it matter?"

I don't know how strange it is to question your own existence. I imagine we must have all done it at one time or another, probably when we learnt about the birds and the bees, all the what ifs, like what if mum and dad hadn't got it together on that night or the car hadn't broke down on them. Or even the race between the hundreds of thousands of sperm that one might ponder on after learning of the birds and bees. Your existence proves you won that race, but what about our parents. Most of you will consider it quite natural and probably know the story of how your parents to be first met, at work maybe? At a disco or a night club or even a friends wedding, now that's always seemed a popular one, but what when even that first meeting seemed very improbable. I can't deny it mine always seemed a little unusual to me. I always thought it would be one of those things that might become clearer as I got older but it just seemed to get more confusing and the more visits to Cyprus I made, the more confusing it seemed to get. The snippets I heard as a child (and they never thought I'd remember).

My grandfather was a shepherd peasant, that was no secret although it's hard to imagine any landowner as being a peasant these days, but from what I can gather it was coastal land, not very good for cultivation and this was before the days of package holidays. The little snippets I heard that made the match seem even less probable and his actions just seem strange.

I had one or more uncles involved with EOKA (pronounced eye-yo-ka) who in the fifties were fighting a fierce campaign against the British, by whom one uncle was hung. From what I could gather it was after or during these events and possibly because of them that my grandfather was to send his family to England. Where to my reckoning he made his strangest decision, he allowed the marriage of my mother at the age of fifteen, to my father, an ex-British sguaddie the family had befriended in England, her birth certificate altered to allow the marriage by British law. Now that is a strange one and apparently it didn't go down too well with many family members and it was to be some time before he became fully accepted into the family. He was ten years older than my mother and taking nothing away from the man he has worked hard to bring seven of us up. I often felt they were (especially my mother) unprepared for such a venture for by the time my mother was twenty-one I was born the fourth of seven children. It's a mystery I grew up with and it just got more intriguing with time.

I can't say I had a wonderful childhood, far from it, I remember my early years too well, it felt like I had two lives in a way. My own family life in our hometown and my life in London with my relatives, often my godparents but just as often with my grandparents. All of which are Greek Cypriots from a village near Kyrenia on the North Cyprus coastline called Ayios Amvrosios or Ambrosias, although the correct way to say and spell it to the locals would be Amvrosios; food of the gods. I found it strange at first that my grandfather should have had such an impact on me, even more intriguing was my ignorance of it, mainly because he died when I was six. It was a big blow to me at the time and I remember the funeral, deaths not something you can really understand at such a young and tender age. Fair and well, granddad was eighty-six when he died but it was of unnatural causes all credit to the man, apparently he'd caught his jacket on the ancient gas stove that he and my grandmother shared in their small flat in Mountain house, SE11. The kitchen at the front of the ground floor terraced flat was directly opposite the bedroom where he went to rest after inadvertently turning the gas on. I asked the usual questions that one might ask at these times, the most natural one being why?

It made matters worse in that my mother's father was the only grandparent I ever really felt like I understood in any way, at any time. Even if there wasn't much to understand, my father's complete family had been an enigma to us all. We knew my father had been evacuated during WW11, during which time his mother had died and his father had remarried, which apparently didn't leave room for my father. After the war finished he returned only to be turned away from his home in Birmingham. When his father closed the door on him at the age of fifteen though my father would turn his back on his father and most of his family forever. It never added to the complications at the time, but the main impact it had on me was that whenever I thought of family beyond my own it would be to my mothers family I'd turn, the only family I've ever known. Which made it more curious as to why I should stop learning the Greek language at my grandfather's death, more curious was the fact that I forgot about it. The irony of it being, he was in my mind the only grandparent that understood English, it's how I remember him, my grandmother bless her soul understood none at all.

Chapter1

June nineteen eighty-seven, there I was sitting on the pub steps, I was twenty-five years old summer was just getting into gear, but I was in my hometown. I had work to start in September-October. I had £700-£800 and those few months free to spend it in. My mind was made up before I'd even finished my first and only pint. I collared a friend into giving me a lift to the train station and an hour and a half later I found myself wondering around London's Soho on a beautiful summer's day looking for travel bucket shops. It was my way of doing it, the hard way again. All I knew was I wanted a cheap and quick flight out of the country. I didn't have a clue where I was going to go. I'd just seen myself handing all my money over the bar at my local pub and that was enough to get me on that train. It wasn't long before I'd found a small office. Peter Pan travels, how appropriate, on the third floor of an old Soho building. I vaguely remember the office. Two desks at right angles both crammed with papers in untidy piles. Each desk had it's own little mess piled to the individuals liking. The wall was covered with world maps marked out with airline flight routes. I remembered noticing a man sitting patiently on a bench by the office, probably waiting for flight details, one man on the phone behind one desk, and another just filing through papers. The air was thick with cigarette smoke. I naturally chose the latter. I had time to light up a cigarette before the man looked up and loosely piled the papers.

"Can I help you?"

"Yes I'd like a flight any Mediterranean destination, one way, as soon as possible"

"As soon as possible?"

"Yes"

"Um, I think we may be able to do Majorca tomorrow, sound any good."

I nodded, it wasn't really what I had in mind but I did say any destination, the man picked up the phone to make his call. I felt committed, so I said nothing, and instead focused in on the other man already on the phone, he was obviously talking to a client I could hear him clearly.

"Got a flight departing Gatwick 9.30 for Athens," slight pause. "No good, ok bye"

"When's that flight for," I immediately directed at him.

"Tonight," he replied.

"How much?"

"Sixty five pounds"

"I'll take it."

"You sure, you'll have to be at Gatwick for seven-thirty?"

I glanced at my watch, 2.30pm I lived a hundred kilometres in the wrong direction, I didn't think too much about it, but I thought I could make it,
    "Better sort it out quick then," I told him.

I hadn't given it much thought and I may not have made it, but as I got off the train at my hometown, less than an hour and a half later. I could hear over the tanoy that the next London bound train due in five minutes would be fifteen minutes late, good old British rail I thought as I ran for a taxi. That gave me twenty minutes to get home, pack a bag and grab my cash from under the mattress and a quick kiss goodbye. There was little time for thought and I found myself getting my breath back as the train left the station, it was just after five, I settled back with no delays I knew I'd make it comfortably.

I never had time to get excited about everything, even though it was to be my first flight. It was one of the smallest charter planes I could imagine. I was sat at the back alongside some holidaymakers totally bemused by the speed at which everything had happened. I hadn't taken into account the fact that I was to be landing in a totally alien environment, in the middle of the night with nowhere to stay and that's exactly how I found myself at four a.m. the following morning. I hadn't even given it a thought until I was actually looking for somewhere to stay. I'd asked a taxi driver at the airport to take me to a city hotel, where I could stay the night. He obliged me, for his fare, helped me with my bag from the boot and was gone. I don't remember the area well, the hotel I remember less, it was well lit up for the night it was also closed "shit!" If I was slightly pissed off, it was with myself I should have asked more clearly, but surely the taxi driver could have guessed my needs. "Oh well" I remember saying it was the sort of time I didn't mind talking allowed to myself and it wasn't the first time I'd been caught out with nowhere to sleep, at least it wasn't going to get cold. I walked to the nearest junction to get an idea of where I was not that I thought anything would help. I never knew the place. I looked up at the street signs "shit again!" they weren't going to be no help at all, all in Greek text, some letters I could make out. I found myself trying to say out loud what the street sign said. I carried on walking and wondered how much of a regret my total ignorance of the language was going to be.

  Now before I describe what happened next I have to explain that with my grandmother being so religious and everything on my Greek side being so proper so to speak. It'd built up a little picture in my mind, as to how I'd perceived Greece and everything Greek, clean and proper in every way a higher and wiser order if you like. So I didn't look too closely at the products for sale at the mobile shop that I wondered across in the middle of the night, like a bright white beacon in the city dark. Someone I could talk to, hopefully, but a light at least. I walked up to the counter, dragging my bag by this time although it opened up to a backpack, I hadn't yet learnt how to adjust it properly so it hurt my shoulders. I stood there gazing at nothing really, just expecting the man behind the counter to come to my attention. I hadn't had time to wonder why he never asked if he could be of assistance, when I became aware that someone else had approached the counter and was standing close to my left. I looked at the floor first to see a pair of high heels and immediately my curiosity was aroused. I followed the stocking covered legs past the glitzy dress following the curves. I knew before I even got to the face that the person was looking at me and it wasn't until I got to the face that I realised under that thick line of mascara and the layers of compact was a man. More surprised than shocked my eyes immediately darted forwards. Now I wanted service just to get away, so for the first time I started to examine the counter to see what I might purchase, quickly glancing left to right before letting my eyes focus on the products in front of me. To my horror what I'd thought were bars of confectionery and packets of cigarettes, were marital aids of every description. Nothing had prepared me for this, it took me about five seconds to realise there wasn't anything I might want to purchase and I could feel the eyes of the transvestite looking at me curiously, too curious for my liking. I turned to my right raising my bag over my shoulder as I turned and walked. Thinking about it now Athens is a very large capital city, but I just had the idea that this sort of thing never happened here. It was getting light before I'd started walking for the port. I'd met an English couple during the night cuddled up on a bench who told me they were getting a ferry to the islands in the morning and as daylight approached, I could just make out the cranes of the port. I estimated they must have been three or four miles away in distance and knowing nothing of the city's public transport system, I made a few adjustments to my backpack then saw no harm in walking. After the sun had turned the sky its bright morning blue I estimated I'd walked about a quarter of the distance before I looked back at Athens. I stopped in my tracks. The Acropolis stood high on its hill, shining in the morning light, could I really leave Athens so soon. My love of all things ancient just wouldn't allow it, for the Acropolis had to be one of the major sightseeing attractions of our ancient world.

From that point, everything seemed to happen so quickly, before I knew it I was at Omonia square and I'd found a cheap hotel room on a busy road just off the square for seven pound a night. It felt like a new day leaning over the balcony, smoking a cigarette, the sight and sound of the traffic was manic, exhaust fumes filled the air along with the constant rumble, but I was happy. Seven pounds a night had got me a bed, my own shower and toilet, a small old wooden writing desk, chair and a balcony. It should have been time to collect my thoughts but I wasn't even tired I'd never done anything like this before and anyone whose done the same will know the feeling. Even a strange city is a whole new experience, a whole new adventure awaited and I'd suddenly found a new eagerness to explore this metropolis.

I was soon to discover Athens has a very good metro system, which would eventually save me from walking to the port, but on this day would take me the few short stops to the Acropolis. I didn't really find the Acropolis itself as awe inspiring as I first imagined, but the view was something else. In almost every direction were the ruins that most school children would learn of. Still intact the original stadium the forerunner of our modern Olympics, over the south wall a magnificent ancient theatre and to the north the church of St. George sat on its hill overlooking the city. It wasn't just the larger of the ruins I was impressed with, but the numerous number of smaller ruins one would see even from the metro, the train would stop at a station and they'd be ruins. But the most fascinating facet of Athens for myself at the time, was the flea market. Now there was a place that I liked, it had a feel to it, which reflected what was being sold. It seemed like you could buy a whole range of various antiquities. From ancient Greek coins to old trombones, some of the stalls and the shops would hold some real surprises.

As for the other facets of Athens, well I'm not the best of people to ask. I remember the postcard I sent to my mother. Although I could understand the preoccupation with the past I certainly didn't feel that modern Athens was any kind of reflection of its ancient glory and three days later I found myself on a night ferry to Heraklion in Crete. A place I would become familiar with over the next few years and I still hold a lot of affection for.

By the time I'd arrived on Crete I was very much enjoying the whole freedom trip. Backpack, passport and even just a little money are all that's needed, the independent spirit soon follows. There are lots of ways to keep your dignity and survive on a tight budget. I considered working through part of the trip to guarantee I could hold out, but after talking to a couple of people working their way, I decided they were simply surviving same as myself. Their only comfort being that they knew where their next meal was coming from, but the pay was so low and often conditions so bad, I felt a lot happier taking my chances.

On my first visit to Crete I can remember the excitement so well. I'd arrived in Heraklion on an overnight ferry arriving early in the morning at around seven. By nine-thirty I'd found a cheap hotel, which I liked, showered and was straight out to explore my new surroundings. With my towel wrapped around my waist, heading east on a 250cc trials bike, I didn't have a clue where I was going and I didn't care, I was young, free and on two wheels riding along the beautiful coast road west, it was a wonderful feeling.

The coast along this route seemed to be mainly high sandstone cliffs with lots of sandy bays. About thirty kilometres out from Heraklion I was to catch a glimpse of one such inlet, whilst crossing a short but high bridge. I stopped the bike and returned to the bridge. There was an idyllic looking beach some three to four hundred metres across with golden sand. I could see some rocks about a hundred metres out, protruding from the base of the cliff formation on the right, they looked perfect to dive from and most importantly, no people. I looked around for a way down and noticed on the other side of the road a foot track that made its way down the steep slope in a zig zag manner, down and under the bridge to the beach, perfect for the trials bike. It was a beautiful location and I'll always remember it how I found it, it was just as I'd hoped. From the beach itself you could see the high sandstone cliffs to the west, along its base could be made out other smaller sandy beaches, totally inaccessible by land. To the east the cliffs stuck out, so little of the coastline could be seen. I swam out to the rocks. The water depth was great for diving. I lazed away the whole afternoon swimming between the rocks and the beach and drying off in between and with the absence of people, it felt like a perfect moment.

It was on Crete that I was to hear something that I found a little amusing at first, it seemed a very minor incident but it would be one that would repeat itself from time to time. The short conversation with an old Cretan went something like.
    "You Greek!"
I nodded well I was of sorts. "Cyprus," I said.
    "Your from Cyprus?"
    "My mother is"
    "And she's Greek?"
    "Yeah but she left," I do remember I never got to finish that sentence off the first time, before he broke in with.
    "Your mother's Greek and you don't speak Greek!" by this time I could feel myself wanting to just turn and walk. His voice and its tone had turned more aggressive and I wasn't used to being spoken to by a 70-80year old man like this, I backed away a few steps before he repeated in his same harsh tone.
    "Your mothers Greek and you don't speak Greek!" regardless of the accent, in word perfect English to make me feel worse, but this time adding without a break in his voice,
    "Your grandfather would be ashamed of you!"
I never quite expected that one. "My grandfather would be ashamed of me," now my grandfather might have had a lot of thoughts on the matter, but I couldn't imagine him being ashamed of me, not my grandfather, I just couldn't imagine it. No one had told me he'd be ashamed of me for not speaking Greek. My very first thought seems quite an amusing one now, you never even knew my grandfather. It was a natural one to think but it hardly seemed worth throwing back at anyone of

course they never knew my grandfather, all I'd told them was that he was a Greek Cypriot and I was a long way off from Cyprus. So how could they know he'd be ashamed of me. It wasn't until many years later I was to realise the relevance of it all and its implications, writing this it all seems so clear, it's nice to know I was so innocent of the facts or just plain innocent. I soon found a response I felt comfortable with but with hindsight I'm not surprised now it shut them up very quickly.

"So where were you in 74?"

"Uh!"

"You heard where were you in 74! If Cyprus is so bloody Greek where were you when the Turks were taking half of our country, I was a child where were you!" and wow! I was not only amazed at the speed with which it'd shut them up, but the way they'd scuttle away after, triumph! Not really, but It just seemed so amusing the way it'd completely turn the moment around at the time. In all my visits to the Greek isles I must have encountered such comments on at least three occasions thrown at me with the same vigour. But more often I'd hear them commenting to each other on it. I'd always know it was my total ignorance of the language that would be the cause of their disgruntlement and they'd be shaking their heads. Once or twice I reverted completely to the Anglophile, that also worked, there's is without doubt a sense of British arrogance that's very useful for these occasions. But from an observers point of view the first response was far more amusing, but also too easy. It did leave a little seed of mistrust in my mind. Well none of them did actually know my grandfather even though he was Greek, it seemed a little like me telling them their grandson might be ashamed of them, it just didn't seem right. But the problem seemed solved so I just put it on record and gave it little more thought.

I left on this trip around the end of June, then the end of July would have seen me travelling around Egypt and well worth a mention in anyone's journals, but only briefly in this one.

I flew into Cyprus on a one way ticket from Cairo in the middle of August with £20 in my pocket and my godmothers address. I didn't know she was expecting me a month earlier, I didn't even realise I was expected. There was no great flood of emotion arriving in Cyprus. A very tight left bank over the Mediterranean but that and the pool of taxi drivers outside the airport are what I remember most and I was also very aware of the fact that I was arriving on my godmothers doorstep broke. The £20 sterling I'd arrived with hadn't converted well into Cypriot pounds and the taxi between Larnaca airport and Limassol was about to devour most of what I had, not that it was of much consideration as I found myself walking around a pretty residential suburb, lost.

"Hey, hey you, what you doing carrying that heavy bag around on your back for?" the voice was mocking, but I'd started to wonder that myself after thirty minutes roaming aimlessly, I was certainly lost.

"Hey come over here and take that bag of your back, you look like a gypsy," I heard jokingly through a vine-covered fence. I could make a handsome Cypriot man out, around his mid thirties sitting in the shade on the steps of his very lush looking, shaded veranda. He beckoned his younger wife to get me a glass of lemonade making a bet with himself that I'd be thirsty. He was right and the shade of those steps called nearly as much as the drink. The Cypriot man immediately moved aside making a gesture for me to sit and at the same time telling me,

"Put your bag down here, looks heavy?"

"It is," I confirmed.

"Been walking long?"

"Awhile"

"You must be hot?" he asked with a smile.

"And lost!"

I had that hot deflated feeling. The heat and humidity was killing me even after Egypt.

"And lost huh," he said showing his amusement. His tone was very comforting and before I could say anything he reeled in with,

"After you've had some tea with us we can look at a map!"

"But!"

"Don't be silly, we're just about to eat tea anyway and of course your welcome too join us."

It was all too pleasant to even attempt any kind of rejection. I felt comfortable enough in the shade with my lemonade as it was and to be fed as well. I remembered thinking how lucky I was to have wondered past this way into the arms of such hospitality. I was concerned about the time but it didn't seem to matter anymore, a nice little oasis, and they hadn't even asked me who I was. The main topic of conversation was about my experiences of Egypt and the Greek isles. It was a couple of hours before I rose to leave, feeling totally refreshed and it was at that point his wife went for the local area street map whilst I fumbled for the scrunched up piece of paper with my godmothers address on. I showed him and he immediately inquired.

"Who lives there?"

"My godmother, Marianna," I informed him.

"Marianna's your godmother?" he asked seeming familiar with her.

"Yeah!"

To which he burst into laughter and blurted something out in Greek to his wife mentioning my godmother's name. She walked onto the balcony smiling, whilst her husband pointed to a house on the adjacent row.

"There, your godmother lives there!" he announced with a big smile on his face. I immediately saw the funny side and with a big broad smile on my face I jerked my backpack up over my shoulder and still smiling I walked out of the garden before turning at the gate, where I waved and simply said a very warm "Thank you." There didn't seem any need to say anything else. The smile said it all. I Walked the short distance to my godmothers garden and opening the gate walked up to the porch to discover no one in. I didn't have to wait long, but I made good use of my time. I thought it cheeky enough turning up on my godmother broke and apparently as I was to find out a month late and now I was draped in full Arab dress, sitting by the door with my back turned to the gate when my godmother arrived home. I knew there would be no way she'd know who it was, but for some silly reason I did expect a guess which never came. My godmother carefully made her way up the garden path. I could make her out through the headscarf trying to peer round. She was far more nervous than I expected, so I immediately pushed the headscarf back over the top of my head as I turned to face her. I thought I looked pretty good with the black robe flowing around and I could see immediately the relief on her face and feel the big smile on mine.

"Marianna!"

I have to say my godmother feels like a second mother to me. Greek Cypriots take the role of godparent very seriously in general, self-included. And I immediately felt that comforting feeling that you can only really feel in the bosom of one's family. My worries were all to be swept away. I'd not actually planned to visit Cyprus at all, it was just close to Egypt from where I'd had a one way ticket bought me. But a phone call and a day later, I knew money to get me home was en-route and my flight tickets were in hand, time to relax?

It was to be a day or two later my ever thoughtful god brother Jim who was visiting his mother had a relaxing walk in mind. I felt silly about the idea of complaining, it had to be a couple of degrees cooler than Egypt but the humidity was crippling my legs. I estimated we must have walked a good five miles in all, it seemed to take about three to four hours, along the promenades and narrow beaches of Limassol's main strip. One amusing incident occurred before I insisted on getting a taxi. My cousin stopped to talk to a chap about my age for a few minutes, they chatted away in Greek. I'd step back a little at these times as I'd always feel a little embarrassed. They said their goodbyes and my cousin and I walked on for a minute or so more before Jim slapped his forehead and called out,
    "Blast!" whilst staring at me
    "What?"
    "That was one of our cousins I should have introduced you," I laughed. It

seemed about right.

Eight hours later I was alone in my older cousin Spyros's darkened flat wondering what had happened to the world. My head was throbbing with a heavy beating. A fever had built up and my joints were aching all over and blisters had started to form in my mouth. I spent the whole night in excruciating pain before finding a supply of distallgesics in the bathroom cabinet, which would mildly ease the pain. My godmother came straight over in the morning and immediately asked me if I wanted her to call a doctor. I said no, I was thinking of the expense and as bad as I felt, I'd never felt the effects before but I took a guess at heat stroke. It all made sense and I knew the best thing for that would be rest and that's what I did for three days before making a recovery and opening the curtains for the first time.

The rest of the stay was much more pleasant, some of my younger cousins were staying with my godmother and I enjoyed the little tours she put on for us up to Troodos and Kykkos. My cousin Jim gave me a guided tour of the Tombs of the kings at Paphos, with which I remember being in awe of. The name is only given to a small part of a very old cemetery. It was used continuously from the 3rd century B.C. for the next six hundred years. Which would have encompassed the period when the Romans were in control of Cyprus and this as well as our own Hellenistic history is reflected in the architecture of the tombs. It's a world Heritage site and well worth a visit.

One afternoon my godmother took me to Petra Tou Romiou, (Stone of the Greek) or Aphrodite's rock as it's most commonly known, as it's from here it's said that Aphrodite the ancient Greek goddess of love walked from the sea, a place that was to stay special in my heart. It's funny how some places have that effect. My younger cousin's had some snorkelling gear at hand, which made swimming around the rock easier, Aphrodite's rock itself lays some ten to fifteen metres out to sea and is around five to eight metres across and some ten metres high. There's a scattering of smaller rocks around and bracing the shoreline is the largest rock of the formation. A very large limestone tortoise shell shaped rock, that stands some twenty metres high and about thirty metres across. A large high rock, with a sheer drop to the sea. The beach is pebbly, large pebbles and a little shingle in places. It was a pleasant afternoon and I had to keep reassuring my godmother it was such a nice day. I spent the time swimming and playing with my younger cousin's. We had the usual packed lunch, after which my godmother told me of a legend that was to enchant me. It's said that if you swam around the rock three times under a full moon at midnight you'll live forever. One of those myths that would appeal to anyone's nature, more of a challenge than anything, but it was a place that I was already fond of, one night, I said to myself, and then to my godmother, "One night I'll be back."

Chapter 2

There have been so many countries and places I've longed to experience since those first glimpses in picture books or more commonly now the T.V. One of these places for myself was Siam as I'd first heard it called now Thailand. I get a warm feeling just thinking of my beach as I still so fondly refer to it. I first went to Thailand en-route to Australia and I've returned many times since and this time I thought I'd take advantage of the long flight, which could easily include a stopover at no extra charge.

It was the19th of October 1993. I flew into Istanbul with a friend for a two-night stop over en-route to Bangkok and I was looking forward to it. I didn't need to have a look in the city guide. I knew pretty much what I wanted to see, although I always hoped to see more and for myself I felt like I was coming to terms with a few things. Like the fact that people are people and I firmly believed that if you look for the good in someone you'll be rewarded and it was with this spirit I landed at Istanbul airport. At Immigration:

"Passport please!"

I handed the unshaven immigration man my passport. It was obvious they never kept a strict dress code here, he didn't even look like he'd washed, his hair was unkempt and he studied the photograph with a cigarette in his mouth, he took his cigarette and stubbed it firmly out in an ashtray as he looked up,

"Where you from?" I smiled. Surely he couldn't be that stupid.

"UK," I told him. He peered closely at me then looked at the passport again.

"Where you from?" he asked a little more sternly.

"UK" I replied slightly confused.

"Where you from?" he demanded again. Now hostility was creeping into his voice and that tone alone was enough to piss me off, but I couldn't believe the stupidity of it.

"Your the one with the passport in your hand, look, read what it says," I pointed to the writing next to the photo, then I just couldn't help myself.

"Try reading the front page," I was already a little confused, but now he was about to make it worse.

"Where your grandparents from?" he asked.

"You don't need to know that," I said feeling more confused.

"Where are your grandparents from?" this time he was snarling and starting to rise from his chair,

"What!" I said surprised at the tone and the whole line of questioning. I was stunned and stood totally speechless, I couldn't believe the question. I couldn't

believe the implications of what he was asking. It didn't matter what my ethnic background was. The horrors that were at that time engulfing Bosnia flashed across my mind. Then the immigration man rose a little further from his chair. This time his glare was more intense, he pinched the skin on his cheek. The snarl had gone from his voice replaced with a more menacing tone as he pinched it.
"Why?"
Now I knew what he wanted to know. I didn't know why it was so important, but I'd done nothing wrong and I certainly wasn't ashamed of who I was and more important, his attempt to put fear into me had just brought my arrogance to the surface. I straightened up, now he'd feel my arrogance in my voice. Proudly and sternly I declared,
"My grandfather comes from Ayios Amvrosios a small village east of Kyrenia!" He flipped. If I was stunned before it'd just got worse, he totally flipped. He was standing in my face straight away, his intense glare exploded into a rage and he angrily hurled abuse at me in Turkish. His face started to change colour. He was shouting so loud everyone around us stopped to stare. The abuse went on for a minute or so and I was totally stunned. Too stunned to respond in anyway. He was still cursing as he stamped my passport and threw it across the desk to me. There was no chance of managing a glare of my own, I slowly walked on, head down not looking back whilst waiting for my friend to clear immigration which he did in seconds, we walked on to the baggage carousel in silence at first.
"You all right?"
"Yeah, bastard!" I hissed sharply. I just didn't understand what I'd done wrong. Paul and I collected our packs off the carousel in silence and made our way to the main doors of the airport, he could sense I was still smarting. We walked threw the main entrance out onto the pavement and into the night air. I stopped by the road and dropped my bag. Paul stopped and I walked across the road to a low wall on the other side. The lights of Istanbul glowed crisply on the near horizon. I hesitated for a while thinking of the blue mosque and some of the other sights that lay there. I took a deep breath. I was still in a daze from my run in with the immigration man, not just in a daze but angry, upset, confused, the hatred in him. I just couldn't have imagined it. I turned and walked back to Paul.
"Paul I don't know what its going to be like there!" I nodded in the direction of the lights.
"All I do know is that I don't feel like lying about where I come from to anybody and I don't know what kind of reception we'll get there," I sighed adding.
"And I know that Bangkok is nine flying hours away and there's a plane leaves in two hours!" Paul nodded with little hesitation.
"Lets go!"
We walked back into the airport building and across the main hall to the Turkish airways desk and took care of the necessary changes to our tickets whilst they

took care of our bags. I checked my watch. Still over an hour and a half to go before take off. I suggested we walked to the coffee bar before going through to the departure lounge. Paul nodded and we turned and proceeded in the direction of the coffee bar, almost straight away to my left, I could see the immigration man who'd caused me so much grief. He'd been watching my actions and was now hurriedly pushing himself up from his chair and starting to head in our direction, he quickly caught up with us, I was still clutching my passport and boarding card in my hand.

"Papers!" he growled. This time his manner was even more intimidating if it could be. I scarcely had time to pass my papers before he snatched them from my hand. I was still confused and upset from his first outburst. It took him two seconds to scan the boarding card before applying a firm grip to my shoulder and in a single movement turned and pushed me in the direction of his desk. He was now far more openly aggressive, pushing me from behind so I kept up a pace, keeping up a constant hurl of angry abuse in Turkish. Again everyone in the main hall stopped to watch the scene. It'd now got to be very humiliating. He pushed me to his desk from where he took a stamp and whilst still standing to the side of me stamped my passport and then thrusting it into my hand. Gave me a sharp aggressive shove, which pushed me through to the departure lounge, spitting at me as he shoved. I stayed silent through the whole ordeal thinking only that he'd pass his hate on to me, just raising a contemptuous glare at the shove, but I couldn't believe he spat at me. I was confused and felt humiliated, but stayed silent, my confusion turned to anger and I took a final glare at the uniform before turning and I walked to get a coffee inside the departure lounge at which the moment was to get its final touch. I asked for a coffee and the Turkish waiter waved me away with a look of disgust before walking off himself, stuff this I thought.

"I only want a fucking coffee! What the fucks up with you people?" I yelled not caring who heard. I was as much upset as I was angry and I wasn't leaving till I got served. A woman walked over and by the look on her face I could tell she didn't want to serve me and she said nothing as she put a coffee down and merely looked at my money, which I placed on the counter. I took the coffee and walked. The only consolation I could find was in Lawrence of Arabia. I'd once read the unabridged version of the Seven Pillars of Wisdom, it took three months and the movie is easier, for want of a better word. I recalled one of his latter victories over the Turks after they'd put him through a personal indignity of his own, and the uniforms had hardly changed. It was the only consolation I could find. I sat in silence waiting to board the flight just imagining the thrill of riding an Arab charger at fall gallop into the ranks of fleeing World War 1 Turks, sabre raised. 'No prisoners! No mercy!' slashing out as I'd catch up with them, mercilessly decapitating those I could get a clean swipe at. I had to stop my right arm from twitching. It actually helped at the time. Well I really couldn't work out what pissed them off so much. I knew my manner was a little arrogant. But stuff it, it was a long slaughter lasting nearly an hour.

I was soon able to put it all behind me in Bangkok, as it's so easy to put anything behind you there. I thought about it a little and I guessed my attitude perhaps along with possible terrorist implications might have made the situation worse. They take almost half of our country off us, my grandfathers' land included, and he's pissed off at me, bloody cheek. Most of all I'd decided I wouldn't carry his hate, no I thought, I'll hate no one, he'll not pass that on to me. Three months later the bitter memory of the whole incident had been washed away by the serenity and beauty of my beach. I did eventually decide that one day I'd like to return. Well you couldn't judge a whole nation on one arsehole of an immigration officer. So I felt certain I'd get a better reception from everyday people, one day I thought. Another conscious thought I'd had was that it was about time I started dealing with the Cypriot bit, for years I felt like I'd been ignoring the Cypriot within, but after incidences like that, it seemed harder.

For those that know yes I was very naïve of many things and it did show and one that I found confusing was why Greeks would tell me that if I went to Turkey it was best to say I was Greek, but why? I'd gave it very little thought, everyone knows that in general there's little love between Greeks and Turks and by this time I'd started to take some pride in what I'd hear from relatives, and other Cypriots. "We used to live all right together." If you asked me about British history I considered myself quite knowledgeable. Maybe I was ignorant of Cypriot history, certainly, I know now to small and very important parts of it, but in the main I felt far from ignorant, here's the basic facts as I knew them relating to our recent history though. I knew pre-74 there had been a bit of killing going on. But I always imagined it was tit for tat stuff. In 1974 the island was invaded and partitioned by the Turks in response to a Greek coup. The impact of this on myself, well I was annoyed to say the least, my grandfathers farm is at Ayios Amvrosios a small village east of Kyrenia and for me, it meant I couldn't go there, which I was very annoyed about. The reasons for this partition from what I could gather, in my own words seemed to be a case of Greeks pissing around again to put it simply. Not meant so much as a criticism to Greece at the time. I had a vague knowledge of the coup, certainly not of the severity of it. All I can say at this point is innocence was a kind of bliss and I was fairly naive in my innocence. But from my perception I considered the partitioning of our island to have been enough punishment for all the people of Cyprus, the problems of before, all seemed so far away from our present situation.

Chapter 3

August 1994, I was thirty two years old, I guess it was safe to presume at this point that there was very little chance I was to suffer the same fate I'd seen so many take by this age, my father included. Life for me by this time seemed far from conventional and more importantly far from boring. August was to see me off on another six-week backpacking holiday to the Greek Isles, this time in good company. Gail my girlfriend for the past year had finished her job a whole month early in eager anticipation of the trip. I should have realised at the time how excited she'd been in comparison to myself. Not only was I familiar with the area we were heading to already, but travelling had become a bit of a pre-occupation of mine and for me airports had started to mean little more than tedious time spent in often stressed out situations or long periods of boredom.

We flew out on a late night flight from Gatwick and funny enough arrived in Athens about the same time as I had on my very first trip. Obviously I felt a lot wiser this time round and told Gail that there wasn't much point going anywhere at four a.m. as there was nowhere to go. I thought about the shining beacon from my first trip. Gail had had quite a sheltered upbringing. No, I didn't think there was anything Gail might want to see. She was ten years my junior and I already knew she didn't hold much of an interest for old relics and ruins. We made ourselves comfortable on some open space outside the front of the airport. The sight of the midsummer crowds coming and going were enough to fill any people watcher's time up, as I am and then around five, five-thirty the silhouette of the mountains to the east started to take shape. First against a very thick dark red sky which slowly turned to a rich amber before being overtaken by light itself quickly turning the night sky blue, about this time I'd noticed the morning traffic had already started it's vicious cycle, vicious on all the senses. Time to go. We were straight into the nearest taxi which we'd shared with a girl doing pretty much the same as us. Waiting to know that the port would soon becoming alive as it does around seven in the morning and it wasn't long before we were on one of the many frequent boats that make the voyage between Athens and Heraklion, Crete.

Heraklion, still very much a small port town not that the port is very imposing. Seven years on some parts had been modernised, but it still had much of the character it held before. It has an airport some ten kilometres east, but in itself is not too commercialised. We stayed in the same hotel I'd found before, down one of the back streets, at the end of which was a number of bars and cafes in the central area. Little noise at night and lots of chic looking Cretans passing the time drinking cappuccino and watching passers by through their designer sunglasses. I did seem to be getting an unusual number of strange looks though. Which I found unnerving at first, but was soon to discover it was because I held a striking similarity to the Heraklion town football keeper. I hadn't realised how fanatical they were about the sport, but it was quite amusing.

The biggest difference for me on this trip, Gail aside. Was budget. We did have one, which was quite a good one and we found very little trouble sticking to it, but we also had a credit card and with the means to go right to the limit and pay it off in one go on our return. This time round things were going to be a little different. We were still backpacking and the type of accommodation used wasn't going to change and there has always been a certain pleasure to sleeping on beaches, if your well prepared and the beach is nice enough, and there were one or two places I was eager to return to.

At this point I have to give a brief description of Gail. At five foot ten, beautiful, long dark brown hair and not only looks fit for a catwalk, but a walk she'd actually acquired for catwalk work. She soon gave it up, saying she resented the exploitation, which suited me fine. My girlfriend for nearly two years one couldn't ask for a prettier or more pleasant travelling companion.

My first mistake. I know too well now not to expect many places to be the same when I return after a few years. One of the sorrows of constantly returning to some places, are the changes that can occur to them.

The beach I'd discovered previously was to be the first stop with Gail, but no trials bike this time, I couldn't imagine doing it in a better manner, until I saw a wonderful battered looking black glossed mini Moke outside a car rental office. The beauty of it being that it was battered, which meant a couple more wouldn't matter. I was even more impressed to learn the standard moke engine had been replaced with a Morris 1300cc engine. That bought a smile to my face, this thing was going to fly. We threw our backpacks in the back, donned our headscarves and sunglasses and were off. It felt so cool and the spirit was there, it was a nice compliment when a backpacking hitchhiker we'd given a lift, asked us if we could pull over, so he could take a photo of us to show folks at home. We found the beach from my first visit, but with a little trouble. I hadn't expected much change due to the total absence of a road to it. Which was why, when I thought I should have been there, I totally ignored a small home-made road sign pointing to a beach. When I realised I must have past it I returned to the sign and looked over the bridge realising to my horror it was the beach. The road that had been laid was little more than a concrete track that most cars would have little trouble on, it seemed to follow the same route as the old foot track. I turned the Moke onto the concrete track and as we got to the bottom, I could see the other changes and probably the reason for the road. A mobile food van had taken up residency. There were no umbrellas at least, but on the beach were twenty to thirty mainly Greek holidaymakers. Off the rocks I could see a couple of men fishing. I'd already described the beach as I remembered it to Gail, so I knew she could sense my disappointment. I'd decided I'd at least stop for a swim, as I approached the beach I could see one of the other scourges that comes all too often with people and that's their waste. I only had a short swim. It disturbed me to see plastic bags and containers lying around. There was simply no need for the waste and the plastic bags are one of the biggest killers of the Mediterranean turtle, which happened to be upsetting me at the time. I couldn't help myself. I took the first bag I found and set about picking up the waste that had been left by the previous visitors. I'd filled a bag and a half when I approached the sandwich van. I noticed up on the cliffs some apartments being built.

"How long have you been here?" I inquired. My voice wasn't harsh but it was obvious with two bags of his rubbish in my hands I wasn't too impressed with his presence.

"Ten years!"

"You couldn't have."

"What do you mean! Ten years I've been here!"

"I was here seven years ago, I don't remember this!" not wanting to call the man an outright liar.

"Ten years I've been here!"

"So you had the road built?"

"Yeah"

"This is your responsibility then!"

I dumped the bags in front of the sandwich bar before turning to walk back to the sea to have a final swim to cool down. It isn't something one should get upset about, I was, but when it come down to it, I felt it little of my business, for me it was just a tranquil place that I thought I'd discovered, for this man it was his livelihood now.

A few days later I got into a conversation with a backpacker who'd taken a very similar route to myself first time out, Ios for the partying and then Santorini for the relaxation. I told him of how I remembered Perissa beach on Santorini, very quaint, with only one eight-room hotel and a camp sight for accommodation. Many of the locals had taken to renting out rooms that they'd had built on to their homes. I stayed in one such place. I remember after getting off the bus from the village of Thira, there was an old Greek woman dressed in black sitting on her garden wall as I passed with friends she inquired if we needed rooms. As we'd been staying in the hotel we thought we'd have a look and what a surprise I'd got. The rooms were very clean and new, each twin room had twin pine beds and a table, the bed linen was clean and the shower worked. Five minutes to the beach and all for under a pound a night. I described the beach to him and told him how it was all so unspoilt, even the restaurants seemed to be extensions of their homes, he listened attentively then looked up at me.

"Don't go back!" I looked at him with fright.

"You've been there?" I asked already knowing the answer.

"Yeah"

"It's changed then?"

"From what you've described I don't think you'd recognise the place"

"How do you mean?" I asked.

"In every way," he said to leave me no doubt.

"It's gone then," I sighed.

He nodded and we changed the subject. I'd heard Santorini had become one of the most expensive of the islands, but I just imagined that it hadn't effected the beach. Santorini has its own little artist colony on the other side of the island, it had become a bit of a chic village to visit and it was only there that I was hoping the high prices had crept in. I had noticed by now though, that even when buying simple things like water that if I stood behind Gail in silence whilst she paid, the price would often be a little cheaper, amusing as much as annoying. Amusing how easily people thieve I mean and never think of themselves as thieves.

The news of Santorini altered our plans a little but I wasn't going to let it ruin things, we toured the north of Crete in our mini Moke, before getting the idea that if we weren't sure where we were going, then we'd go anywhere that took our fancy. We knew we wanted to end up in Kos to visit friends and until then we spent our time chasing postcards so to speak. It was a lot of fun. We'd find postcards of places we'd like, mainly in Crete and go. It was a good way to see the island and I dare say we'd have never gone to Sitia on the north east of the island otherwise, it seemed that most of the holidaymakers there were Greek. Now shortly before I embarked on this trip I remembered watching the chief prosecutor of Rhodes on TV saying that incidences of rape on his island were mainly the fault of the tourist women dressing in a provocative manner. His ideas were to me pathetic and I saw little bashfulness on these beaches, I wondered what his response might be to a Greek woman being raped for the same crime, looking provocative, define provocative to a man with a hard on.

By the time we'd got to Sitia, it had been an idyllic trip, but for one problem, which had even started to feel oppressive. I noticed I'd been hearing something I was very surprised to hear from Greeks. Gail had first heard it when she accidentally walked into a Greek woman sweeping.

"Bloody Europeans!" she snarled. Gail seemed upset when she told me.

"It was the ugly way she'd hissed it, bloody Europeans! Bloody Europeans! She just kept repeating it," recalled Gail.

"Bloody Europeans!"

It wasn't just a single incident or just Gail that heard it. In fact she was to shortly have another similar experience and I spoke to a Dutch man in Sitia and he'd heard the same comment several times. For myself I couldn't understand it, I'd certainly never heard it before and they themselves were now European but it was something I think a few people may have heard that year, for myself it took a little while to work out.

It was on Kalymnos a small island near Kos in the Dodenacesse that it really hit me. I'd seen a couple of little signs but the implications didn't really emerge in me until this one sign, why this sign? I don't know. Maybe the care that some private individual had put into hand painting the two by four-foot placard. Or the plain and simple message it gave, but when I saw it, it was to stop me in my tracks. The sign was a simple one with a simple message. But at a time when the situation in Bosnia still hadn't improved and daily we'd been barraged with the sight of men, women and children suffering to such a degree in central Europe of all places. I don't think I need to describe the feelings that I felt, the sign simply read;

MACEDONIA
IS GREEK.

It scared me at first and then anger started to set in. Gail didn't understand why I was so worked up when I got back to our chalet, where I went straight into one.

"That's exactly the type of nationalistic bullshit that got Cyprus into trouble!"

"What's up?"

"You not seen that sign out there?"

"No, what sign?"

"Macedonia is Greek, fucking bullshit!" I was infuriated.

"Oh!"

Gail wasn't too interested in politics so I decided to fill her in on the details as I saw them.

"Macedonian's are seeking to establish an independent state in their homeland now that they've got their independence from Yugoslavia!"

"And?"

"And Greece say's that if they call themselves Macedonia, Greece will invade them! The fucking mentality of it!" I sneered " I just can't believe that people on the street endorse it, I just can't believe it! Bastards!"

"Why?"

"Why what?" I asked.

"Why would Greece invade them?"

"That's the most pathetic part, to protect their fucking history!" I started to calm down so I could explain the situation.

"Right most people regard Alexander the Great as one of the greatest men that ever lived, ok!"

"Yeah."

"Greeks cannot consider a world where Alexander might be considered anything else but Greek right." Gail was listening, but I wasn't sure if she really understood. I continued,

"And whilst there is no Macedonia, it's how people will regard him." I paused slightly to explain it as I saw it.

"But he was Macedonian and now that Macedonians actually have the freedom to call themselves Macedonian, some Greeks it seems, are scared that people will regard Alexander as Macedonian first and not Greek, but no one can take the Greek out if him," my temper built up again.

"They actually want to invade the country, with everything that's going on in Bosnia! They actually want to invade a country for simply calling themselves what they feel they are, I don't fucking believe it!"

I sat down on the bed and dropped my head a little and stared at nothing. Before saying to myself again,

"I don't fucking believe it!"

I'd started to go into thought about it, I couldn't believe a people could be so nationalistic. I couldn't believe the mentality behind it. Even listening to events unfolding whilst in England it hadn't really sunk in. I couldn't believe what I was hearing then. But seeing the sign had drove it all home in me. Even more pathetic I felt were the politicians behind it all, the implications of what I was saying I felt had gone right over Gail.

"I don't know if you understand what I'm trying to say Gail, these people actually want to invade another country to protect their history!" by this time my tone had become subdued. Visions of Bosnia again crept in, slowly and more sadly I finished with.

"Gail, invasion means war and everything that goes with it, the devastation the heartache, innocent dead women and children, look at Bosnia, they'd create that again and all for the memory of one man, how great could that make him," I paused for a moment. Then with far more sorrow than anger,

"Bastards!" I could feel the tears starting to build up. I finally sighed, dropping my head to stare at nothing at all. My thoughts drifted to Cyprus. My head dropped further, and an intense sadness started to overwhelm me as I started to consider the effect that such Greek nationalism had had on Cyprus and its terrible implications for our country and our Turkish Cypriots to whom I'd suddenly felt defensive about. I could feel my emotions starting to build up, I took a deep breath whilst thinking to myself 'get it together' which I did, turning the sorrow into a mild anger which felt better for me. I raised my head slightly still focusing on nothing in particular, then slowly shook my head and feeling my resolve return told myself firmly.

"These can't be my people.....never!"

Chapter 4

No greater sacrifice can a man make than to lay down his life for his beliefs?

My next visit to Cyprus was in October 96. I arrived on the 10th October still fired up two months after what many regard simply as the flag pole incident. The whole affair had enraged me. A few days previous to the incident a Greek Cypriot had been battered to death with pickaxe handles by Turks, whilst demonstrating in the DMZ in Nicosia, against the occupation by Turkish troops. The whole incident had occurred in full view of other demonstrators and the world media, who gazed on from a very short distance away behind the safety of the badly kept fencing that partitions the area off. After the funeral another group of protesters had gathered this time with one aim in mind, to remove the Turkish flag that fly's from a flag pole in the same area as the beating, it was to prove a futile attempt. Flagpoles aren't the easiest of things to climb at the best of times and not surprisingly no one was to get close, but one man was to lose his life, taken by a shot through the neck from a Turkish border guard a third of the way up the pole. The Turks had made it quite clear that they would kill anyone who tried to interfere with the flag in any way. I'd watched these events unfold on British TV and I was incensed, not only that, but something was happening that I could relate to, demonstrations, stone throwing, civil disorder so to speak, yes, these were all things I had some experience of from the late seventies and very early eighties. It had felt necessary at the time in Britain to demonstrate not only against extremely oppressive policing, but maybe also in a way to be recognised as the force that young people are. Things were very much different from today, where the young are held in higher regard and there is a certain thrill to it all. My ticket was booked and I was off. I'd thought about taking a good catapult and a bag of marbles with me. As most schoolboys will know a catapult can be a formidable weapon and without doubt a good shot to the right spot could easily inflict serious injury. I'd noticed from the TV pictures that the flagpole itself was well within range and so would any Turk in the near vicinity. I looked forward to the idea and hoped so badly that protests would be continuing after I'd arrived. I'd even given the flagpole itself some consideration, if things were still happening, I considered that a prime target. I'd seen from the TV footage that no one would have a chance of successfully climbing the pole and even reach the offending flag, but merely reaching the pole itself wouldn't be such a hardship. It was not only possible to reach the flagpole, but just as important was its close distance to the protective fencing. I'd made up my mind if the demonstrations had as I'd hoped continued I'd make an attempt on the pole. I imagined how nice it would be to climb it, even if the shot came after reaching the flag itself, just a good grip on it and it would come down with the body. But a much better alternative to myself at the time was the flagpole. If the flagpole itself was wood then it would also burn, an open petrol container at the base of the flagpole and maybe even a few petrol bombs, I couldn't see why not, if it worked it would work well. I just needed demonstrations to continue.

It had started to become very frustrating thinking of the situation there, nothing had seemed to be resolved, and progress was nil. By this time I'd started to feel more emotional about the whole situation. More frustrating was the ever-growing desire to return to my grandfathers' farm, for some reason it was becoming more and more important to me.

I arrived in Larnaca at around one in the morning. The protests had as I'd feared become more subdued. I'd decided to spend a couple of days in a hotel in Lanarca before going to my godmothers in Limassol. If things were to start again I'd go straight to Nicosia instead. There might not even be a need for my godmother to know I was there. I could imagine her thoughts on my ideas regarding the sacrifice I'd be prepared to make. I took a taxi from the airport and gave the driver the hotel name. It was a pleasant fresh night so I opened the window, as the air conditioning wasn't needed and asked the driver if I could smoke, he nodded. I took out a camel light and offered the driver one, which he took.

"Here on holiday?" he inquired. He had a very firm voice and like many Cypriots his English was very good.

"Sort of, but came out mainly because of the flagpole incident," which now seemed a bit irrelevant being yesterdays news, I continued.

"It pissed me off so I thought I'd fly out just in case," in case of what I didn't know.

"Fucking Turks!" the taxi driver hissed. Not loudly but more than a little menacingly.

I seldom talked about the situation with anyone other than my relatives in Cyprus, so I was eager to hear any sort of input on the situation. I'd started to feel more and more a victim of the invasion, so I thought I'd reveal my personal loss.

"We lost my grandfathers farm in the invasion, at Ayios Amvrosios near Kyrenia, I want it back!"

The response sent me cold.

"I lost a father and a brother in the invasion and I've never them seen since!" his hatred surfaced in his voice and his face had taken on more than a snarl as he manoeuvred the car around the city streets, he continued with,

"And I swear! I swear that I promise! I will do harm to any Turk I ever meet! Ever!" shit, I thought. Glad I'm not a Turk. It wasn't just the harsh return. What struck me most was the hatred in his voice. The intensity of it even scared me. I knew many had lost family members, we were more fortunate. The hotel was close and I didn't really want to continue the conversation. The hatred I could sense from him scared me, I just remembered thinking how I'd hate to be that first Turk he meets. I slept lightly that night, the words of the taxi driver repeating themselves on me, it felt a little disturbing and it's not something I'll ever forgot.

The hotel in central Larnaca was a reasonable tourist hotel, most of the tourists having left. I found a place where I felt comfortable eating, a couple of minutes from the hotel and I also found myself deep in thought, over a half bottle of ouzo and some water. It was the changes in myself that I was considering. Ten years previous I'd not have flown out for the flag pole incident, I'd kind of managed to keep the Cypriot within pretty much suppressed, if that's the right word. I thought one reason being that we were from the north, as an adult I could see how emotional and confusing the situation was. I couldn't imagine a child wanting to take it all into serious consideration. When I'd finished thinking, the ouzo was gone and the water still three quarters full and I left the restaurant without even feeling the alcohol.

The rest of the time was to be spent at my godmothers and despite the frustration, it was nice, as it was off-season. My godmother and my godfather are both retired having made their money from selling fish and chips from a couple of shops that they'd had in London over the years. The most memorable for me being the Dolphin fish and chip shop on The Kennington Road, it was often during this period as a child I'd find myself in London usually for the holidays. I remember the period well from the late sixties through to the early seventies a little from before my grandfathers' death. Although I have fond and firm memories of my grandfather, he was from my point of view the most fun to be around. Although I had quite a few relatives around the London area and a few cousins closer to my own age I do remember how much happier things seemed to be when grandad was about. Maybe it's just how I remember him, but as a child you could do no harm with grandad. He seemed to be happy around you and it was unconditional happiness. I was a normal child when it come to many things, so the bomb site across the square from the flats would be a favourite playground until they were demolished. Every one would go ballistic if we were caught playing in them. But grandad, I wouldn't mind being caught by him, he seemed to even enjoy the telling off he had to give. What a difference that must make to a child. My memory of him taking his time with his walking stick and his peaked cap coming through the gateway to Mountain House, a block of terraced flats that still stand in SE11 is still so strong. Just to see the change in him as he approached to find his grandchildren waiting for him. He'd speed up a little and it's like I can still feel the happiness in him, a big broad grin under his thick bushy grey moustache, raising his walking stick in the air.

"Yeah it's grandad,..............!"

He died when I was six.

If I think back to the time I can remember how wrong it felt. It didn't even seem like his time and it was the last thing I expected. He was elderly, eighty-six when he died, but it was of unnatural causes. Apparently, he'd inadvertently knocked a gas switch on before taking a nap. I remember looking at the large old bed on which he slept for the last time, there wasn't the fear children might normally associate with such things. Someone asked me recently if I missed him, I told them I didn't see how I could if he died when I was six, but I do, perhaps now more than ever. After my grandfather died my grandmother quite rightly became the focus of the family's attention. My grandmother bless her was very different from my grandfather, as much as I love her and the bond is strong, the relationship with my grandmother was very different and whilst in London she would be a major influence in what I did. The church was one of those influences in my grandmothers' life, which meant mine as well, which had its pitfalls. The average Greek Orthodox service lasts a couple of hours at least, and that would be twice a week and fasting would start the day before, which we had to adhere to. I can't say I really minded much at the time, there are some things you can eat, not a lot though and the most amusing part would be on the way to church. The surveillance to insure that none of us disappeared into a sweet shop, not that I would have. I do remember the frustration that I'd feel only later on in life at my total inability to communicate with grandma. Regardless of the time I spent alone with her I learnt nothing. I mean nothing. I'd be more than happy to make up for it by being an altar boy for a day. It was the sort of thing that made grandmother proud. Her faith was very strong. After my grandfathers death she kept an oil wick burning constantly, twenty-four hours a day in a cupboard decorated with religious icons in memory of him and every day she'd burn incense around the flat in a tea strainer, to ward off evil spirits. They do it in church, but not in a tea strainer obviously. It was just a sight I got used to. My ever-shrinking grandma dressed in black waving a smoking tea strainer around. Things did change after grandad died.

I have good memories of my godparents as well in those days. They lived ten minutes walk from my grandparents in a three-storey house just off the Kennington road. I remember how hectic it used to be around the house at times. My godparents worked very hard building up their fish and chip shop business, which seemed to me to be the probable cause of a lot of my godfathers stress, he doesn't know this yet but he used to scare me something silly. Now that's something I should have told him a long time ago, he's far more chilled out now he's retired, but it was probably just his way of getting things done, I used to try avoid him. It's nice to see him now relaxing on the balcony with his fly swat, often with something funny to say, he can still scare me a little though, must be the memory of it. My godmother on the other hand had a soft spot for me and always let it show. She had the same pressures on her but it would always be the affectionate side that I'd see. Then there are their children, my cousins and god brothers and sisters. The best part about such a large house was the space, even with so many children, my godparents had their lounge room and we had ours. These and many other members of my mother's family were the only family I'd ever known and I love them all very much. It's been a strange upbringing, I do feel so strongly linked to my Greek heritage. It just can't be helped. I'm not religious but if I were to ever marry it would be in a Greek Orthodox Church, they're such celebrations and I like the emphasis and the importance of the family ties.

At seventeen, grandma asked me through my mother if I would go to Cyprus to do my national service, which would last six months. Now I did considered it I'd recently enquired about the British army and alright there was a bit of a difference to the Cypriot National Guard. I didn't speak Greek for one, which would have made life a little harder. But it would be for only six months, I considered it all right, for about two minutes when I asked a question the answer to which, seemed to make a lot of difference at the time and that's the pay, eight pounds a month. I suppose my grandma thought it seemed the right time for me to go but I was seventeen and it was 1979 and like my many of my generation a little rebellious at the time. I felt awkward about refusing but no way was anyone going to get my butt for eight pound a month. I didn't like to upset my grandmother, but it did seem like she was asking a bit much at the time, asking me to uproot to a country, which even though I felt familiar with I'd never been to and join their military service. For less in a month than the dole paid in a week. So I promised her that if Cyprus had trouble and needed help I'd be there, it was the best I could do. When I was asked a short time later if I was ready for an arranged marriage, my response was that little bit harsher, no way. Not to make anyone happy was I going to do that. It neither seemed fair on the other person nor myself. As you can gather grandma was very traditional. I think if it had have been my godmother asking me to do my national service, it might have got a different response such are my feelings for her.

The time that I was to spend at my godmothers in Cyprus, was time I enjoyed even with the strict house rules and it was to leave me feeling a lot closer to my godmother. I think it was the time itself. I remember telling her over the dinner table on the balcony one afternoon how frustrating I found her at times.
"Why do I frustrate you?" she asked.
"You sound like my mother but I can't have a go back at you like I do her," I said as a gentle smile passed both our lips and an affectionate gaze filled me with

a warmth that I'd found rare in my childhood. My mother possibly through lack of affection in her own childhood had seemed too dominating, but as I'd grown older I'd turned the table on her. I spent most of the time with my godmother talking mainly about the situation in Cyprus, it seemed to dominate the majority of our time. The Turkish border guards had by this time shot an innocent man in the buffer Zone. He'd been out picking snails with some family members, from what I could make out he was shot in the back whilst walking out of the buffer zone. It was a terrible injustice and not a rarity in Cyprus at least the third person to die in such a way that year. I was angrier knowing that the UN forces even had to get permission before retrieving the body and to just incense me even further, I could see it was all affecting my godmother, now that really pissed me off. Then I was to learn of another demonstration in Nicosia, this time it was schoolchildren, but I wanted to be there for any protest. I was feeling militant, and even a protest by school children seemed like more than a good day out.

"Marianna, I'm thinking of going to Nicosia tomorrow."

"What for?" she enquired.

"There's a demonstration at the line, I want to be there," I said.

"No, you can't go!" she told me sternly.

"Why not? " I asked.

"I don't want you to go!" she said disapprovingly.

"But why not?" I was expecting my aunt to disapprove.

"You might get hurt," she said.

"Maybe I think it might be worth it!" I pleaded.

"No, I don't want you to go!"

"I don't mind aunt, I really don't!"

"No!" she said firmly.

"I don't understand, you let children demonstrate when we should be with them!" It seemed a fair attack and it reflected how I felt.

"I don't want you to get hurt," she said softening her tone.

"Marianna if I got hurt it would get coverage!" I continued. "All right so someone got killed trying to climb the flagpole, but it got on World Wide TV, people knew about it!" I thought about the man shot in the buffer zone and the others who had died earlier in the year under similar circumstances. I'd heard nothing in England.

"I'm a British citizen if I get hurt it'll be different! If it gets world-wide coverage, it helps, it'll be worth the sacrifice!" I told her pleading my point. But I knew then that I'd shown my hand. I knew at this point my godmother would never let me go now and I knew I wouldn't defy her. I let her know that I wasn't happy about her decision but at the same time I knew she wouldn't hit back at me, my personal frustration was showing. I carried on,

"I understand your concerns aunt but I just think the world needs to know what's going on and if it means making personal sacrifices then….." I could see the talk was upsetting her. I thought about the family of the snail picker and their grief and immediately I understood. There was a brief pause more like long sigh within myself.

"It's just all so frustrating, how can they shoot anyone for picking snails?"

"It happens a lot," my godmother sighed.

"Too much! It's not even marked out, how are they supposed to know they're in it!" meaning the buffer zone. I was furious at it all, at the Turkish border guards in particular. I liked the idea of taking a high powered rifle of my own to shoot back with. They seemed to get a lot of pleasure out of shooting unarmed civilians.

"Bastards! How do they get away with it!" now I never normally swear in the presence of my godmother but I knew she'd understand. We were standing on the balcony of her Limassol home it was a fresh starlit night, after another brief pause she revealed to me.

"At night when they get bored they come across the border and shine their torches in peoples houses."

"No!" I hissed. Now that really pissed me off.

"They're taking the piss!"

The idea of Turkish troops coming over the line at night to torment the scared villagers in the area really got me. At this point I'm thinking ordinance survey maps of the area and what would be the easiest way to get a semi-automatic rifle. I remembered seeing a gunsmith in town, surely I thought I could get one to sell me a rifle for the specific task of killing Turkish border guards. It was to start an amusing line of thought going with myself approaching a Cypriot gunsmith,

"Hi, I need a good rifle, high powered, semi-automatic for killing Turks with, just thought I'd go up to the hills for a couple of days"

"Hmmmm for killing Turks with huuh, let me see!"

At this point I really couldn't see a Cypriot thinking of the legal side, seemed about right to me. It was a very frustrating conversation. My eldest god brother Spyros arrived and entered the conversation without really knowing what had been said.

"Huh what you talking about?" he asked.

"The situation," I replied.

"Yeah its them bloody Turks! And them Greeks! All the bloody same!" he reeled off with.

I looked at him, surprised. My godmother silenced him.

"Don't you talk like that!" it was said harshly but we were having an emotional conversation on the situation. I felt sorry for him at times. He just seemed to say the wrong thing at the wrong time too often, but usually quite amusing. I thought about the situation again and how helpless the Cypriot people were, the British it seemed couldn't be relied upon in the area for anything.

"We need to be strong godmother! We're not a poor country we need to build up our defenses!"

"You think so?" she asked.

"Yes we're not a weak people we must show them, we won't take it!" I thought about the psychological damage being done and its effects and I knew my godmother was frightened as well, which I didn't like. I could see her thinking about it.

"Marianna Turkish troops are just a few miles north and they're terrorising our people, in the world we live in today, no one keeps what they've got by being weak and not when it's Turkey," I said finishing with. "Everyone knows what they're like, no one should have to live in such fear!"

My aunt was quiet and deep, deep in thought.

"No," she said. Then sighed as she added quietly,

"We used to live all right together."

It was a depressing and frustrating conversation that wasn't going to solve anything, but just unearth more frustration, time to change the subject.

"Are you going to church Sunday aunt?"

"Yes"

"I'll take communion with you then," I said. My cousin looked at me inquisitively, as I knew he would.

"What you going to church for?" he asked.

"I want to," I replied.

"You're not religious," he said with a smile in a slightly mocking manner, perhaps considering it more than I had.

"No, but it's how I like to remember grandma, I go to church!" I said with a smile. Normally I'd just light a candle but I didn't mind the idea of a service, although I hadn't really considered it. I just knew I wouldn't be doing anything else and for me it would also be more quality time with my aunt.

"Ok," said my aunt and then followed with.

"I won't expect you to fast, not the night before, but I don't want you smoking in the morning before we go to the church."

Oops! I forgot about the rules, and here my godmother was a little firmer, she made a blowing motion into her cupped hand and smelling as she did so and saying,

"We don't want the priest to smell smoke!"

I started thinking instantly of mouth washes, I'm at least a twenty a day person, two before breakfast and my aunt seemed to have an uncanny sense of smell, coming from my grandma perhaps. I nodded in agreement, no reason why he should.

The rest of the week was a real eye opener for me and just from watching my godfather every day I felt like I was learning an important lesson from our past and in the most amusing manner. He would be up and out of the house well before I'd awake on most days. To return early afternoon with his natural bounty and I'd sit on the balcony after a lazy morning and watch my uncle with what would later be our tea. Everything from small birds caught on bird sticks to a variety of nuts and roots, none of which you'd be likely to find at a market, but as I was soon to discover all quite good eating. I hardly saw the need for my aunt to go to the shops, my uncle could hardly have guessed how interested I was, if I enquired he'd show me what come from where. But I think he seemed to have been a little surprised that I was so interested, it was part of our history though. The Cypriot people are very much a rural people and looking at the brown sun scorched hills in summer, it was always hard to imagine that such a feast would be out there, and these would be foods that we'd have eaten for possibly thousands of years. If ever I'd ask he'd always impart his knowledge to me. But there was one important part of our history that my uncle would make me aware of my ignorance of occasionally and that would be the Greek language.

Sunday came and seven a.m. I was smoking my first cigarette of the day. Leaning far out of the bedroom window so none of the offending odour would be noticed. I looked over to the balcony, shit! I couldn't believe my godmother was standing there looking straight at me, thirty four years old but my godmother could still make me feel like a child, if she disapproved she wasn't going to make me feel guilty about it.

"Morning Dimitri!" she called out. I like my Greek name far more.

"Morning," I replied with an embarrassed smile.

"I'll put some coffee on, you shower now and get ready ok!" she called out.

"Ok," I replied. It wasn't a request.

My godmother turned and walked out of sight to the kitchen, whilst I finished my cigarette before flicking it over the low wall that surrounds their large bungalow. I fully expected her to chastise me over the cigarette. I showered and dressed in a light cotton summer suit that I'd bought off the shelf in Bangkok and tied my long black hair right up into a bob to keep it tidy, I knew how important appearances are at these times. We left the house in my aunts car at around seven thirty on a bright Cypriot autumn morning. As we parked the car she informed me we might be a little early, which seemed about right to me. Until we actually got to the church, which to my disbelief was packed already. My godmother knew I might be more comfortable with seating, which we found on the top balcony of the church. The church itself was by no means small, but the congregation would be the envy of most clergymen. It really is a sight to absorb, the church was full and the standing worshippers not only filled the entrance, but I knew from previous experience that there would be a large congregation gathered around the entrance. A lot of the time I was too in awe of the congregation to notice it was time to cross myself as you do at various times during the service. I was glad I'd made the effort, I may not be myself religious but I do have a lot of respect for religion and more so the power of faith and here it was strong. The Cypriot branch of the Greek Orthodox Church has been autonomous since 488 AD. After the discovery of the tomb of St. Barnabas and St. Paul was also received and preached in Cyprus. The service itself included communion and lasted about two and a half-hours, which might have passed quicker if not for the clock I'm sure I could see. Either that or I was constantly gazing at my watch but I couldn't remember minding too much at the time. I knew why I was there and it was working. After the service on the way back to the car my godmother revealed,

"You know I am very proud that you come to church with me this morning." If that alone wasn't worth it, but I really did have other reasons.

"I don't mind aunt, I'm glad I came," I shrugged.

"Like I said it's for grandma, it's how I like to remember her."

It worked as well. If anything would remind me of a time when grandma was here it would be church.

We returned to my godmothers for the day, it had been pretty much a holiday around the house. Come lunch time my godmother got the capers out to eat with dinner, which I confess to having a craving for at times, like a lot of the time with my meals in Cyprus. It's a pickled thorny bush, it tastes a little like pickled gherkins, the seed pods are what most people see and eat from jars, but I preferred the bush itself and my godmother was preparing me a large jar to take home. It had been a relaxed day lazing around and watching TV when later on, my cousin Spyros appeared.

"Hey Jim, do you want to go down to the tourist strip for an hour or so?"

What! I thought, now that might not seem an unusual request, but I wasn't expecting it. Drinking is quite accepted at home over dinner or the couple of beers in the evening, but the idea of going to the bars whilst staying at my godmothers, it was unknown to me. It was forbidden. Under her roof you are under her rules, which I wouldn't question.

"Yeah why not?" I said bemused.

This was going to be interesting I'd never been out for a drink with Spyros before. Not for any known reason, other than the fact that I'd never known him to go out for a drink at all. I knew he had to work but I knew that wasn't the reason he never went out.

"Give me five minutes to get ready," I told him.

Now here I have to describe my cousin Spyros a little, as I can't imagine anyone else being like him. He's in his early fifties, a wonderful person whose words often seem to belie his real nature, mainly in what and how he says things, a cynic at times although I could understand that part of him. He always seemed to me, to be unsure of what he wanted from life. His indecision would be beyond frustration at times to the point of amusement. I didn't even know he'd been married twice. When I asked him about the marriage I knew nothing of I wasn't surprised I'd heard nothing of it, as it only lasted two weeks. I remember I couldn't help but giggle when he told me.

"Well I changed my mind didn't I," that's Spyros. We were going to the tourist strip on his moped. No fancy Med type scooter but a one seat Honda 50cc, it was quite amusing trying to hold on with my feet up. But I was surprised when he stopped a mile or so short of our destination.

"Why you stopping here?" I asked.

"Ah it's the traffic I don't like to ride along here especially with you on the back, it's too busy," he grumbled. He wasn't the most confident of riders even though he'd always been riding a moped. It took us a good twenty minutes walk to get to the start of the bars and we strolled along until we found one I liked, a nice spacious bar with a couple of women walking around, we took our places on stalls at the bar.

"Two keo's and two B-52s please. Oh and two straws I want them flaming!" I told the barman. He pulled the two beers and then produced the short cocktails. My cousin viewed them like one would a very unsavoury looking dish that you might find in Asia.

"What's that?" he asked. Sounding disgusted with what he could see.

"Cocktails," I told him.

I proceeded to burn the sambucca that layers the top of the drinks in one glass, then once it was burning with its blue flame I plunged the straw to the bottom of the glass and sucked up the contents in one. The last thing to hit the throat is the flame. I sucked back savouring the taste.

"Not bad," I said looking up with a smile.

My cousin was looking at me with a look of disbelief on his face.

"Here this ones for you," I said pushing him the glass.

"I don't want it! What do you burn it for?"

" It helps, here try it"

He shook his head, I knew he meant no, so I didn't even attempt to entice him.

"Ok more for me!"

I set light to the remaining cocktail before sucking it up and ordering another. I was starting to enjoy myself. The beers went quick whilst we chatted. We'd started our second beer when a girl walked over to the bar to stand at my cousins' side. I looked past my cousin at her. She was quite attractive. My cousin peered at her about the same time as she raised a smile at him. To which he pulled a slight face and to my bewilderment turned his back fully to her, completely cutting her out from any possibility of any conversation. I smiled and shook my head, the beers were almost gone but the night was young.

"Another beer?" I asked. Spyros looked at his watch, then exclaimed.

"No we're going to be late already!" late for what I thought.

"What do you mean?" I asked.

"It's a quarter past nine and I promised my mother I'd have you home by nine thirty," he told me before he supped up the last of his beer. I watched him empty the glass feeling a little bewildered at what he'd just said. Then he confirmed it with.

"We have to go!"
This wasn't sinking in very well. I was now being harassed into finishing what I had of my beer,

"What do you mean we have to go!" I demanded. I was not only confused but I'd just started to get going. The bar had started to fill up and there were by now plenty of females walking around. Spyros started to lead the way. I was still in disbelief. We got out on to the main strip and he picked up his speed, but I had other plans.

"Spyros what do you mean we have to go?"

"We have to go, I told my mum I'd have you home by nine thirty."

"You did WHAT!" I hollered after him.

"I told mum that I'd have you home by nine thirty and that's where we're going!" he told me firmly. Now I knew he was serious.

"WHY?"

"Because that's when she wants you home for," he said as simply as that. We were now walking along at a faster pace with me holding back and trying to slow him down to talk this over.

"Spyros what did you bring me here for if we've got to be back for nine thirty?"

"An ice cream."

"You what!"

"I told mum I was bringing you out for an ice cream," he said. Looking back at me. Now I was pissed off.

"A bloody ice cream!"

"Yeah I thought you might like to come down here for an ice cream."

"The last thing I wanted down here was an ice cream! You phone your mother up and tell her we're going to be a little late!"

"Can't do that"

"What do you mean you can't do that, you can, you will!" I shouted at him.

"Can't do that, she told me to have you home for nine thirty and that's where we're going," he kept walking, I really couldn't believe it was happening,

"You go home and tell your mum I'll be home about midnight and to leave the key under the mat."

"I can't do that," he said.

"Why can't you do that?" I demanded.

"Can't go home without you, your in my care!"
Now as flattered as I might feel, I found the idea of being in the care of Spyros way past amusing.

"I'm thirty four years old I can take care of myself!" I told him letting my feelings show.

"Not here you can't," I thought immediately of my life and some of the places I'd been to.

"Spyros I've been round the bloody world what do you mean not here?"

"Not here, here you're my responsibility!"

Now that hit a raw nerve, the idea of anybody being responsible for me, but myself, was far more than I could consider.

"No one! No one! Is responsible for me Spyros!"

I might as well have been talking to myself, he wasn't going to have it and when we got home at ten I could see why. My godmother was very angry with him. He received a fierce barrage of abuse that I couldn't understand but certainly felt guilty for.

"It's my fault we're late aunt."

It was all a bit late now though. I could understand his earlier fears and I was feeling very sorry for him. My aunts' protection for me seemed a little extreme, but I understood, if I consider our relationship I knew she possibly regards me like her youngest son.

Chapter 5

It wasn't to be long at all before I returned to Cyprus, but if I learnt one thing from my previous visit it was not to get too emotional about events. Things still troubled me, nothing had changed but my attitude a little, and the next two visits were to be time out for me to explore and search out other facets of Cyprus. Perhaps what I meant was I wanted the freedom to enjoy Cyprus in pretty much the same way as millions of tourists every year. My choice of timing for the first of these visits was a bit unlucky though. February 97 I'm told had seen some of the coldest temperatures in over fifty years and it was cold, the wind had a bitter bite to it. I'd flown into Paphos and spent the majority of the time at a very pretty central Paphos hotel called The Pine Mansions, I'd decided not to visit my relatives and I felt a little bad about it and I didn't even let them know I was in the country. It was a pleasant stay, I'd pass most of my time talking to the mainly elderly tourists and with pleasant but short strolls around Paphos and some of its museums, avoiding the outside ones. The museums are plentiful around Paphos and these few lines don't give them the credit they deserve but my next visit was to be a little different.

September 97 and this was to be nothing more than a holiday in a country I felt at home in and one of the pleasures of this visit was to bring with me a friend from England. Allen who was staying a week of the two weeks that I was to be there. Now Allen and I already had a bit of previous holiday history together. Sometimes with his family, but once or twice on our own which often got a bit crazy, fun but a little crazy and in that sense this was to be no different. We flew in, tickets only and arranged our accommodation on arrival. There's very little trouble finding cheap holiday accommodation at this time of year and we quickly settled into a large two-bedroom apartment with a TV no less, not that it was going to be needed. It was on the main beach road a couple of miles east from the majority of tourist facilities, which wasn't going to be a problem to us, as we'd hired a jeep out for a week.

First night out and some might say we got into a little bit of trouble, it didn't take long. We went to the same bar that I'd previously frequented and hit the B-52's, I remember the waitress telling me we'd be sick.
"No way," I said downing the third.
We were probably drunk pretty early in the evening but there was room for more and we stayed till quite late. After which we left the bar to return to our apartment in a taxi. We were slowly cruising up the strip when the taxi driver spoke,

"You like girls," he asked. I was sitting in the front. I nodded a natural nod. I knew what was coming next.

"You like I take you to a place, nice girls a hundred pounds all night," he told us. Taxi driver turns pimp it happens often enough, usually when they stand to make, but Allen had heard it in the back and I don't think he wasn't ready to go home.

"Come on Jim let's go!" he called out from the back. I smiled. I didn't have a hundred pounds on me anyway but,

"What sort of girls?" I enquired.

"Nice Russian girls, nice, only a hundred pounds a night or only look if you want," he'd said a key word for myself.

"Only look if we want?" I asked. Well there's no harm in being an observer.

"Yes if you want only look, if not whatever," I knew I should have been thinking about it but,

"Can we buy drinks?" I asked.

"Yes, yes you can buy drinks," he said excitedly.
There was no need to ask Allen what he thought, as he was already heckling from the back, so I knew what his answer would be.

"You want to go I take you, I take you," the taxi driver said eagerly.

"Ok lets go," I told him with a flick of my hand.
The driver made a hundred and eighty degree turn on the road and was now speeding in the other direction. I figured I had only forty pounds on me, which would be all I could spend or lose, what Allen was thinking I didn't know. The taxi pulled up outside the club and we walked straight in, so this is the sort of place I was protected from perhaps. As we walked in there was a dance floor in front of us to the left with some seating around it. To the right there was more seating and scattered around were some girls in lingerie dancing around poles, most of them looked pretty bored. Well I was on limited resources but I was going to enjoy the experience. I sighted a pretty blonde sitting on her own to the right and I thought she'd do for company, Allen disappeared to the left. I sat down next to the pretty blonde in her fine lingerie. The music was loud 'don't speak ' was playing.

"Hi," I said as I sat down.

"Hello"

"Do you speak English?" I asked.

"Yes"

"What's your name?"

"Ellena and yours?"

"Dimitri but Jim's fine, where you from?"

"Siberia," she replied.

"Siberia eh!" now I regard meeting people from far away places as good as travelling.

"You're the first Siberian I've ever met!" I told her, she smiled.

"Do you like it here, in Cyprus?" I asked.

"Yes."

We could just make a conversation over the noise. A man came over to take our drink orders.

"Scotch and lemonade for me, do you want a drink?" I asked.

"Yes please"

She made a sign to the waiter who walked off and returned with my scotch and a coke for the girl and we carried on chatting. After another drink and a little later I noticed Allen disappear through some curtains behind me with a girl, I thought perhaps to a room, but he reappeared less than a minute later with his hair a little ruffled and looking confused. He returned to his seat out of sight of mine. A moment later the girl asked,

"You like I dance for you?"

"No," I was happy enough talking and there were plenty of girls that I could see dancing already.

"I dance for you?" she asked again.

"What for?"

"Twenty pounds," she replied. I burst out laughing it wasn't what I was asking, but I found it funny.

"No I don't want you to dance for me and especially not for twenty pounds"

"Why not?" she looked a little offended, but it never mattered to me. I wasn't about to pay a girl twenty pounds for dancing for me.

"In six weeks time I fly to Thailand, where a girl will love me all night for twenty pounds," I said. But I knew that wasn't the reason, so I told her.

"I'm not business," whilst living in Sydney I had a drinking companion who was a prostitute you tend to learn a lot and look at things from a different perspective.

"No, not business!" she defended herself with.

"Yes it is and I'm not! Drinks ok, but I'm not business!" I emphasised with my voice.

"No! Not business!"

"This is! Here it is!" and then I continued with.

"But if you want to meet me tomorrow away from here no problem, but here it's business and I know it!"

She looked off into the distance, I could see she was thinking about it then she said.

"Hotel Essex at three o'clock!"

I don't think she understood what I meant but I was having fun now.

"No six!"

"No three!" she replied.

"Can't do."

I wasn't about to change any plans for the next day. We chatted on a bit more before my glass was empty.

"Do you want something else to drink?" I asked. Thinking she might want a change from Coke.

"Champanyar!" she announced loudly in her Russian accent. Champagne I thought, before I was even going to buy a glass of this I wanted to know the price of the bottle just to get an idea of the prices, which I couldn't cover.

"Oee!" I called at a waiter. He walked over, a young lad with a tea cloth over his arm.

"How much for a bottle of champagne?" I shouted. I couldn't quite hear his response.

"How much?" I shouted again over the music.

"One hundred and eighty pounds!"

"Stuff the Champagne and bring me another scotch!" I didn't even order another drink for the girl it seemed like a waste of money to spend it on coke. I explained this to her and surprisingly enough she wasn't offended, shortly after the waiter came back and leant over close to my ear.

"Would sir like to come through to the back room to pay his bill please?" boy if that didn't sound ominous enough.

"Not really," I replied.

"Please!" he responded more firmly, I knew it wasn't a request so.

"Ok," I said. I didn't really want to get up yet but it seemed like part of the routine. I got up and behind where I was sitting to the left of the exit, was an office door. I walked into the small office. There was a man sitting behind a desk and the taxi driver who'd given us a lift was sitting on a bench to the right of the office entrance, a short stocky gorilla type looking man with a tight perm walked in behind me. I got the strong impression by his accent that he was, if not Russian then East-European. They certainly weren't all Cypriots,

"Sit down please," said the man behind the desk.

"I'd rather stand for this bit thanks," I told him. I wasn't going to let height be an intimidating factor, which it wouldn't be. I'm by no means tall but I stood six inches over the gorilla.

"We have your bill for you to pay," said the same man.

"Oh yeah how much?" I enquired.

"Sixty pounds"

"How much?"

"Sixty pounds"

"How did it get that high?" I asked sounding surprised which I was, I wanted to see how I'd spent sixty pounds on a couple of cokes and three scotches.

"Here are the prices, they are displayed at the entrance according to law"

"Yeah and how did I spend sixty pounds?"

"The drinks for the Artistes are twenty pounds," shit I thought pricey coke. Of course I should have known where I was. He showed me the price list and the bill. I wasn't about to check if it was displayed at the entrance. The bill wasn't right anyway, which was totally irrelevant. I knew I couldn't pay it, which meant that it was going to get a little amusing.

"Well that's all right," I said as I got my wallet out and opened it up.

"But I've only got forty pounds on me, so it's all you can have," I told him casually. The man behind the desk looked surprised.

"That's all you have?" The gorilla was looking around as if he might find more on the floor around my feet.

"It's all I've got so it's all you can have," I told him.

"No credit cards," he asked pointing to a sign on the wall behind him, I didn't think he'd get too upset over twenty pounds.

"Nope," I had my wallet open

"You Cypriot?" he asked like it mattered.

"Yes," I now found the situation too amusing to feel harassed.

"Nothing?" he asked again, if he was upset about it there was nothing he could do, the gorilla had come around.

"Nothing!" I said.

"What's that?" he asked pointing at my lucky dollar.

"No that's my lucky dollar, you aren't having that!" I had to satisfy him it was a single dollar.

"Here just one dollar and you can't have it, are we finished?"

"You have no more money on you?"

"No, that's it can I go finish my drink now?"

The man behind the desk nodded, boy that was easy I thought, the gorilla was already sitting next to the now despondent looking taxi driver, no commission from my fare I thought. I left the room and saw Allen sitting with a girl. I walked over and whispered in his ear.

"It's a honey trap!"

I really thought that would be enough warning and returned to my seat. A minute or so later I watched Allen being led into the office. Now Allen's a little different from myself, more abrupt perhaps. I used to think he was just a coarse person, until I went to his hometown between Bradford and Leeds to find out it was how everyone was there. He'd been in the office for a minute or so when I heard a commotion going on behind me, I looked around and smiled. Allen had his back to the entrance with about five guys forming a half circle in front of him, I guessed they must have got a different response from him. It looked like a · fighting stance. I watched from my seat amused, very much amused. The men around him were thinking about what to do. A couple of them were hopping from side to side. Allen sprung forward and kicked out at the nearest man to him then immediately lashed out at another with his fist before taking note of the exit behind him and using it. Two or three men ran out after him, but I knew he'd be safe on the main street. It had altered the evening a bit though. The taxi driver came up behind me.

"Your friend, your friend has trouble!"

"Has he?"

"Yes your friend has bad trouble, you stay at the Mediterranean hotel?"

"No you think we stay there," I said not feeling concerned so I told him. "And from what I saw my friend has little trouble."

He walked off, even more despondent. I stayed another ten minutes or so to finish off my scotch and left the club using the last of my change to get a taxi back to the apartment. When I got through the door of the apartment Allen was pacing up and down the room furiously.

"Bastards, did you see me in there, bastards!"

"What happened?" I already knew it was going to be an amusing story.

"They took me in the office and gave me the bill."

"How much?"

"Two hundred and sixty pounds," I nearly wet myself laughing and curled up on the sofa.

"You didn't order champagne did you?"

"Yeah!" I smiled at the thought.

"Didn't you hear me tell you it was a honey trap?"

"I don't know what one of those are, did you see me outside!" I was finding it more and more amusing.

"Only in the club, I was happy chatting to one of the girls and I knew you'd be all right, what happened in the office?"

"I walked in and sat down."

"You sat down?" I looked at him surprised.

"Yeah I wondered what was going on but I didn't think nothing of it, until they told me the bill."

"And then what happened?"

"I flipped and told them to call the police, and that was it! I saw them twitch when I said that so I knew they wouldn't!"

"What happened then?"

"There was some short guy with a perm blocking the door"

"The gorilla"

"Yeah, we argued over the bill a bit more and then they started to get heavy"

"And?"

"And I kicked the gorilla straight between the legs and run out of the office!" he huffed.

"I weren't going to pay it, bastards! Did you see me though!" Allen was still worked up.

"I saw you outside the office, I knew you'd be all right and I knew they wouldn't chase you on the main street," I lay back to reflect on it all.

"Anyway I was quite happy chatting to the girl I was with, Siberian!"
"Bloody joke they were as well!" he tore in with.
"Why?" I asked.
"She took me behind these curtains!"
"Yeah"
"Then she got her top of and bashed my head about with her tits!"
"She did what?" I asked. There were tears in my eyes from laughing.
"It's what it felt like! She took her top off and juggled her tits across my face for about thirty seconds and charged me twenty pounds for it!"
That was it for me I had tears in my eyes and a pain in my stomach from laughing so much.

The next day we took our hire car to Polis in the north west of the island for the day and in the evening I took Allen to meet my uncle Georgio and his wife Marie, who had a smile for me that I could never forget. She'd just sit and hold my hand and talk away to me in Greek with this big warm smile whilst occasionally beckoning me to eat, she was lovely. I hadn't really known Georgio and Marie for long but there's a warmth I got from them that I'd found rare from most of my relatives, they're elderly and run a grocery store on the western side of Limassol town. My cousin had told me it had been abandoned by a Turkish family, I safely presumed after the Turkish invasion, at the same time Georgio and Marie were both living in the North when the invasion drove them from their own homes. I liked Georgio instantly, I'd found some of my mother's older brothers weren't so easy to get along with, but Georgio was different and with him and Marie I'd confess to feeling very bad about not speaking Greek. It was myself, not only would I find it embarrassing when my uncle would rush to warmly greet me in Greek and I'd have to immediately request an interpretation. But I had an urge and a desire to communicate with them. This visit was complicated a little by the absolute necessity for Spyros to be there to act as an interpreter. Which can be a complication if you know Spyros, but in the nicest way.

Early evening we dropped Spyros off and headed into town and went naturally enough back to the same main strip cocktail bar, which was and still is a bit of a regular to me. Allen disappeared for a while when I took notice of the barmaids. I don't know which I was to ask first, Kyp or Christine but either way the response was the same and both came within minutes of each other like savage attacks.
"Hi where you from?" I asked already knowing the answer.
"Cyprus." was the simple response.
Now I can't believe the next question was a natural one for me to ask then, but it was. The response from both girls was the same when I asked it, but it was the nasty sneer that came with the answer that really made it feel like an attack and it struck deep.

"Greek or Turkish?"

"Cypriot!"

Now it wasn't what they said but how they said it. With a sneer, that was like saying. "Would you make the difference?" and they didn't seem happy about it. I was impressed although I was probably looking a little sheepish and stung from the severity of the attack. I watched them for a little while, they were Greek speaking all right, but I liked what they were saying. I remembered thinking that it's a response that would do for me from then. Well yeah we were Greek Cypriots, but here you have to excuse my choice of words, well, stuff it! For me it had started to be a case of see it, be it, if you like, and when I'd realistically considered a unified Cyprus, then we had to accept that one fifth of our population are Turkish..... Mmmm big change of thought necessary, Greeks don't like Turks, and vice a versa but they don't have to live together and if we wanted the north back, then we would have to live together, the difference would cause problems and this was the solution for me. It also got me thinking about the north again and wondering how to pass my time after Allen had gone, and the more I thought about it the stronger the desire had become to go. I chatted to Sergio the barman at the same bar about it and as he pointed out and as I knew I'd have to sign the Denktash agreement, which is a bit of paper saying you recognised the Turkish republic of north Cyprus, which most have a problem with.

I decided I'd seek family support after Allen had gone. The urge to go to my grandfather's farm was just getting stronger with every visit to Cyprus. I knew Turkey had partitioned the island off, but I knew that Greeks were messing around in the country beforehand, so perhaps the blame should be shared a little and after the emotional visit a year earlier I'd thought long and hard about things. I just wanted to go and walk where my grandfather once walked, not only around his farm but to be able to look out at a view and the scenery that I know must have meant so much to him. I didn't regard it as a way of trying to get closer to my dead granddad. I feel close enough, especially now. It's hard to explain, but if I said when I go to church my grandmother is with me, then would you understand that only when I looked out from Ayios Amvrosios south to the mountains and north to the sea would I feel together with my grandfather again.

The rest of the time with Allen passed without too many mishaps. We found a local restaurant with a friendly and funny proprietor. Frequented our now local cocktail bar quite often and for something a little different I'd suggested to Allen that we go to the Turkish baths in the old quarter, we'd seen a home made sign pointing to one whilst driving around. The idea of a steaming Turkish bath to give the body a good cleansing was appealing and letting the imagination run a little wild, I even hoped there might be a possibility of a Turkish massage. I was also to see somewhere that I knew I would like to stay when Allen left. Funny enough we both showered before we went to the baths not that I thought about it at the time. Allen rolled a joint of marijuana, which we both smoked before we left. Now I'll say here that possession of cannabis is a very serious offence in Cyprus. We found the old baths about 5pm not that I thought the time would matter, either they would be open or not. They were open, the building itself looked medieval, it was old, the walls would have been at least 45cms (16inchcs) thick with a high ceiling. I thought it was probably as old as the medieval mosque nearby. We walked in through the large main entrance down a couple of steps into what I'd guess you'd call the main reception area, it was more like a small hall. To the left as we walked in were two, very elderly, Cypriot men sitting on small wooden chairs at a wooden table smoking and chatting away and paying no notice to us whatsoever. I tried to make out their language. It didn't sound Greek so it felt safe to assume that they were Turkish. There was a wooden door on the opposite side of the hall, which I imagined led off to the baths. To the left of the seated men was a tall drinks cooler with a few assorted bottles and cans of soft drinks and to their right was a wooden clothes horse laden with small towels. And around the bottom were a few pairs of shoes, which led me to believe that there were other people already in the baths, which meant they were certainly open. The two elderly men only broke their conversation when we actually interrupted them.

"Hi, we want a Turkish bath," I announced pointing to the door at the same time. They both just looked at us. The expression on their faces hadn't changed. It was like not a single word was understood, I repeated keeping it clear and simple and they just carried on with their conversation. This might have seemed a little ignorant but it didn't feel like it and the fact that the marijuana had taken effect was making it purely amusing.

"B-A-T-H, T-U-R-K-I-S-H B-A-T-H," I said very loud and slowly. They both paused again from their conversation and both raised a head like they understood, but that was all they did, before they continued talking. It was like they weren't even working there, so I enlarged, speaking slow and making hand movements as if they'd help.

"T-U-R-K-I-S-H B-A-T-H," I said again then followed as much with hand signals.

"T-U-R-K-I-S-H B-A-T-H, H-O-W M-U-C-H," I said pointing at Allen as I did. Success the man on the left raised up three fingers, great I thought now we're there. I told Allen my translation not that I thought it was needed.

"We're in, three pounds, seems all right," I was nodding for approval from Allen. He was finding it as amusing as myself, I clarified the price again before paying the old man.

"T-H-R-E-E P-O-U-N-D-S , F-O-R T-W-O," quickly pointing back and forth between Allen and myself. This time I was to get a response, which was completely unexpected, the old man held seven fingers up.

I looked at the fingers totally bemused. I knew he must have understood me the first time, so even if three pounds was for one, how did it get to seven for two. Now at this point I knew it was a blatant rip off but the cheek was amazing.

"Allen the price just went up to seven pounds," I said not being able to hold back a smile. We both agreed we would pay, we knew they were over charging but we decided the amusement it was providing was worth it. We paid the money and followed the old man through the door to another large room. This one was square, each wall about 5 metres long. Running around the sides of the room was a raised platform on which were very small low partitioned changing compartments with curtains across each compartment, on the other side of the room was another exit presumably leading to the baths. Allen and I chose our respective compartments, but we were still a little confused as to the routine. There was a small towel in each compartment and we both had a bit of a giggle talking over how strange the men at reception had been, but how amusing it had all seemed. When we'd stripped right down we discovered just how small the towels were, they were like tea towels, just big enough to put around our waists which was all we could do with them. So there we were, both ready, standing there with nothing on but these very small towels wrapped around our waist, the floor was cold stone slab, the same as the walls and the whole place had an echo to it, the amusement of the whole situation hadn't worn off.

"I guess that's the way," I said pointing through the other doorway, which we brazenly made our way through holding our small towels as we went. This door was to lead to a passageway, on the left we passed a sauna that wasn't in use and not for the first time we noticed how quiet it was apart from ourselves. We got to the end of the passageway which left me totally bemused again, we found ourselves in what to me looked like a sluice room. The stone walls had lost their height as soon as we'd walked into the room. The ceiling in here was about two metres high. The room was about three metres by three metres square and at the centre of each wall on the floor was what appeared to be the oldest stone bidets I'd ever seen with two taps above each, scattered around the floor were a few small plastic bowels.

"No this can't be right," I said. "We must have got lost."
We stood there shaking our heads in disbelief. It was a funny sight with our towels. I told Allen I'd find out where we went wrong and went off to the reception hall to seek assistance, I returned a few minutes later with one of the old men in tow, insisting he came with me.

"L-O-O-K!" I said "N-O S-T-E-A-M!" I then made a gushing noise and baked the noises up with a hand motion, needing one hand for my towel.

"W-H-E-R-E?" I growled. Giving away a grin. The old man seemed to click and got excited. Without saying the words he made the noises that sounded like yes, great I thought we're finally there and fully expected the man to lead us off. But to Allen's and my amazement he was just going for one of the plastic bowels, which he returned to the basin with and proceeded to make the motion of pouring water over his head.

"You have got to be kidding, I JUST HAD A SHOWER!" I shouted at him. I was stunned and so was Allen but the marijuana was also a dominating factor and we both burst into laughter. The old man was finished giving us a display and left us with a big grin on his face. We knew then our Turkish bath just wasn't to be and returned to the changing room, but the amusement of it all hadn't worn off. We told the old men as we left, the money was worth the experience and they still made no sign at all of understanding a single word we said, which in itself was amusing. We decided afterwards if anything we'd got there late, there were no other people there and they were probably the caretakers.

I knew well before Allen left what I wanted to do. I just hadn't wanted to get him involved while he was there. I checked out of the apartment and in a hire car that I'd taken, drove down to the old town to take a room in an old hotel I'd seen, it had more than enough character to attract me. It was an old building, the Hotel Hellas. The rooms are very small and the walls mainly plywood and to get to the shower you had to walk through the old reception hall, which always had some life in it. It was a bit of a drop, but possibly one I would've chosen anyway, for £3.50 a night, it suited me and now I had no ties and my bag was in the hire car.

Since the brief conversation with the barmaids I'd had the north on my mind again "Cypriot," as much as I returned. There is only one part of Cyprus that I really yearn to visit. I'd grown up with an oil painting of Kyrenia harbour and the mountains in the background and I knew my grandfathers' village was close. I knew the communities had gone but I imagined my grandfathers' farm still standing, maybe with someone living on it, maybe, but I'd already started to come to terms with that one. My relatives couldn't seem to understand the attraction or the way it seems to draw me. I'd arranged to pick my cousin up to take him over to see my uncle Georgio, if I'd known my godfather was at home, I would have gone straight to see him but for some reason I'd just naturally assumed that he'd be away with my godmother. So I regarded Georgio as the nearest family elder at hand so to speak. I'd told Spyros that I'd need him to interpret for me and that I had something specific to ask my uncle. We arrived early teatime. My aunt wasn't present, when I was to get down to the serious questions. We were standing,

"Spyros ask uncle if I can go to the north?" my cousin spoke to my uncle for a short while, then turned to me.

"He wants to know why you want to go to the north?"

"Because it's where granddads farm is and I want to see it," Spyros translated this then quickly replied with.

"He say's that there's nothing to see." How many times had I heard that one and it was so frustrating, how can you really explain to people what a strong emotion it was,

"Tell him I don't care if there's nothing to see, it's something I want to see for myself." Spyros spoke for a short while then responded with.

"But he say's you'd have to sign the Denktash agreement."

"I know that, it's why I'm asking for his blessing on it," I already knew where the conversation was going to go now, I saw my uncle shake his head.

"He say's he can't give it," my frustration quickly set in. I shook my head.

"I might as well go across with the smugglers!" I snapped. I thought that wouldn't meet much resistance, which it never, but I knew I never meant it. I sat down my frustration now showing but at the same time I could feel the frustration in my uncle, I wasn't happy, but I did understand. I was sat and still looking down when I said.

"Ask uncle if he can draw me a map of where the farm is, one that I can use at sometime with approximate distances from the village, road junctions etc. Ask him if he can do that for me?" Spyros spoke to my uncle I looked up to see my uncle nod, my cousin turned to me.

"Yes, he says he can do that." It's something I thought. I didn't get the pen and paper out though. I still had to work out how I was going to get to the north. But the map promise was one I thought I'd hold my uncle to. I was just glad at that point that he could give me that information. The conversation was soon to end and I left my uncles under a sombre cloud to go to the cocktail bar. Promising him that I'd return to visit him before I left Cyprus.

I now decided I would go straight back to my holiday, it seemed worth a try. But I thought I'd check out of my hotel in the morning and drive the car to Polis for a few days. The distance from Limassol seemed to be appealing and I quite liked the beach and the sedate town. I got to the cocktail bar to meet up with a Swiss guy called Bill, whom I'd met a couple of days previous. He was going to try to get the money back on his apartment, which he was full of complaints about to leave him free to travel. I'd told him of my rough plans but up until that point they'd just been contingent, Bill was in the cocktail bar.

"How did you get on?" I enquired.

"No good, I have not been able to find the person who deals with the money"

"I didn't think you would, don't worry about it, keep the apartment I have the hire car for the week anyway, so let's get some use out of it," I told him adding. "Wherever we go we can get a room for five pound a night each, go halves on fuel," I shrugged my shoulders.

"And go a roaming, what do you think?" I asked him.

Bill smiled and nodded. He was up for it and he made for a good travelling companion apart from his constant choice of techno for the stereo. We drove north past Paphos and on to Polis where we took a small twin room over the home of an old Cypriot woman named Kaloo. It was her room and even though she spoke very little English, we knew she was going to make a pleasant landlady for a couple of days. She was a talker and she didn't mind if you couldn't understand. She was happy and it seemed contagious around her and with the talk usually came coffee and pastries to eat, which she'd always make hard to refuse.

The beach at Polis is nice if not for the colour, for it seems a shade of grey at times depending on the sunlight. From the water line it's very pebbly, which can make walking in the sea harder but regardless, the beach is pleasant. The road to the beach itself leads through a wooded campsite on the edge of the beach with full facilities and a sandwich bar that looked like it had been there for some time. There were signs of organised barbecues and a banner that announced a weekly volleyball competition with a hundred pounds prize money for the winners. Bill and I were to spend a fair bit of time on the beach, which I seemed to be drawn to, day and night. The moon was filling up, I knew another day or so and it would be full, I thought of Aphrodite's rock.

The town of Polis is quite small and it's got that pleasant relaxed Mediterranean feel to it. In the early evening the cobbled square is alive with waiters nipping in between tables and diners enjoying their meals. We chose a restaurant outside the main square, which was a little quieter and after we'd eaten we walked through looking for somewhere to drink. I noticed two young female tourists sitting together. At a guess I would have said German, but it seemed to matter less with Bill, he spoke smatterings of French as well as his Swiss German and a little Russian, the idea of which I found amusing.
"Bill go and ask those girls if we can join them, while I get the drinks." Bill looked at me a little uneasy of what I was asking him to do.
"I can't!"
"Don't be silly of course you can!"
"I can't!"
"You get the drinks then and I'll ask them," I told him giving up.
"Ok," Bill's shyness was too much at times. He walked off to order our drinks.
"Would you girls mind if my friend and I join you?"
"No not at all"
"Thanks."
I introduced myself and Bill soon appeared with our drinks, they were as I guessed German. We chatted for twenty or thirty minutes. I chatted less. My German seems to dry up a little after a few drinks and unlike a lot of Germans I'd met, their English was very bad. We were soon joined by a middle aged Cypriot man looking for pleasant conversation perhaps, but he was soon to get more than a little annoying for me.
"Your Cypriot eh?"
"Yes," I said.

"You don't speak Greek?"

"No"

"Why not?" he asked. I was thinking this was the last thing I needed.

"Just the way things worked out I guess," I told him. Already showing how I felt about the conversation.

"You Love Cyprus?"

"Yes," I nodded.

"You love Cyprus why don't you do your national service?"

"I don't need military training," I didn't see any need to enlarge on that one at all. By now I was having a conversation I really didn't want. I knew the man was playing on this for the benefit of the girls.

"You know everyone here does their national service"

"I know," I said.

"Me, I do mine, and you know what we do if the sirens sound?" he'd just got my attention with that one.

"No, what will you do?" I asked, showing my interest.

"If the sirens sound, we go to the army camp, and we leave together!"

"You leave," I could not believe what I'd just heard but my tone hadn't changed.

"Yeah we leave."

"Then maybe it's better I don't do my national service," I said with a piercing look. It was to me one of the most contemptible things I could have heard. I thought of my promise to my grandmother and I made my disinterest in him obvious by pulling back my chair and turning to Bill. The Cypriot soon took advantage of this and turned his attention to the German girls and to my relief he spoke very good German having worked there and was intent on trying it out on them, which suited me. At the end of the evening the girls came back for a bottle of wine, but my German doesn't improve with alcohol and I never expected their English to, so I soon found myself asleep.

After a few days we drove back to Limassol. We had Bills two-bedroom apartment that I hadn't seen to return to. So when we gave a lift to a couple of female German backpackers, who'd got soaked in pouring rain, I thought of my backpacking days and offered them a room in Bill's two bed-roomed apartment, before asking him, which I knew was cheeky, but I knew Bill wouldn't mind. It would make a nice change and I told him they were prettier dinner companions. Bills apartment was quite nice and he hadn't told me there was a swimming pool there. Now that could make or break a holiday. The girls left the next day and I tried to relax by the pool but I found myself often drifting away with dreams of the beaches around Kyrenia and Ayios Amvrosios. It seemed like every time I came here, I'd find or see something, which would leave attempting to asses the situation from different perspectives and the girls in the bar had done it this time.

It wasn't that I'd ever considered Cyprus as anything other than independent. But it was as if they'd enforced that concept by not differentiating between heritage when it come to being Cypriot and there was another thing that impressed me, they weren't afraid to say it.

I spent most of my time from then sitting by the pool listening to British Forces radio, which always gave me the impression that Cyprus is good holiday destination for them. I found my thoughts focusing on the islands problems again. A tourist caught me by surprise by the pool.

"How long have you been on holiday?"

"Holiday ...is it?" I said. I'd forgot it was.

I never did return to see my uncle before I left, but if I felt a bit guilty about it, then the frustration I felt seemed to say it was ok.

Chapter 6

Now I'm not quite sure why I do some things I'm certainly not sure why I went to Kos when I did. But have you ever had one of those feelings. Well they're the sort of things that I'd found myself travelling on lately, feelings, as I said I don't know why I went to Kos. It was early June nineteen ninety-eight, it just called and I went.

I found myself settling down on the floor of the departure lounge at Gatwick airport for the night before an early morning flight. If I was wondering what I was doing then, then twelve hours later would find me cursing what I was doing, as midday the next day found me walking round the back of Kos town. Misdirection had sent me totally in the wrong direction as I found out after walking a good hour and opting for a taxi. I was going to visit my god sister Nikki and her husband and the countless other friends that I had accumulated over the years in Kos and to add to any excitement I knew I wasn't even expected. Nikki is my god sister as my mother christened her. Her family lives in my home-town and are Greek Cypriots that my mother first befriended many years ago. It was one of her cousins that was shot whilst attempting to climb the flagpole in Cyprus in ninety-six. She came to live at my mother's house for a while, very much part of an extended family. She's a hairdresser by profession. Trained to instructor level at Vidal Sasoon's before embarking on her travels. Which at some point took her to Cyprus where she was to meet Christos her Cypriot common law husband. By all accounts it was a fiery first meeting between Nikki and Christos mainly because the police were in the process of arresting him and not being too polite about it, which was probably what attracted her to him in the first place. Christos is a real character. He comes from the mountainous Troodos area of Cyprus but looks more like he's come straight from the mountains of the Himalayas (only in denim) where he tends to spend much of winter, after his shopping in Asia is finished. They spend approximately six months of the year on Kos selling street jewellery and the rest of the time in Asia buying the jewellery, made and unmade that they'll sell the following year. They have a four year old boy Costas who seems to have adapted well to this life, but due to his age will soon require a more static base for his education. Christos had not been able to return to Cyprus for a couple of years through fear of arrest. Before he'd left he was accused of growing a single cannabis plant. I dare say it may be true, apparently the police and National Guard had actually staked out this single plant and had seen Christos caressing and talking to the plant, it all sounds too funny to take serious, but on Cyprus it is.

This was at least my forth visit to Kos in as many years and it was always with Nikki and Christos that I'd stay, Nikki was working around the house when I arrived, it was all hugs and kisses.

"Jim what are you doing here? We wasn't expecting you!"

"I didn't know myself I was coming out until last week."

"I'm so glad you came, how long you here for?" she asked excitedly.

"Ten days"

"Christos is going to be pleased to see you."

"Where is he?"

"He just had some things to do he'll be back soon."

"Have you started work yet?" I asked.

"No"

"Why not?" I enquired.

"Because he's waiting for the others to arrive they'll be here in a few days," she informed me.

"Why is he waiting for the others?"

"Because they've given us all really shit sites to sell on and he's waiting for the others to arrive so that they can all go and complain together."

"Where have they put you?" I asked.

"Outside the toilets!"

"Where?"

"Outside the toilets below the tree!"

"Where no one can see you?"

"Yeah"

"I'm not surprised you're complaining," I said hardly blaming them.

"Yeah it seems to get worse every year!"

"What about a shop, have you thought about it?" I enquired.

"Yes, there's one in the square we've been looking at, but the man wants five thousand pounds before we even move into the place, Christos seems uncertain but he's being so negative."

"Five thousand, that's a lot, what's the rent?"

"About two hundred and fifty pounds"

"That's not too bad, what's the location like?"

"Good! Right in the main square, we'll show you when Christos gets back, you hungry?"

"Too right!"

Nikki's a great cook. The house that they were renting was bigger than on previous years. It was a bungalow with a low white brick wall, topped with iron railings around the perimeter of the house and garden. As you walked through the front door immediately on your right is the kitchen the smallest room in the house about two metres across by three metres in length. Everything in the kitchen seemed quite modern except for the washing machine and a small two ring electric cooker, which sat on top of the washing machine. The cooker itself was about the size and shape of a large microwave oven as it had a grill and an oven incorporated into it, but it seemed surplus to their needs due to the fitted gas cooker to the right of the entrance. Directly opposite the entrance to the kitchen and next to the washing machine was the workroom where Christos had spent hours making the jewellery that he should be selling. The room was about three by three metres square and the far wall was shelved from about a metre up, below the shelving was a large chest of draws. Along the wall opposite, but nearest the entrance on the left was a z frame bed, my bed for the next ten days and between the bed and the chest of draws was the workbench underneath the window with it's assorted tools and drills. Back to the hallway past the kitchen on the left was the main bedroom and directly in front was the large square lounge. The dominating feature in this room at the time was part of Christos's stall, which was opened out as he'd been laying out his displays. The stall itself consisted of four large wooden display cases that opened up to lay two horizontally and two vertically. It was quite a display set off by a large wooden carved head of a Native American Indian hanging from the top centre, but the jewellery was way beyond what I was expecting. I knew most of it was genuine silver but I told Christos that the quality of most of the pieces were far better than previous years and good enough for a shop, I was quite astounded by some of them. The rest of the room might have seemed drab compared to the display, but wasn't. There was a pair of patio doors on the left as you walked in with the garden beyond and on the right, sparse, but comfortable seating and a stereo on some shelving in the corner. The house was comfortable enough if I wanted to spend time there, not that I planned to.

At the time the shop had felt to me to be the reason why I'd gone to Kos. Christos was pleased to see me but we didn't really get the chance to talk properly for a day or two, mainly because of Nikki's and my pre-occupation with the shop idea, not that Christos wasn't with us. It just wasn't one of his main priorities, but it took me a day or two to see it. The shop Nikki had spoken of was in a prime location and I knew I could help them with the reserve. But Christos had seemed pessimistic about the whole affair from the start. At first I just thought it was the one shop in particular and I wasn't surprised after talking to the owner in Athens and the restrictions he was putting on whoever rented the place. The restriction that would hurt most was not being able to make use of the area immediately outside the front as other shop owners could. This was an obvious disadvantage and as Christos had pointed out, no matter how good the location, it would be no good if people could not see the shop existed and amongst the clutter from the other shops that looked a possibility despite it being on a corner.

Here I should explain that most of their income would be made between June and September and as it was now early June it seemed to add to the importance of getting established in some form of premises as quickly as possible. So the next day we were to look at some other locations. The council had given them such a bad spot, all the street sellers were usually positioned together, but this year not only had they been split up, but some had been given one of the worst possible sites in the town. Outside the toilets below from the tree Hypocrites was said to teach under. But way below on the main street, just on the edge of the port. Not a good site for passing trade. No matter how many lights Christos would set up, they'd never get seen due to the two high walls either side of the road, one being to the ancient port castle. To my surprise when we looked around the perimeters of the town we were to find more than a couple of premises that seemed suitable for a shop. Nikki was also emphasising how much she wanted a hairdresser's and there in front of my eyes were two empty shops in a quiet passageway near the main tourist shopping area, both next to each other. They seemed perfect to me especially as there was no reserve needed and the rent was cheap. Christos and I went alone to look at the shops, but as I inspected the premises my imagination seeing how they could look, Christos seemed totally disinterested and wondered across the way to look at a shop nearby that his friend had recently opened. I walked over and gazed around the shop for a short while, looking more at how much work had gone into fitting it out. It looked quite good for a shop fitted out on a budget and I was most impressed. It was painted in a light sky blue, with a little bit of painted carpentry hiding a few possible ugly spots but the shops contents barely interested me. A mixture of cheap Asian and Indian bric a brac. I suppose it would be easier to describe it as hippy junk, joss sticks and little bits and pieces. It might interest some people but to myself there was nothing new, it looked just like a number of places I'd seen in England and most of the items I'd either purchased or at least seen in Asia at a fraction of the prices now being charged. I'm not very good at even attempting to look interested at times like this and not wanting to seem rude to the shops' owner I made my excuses and sat out of sight around the corner and waited for Christos. Nikki had been complaining that he was being very negative in his approach to it all and when we got home I told her that I agreed.

"How did you get on?" she asked.

"No good Christos doesn't seem interested at all," I told her.

"No I told you he's being very negative about it!"

"You're telling me!" I thought of the total disinterest he'd shown.

"I've told him I want to make extra money from hairdressing and he doesn't encourage me at all, he just doesn't think I can make money from it, but I cut good hair!"

"I know that, you're the only one I let touch mine"

"I make little bits here and there but it's not enough, there are things I want, I want to be able to buy things without going to Christos!"

"I can understand that," I said.

"I want better for myself, for us! But he just doesn't seem to listen! I want to be able to buy things when I want, like a new dress," she told me adding. "I had to order the one I wanted so I could pay it off!" That seemed reasonable to me, but it did seem strange, either the dress was expensive which was unlike Nikki or Christos had got very tight which didn't seem like him.

"And I need a new pair of scissors mine have had it and I need them for my work, Christos says I just have to make do, but he doesn't understand how important they are to me."

I just nodded, she did cut good hair and most people that used her for their haircuts had no idea of her training. I felt she could make some sort of an income from it, but this was their own domestic affairs' to me. I could tell Nikki was upset about it, but I just wanted to know what was going to happen in regards to the shop. My time was limited and I wanted to help out if I could. Later that afternoon I had my first real talk to Christos about it all. It was clear then the shop wasn't going to happen and things weren't well between Nikki and himself.

"I don't know what's wrong with her these days," Christos's English is very thick, but good even if sentences are often simplified.

"Oh, she just feels it's the right time to settle and a shop seems like a good idea."

"Yes, yes I also want a shop but its not the right time now, we don't even know if we want a shop in Kos. I like Crete, but Nikki all the time now she wants, I want this, I want that and why I ask her, why all the time she wants now when she was happy before?"

"I think she's thinking of Costas and his education," I told him considering it.

"Yes I know this, I also, but Costas goes to school next year and until then we have a good life, I tell Nikki this and she doesn't listen, I tell her next year that's it! Costas starts school our lives change for sure but until then, why does she want these things?" I could see he was a little upset at everything expected of him. He continued,

"I tell her we have a good life! I think many people would like to have a life like ours, next year it changes for sure! But why rush to it!" he sighed. "When our life changes she will miss this and I don't even know if I want to stay in Kos, I think I like Crete more." I'd heard Nikki mention Crete with more affection as well and I agreed that it was a nicer island.

"I want to spend more time looking there first!" he finished with. I had to agree with him and it did get me thinking about how good their life was. Five or six months in the Mediterranean, a month shopping around Asia with a stop off at a beach and then to their Himalayan retreat. Which I'd seen many photos of and looked beautiful, clean, and the views were spectacular and I knew that the life suited Christos. You just needed to look at him with his long black hair and full black beard to know he'd feel comfortable there. He'd certainly taken on the appearance of one of the locals, except of course for his denims. But most importantly at this point, he had seriously thought it through, we were having a conversation we should have had a couple of days before, it would have saved me a little stress.

"You have thought about this then Chistos?" not that I needed to ask.

"Yes!" He said in a way, which seemed to force it home.

"Yes I think about it often and I just don't think the times right, not now!"

From what I'd heard during our conversation I had to agree with him, he had not only thought it through, but his conclusion was one I couldn't disagree with, the life they had was good. As for settling down, Costas would be at school for a long time and that would bring big changes with it. He was right, they would miss this life when things change, or Nikki would. I knew Christos would still be spending his time in Asia, he had to, to buy his jewellery. It would be Nikki that would be more tied to the one place, I didn't know if she'd really considered that, so I finished the conversation on a lighter note.

"Ok! So no more shop hunting. I'm back on holiday!" I said Gleefully, and so I was, off to get a hire push bike and intent on enjoying the rest of the holiday. I gave a little thought to Nikki and Christos's home problems. I knew it wasn't just the shop business that was annoying him but it seemed domestic. I just hoped they'd work their way through it, and anyway, I couldn't think of anything else I could do on that one, it seemed more personal. I was soon to tell Nikki of my findings.

"I had a talk to Christos earlier, about the shop business."

"What did he say?" she enquired.

"Well we had a good chat about everything," and after a slight pause. "I've got to say I think he's thought about things and he's right about waiting as far as committing yourselves."

"You think so?"

"Yeah I do Nikki, Costas starts school next year, your lives will change forever whether you like it or not, he does want a shop but he's not sure if he even wants one on Kos," I told her finishing with. "It seems he prefers Crete as well."

"You don't think he's just being negative about everything?" she asked.

"No he's thought about it and I've got to say I think he's right."

"You think I should forget the shop then," she said letting her sadness show on that one.

"For now, he does want one, but not now and I think he's right about not committing at this point."

I knew she would be hurt at that one, because it was also saying I didn't think it was a good idea for her to open a hairdresser's, her place of her own which I said I would help her with. Help, she knew, now wouldn't be coming. That was about all I had to say on the subject which I felt more than a bit sad about at the time, I knew she wasn't happy and we were quite close but if it was her relationship that was in trouble I didn't think I could help. I couldn't say I knew Christos very well at that point but I knew him well enough to know that he knew what he was doing as far as business went and I could find little fault in him, not saying he's perfect, but who is?

So back on holiday, well I suppose so. The hire bike helped, I'd hired a female mountain bike. For the first time in my life I found myself wondering what we actually need the crossbar for. I had money of course, but I'd badly sprained my right ankle before going to Kos and it was troubling me enough to put me off most activities including swimming, even though it might have done me some good. But not only that, nothing seemed as it normally was, few of the street sellers I knew were working, most of them weren't even on the island yet. There were others I knew, Fanouri for instance, but he'd be out on his boat with the tourists on their three islands' tour, it was a big yacht built in Bodrum. I knew if I just turned up I could go out with him any time but my ankle was ruling that out. So I thought it best to get into a routine and found myself hoping I wouldn't get bored by the last few days of my visit, which was a possibility.

By this time I'd met Helen a Danish woman that Nikki had befriended, she had a child close to Costas age by her Greek husband with whom she owned a bar. She was friendly and I'd often see her in the mornings, when the children would be put on a minibus for nursery school after which she and Nikki would go for a morning swim. I had a couple of brief conversations with her during which, one thing I did hear and thought a little of at the time with my talk to her, was someone other than Nikki who seemed to put a bit of emphasis on being positive. Here I'll have to say that Nikki is one of the easiest influenced people I know and has suffered because of it, at the hands of one or two religious sects which makes me a little protective of who I'd want influencing her, and friends are influential. But I liked Helen and was pleased that Nikki had met her. I told her that I'd pay her bar a visit one night and I looked forward to meeting her husband.

I worked quickly into a routine, bearing in mind that Christos and Nikki had things to do and one which would get me out and about for most of the day. In the mornings I'd started to visit a woman that Nikki had recently met and made friends with. She worked in a bikini shop about a kilometre away from the house, on one of the roads that led to the port. The road itself, even though in a tourist area had a very relaxed feel to it, there was a mixture of tourist shops and bike hire places and further on closer to the port some bars and restaurants. The shop itself is small but indiscreet in its colouring, bright Canary yellow. They'd made use of the five or so metres of pavement outside the front of the shop with rails of bikinis and swim suits under the cover of a protective awning. But out the back was where whoever was working would spend most of their time. Under the cool shade of a very, very large parasol with three-quarters of the area protected by the shop and two canary yellow walls leaving the back open to light. In the middle of the area was a medium sized white round plastic garden table and some chairs. Over the table was a white tablecloth and in the centre of the table a flower in a small glass vase and around the perimeters of the area a couple of rubber plants, and one or two small potted trees. Which made it look an appealing place to sit and chat with Nikki's new friend Jean. I wasn't bashful about introducing myself to her. Nikki had told me to drop in on her or Angie the shops owner, both Australian Greeks anytime and that they were looking forward to meeting me. Jean just happened to work the shift that fitted my routine at the time and she was very easy to get on with. I got quite a shock when I first saw her. She could have been the much older sister of one of the barmaids from Cyprus and they were both from Melbourne. Only Jean looked a lot more haggard although she still had some looks about her under the makeup. You could tell she was one of the people that tend to ignore good advice and sit in the sun too long, drying them up for good. She dressed well and was outgoing and pleasant company, long hair usually tied up and she might have once been a brunette, I couldn't tell as the sun had bleached her hair a reddish colour. I was to spend a few mornings with her just passing the time chatting about nothing in particular. I took an interest in the book she was reading. She informed me Angie had given it to her and that was where she'd got most of her books. It wasn't long before I was to meet Angie, just a few days. She stopped off on her push-bike whilst Jean and I had been chatting. She had her son with her and was showing off her new running shoes and announcing to us that she'd decided to take up power walking at six in the morning. Taking an erect pose as she did so, breathing in deeply, straightening her back and pulling her hands up to her chest and pushing her elbows out and seeming to stretch as she exhaled. Looking off into the distance with a demure but slightly smug smile on her face as if she was facing the sunrise that she was describing. I watched more amused than anything. She was quite an attractive woman possibly the same age as Jean, about mid thirties. But without the same sun ravaged skin, which was in very good condition. Olive skinned and black hair which she wore tied up, both women had good figures, but Angie seemed to show it off a bit more without really trying, through the tight jeans she wore and the tight white top. We only spoke briefly. She had more of a well spoken, but Greek accent, than an Australian one.

After a couple of hours chatting to Jean I'd ride down to the small port and around to the western side and along the ancient castle wall to see what visiting yachts were in and where they'd come from. I'd enjoy conjuring up visions of the voyage that some of them must have made, some days there were some of interest. After a wander around the port I'd make my way to Cosmos, the bar was called. A young Dutch fellow and his Greek girlfriend who had an evening job in another bar ran it. I imagine to help make ends meet it was their first year in business. Here I'd make it a habit to stop for a couple of toasted sandwiches and some cold drinks. I liked Sonny the Dutch fellow who run the place and it looked like he could use whatever business he could get and I was more than happy to throw a little of mine his way.

It was on the fourth or fifth night that I found myself in Helen and her husbands' bar. I hadn't yet met Nicholaos, Helens husband but had expected to. The bar itself was quite open at the front with a standing area and some high tables and stools. The small dance floor and second bar was sectioned off about five metres from the entrance with a varnished wooden partition down the middle and wooden sliding doors at the front. I couldn't see much more at the time, it was too crowded with a mixture of young Scandinavian holidaymakers partying and several young and not so young Greek men. One of which was Nicholaos whom I was looking forward to meeting. I didn't feel comfortable though. I certainly had no reason for feeling uncomfortable at that point apart from my manner of dress perhaps, which was very casual or maybe that as happy as I was to be where I was. I couldn't compete with the enthusiasm of the revellers around me. I was standing close to the bar and Nicholaos was pointed out to me by Helen as she made her way through the crowd, she didn't stop long just a quick but warm introduction and she was off to play the ever attentive host. Now at this point along with Nicholaos had come a crowd of well-dressed, smooth looking Greeks, which made me feel less comfortable. I know for some unknown reason, I was feeling defensive. Nicholaos turned his head toward me so I could hear him over the music and the revellers.
    "You're from Cyprus?"
    "Yes," I replied. It felt totally natural saying it.
    "You don't speak Greek?" he asked a little surprised.
 Now I still to this day can't understand what made me reply in the harsh and short manner I did and the words I spoke surprised me even more.
    "As a Cypriot I will not have a Greek telling me what language to speak!" I said way too harshly.
    "I understand," replied Nicholaos slightly embarrassed. I didn't, I didn't know why I said what I said or why the harsh tone in which I said it. I decided I'd work that one out later. Nicholaos turned back to me and inquired,
    "Want a beer?"
I nodded. "Thanks."
I felt a bit awkward talking to Nicholaos or attempting to over noise after the way I'd responded to him. I certainly didn't mean it to come out so harshly. I wanted to apologise if I sounded offensive but with the crowds and the noise, any kind of reasonable conversation was out of the question. The best I could do would be to accept a couple of drinks show my appreciation and leave. I thought I might mention it to Helen or something. I did feel a little bad about it if only because

from first impressions Nicholaos is a very likeable person and I felt that was confirmed at other times when I met him, but it was done and I couldn't undo what I'd done, not on that night anyway. I figured that with nearly a week left I'd get a chance to talk to him properly.

The next couple of days drifted past and not as well as they could have. Things seemed to be deteriorating further between Nikki and Christos. I didn't find it bothering me too much, I had my own room so I could shut the door if I wanted to but I was hearing some very strange things from Nikki. She had got a little more demanding in her needs and I don't mean her emotional needs so much. I could hear her asking for better material things to replace what they had, but here the main consideration had to be given to the fact that they were far from settled. I was lying down in my room early one afternoon when one such incident occurred, Nikki and Christos were around the house. Christos was preparing his stall, he'd decided he'd just set up wherever suited him until he was moved on, most importantly he knew he needed to start the money coming in and Nikki was doing some domestic chores. My room was peaceful, directly next door to the kitchen. But I couldn't hear anything from there as I closed my eyes and drifted away to the low and sedate music that I had playing, feeling a little light, but cosy, from a glass or two of wine. When, without any warning whatsoever, a noise that I can only describe as sounding like a very old jet engine going straight to full thrust pounded through the room. A very old jet engine because of a very loud metallic banging sound that came with the roar. It jolted me into life and brought me around in a flash, I was straight on my feet and to the door. I had no idea what the noise could have been it was so loud, but as I opened the door it was immediately apparent, although still a little astounding. The washing machine had gone into spin with what I imagine must be a drum more than a little off balance. In the few seconds it had taken me to get to the door and open it, the machine had rumbled and bounced forward some thirty centimetres. And to make matters worse not only was the compact but heavy two ring grill and oven on top but the stew in the oven was splattering out through the now open oven door. My first thought was to grab a hold of the washing machine, but almost instantly realising there was only one option and a far easier one. I reached up to the plug that was inserted in the kitchen wall by the doorway and removed it. At which the grinding and rattling was almost instantly silenced. The difference in the noise level was amazing and a moment later Nikki was on the scene closely followed by Christos, who stood at the kitchen doorway. Nikki was getting upset, immediately starting to attack the mess and at the same time apologising. I took a step back still stunned that it was just the washing machine. I'd heard faulty ones before but that was loud, very loud.

"I'm sorry Jim!" Nikki almost screamed and cried at the same time.

"It's this bloody washing machine! I told Christos we need a new one but does

he listen, NO!"
Christos was leaning against the doorway, he said something quietly but defensively in Greek, Nikki replied in English.

"I told you ages ago we need a new one but you never listen!" she was getting more upset, I thought I'd try help,

"Nikki I don't think the cooker on top helped, it's just the drums a little off balance."

"It's this washing machine!" she replied as much to herself, she was now getting angrier as she carried on wiping the stew away from the sides and the floor.

"You want clean clothes to wear, you get me a new washing machine! Or you can clean them yourself or would you rather I wore them down on a rock as if we were back in India!" Nikki screamed at Christos. I really didn't want to say anything but when she said that I had this instant picture of Christos walking up a Himalayan mountain track with a washing machine strapped to his back, scrubbing on the rocks sounded better to me, not that I was about to say it,

"Is there not a launderette you can use?"

"No and I don't have the time anyway Jim," she sounded more upset when talking to me but it turned to anger when she spoke to Christos. I felt like I had to help but I couldn't see any point in a new washing machine and I knew even a second hand one would cost money they could barely afford at that time. Nikki was continuing her barrage on Christos, this time attacking him for not giving her enough time to make her own money from haircuts, not that she saw any chance of that with her old scissors. Christos was now starting to get angry himself, I didn't want to take sides, I could write more of what was said but I'd already switched off and decided it was time to get out of the kitchen, literally. I took a slow ride down to the port thinking about things and a conversation I'd had with Nikki a day or two earlier. She apologised to me for the situation between her and Christos. I'd told her there was no need to as it really wasn't affecting me, I thought it might be time to tell her it now was. But I really couldn't work things out. I'd known Nikki for many years and material things had always been of the lowest priority. I started considering the changes that she'd been through, a child for instance would bring on changes, but the vision of Christos with the washing machine on his back was an amusing one. I really didn't think they were going to last. It seemed so many little things compounding. But I didn't feel I could help. It just seemed like one of many relationships I'd seen dissolve away, and I knew that Christos would only take so much. My helplessness on the matter helped it all drift to the back of my mind by the time I'd got to the port. I rode slowly round to the western side to see what boats were in, there was a small, but nice little nine or ten metre yacht that I'd noticed there every day, but it had been gutted by fire the night before. A lot of the interior had been ripped out and the cockpit was blackened and the sail had started to melt around the boom. I looked at it for a short while. She was very similar to one I'd once owned with a friend, a nice boat and easily manageable.

I considered the impulsion that had brought me here. I'd had many pleasant trips to Kos but I normally visited at the end of the season when things are more relaxed. I'd felt something had drawn me here but I was lost as to what. I slowly rode further around the port pondering as I rode and then I saw a yacht worth a stop. One of my favourites not that I could ever afford one, a Moody 46. This is a yacht that even with my limited sailing experience I knew would take one anywhere and a boat for all moods if you like. A good looking cruising vessel and very capable. I hadn't got off my bike, but I was just admiring the boat when a young looking fellow approached and started to pull himself up on to the bow. I could tell the boat was from England but her homeport wasn't painted on her side as is often done so I thought I'd at least inquire.

"Where you out of?" I asked.

"Southampton," he replied. I just nodded and carried on admiring.

"She's a beaut isn't she!" he added.

"Sure is!"

We made pleasant conversation for a short while. His name was John, he and his girlfriend were crewing the boat for the owner who they were to meet in Kos. Their gear cable had broken on the way in, which was why the boat was moored bow to port as opposed to stern to port, which is more common. John made an immediate impact on me, I think if only for the time he gave to a total stranger. I knew that a boat like this would attract a few admirers and most owners didn't seem to make this much time, but when I left him ten or fifteen minutes later I felt like he'd picked me right up. He'd told me his girlfriend was sleeping, but to call back another time, just the idea of a beer on board was nice. Some people buy these sort of boats, just for drinks on board without ever taking them out, but this wasn't one of those and just from talking to John you could tell that despite his age he had experience. I rode back towards the house in a different frame of mind, it's nice how just a brief chance meeting could change a day. I had three or four more left and I figured I might be spending more time at the port. I wasn't in a hurry to get back to the house and it seemed a perfect time to stop by and spend an hour or so talking with Angie. The set up at the back of the shop was a nice place to pass some time. I rode up on my bike Angie was on her own standing by the table. I put the bike on its stand.

"Hi, mind if I sit with you for a while?" I asked.

"No, not at all."

I sat down at the table. Angie was dressed as before. She took a gaze through the back door of the shop for any customers and then slowly made her way around to the other side of the table. Her actions seemed slow but purposeful and her pose very erect and she still had that demure but smug look on her face, how did she do it? She stood with her back to me for a short period and then turned. She walked around a chair at the table and before sitting she looked up with the same look on her face that she'd had when she described the sunrise on her early morning power walk. Looking not at me, but straight ahead, she took a deep breath as she placed her hands on her hips sliding them down her thighs, as she sat and announced, still looking straight ahead.

"I am so full of positivity that nothing could sway me," slight pause before looking at me.

"I am so full of positivity that I see negativity whenever it is around me!" she said it so smugly. I thought of one or two things that I could have said and wanted to say, but I held back.

"How is your power walking going?" I asked with a smile on my face.

"Good, very good"

"Good, I've heard so much about you I thought I'd stop by for an hour or so, it's a nice little shop you have, how long you been here?"

"About ten years," she said adding. "It is a nice shop and it does well!" with a slight nod and a look to suggest that business was not only good, but so was the money and the smugness seemed to increase.

"Yes, it helps to pay for the things I want," she said.

"Good, good, you seem very happy!" I did mean smug. The way she was talking was beyond belief.

"Yes it pays for everything I want and that's important to me!"

"Of course, it's good to be able to have the things you desire," the conversation was going well.

"I like to have the best, I think it's very important to always have the best of everything! I travel first class and when I go shopping I always buy the best!"

"Your money, you like to read a lot as well?" I asked. There was an open book on the table.

"Yes I like to read," her voice changed to a lower tone.

"I don't just read my books though, I study them!" she told me, letting her tone deepen.

"Really," I said taking an interest.

"Yes when I get a book I like, I study it, I make notes and sometimes I'll study a book for six months or more, Yes books are very important to me," she said seriously.

"Ah its good to read," I said not that I'd read a book for a while.

"And when I've finished my books I give them away to my friends for them to read."

"Uummm!" I just nodded as I listened.

"Yes only recently I cleared out all my books and gave them all away to my friends," she got up to survey her shop again. All her movements seemed so purposeful as if there was a TV camera constantly on her. She walked to the door of the shop paused for a moment and turned and without any prompting at all announced.

"When I die I am going to leave ten percent of what I own to my favourite church! And the rest I will leave to be divided amongst my friends!" I think that was supposed to be a show of generosity. She swayed back over to the table and sat down again. I hadn't liked what I'd heard.

"I feel happier doing something while I'm alive Angie, I've a sponsor child and I donate to a couple of charities, it's not much but it helps." Here she put her hands together and solemnly said.

"I pray for the hungry," I leant forward and said as solemnly.

"That's very nice of you, but it really doesn't put food in their stomachs." I did not like her idea of charity at all.

"So are you enjoying your holiday?" she asked changing the subject. I actually regarded it as more of a visit than a holiday but replied.

"Yeah it's ok, it's always nice to catch up with friends," I told her. "I've just been to the port I like sailing yachts, there's a couple of nice ones in at the moment."

"You like boats?"

"Yeah, just looking even, although I do like to think I'd be able to buy one again," I told her adding. "I used to share a small sailing boat," her tone immediately picked up.

"Oh if you like boats you should go to Bodrum! There they make some of the best boats in the world," she said ecstatically adding. "Many people go to Bodrum to buy boats. I've been to Bodrum myself many times! It's beautiful there!"

Bodrum is of course in Turkey, but just a few miles from Kos. At night when you look out to sea you'd almost believe the town was on the same island it's so close. I had considered going there this trip, on one of the numerous ferries that went to and throw but the thought of my last visit to Turkey had daunted me more than a little.

"Yeah, so I've heard, I don't know I had a bad experience when I went the last time."

"You know it's better to say your Greek if you go?"

"I know, people keep telling me," why though I still didn't have a bloody clue and I knew if I asked, like others she'd just say because it is, I added.

"I don't know, I've thought about it," I told her. I started wondering if a different attitude at immigration would help. I really didn't want to lie about my heritage. I had a vision of what response I might get if I was to be more open and polite like.

"Where are you from?"

"Cyprus," but courteously with a smile or something, or maybe even lie to him, just to meet the people, I was sure they would be different. The idea of lying about it hurt though. I returned to the conversation.

"I don't know, they gave me a lot of shit before and I don't want to lie to them."

I went on to tell Angie in some detail about my very brief visit to Istanbul. Recalling some of the details just brought it all back to me, by the time I'd finished my head was hung a little lower thinking of the way I'd felt abused. Angie moved her head a little closer to the table, what she was about to say was to completely stun me, slow and firmly she said,

"I think you are negative about being Cypriot."

"What!"

"I think you are negative about being Cypriot!" she said more firmly.

"No way!" I was immediately defensive and told her.

"If I was being negative about anything it was being questioned about my heritage by an immigration man, that's bullshit they've got no right. Fucking cheek they take half of our island and then I get that shit," her response came like an attack.

"Forget the north! Forget it! You've lost it! It's gone! It's not yours anymore!"

"You what?" this was something I could not comprehend anyone telling me, let alone a Greek.

"I said forget it! It's not yours anymore, it's gone!" I was stunned to say the least. Turkey had only partitioned our island off because of a Greek coup that had overthrown the Greek Cypriot government, a case of Greeks pissing about in our country again and upsetting our Turkish minority. I'd never felt bitter or hostile about it. I thought it silly. But hearing this after their silliness had cost us, cost me even, so dearly, I was stunned into silence. I'd sat for a brief period when a very well dressed Greek woman approached and said hi to Angie, I sat with my head down contemplating what I'd heard and a little upset about it. I could hear Angie and her friend talking about nice clothes and expensive watches for their men. I looked up and Angie introduced me to her friend.

"This is Dimitri he is from Cyprus." The woman immediately smiled and started talking away in Greek to me, none of which I understood of course.

"I don't speak Greek."

"What! You don't speak Cypriot?" she replied. Fucking unbelievable was all I could think. One woman was giving away half our island and another is claiming it.

"On Cyprus we speak many languages!"

It went right over her head and she carried on talking to Christina, I'd heard enough. I waited for a couple of minutes and said I was leaving, we made short but courteous goodbyes and I rode back to the house still stunned from everything I'd just heard. When I got to the house the place was fairly quiet. Christos was out and Costas was at nursery. I didn't say anything to Nikki at first but went into the bedroom and sat on the bed still turning all that I'd heard over in my mind. The Cyprus bit hurt, it hurt a lot, I called to Nikki.

"Nikki will you come here please I want to talk to you," my voice was firm, she came to the open doorway.

"What's up?"

"I've just been having a chat to Angie"

"Oh yeah how did you get on?" I ignored the question.

"How long have you known her for?"

"Three weeks, why?"

"Three weeks," I repeated. It wasn't long I thought.

"Yeah I met her at the same time as my friend committed suicide on Kalymnos," she informed me. I remembered Nikki telling me about a close friend hanging himself.

"How often do you see her?"

"Everyday"

"Everyday!" I looked at Nikki inquiringly.

"Yeah I've been spending half an hour or so with her everyday"

"What do you talk about?"

"Lots of things she's been really helpful to me"

"What sort of things?"

"All sorts of things"

"Like what? Tell me," I said.

"She tells me how I should dress, the sort of things I should do. Being positive and getting the best for myself," I cut in,

"And nothing but the best is good enough for you?"

"Yeah!"

Nikki looked at me slightly surprised, I threw her a disapproving look and she knew a disapproving look from me when I gave her one.

"What's wrong?" she asked looking concerned.

"Has she given you any books to read?"

"Yeah!"

"Can I have a look at them please?"

"You've seen one of them, it's there, I'll get the other one"

She pointed at a small book that I'd been flicking through it was called creative visualisation. I remembered thinking it was harmless. I'd actually made a note of it in my notebook writing ' I didn't know there was such depth to something I've been playfully doing for years'. She returned with a much thicker paperback in her hand which she passed to me as she sat on the bed, many paragraphs were spotted by pen marks where someone had been studying it.

"You've been reading this?"

"Yes Christina told me to study it." I flicked through the book whilst Nikki sat in silence. I studied a few parts before getting an idea of what the book was about. I read a passage out aloud "it is not only a sin to be poor but an even bigger sin to be poor when you could have been rich," and it was money it was referring to. I considered the book disgusting it seemed to make a mockery out of religion to comfort the rich.

"Nikki you've been studying this?"

"Yes, Christina tells me I should study everyday, she encourages me to write about it as well, what's wrong?"

"This book is the biggest load of bollocks I have ever read! No way can I allow you to read it. I'm not surprised your life's fucked up at the moment!" Nikki looked at me starting to take in how I felt, but for me it had all fallen into place.

"You've been making notes and studying this?" I asked. My tone was not a pleasant one and it was to convey how I felt.

"Yes," I think she knew what was coming next.

"It's fucking brainwashing you! Now I know where all the shit you've been coming out with is from!"

"You mean?"

"Yes, all this, I've got to have the best shit! I've been wondering where you've been getting it from!"

"Oh no" she sounded like she had a headache, it might have been hurting, I don't know,

"Yes Nikki!"

"I think this shit has been the cause of a lot of your problems lately!"

"You think so?" she was getting emotional now. "You think it's why I've been so confused lately."

I nodded, I knew at times when people were being influenced like this the confusion would be there.

"Most likely, yes I do"

She burst into tears, through the tears I could hear her saying.

"Not again, not again."

Over the next hour or so we talked it over and I felt my feelings confirmed. We talked about how it had been affecting her relationship and her new found desire for the best and nothing but the best, was, I hoped being crushed and ground into the earth. As we talked, she could see how her demands were affecting her relationship and then to the next stage, a bit of protection.

"Nikki I want you to be angry at Angie!"

"Angry?"

"Yes very bloody angry! She nearly destroyed your relationship Nikki I want you to be angry with her!"

I still had to impart on her what I'd been told about Cyprus.

"She told you what?"

"She told me to forget the north as it's not ours any more!"

"No!"

"Yeah"

Soon the next stage, telling Christos.

I sat down alone with him and explained what had been happening regarding Angie's influence over Nikki, the Cyprus bit wasn't needed for Christos to get angry, although I knew it would feed the fire. His first response was extreme anger but he calmed down whilst I called Nikki, she came to the door with a sheepish look on her face.

"I've explained everything to him," I told her.

She entered the room and approached Christos before falling into his arms and breaking down into tears, now Christos's anger surfaced.

"Fucking bitch!" he screamed.

"She interferes with my family! I put a fucking knife to her throat! I go see her, NOW!"

"No Christos! No! There's a better way!"

"No! She makes me fucking angry! Now I go see her! I tell her what I think!"

"No Christos I can see you're angry but it's not the way!"

"Then how?" he asked suppressing his anger slightly.

"She will know Christos! She will know but not this way," I said assuring him with my eyes and putting my hands out to calm him down.

"How?" he enquired slightly confused.

"Tomorrow her best friend comes here for dinner, yes!" he nodded and I continued.

"Christos, I tell you for sure Angie will know how angry you are through Jean," I looked deeper at him.

"How will she know?" he enquired looking deeply back.

"Trust me, she will know through Jean!"

"I don't see how," he said pulling his head back.

"There's a way, if it doesn't work you can do it your way, but let me try this way first."

Christos looked cautious about it. I could understand him wanting to confront Angie. But as I was to later tell Nikki it's not something that anyone could ever prove as in some ways it could be said that it was all in her head, which it is, but that's where our most important part of our body is, the mind.

"Ok we see!" said Christos.

"Right!"

I did at this point feel a little sorry for Jean, but it wasn't to last.

Now if I sounded confident about what I was going to do I don't know why. I knew it could be done. I just never had a clue how I was going to do it though and now my time was starting to seem short, just three more days, this one inclusive. Jean was coming to dinner tomorrow evening but so were a couple of loved friends Marie and Rafael and I didn't want them involved. So dinner times were altered to allow us to have dinner with Marie and Rafael in the afternoon and Jean was due at ten. But I still hadn't worked anything out by the time I'd wondered home from a bar about eleven o'clock that evening. There was a babysitter at the house sitting in the lounge reading, as Nikki was helping

Christos on the stall. I didn't stop up, but went straight to my bed put some music on and then just felt an urge to write. I'd been brooding all day "forget it, it's gone, it's not yours any more" just repeating itself again and again. It hit even harder to hear it from a Greek. But to hear it at all and I was the one accused of being negative about being a Cypriot. What did she know about being a Cypriot or about me for that matter? I had a pen in my hand and was looking for some paper, when I saw Costas's blue school writing pad. I didn't think anyone would mind and if they did then I'd buy a new one. I wrote and wrote, two or three hours later I fell asleep after putting the final full stop to what I'd written, too tired to read it, I closed the book and slid it under my pillow, dropped the pen on the floor and slept.

Next morning I awoke just before midday. I didn't get off the bed, there was no top sheet as it was so warm and I slept in my shorts. I just rolled onto my front, pulled the blue book from under the pillow and read. It seemed to start confident enough. My granddad was in there and if there was anything negative about this I couldn't see it. I leapt off the bed pleased with what I'd written, I threw the book onto the bed and decided to sort out some breakfast and have a shower before revealing my work to the others. Less than an hour later we were all in the lounge. Christos was sitting down. Nikki came in and stood next to him. I told them what I'd spent the early hours of the morning doing, I didn't feel any need to explain why I wrote it, but I knew it was some kind of personal testimonial as to how I felt about being Cypriot. I was nervous about the response from Christos and I also knew that they might be a little biased towards it simply because it came from me and the good communication progress that they'd made since my revelations. His, would be the one whose response I'd gauge carefully. I had my audience and I read my piece, it took ten or fifteen minutes at the end of which, there was silence, it seemed like a long silence when Christos turned to Nikki and said something in Greek, she looked up at me and translated.
"Christos says that it made the hairs on his arms stand on end." Yes! Wow! That had such an effect on myself and I could feel a big sense of relief, I couldn't have hoped for a better response. Soon after I was gone, off to give Angie my response to her telling me I was negative about being a Cypriot and feeling good about it. I got to the shop where she was sitting at the table reading. I put the bike on its stand and took the book from the basket behind the bike seat. I took a deep breath telling myself to keep my composure.
"Angie, mind if I read you something I wrote in response to you telling me I was negative about being a Cypriot?"
"What's that?" she asked looking up.
"Something I wrote in response to you telling me I was negative about being a Cypriot."
"Oh! not at all," she said surprised. I started the piece still fuelled by the

confidence from Christos's response. I read away.

My name is Dimitri Jordan I am 36 years old. I was born in England and my father and his father are English. I am proud to be English but my heart and soul does not belong to England alone. My mother was born in Ayios Amvrosios a small village some 16kms east of Kyrenia. Some say I take after my mothers father, a man I loved very much. I'm proud of my mothers father and of her mother and both of which were once proud to call themselves Cypriots of that I'm sure. In 1974 my grandfathers' farm and home were taken in the invasion and I know our loss is little compared to some, I am just grateful my grandfather never lived to witness this tragedy, my grandmother did. My mother was married to my father in England at the age of 15 and regardless of some attempts by relatives only my eldest sister speaks Greek as she was sent to a Greek school in London. I did not see the need to learn another language (although it was never far from my lips) my grandfather spoke very good English. My grandmother once asked me when at the age of 17 if I would go to Cyprus to do my national service. To me the idea seemed horrific, mainly I think because of the little pay the soldiers received. I said I could not but felt that my grandmother wanted to feel proud of me and I made a promise I do not intend breaking. That if Cyprus has trouble I will be there and I will fight to keep the country free of any tyrannical rule by any country. What I meant was if the Turkish government wants more of Cyprus then over my dead body, not something I say lightly.

In 1986 I started to travel (which although took in Cyprus I saw the visit as purely coincidental to my travels and had little significance to me). I traveled frequently to the Greek Isles where Greeks would tell me I should be ashamed of myself for not speaking Greek and worse still that my own grandfather would be ashamed of me. This I confess to finding confusing, my grandfather although a mere peasant shepherd and of Orthodox background, he never, ever, to my memory tried to enforce or even encourage me to speak Greek. Something I now thank him for, it's a language I can learn easily, the alphabet I've always known. After a short while I found a response which felt good, I'd ask them where they were in 1974, for I was a child and that if they considered Cyprus to be Greek (as part of theirs) why they never went themselves to fight for what they considered theirs. For now I am a man, I would fight for both Cyprus as well as England but not just for a promise.

In the last 3 or 4 years I have made a few trips to Cyprus but this time my trips were anything but coincidental. My last 2 visits I've made I've not stayed with relatives, many of whom follow the old ways, which I have much respect for and the church has become a place where I may be found in memory of my grandmother, for I follow no organized religion. But the extra freedom gave me the opportunity to enjoy other facets of Cyprus. In a bar in Limassol (which is a good place to talk to the young) I met two Cypriots one was born in England and the other in Australia. They both told me they were Cypriots I asked (rather naively) Turkish or Greek their response stunned and struck deep within me they are Cypriots (even though they were Greek speaking and probably christened Orthodox) first and foremost not Greeks not Turkish. Their response was harsh and struck deep and from then I vowed the same response.

One only needs to read the political history of Cyprus before the invasion to know the damage done by both Greek and Turkish influences. I now, and for some years have believed that those that would have liked to have made Cyprus little more than an extension of Greece, gave an excuse the Turkish government made great use of. And with the wheels of propaganda and the support given to Turkey by the most powerful of nations, found a means to justify taking what we know is the best part of a most beautiful country and my grandfathers' home I have never seen.

My visits of conscience to Cyprus began funnily enough after an attempt to visit Turkey (despite being brought up with the horror stories) I was and still am of the opinion that people are people and if you search for the good you will be rewarded. I arrived in Istanbul for a 2 day visit and I looked forward to seeing a city steeped in history and yes, to meet the people as people and I expected a rewarding trip but I never expected to encounter such hatred and bitterness before I'd even left the airport. At immigration I was asked where I was from. I thought a man in possession of my passport could tell. It's a British passport which clearly states ones place of birth and I told him so (with hindsight I could see a bit of British arrogance, mixed in the blood) and I also asked the immigration officer to read the first page. To my horror he then asked me where my grandparents were from. This in my opinion is not a question that should have been asked and I told the immigration officer that it was not necessary for him to know this information (and with the horrors of Bosnia so close I did not like the implications of his line of questioning). This angered the immigration officer. I was stunned and after more abuse I told him and I told him proudly what he wanted to know and then his hatred really surfaced, he stamped my passport with much abuse and I remembered thinking his hatred he'd pass to me. I never left the airport proper the trip to Istanbul was a stopover en-route to Thailand, what I'd experienced embittered me. I looked at the lights of Istanbul and despite knowing that the experience that I'd just encountered was unlikely to be repeated I'd lost the desire to visit such a place. I now know the man at immigration had temporarily filled me with bitterness and I knew that Thailand was only 10 hours away as the next Bangkok flight was leaving in less than two hours. And after what I'd encountered the warmth of the people of Thailand became ever more appealing, no ignorance, no fear. I went to the airline desk and made the necessary changes to my ticket so I could be on that plane and I then proceeded to the coffee bar before going through to the departure lounge. I never reached the coffee bar. The immigration man who gave me such a hard time left his desk, stopped me and physically forced me through to the departure lounge. Spitting and cursing me (though I know not what he said) a bad experience. For a period he filled me with hate for him and all of his. I thought of T.E. Lawrence and how appealing some of his latter conquests over the Turks in Arabia, no prisoners and with these thoughts I left Turkey. Only for a brief period could I feel this hate, anger in my opinion is a force that can be used positively, defensively, but hatred is a negative force that I cannot hold for any man and 5 years on I know I am the better man for it.

I write these words whilst on the Greek Isle of Kos, a few days before writing this I went to a friends bar where I was asked by a Greek man whom I found I liked, why being a Cypriot I never spoke Greek. I responded too harshly for such an innocent inquiry and told him that as a Cypriot I would not have a Greek telling me what language I should speak. By this time I now view Cyprus as a country that owes very little in the way of alliance to Greece. She cannot protect us and will not and too many Greeks are of the opinion we are theirs, a view many may not like and this I understand, but I was shortly to have a conversation which endorsed my personal opinions.

I spoke to a proud Greek woman on Kos. She has a profitable business and has all the material trappings that make for a comfortable life. When I told her of my incident in Istanbul she immediately pointed out to me that I was negative about being Cypriot (to which this is the response). I said that my attitude might have been a little negative, but in response to the immigration officer I felt justified, this woman then went on to tell me to forget the north (I was stunned). She went on to tell me, it's gone, forget it, it's not ours anymore as if we'd sold it or simply handed it over and something I could simply forget. Shortly after a friend of hers arrived and spoke to me in Greek when she learnt my mother's Cypriot, I told her I don't speak Greek, to which she replied you don't speak Cypriot, at that point I felt my feelings on Cyprus were confirmed, are we not a country of more than one language.

I live in hope that what was taken will be returned and furthermore that one day when Cyprus is no longer a divided country, all Cypriots regardless of what language they speak and whatever their religion, they will regard themselves as Cypriots first and foremost free from the external influences of any country be it Greece, Turkey or Britain.

I have a hope that one day I will be able to return to my grandfathers' land and for myself, if, when I arrive there I find that my land is tended and my grandfathers house is inhabited they will acknowledge my rights as I will acknowledge theirs. For 24 years have passed since the occupation and any man or woman who may have been born there will feel that it is as much theirs and in my opinion rightly so, for it would be their birthplace and I know the importance of that. But if we can acknowledge each others deepest emotions we will see that if not the homes (through size) then the land is part of us and can be shared easily if each and everyone of us can put behind us the hatred, the fear and the ignorance that have troubled our forefathers for so many years. A united Cyprus in every sense and one to be truly proud of.

No I do not feel negative about being Cypriot, just towards the influences of those be they Turkish, British or Greek that would hold our country in the belligerent state she lives in, if only in the mind.

At the end Angie nodded her head then said.
  "You know it's good that this has come from our conversation, but it's a little bit anti-Greek!" I didn't actually think it was, but whatever.
  "Like it says, it's against anything that holds our people in the state they are and I don't really think I want to continue this conversation any more Angie, I haven't really got much I want to say to you."
  With that I left. I simply didn't want to be in her presence any longer, I could feel my emotions quickly surfacing and had to get away, but I hadn't felt like I'd achieved anything either. I left Angie and rode towards the port feeling very despondent.

At the port, John and Vicki cheered me up a little, I'd gone on board for a couple of beers after spending the first thirty minutes trying to hold the bow of the yacht away from the stone port wall. Other yachts were constantly getting caught up in each others anchor lines, which all went out towards the middle of the busy but small port. In the hour or so that I spent on the boat there was a couple of other yachts that again caught themselves on the Moody's anchor line. At this point I didn't envy John and he made no secret of his desire to get the gear cable replaced and get out of there. But despite everything they were good company and a nice couple to talk to, both young, in their early twenties and simply taking the yacht wherever the owner wanted it. They told me of the owner putting them both through their diving courses and fitting them out with diving gear which was nice to see, but watching John on the Moody I considered the owner to be the lucky man to have found him. I couldn't stay with them too long, as dinner was being served up soon and there was something I had to do and suddenly it felt urgent.

When I got back to the house Nikki was there alone in the kitchen, which made it easy for me to talk to her from my bed on which I was sitting. I was embarrassed about the fact that I'd written that I knew the Greek alphabet, which wasn't quite true. Part of it was actually all I knew. I couldn't even count to three I was actually terrible with Greek full stop, but I was now determined to finish the alphabet.

"Nikki do me a favour?"

"What?"

"Help me finish off the alphabet"

"What the Greek alphabet?"

"Yeah I think I know a most of it I just need to finish it off"

"Ok, tell me what you know"

"Ok alpha," I went through the alphabet as I knew it stopping at Ipsilon. "What am I missing I know it ends with omega."

She looked at me surprised.

"What's up?" I asked.

"You said it so fluently!"

"It's just how I know it, what am I missing?"

"Phi, khi, psi."

I looked at Kyp expecting a little more.

"Is that it?" I asked surprised.

"Yeah."

"Shit!" was all I could say.

"What made me stop learning at Ipsilon," I was stumped over why I never learnt those last three letters of the alphabet. But it wasn't three it was two I actually slipped Psi in the wrong place, and missed out Xsi because I didn't know where it went, I'd just said it so fast that I think Kyp had missed it.

"That's it!"

"Yeah do you want me to get you a book."

"If you like," I said. I didn't really care though, I was stunned. I couldn't get my head around the idea that I'd got to be so close to the whole of the alphabet and stopped. When I could remember as a child learning the Morse code and even though I'd long since forgotten it, I remembered I made sure I learnt it A-Z. Just as surprising to me was that I had no idea I was so close. Nikki brought the books, which I looked at, but took little notice of. I was still trying to work out how I'd let it happen and was still wondering about it at dinner time when Marie and Rafael arrived and then Nikki's food took over and I put it out of my mind for a couple of weeks. Rafael and Marie had both arrived for the summer season and I'd known them for a number of years, both very sweet people. Marie had been told of my revelations by Christos, who was now convinced I'd saved his relationship and at three o'clock the previous morning had gone home to make me a beautiful necklace, which she gave me before dinner. The rest of the day went quite fast and before I knew where the time had gone, I was sitting with Christos at his stall in the town, it was well lit up, powered by a little petrol generator placed about five metres away. Little had been said concerning Jean or Angie and I wondered if it really mattered now. But around ten thirty I walked through the door of the house. Jean was sitting at the kitchen table with a bowl of cold black eyed beans and cabbage soup, quite appropriate I thought, but I really couldn't be bothered and I had no idea of how I was going to achieve what I'd told Christos I could and would. I told Nikki that I'd baby sit to allow her to go to the stall to sit with Christos and then I set about trying to get rid of Jean funny enough. I sat on the end of my bed in sight of her and stretched yawning at the same time making a comment about being very tired in an attempt to get her to leave, she wasn't going to take it or was she.

"What are you tired?" she asked.

"Yeah!"

"Out on the beer last night Ah?"

"No actually I was writing an essay in response to something Angie said"

"Oh yeah what was that?"

"That I'm negative about being Cypriot, do you want to hear it?"

"Yeah, why not?"

I read the piece to Jean at the end of which she tried to defend Angie for telling me to forget the north, which surprised me and I wondered if she'd even listened to the piece.

"You know she never meant what she said about Cyprus"

"No I don't believe that, not only did she mean it, but she also emphatically drove it home." Then she was to say something that I'd never considered before.

"How comes your Grandfather spoke good English if he was just a peasant farmer?"

"I don't know, I just know he was a very intelligent man."

She had left me with one that I hadn't considered though. From there she went straight into an attack on me for the actual piece I'd just read. I was now wondering if she'd listened to it or been told of it by Angie, it sounded a little rehearsed, which flattered me a little, but the attack was from the direction I was expecting, telling me that Cyprus was Greek through a five thousand year history. It was the most natural attack for a Greek and if you'd have asked me about our history I would've said it goes back some five thousand years with Greece. But as I pointed out to her it wasn't our history I was concerned with. But our present, and our future. Being constantly told 'we used to live alright together' can bring some hope that we might again and when considering a unified island our Cypriots of Turkish heritage as I'd now started to consider them. Wouldn't I know feel happy about living in a Hellenistic society that takes its cue from Athens and there's enough Greek in me to understand why. Jean was meeting good resistance mainly because she was so ignorant of the basics of even ancient history and I didn't mind telling her, but she was also making the mistake I wanted to hear and at a great time just as Christos walked through the front door. She kept telling me not only how I was feeling, but also how I was thinking and Christos was just in time to hear her first telling off about it.

"Jean I don't mind telling you I think you're talking shit! But one thing you're doing that I don't like is telling me how I feel and what I'm thinking! Stop it now!" I said it firmly, but whether she took it in or not, I don't know. But to make matters worse for herself she was getting very worked up and I noticed it early enough to keep my composure, whilst she seemed to be going into overdrive. The whole time Christos was leaning against the doorframe taking it all in. After a good hour or so of very heated debate Jean was on the defence again and losing badly. Here she was to get her last warning about telling me how I felt and what I was thinking. I knew now though that this wasn't just over Nikki, but it was working out well.

"Jean your not qualified to tell anyone what they're thinking or feeling and you haven't got a clue what your doing when your doing it! Imposing yourself on someone else!" These were the sort of comments, which were going straight over her. I'd thought I'd heard enough when she made a last and final attack about Cyprus. Declaring again that Cyprus was a Greek island because of our five thousand-year old historical links. To which I attacked in the same manner as before, tempers were getting frayed.

"Jean I've told you before! And I'll tell you for the last time! It's not our history that concerns me but our present and our bloody future!" by this time she was hissing her response.

"What future! What you got! You got a fucking line running through your island! What you got? You got nothing ah! Nothing!" she said it spitefully. That hurt, she was directing it at me personally, but I knew Christos would feel the pain of that one as well.

"We've got hope Jean!" I said quietly. It was all I could fall back on. I walked over to my bedroom and sat on the bed as I did I took the offensive book from under the bed.

"Jean before I finish this conversation and it is finished! I take exceptional offence at this book!" I held it up.

"I take extreme offence at this book being given to Nikki and it's going straight in the bin! And I have never done that to a book before!" she took that in good and well. It was the first time she'd been quiet for an hour, as soon as I dropped the book though I could hear her voice again. But I'd heard enough. I was upset but I wasn't going to show it, Jean talked on whilst I picked up my cigarettes and lighter, got to the bedroom door, turned and slowly told her,

"Jean I told you. This conversation is over, I have no more time for you, not only are you talking shit! But you are shit Jean! You are shit!" with that I shut the door and sat on the bed and waited for her to leave, which she did very quickly. I pulled the door open. Christos was standing there not very happy.

"Now from what I hear and from what I see, I say they have no more contact with my family!"

"From what you hear and from what you see Christos, you can," I said. I felt like I'd achieved something. At least it had gone better than I thought it would. The next day when Nikki had gone to Angie's to tell her she had to cancel any babysitting plans, Angie had seemed worried.

"I hope your husband doesn't think we're influencing you Nikki, we wouldn't want that." And then the classic,

"We were only trying to help you!"

It felt good to know that I hadn't even had to say it, that felt good, but it didn't help the pain I was feeling about now two Greeks telling me that we'd lost our north and it was gone. When from my perception it was Greeks who'd been as much to blame as anyone, including the Turks. The next day Jean was heard to even take our hope away which felt like a twisted knife, this was to bring on a radical change of feelings.

My time in Kos was almost over, Christos couldn't thank me enough and constantly I was being told that if I hadn't of arrived when I had, then him and Nikki would surely have finished. John and Vicki's presence was a bit of a blessing on the last day. After pulling the Moody clear of an ugly cruise boat that resembled a cross between a metal tug and a very small Nile cruise boat that had literally dragged the moody off its mooring. I was happy to settle down with them for a couple of hours, feeling totally away from all that troubled me. Maybe one of the nice things about having a boat to drink on is that you can feel like you've escaped, without even leaving port, enough justification to buy one if you have the money. I got a chance to say goodbye to Nicholaos before I left, one regret I'd had was not getting a chance to spend a bit of time with him, he interested me and I took an instant liking to him. It was a brief goodbye but heart felt.

"Nicholaos I've come to say goodbye and I want to apologise to you, the first time I spoke to you I was bit harsh, I don't know why, I'm sorry."

"It's OK I understand"

"I just thought I was a bit harsh."

"No, have a good flight." I knew he'd heard what I'd been told about Cyprus and he must have known even from two silly women, it must have hurt.

A final word about Nikki's hairdressing scissors. Well a new pair like she wanted and already had was going to cost over three hundred and fifty pounds. When the old pair merely needed sharpening, price fifteen pounds and I was happy to bring them back to England and send them back sharpened and ready for another couple of years use. I thought about whether it was the reason I'd been drawn to Kos, for Nikki and Christos, maybe it was. But I was starting to get the feeling there was more to my visit than saving their relationship. In two days I'd wept twice for Cyprus, something I'd never done before.

Chapter 7

I was being honest when I told Nikki that I was pleased I'd gone to Kos, but if that was the case then I was far happier to get back to England. It was a Sunday morning and I cleared Gatwick immigration at seven, which meant I got to Kings Cross train station for around eight a.m. I felt a strange sense of purpose as I boarded the train surrounded by the walking casualties from a Saturday night on the town. I'd been up all night, but sleep wasn't to drape itself over me as often on these train rides. With the sense of purpose, I felt awake, wide-awake, but it wasn't the bright summer's morning light that kept me awake, I couldn't sleep if I'd tried. A whole train of thought was running its own course through my mind.

I'd always felt it was harsh of the Turkish government partitioning the island off because of the Greek coup, although nothing I could think of justified the ethnic cleansing of the Greek Cypriots from the north, it had seemed harsh under any circumstances. But exploring my own personal feelings towards Turkey from a Greek perspective I had to say I could understand it in part. If I consider our ancient history, some of our finest ruins lay on Turkish territory. Seized during the Ottoman period like many other countries perhaps, but unlike most other countries, much of it was never returned to Greece. It does leave you feeling a bit cheated and I can't believe other Greeks don't feel the same way. It always felt sad to see Turkish holiday posters with our ancient ruins in them, with some slogan 'COME AND SEE THE HISTORY' our history and we despise them for it. The Turks are a nomadic people from the east and only migrated west if you could call it that fairly recently historically speaking which goes further against them, the animals from the east as I've often referred to them myself. Under these circumstances I could understand Turkey being a little more than unhappy about Turkish Cypriots living directly under Greek rule.

I'd recently been analysing it within myself, the hatred that is. It seemed more like resentment turned into a terrible bitterness. I could have happily gone to a hill in Cyprus and shot Turks all day. Some might say it's natural considering their behaviour in Cyprus, but I had to be honest, I knew it existed before then. As a child my mother's horror stories were of Turks chopping up children, they were the bogeyman and there was always Istanbul and that was way before the partition of Cyprus by them. The hatreds deep and often hide's under a rock so to speak. I pulled the rock over and lay it out in the light to be examined. It is fairly much how it felt and in the light I saw it for what it was, resentment and bitterness from a lot of history, it's gone now, blown away with the wind, no one should dwell on history like that.

So that was history, it was said and done so to speak, and Turkey and Greece had demographically confirmed this by a mass resettling program carried out in the twenties. Greece obviously knew and accepted that these territories were lost forever, but it left a lot of Greek descendants in Turkey and vice versa so they were repatriated by religion. This was something that had obviously never happened in Cyprus. The harsh bit seemed to be that the Greek coup fell apart and Turkey kept our north, but isn't that Turkey for you I guess. But it seemed true to say that the Greek coup was as much to blame for bringing the Turks. Then considering the political climate and the fear that Cypriots lived under, I thought about the flagpole incident and the snail picker and my godmother telling me that Turkish border guards crossed over at night to harass the villagers. This would keep the people holding tightly onto Greece, her being the only country to openly declare that she would stand by Cyprus. Which I have to be honest about, I considered this more of a gesture than anything, as she was as much to blame in the first place and couldn't protect herself from Turkey, let alone anyone us.

I had wondered why the British hadn't intervened, but I imagined they were happy just to keep their Sovereign bases and didn't want to interfere. I had wondered how the Queen had got to keep title bases there, but the British did have a habit of claiming anything for Queen and country so to speak and I guess the bases on Cyprus were our contribution.

So theoretically speaking if we were able to show Turkey that we were not only Cypriots first and foremost something, which I considered many of us to be. I'd not only been thinking of the bar-girls but a couple of times I'd heard Greek Cypriot lads openly curse the Greeks, it sounded like frustration at the time. I'd just smile, I understood how they felt, there are times when Greece seemed to have way to much involvement in our country, without taking into consideration what many must think of them for the coup, which brought about partition. But the most important part was that I firmly believed that they considered themselves Cypriots first and foremost as I did myself, and indeed like the bar girls would shrug the title of Greek first and foremost. It showed pride in the country.

Now speaking as a Greek Cypriot we are the greater people on the island numerically speaking and it was the Greek bit that I believed that Turkey feared most, but I understood that, no way could they allow their own people to fall under the influence of Athens. This all brought me right back to the piece I'd written on Kos, absolute forgiveness replacing resentment, a big change of thought but that's all it is and if we were serious about a unified island then we would have to start forgiving sooner or later or it wouldn't work. I was brought back to the conclusion I'd come to, that I couldn't believe that the Turkish Cypriots were any less frustrated than ourselves'. There was an ever-growing feeling inside of myself that Turkish Cypriots were indeed suffering as much as we at present and with Cyprus soon to enter the EEC, the benefits for both sides were great. I thought of our flag, a gold filled outline of our island country with two olive branches of peace entwined beneath it, to truly symbolise the two communities in a united Cyprus. I'm sure I don't need to explain the importance of your own flag to yourself and ours is one that I'd not only started to believe in, but also aspired to achieve.

I thought of the taxi driver in Lanarca and his hatred, it'd scared me. But I couldn't believe his pain wasn't greater than his hate and it was the pain that needed healing rather than feeding the hatred, I was sure somewhere in the north there was a Turkish Cypriot who'd lost as much. I couldn't help but draw similarities between Cyprus and Northern Ireland because of its mixed people and the depth of hatred that could manifest seemed similar to that between Turkey and Greece. Although I would tell people it was worst, but to be able to look to your past and truly learn from it, rather than attempt to build a platform to justify it. Would make the people whatever religion or race a great people in themselves, not measured by size, but in ways that in this world today, many should take example from.

I couldn't help but direct this feeling to my own people, the Cypriots. There had been so many changes in myself in just the last two years. Born and raised in England and I'd always say I'm proud to be British and still was proud to have a vestige of such a great union. I may have been born to an English father, but there was an inexplicable force drawing me to my past. My Cypriot past and my heritage, but the experience in Kos (and I hadn't forgotten the Macedonian affair) had all enforced the Cypriot to move away from the Greek within me and out of the perpetuated cycle of hatred between Greece and Turkey. The only way to a united island.

I thought of the promises to my grandmother. My emotions and the personal commitment I felt I'd made to a country I'd never seen before I was twenty-five and wasn't even sure if I understood, but had always carried with me wherever I went, whether I wanted it or not. The colour of my skin, in my eyes a constant reminder of who I am and what I am. The end product of generations of British and Greek Cypriot forefathers, yes, but it was my Greek Cypriot ancestry whose calling was strongest and not just for the colour of my skin. I couldn't help but be drawn to that heritage like a moth to the flame, even though I don't speak Greek, which no longer seemed to matter. I'd felt like I'd began to discover an identity which had been calling to me for as long as I could remember, but I always resisted and I never knew why. I felt far more proud about being Cypriot after Kos, unashamed to even cast aside the title of being British first and foremost and that was something that I could never have imagined before. I'd grown up with so much pride in being British and even though I still felt it, I was choosing an alternative future, but taking with me all that I'd learnt from being British, and I felt that that was nothing to be ashamed of.

By the time the train had pulled in, I'd realised the frustration was creeping up again, the line would still be there. Turkey wasn't about to withdraw because one Greek Cypriot had decided that he was not only happy to forsake the title of Greek. But to share his land and forgive them for the pain they'd put us through, for the sake of a united Cyprus. I decided to put those thoughts away and get on with some reality. I'd brought Costas book home with me and as I unpacked, I simply threw it onto a pile of other books and paraphernalia under my P.C desk.

The only thing I was now certain of was openly rebelling against the title Greek and I felt with good reason. I knew it was going to hurt some family members, but they hadn't heard what I'd heard and I'd tell them so. It was simple I'd heard two Greeks give my country away, so I give them their title back, I didn't have a problem with that and anyway I don't speak Greek.

Then the news, and what news it was, before I'd gone to Kos I knew that the Cypriot government were attempting to buy American made surface to air missiles. Although I also knew that the U.S.A. were going to put a block to them, which they did, which infuriated myself and others, I'm sure. But what news to hear on my return, it was now confirmed that Cyprus was to take delivery of Russian built S-300 surface to air missiles. YES! The best place for myself to get information was off the Internet and it was there that I'd read Muratov's speech, Muratov is Russia's ambassador to Nicosia. Turkey said that they'd destroy the missiles, it had caused a bit of a crisis, but Muratov had described the crisis as artificial. He said he was confident that Turkey would not strike and had also said. "In any military adventure on the island, the weapons would strike the one who started the event," an event, that seemed amusing. I'd never heard military conflict described as an event before, anything that sounded like change seemed welcome though. He'd also said that. "Russia advocated a just and lasting peace in Cyprus and it could not allow the independence and territorial integrity of the republic of Cyprus to be destroyed," now if that wasn't music to my ears better was to come. I have a friend, Dawn whose father is an ex British army officer living on Cyprus. She'd just returned from there and had come round for a visit when we'd got talking about the subject. She'd told me that whilst sitting in her fathers garden a Russian military plane had flown low overhead, with its undercarriage down to land at Lanarca airport.

"What's that?" she'd asked her father.

"Oh it's the Russians," he replied.

"Russians?"

"Yeah they keep saying that they're getting lost."

I joked with her about them checking out the best base housing for themselves' but when I was told that, it made me think of how much Russians seemed to be investing in Cyprus and it did seem considerable. They're not all broke and I can't say I cared how it was made or where it came from.

It was not the mere fact the planes were there, but planes that are getting lost won't have a flight plan and unless they are seen, they aren't really there, are they? In all the realms of possibility and probability, if Russia was serious about their offer I knew what I'd be thinking if I were running Cyprus. I'd want to make the possible more probable. Greece was naturally saying that they would defend Cyprus and we had our pact with them but Russia is possibly the only country in Europe that could handle Turkey.

During the cold war Turkey used to receive a very large payment from the U.S.A. in military hardware to hold the southern border area of Russia. This had made Turkey possibly the strongest nation in the area. Far, far stronger than Greece, even much of Europe, excluding Russia of course. Turkey had some thirty thousand troops on the island, since the missile announcement they'd moved another ten thousand troops on to the island. Enough to hold in case of an attack until reinforcements could arrive? I noticed that they'd established a new Aegean Sea army with some two hundred-beach landing craft, if that was to be there reinforcements then I wondered if air support, which Russia could provide, would perhaps stop them. I knew we could put up a match for those forty thousand troops, if it was possible then it could also be made to be probable. I considered how long it might be before our missiles were used to bring down a Turkish plane, not long if I had my finger on the button. Yes! It would be good to get a Turkish F-14 getting too close having our own no fly zone, and the ability to enforce it.

Now more than ever, I felt the piece I'd written on Kos had a use though. I could see Costas book under my desk, but I couldn't just see it, I felt it, calling to be used. It stuck out in its bright blue cover, I pulled it out and started typing onto the P.C. what I'd written. I felt like I had something to say and the message wasn't just to Greek Cypriots but Turkish Cypriots also. If I could get it on to the P.C then I could e-mail it to whomever I wished. It felt good to get it on the screen but by the time I'd finished it had left me with a question and it wasn't mine it was Jeans.

"How comes your grandfather spoke good English?"

My answer had been that he was an intelligent man and I couldn't remember us speaking anything but English. But even if he was an intelligent man the idea of him speaking good English was a strange one. It might not seem so to some, but to get an idea of what was meant you'd have to go to either a very rural area of Cyprus or Greece for that matter, find a shepherd and try have a chat with him. There aren't many shepherds that speak anything other than their local dialect. My grandfather had come to England in fifty-nine at the age of seventy-seven and had spent his life in a rural community. It would've been very rural, particularly up to fifty-nine some might say backward, but to myself just country. That got me thinking, but I had to be honest with myself. One truth was I couldn't remember granddad ever speaking Greek to me and we always understood each other. Hmmm........ memories of a six year old, 'can't wait until granddad gets home someone to talk to', sitting on the steps of mountain house waiting for him and other memories,

"Granddad can I have some bread and jam please?" he understood and he'd know what I wanted. But how much do you need to know to speak to a six-year-old, but on the other hand I wasn't a stupid six-year-old. I phoned my mother. I'd already told her that I was now a Cypriot first and foremost, I was a little bolshey about it, so I wanted to be careful how I worded this one.

"Mum, I want to ask you something about granddad"

"What do you want to know?"

"Well I only remember speaking English with him"

"Your granddad never spoke English," she replied. Couldn't be so I thought.

"Mum I don't remember speaking anything but English with granddad!"

"Well everyone knew you used to communicate well with him, but he never spoke English"

"What do you mean he never spoke English? I only remember speaking English with him!"

"He only spoke three or four words, he was a peasant farmer Jim," I was starting to feel irate.

" I know that mum, but I remember speaking English with him! I can remember! I used to talk to him and he understood!"

"Oh he understood everything alright, he just never spoke it".

"What do you mean he understood everything alright but never spoke it?" that didn't sound right. My tone sounded harsh but it was more surprised.

"Oh he understood everything well, but he only spoke a little, I don't know Jim it was so long ago." Now I could hear my mother getting a little stressed at my questioning. As I'd got older, I'd also got harder on her and there were times when I would tell her things that I thought she should hear but wouldn't like. I had an unhappy home childhood and it was my revenge I guess, but it did upset her and I hadn't meant to this time.

"Ok mum, it's ok talk soon"

"Bye"

"Bye"

I was stumped and after five minutes of deep thought back on the phone, but sweetly.

"Mum tell me a bit about Granddads life?"

"Well there isn't much to tell, he was a well-respected man in his community, a very tolerant man, well liked and," nice as it was I'd heard all that before.

"No tell me about his life"

"Hmm like I've said before there isn't much to tell, what do you want to know?" she asked. There had to be something I thought, this time I kept my tone soft and gentle.

"Anything Mum, anything, he was eighty six when he died"

"Well he was married three times"

"Three times!" I repeated. My tone picked up immediately, that was a surprise I knew Grandmother had but this was news for me about granddad, my mother was one of three children by him.

"Yes"

"What happened to his other wives?" I knew divorce was extremely rare.

"Well I don't know too much, I think one died and I know that one of them had to go into an institution, she wasn't well," I knew what my mother meant by institution.

"She was institutionalised?"

"Yes"

"Poor granddad," then a slight pause.

"What else mum, anything?"

"Oh there's not much, oh he went away somewhere with the British army"

"The British army took him away!" that was a bigger surprise.

"Well he went away from the village with them but that was a long time ago, I don't know anything about it, he never talked about it."

"Who does?"

"Try asking your uncle Yannis"

"I will, thanks mum"

"Your welcome."

What did the British army want with a shepherd peasant? My first thought was a cook or something silly, the thought being silly in itself, I knew that they had their own cooks. So, what? I thought the years through, he was eighty six when he died and that was in sixty eight, it must have been a long time ago, possibly around WW1, that would have put him in his mid thirties. But if he was anything like myself I knew he'd have passed for being in his mid twenties. I needed to phone my uncle anyway. Yannis, my mothers' full brother is a well liked uncle to us, in his mid fifties or early sixties I'm not sure since he started using black hair colour. A bit of a wide boy, he seemed to have his fingers in so many pies, I got him at his hairdressers.

"Yannis, first I want to tell you that I no longer want to be referred to as a Greek Cypriot any more, just Cypriot, Cypriots fine!"

"Why?" he sounded bemused.

"I had a bad experience in Kos and I heard two Greeks tell me some bad things about the north, they said it's not ours anymore."

"They said what?"

"They said it's not ours anymore, it's gone, they gave away our north so I give them back their title."

"Oh, they were just stupid cows, don't listen to them."

"Stupid or not, I heard them and I don't like it, anyway I don't speak Greek."

"Oh, don't feel like that," he said trying to bring me round.

"I do," I replied thinking I'd change the subject. "Yannis I want to ask you a couple of questions about granddad."

"Your granddad!" he sounded surprised "What do you want to know?"

"My mum says that he went away somewhere with the British army, do you know anything about this?"

"No it was a long time ago, they took him away for a while," my uncle informed me.

"Well where did they take him?" I asked.

"To the States," my uncle replied. I was stunned and not expecting that at all.

"What the United States..........America?" I said bemused.

"Yeah, America"

"What the hell did they take him there for?" I was showing my bemusement.

"I don't know Jim it was a long time ago"

"No idea of how long for?"

"No I don't know anything about it, it was a long time ago"

"When was his birth date?" I asked. Thinking about doing some personal enquiries.

"I don't know"

"You don't know?"

"No, no one knows"

"No one knows! No birth certificate or anything?" I asked knowing the answer.

"No birth certificates in those days," my uncle informed me.

"Well when did he celebrate his birthday?" I asked.

"He never," Yannis said, strange I thought.

"Ok let me just confirm the years then, what year was he born?"

"I don't know!"

"Yannis he was eighty six when he died!"

"Oh, eighty six or eighty eight I think!"

"No Yannis eighty six I remember and he died in.....?" I paused waiting to let my uncle fill in the year,

"He died in sixty six," my uncle wrongly informed me.

"No Yannis he died in sixty eight I was six, I remember!" This now felt tiring.

"Oh, you remember!" he asked surprised.

"Yes of course I remember!"

"You know then," he told me. Of course I did but I just wanted it confirmed.

"Thanks Yannis!"

"That's ok," he said as he hung up. I put my receiver down and thought for a moment then picked it up again and pressed redial.

"Uncle what was Granddads full name?" I asked.

"My fathers full name?" my uncle sounded surprised.

"Yeah and spell it," I said wanting to ensure I got it right.

"Ok Dimitri," I didn't need that spelling.

"Yeah I know that one what's the surname?"

"Htenary, H.T.E.N.A.R.Y." I spelt it back to him, then a little more confusion.

"But he changed his name," my uncle told me.

"He changed it," I said thinking this wasn't getting any easier.

"Yes it's not unusual he took his brothers first name"

"And what was that?" I asked.

"Adamou, A.D.A"

"I know how to spell Adamou, Yannis," I told him.

"You know it?"

"Yeah thanks," I said feeling a little confused. I sat taking in everything I'd heard. First my mother telling me my grandfather never spoke English as I remembered him, but understood it well and then this. I'd decided it was a lot to take on board and attempt to analyse overnight. This all made it seem so much more intriguing. I had a personal theory now but there were other possibilities, but the news about him being taken to the United States merely went to confirming my theory. I don't know what he went there for but the only thing I could think of and still believe is intelligence work, which would make so much sense.

The British were at war with Turkey around the right time (WW1) and my grandfather would have been familiar with their ways, but what use granddad? I really didn't know, but it might have explained one or two things. I'd always got the impression that he knew more than people thought he did. My father describes him as shrewd. Grandfather certainly had different ways about him. There was one thing that I knew for sure though and that is one that I'd learnt from travelling myself, travel can open and broaden the mind immeasurably. It all depends on how much effort you put into understanding different people. It goes a long way in helping to overcome certain bigotry's and I was not only starting to believe that it had an effect on how he acted and far more important to myself. I was now of the belief that my grandfather not only saw the depth of the hatred being constantly perpetuated between Greece and Turkey for what it was. But perhaps acted on it to separate himself from it. I believed I might be an end result of these actions, this felt important to me.

It certainly gave me something to think about and in the meantime I telephoned my god brother and Cousin Jim in Melbourne where he lives and works as a computer programmer, being a maths professor, it was a natural subject I guess. We had a good long chat about things, we joked about it being at my expense and he told me he was going to be visiting Cyprus at around the same time my parents and my sister were going to be there. I told him to let me know and maybe we'd meet up. The idea of seeing my cousin again after over ten years was well worth the visit. I sent him an e-mail with my theory about the arms build up and the difference Russian help could make, including the piece I'd written in Kos to him as an attachment, and told him.

'With all my trips to Cyprus I found a lot of people making a lot of excuses to do nothing self included and please no cynicism without practical criticism. And let me know when you think you'll be in Cyprus maybe I'll make it a long weekend, love you Jim'.

I'd also sent one to a journalist in Cyprus, at the Cyprus Mail. More for ideas than anything The Cyprus Mail is an English language Cypriot paper available on the net. It felt a bit cheeky, as I was very familiar when I wrote. He was an English-speaking journalist called Charlie. I simply picked him out not only because I knew he spoke good English. But also the reporting I'd read by him was about football and England in the world cup and they'd just been knocked out, like I wrote to him.

'Footballs over Charlie let me know what you think of this?'

I really felt like I had something more than an essay that I'd written because a Greek pissed me off, far, far more and e-mail seemed great, almost like I could hassle anyone online that took my fancy. My next task wasn't one I was looking forward to but I believed in what I'd written and the more I examined the hatred between Turkey and Greece and it's perpetuation, I not only wanted out, but wanted to see the Cypriot people out of it. I now felt sure that both communities weren't feeling much better than the other about it all and I wondered about the time when they used to live all right together. I just wanted to point a way back to it. I phoned up my godmother.
"Hello"
"Hello, Marianna, its Dimitri, how are you?" I enquired.

"I'm ok," she sounded anything but ok but I wanted to get this over with.

"Marianna I had a bad experience in Kos with two Greeks," she stayed silent so I thought I'd just finish it.

"Marianna I don't want to be referred to as a Greek any more."

"No," her voice sounded hushed. She didn't even resist me but I knew it must have hurt her, far more than it was hurting me, which hurt me even more, at the same time I wanted to say what I felt.

"No Marianna I heard two Greeks give northern Cyprus away and I didn't like it, are you sure you're alright?" I wanted to change the subject.

"Mmm I'm ok," she said sounding very down.

"Mums going to be coming out at the end of the month, I thought maybe I'd join them," I told her.

"It's not a good time to come," she said nervously.

"It's not?" I asked surprised.

"No," she said. I realised straight away the missiles were scheduled to arrive in August and with Turkeys threats she would be nervous.

"Marianna it'll be ok!" as if my few words would help.

"You think so?" she asked.

"Yes I do, don't worry it's ok," I told her as reassuringly as I meant it.

"Ok," we said our goodbyes and I sat down. The fear I sensed in my godmother upset me and drove home just how serious it all seemed or could even be. The missiles were very shortly put back to October and then beyond. I soon got an e-mail from Jim, which put a bit of a damper on my thoughts.

Hi Jimmy,

Sorry I didn't reply earlier but I check my personal e-mail only once or twice a fortnight.

I find your comments on the Cyprus situation naïve and overly optimistic. As far as Russian support goes, don't count on it. Before the 1974 invasion, UK, Russia (USSR) and USA all warned Turkey not to invade Cyprus but did nothing about it when it happened OR since.

The situation now is one of Corrupt Turkish Cypriot leaders and economics. The Turks before the invasion, when there was relative peace, could not influence the direction of politics or economics in Cyprus simply because they were a 17% minority. Denktash could never have been a president and he and his cronies would never have had the influence over the Turkish Cypriots that they have now. You only have to look to the massive weight gain that Denktash has put on since 1974 to see that he is living the life of luxury and he will not give it up. Even now the Turks bikker about Cyprus joining the EC, They oppose it because the Greeks would get a better economic future that is denied Turkey. Another reason why the Turks will not compromise is that they would also have to give up at least some of the properties that they've stolen from the Greeks.

No Jimmy, I do not hold up much hope for Cyprus while Denktash is there and while there is no effort by the UN and the Security Council to put any pressure on Turkey. They only need to bring economic sanctions against Turkey to back up their resolutions and you can bet there would be a solution in Cyprus in no time.

I appreciate what you are trying to say but you do not have the memory, or the "Greek" background, to have a grassroots understanding of how the Greeks and Turks view themselves and each other.

During the Ottoman Empire, the Greeks were Forbidden to speak Greek and the language almost died out. That is one of the reason all Greeks are encouraged to speak it and not doing so is regarded as an act of betrayal.

Anyway take care

Jim.

I sent him an immediate reply;

Hi Jim,

I understand the importance of the language I did not realise the Ottoman Empire banned it. But I do feel I was bought up with a little understanding of how Turks and Greeks view each other and of the bitter hatred that has existed for so long which is one reason why I feel we should pull out of it. I'm not talking about denying our history but more to a better future learning from our history, we'll never get them back for what they've done in the past. But what I feel, is that as a united Cyprus we need to be able to show that we are prepared to forgive, as you said 17% of the population are Turkish. Wouldn't it be more helpful if we started referring to them as Cypriots first, Turkish speaking maybe but if we only intend regarding them as Turks, how can we ever hope to live in a unified Cyprus. As for Denktash I (personal view) think he's a frightened little fatty. He more than anyone will draw the line and tell the world we are Turks and they are Greeks and if anyone wants to mess with us Turks we have lot's of sons of Otto over there to help us. I really think that he knows as much as anyone that to propagate this hate will do more to keep a line through our country than barbed wire. Cyprus is a wealthy country and will prosper more in the EU and from what I've read of Denktash's government economically, they are not in very good shape. Maybe I am a little naive but I still find it hard to believe that Turkish speaking Cypriots feel comfortable with their situation, yet would find it hard to turn to a country where 83% of the population seem to hate them. Naive I may be, but I don't believe much good ever come from this sort of hatred, if we are to forever label our Turkish speaking Cypriot's with the same face as Turkey, Cyprus will never be a united country. Regardless of their past we should show them we are willing to invite them to join us for a better future. But next point, as this is all academic

while there is a line through our island (although I do feel it is a message Turkish-speaking Cypriots should hear and hear clearly). One of us holds a lot of hope for a united Cyprus and it's not one I'll let go of. My only frustration is finding few that will share such an optimistic approach. I have made no secret of my desire to cross over the line officially or not and I do believe much change will come to Cyprus. For better or worse, the defence that Russia will be offering our country will only open up the area to new hostilities in my opinion. For the first time we may be free to run covert operations in the north without fear of unleashing more problems to the south. Russia has shown her willingness to defend Cyprus, lets take advantage of it, one way or the other and I don't think the Security Council or the UN will or can do anything. In 74 the political situation between Russia and the west was, as you know a completely different story. Russia could not do anything before even if she really wanted. Turkey's strongest defence was a N.A.T.O. whose main concern was holding the USSR in check. It's now a completely different situation, Turkey used to get $3bn a year from the U.S.A. to make sure she could keep a strong military presence on her borders with Russia and from what I've heard the U.S.A. also benefited from the invasion. The military situation is completely different now, I believe Russia is the only power in the area to be able to dictate certain policies to Turkey. Just as they are doing with the S-300 missiles, lets wait and see, I don't think it will be long before things start to evolve and if the reunification of Cyprus is not on their agenda. I think there is a way of changing their minds. I think economics as well as strategy takes Russia to Cyprus and I think for both reasons they will (if they have not seen it yet) see that they as much as anyone, will, or can, profit from a unified Cyprus.
Love Jim

I had to confess, I found the language bit a little sad if true but at the same time I found it amusing. The idea of a Greek not speaking Greek is funny, like why would a Greek grow up speaking any other language. Except of course under Ottoman rule, but that was history. From Charlie at the Cyprus Mail I heard nothing. Not even, an acknowledgement but I suppose he might have thought me rude. The conversation I was about to have with my sister was to push all this to the back of my mind. Gina my eldest sister is six years older than myself and spent a couple of years living with my grandmother in London after my grandfathers' death during which time she went to Greek school.

"I've been talking to mum about granddad."

"Oh yeah, what about?" she was pulling washing out from the washing machine as she spoke.

"I was telling her that I can remember granddad speaking good English."

"Oh he only spoke three or four words, but you two used to communicate well though," she said as she pulled washing into a basket.

"Yeah, I remember, I've been thinking back a lot lately," and then added. "I always remember granddad being so happy when he was around us, just playful, like you couldn't do no wrong, not that you wanted to."

My sister was smiling. Probably with the memories coming back when she said without looking up,

"Remember him teaching us to count?"

The memory hit me and shook me at the same time me, yes, I did. It was the way he was playing with us whilst teaching us that she was referring to. I remembered him sat on the bed with my sister in front of him and they were playing as he was teaching. What a shock to realise and remember my thoughts as I played on the bed 'Alphabet first numbers next' and granddad was teaching me.

"Yeah I do, but I wasn't taking any notice I hadn't finished the alphabet," I remembered again thinking alphabet first, numbers next. I was up to Ipsilon and I can't count to three in Greek, grandfather would I know shortly after pass away. I could feel the sorrow building up in myself, but I didn't want to show it. I didn't even attempt to analyse there and then why I couldn't remember something so important, him teaching me Greek. I was just stunned to hear a truth that I'd forgotten for so long and why? Why didn't I remember?

A couple of days later I was off to Helsinki to visit a friend for a long weekend. On my return my parents and my youngest sister were at Stansted to pick me up. It was only a couple of days before they were to fly to Cyprus. It was my father who spoke,

"We spoke to your godmother yesterday," he told me.

"How is she?" I asked a little concerned.

"Good, she says Jim's flying to Cyprus."

"When?" I yelled from the back of the car.

"First of August, I think it's the first or second," my dad wasn't sure but that was a week away.

"Shit! I asked him to let me know! When you flying out?"

"On Wednesday"

"I'll book a ticket to join you for a week, as soon as I get home."

My ticket was booked that day for the second of August. I still had a lot of faith in the idea of what I'd written in Kos. I couldn't help but believe that there wasn't something of use that could be drawn from it. It wasn't meant to be anti Greek rather pro Cypriot although two Greeks on Kos had thought so, but as a Cypriot I had to believe in it. It was a couple of days before I was to leave, when I went on line to check my mail box again and decided I'd read the newspapers. Now I already thought things were looking rosier for Cyprus, well I considered almost any change as rosier and the arms build up met my approval. Now the news in front of my face was something to truly celebrate, this would be a real blow to

Turkey. The European court of human rights had awarded a Greek Cypriot Titina Loizidou over three hundred thousand pounds in compensation against Turkey for 'prevention of enjoyment of her property'. It was the courts final decision on a case that first appeared before them nine years previous. Here was beautiful news to read. The court held Turkey solely responsible. It not only opened the door to thousands to sue, but it seemed to me, to be one of the most positive steps taken by any power against Turkey and the European Union although I considered it far from perfect, it is a power to be reckoned with. At the same time I considered any hopes of Turkey joining this now great union washed away. They are far from ready in most people's opinion and they now seemed to be taking a battering on the European circuit. With this in mind I went searching through the internet and ended up back at The Cyprus Mail, but this time I took a bit of time and realised, oops! I'd broken protocol. There it was in front of me were instructions telling me all letters and whatever should go to the editor, my mistake. So I got on the keyboard and sent the editor a long e-mail with my views on almost everything from the arms build up and the difference Russian air support would make along with the piece that I'd written on Kos. I felt committed that's for sure, I also told him that I was going to be in Cyprus and would appreciate a chance to meet someone and debate the issue. That was naïve of me.

Now I know what I wrote in Kos, but one of those snippets I'd heard as a child was that my granddad had actually left the farm to myself and my immediate family, not that I knew why. Things were to soon change and we were then told that an aunt was looking after it and then that it had been left to my uncle Yannis, which most of the time seemed irrelevant due to the occupation. I went for the phone filled with excitement.

"Yannis have you been keeping up with Cypriot news?" I knew he would hear the excitement in my voice.

"Oh yes, I try, why what's up?" he enquired.

"The Loizidou court case," I had no idea of how to pronounce the name right.

"The what?" he asked confused.

"The Greek Cypriot that's suing Turkey for the occupation," I said.

"Yes I know about it," he replied. I could tell he hadn't heard the final ruling.

"Well get on the phone to your solicitor, and find out a bit more, it's just gone through!" I told him excitedly.

"What do you mean?" he asked.

"The European court of human rights has made its final decision, she won over three hundred thousand pounds plus expenses, and it's not compensation for the land Yannis," I wasn't hiding my excitement. "It's just for non access! The lands still hers, but Turkey has to pay her now for non access!" I paused for a moment to let Yannis take it all in.

"It's gone through?"

"Yes! Its through do you have the will, the papers for the land?" I asked.

"Yes, Yes I have them," he told me.

"Well get on the phone and sue, and tell the others to sue as well. If everyone sues it could cost them billions and phone your brother in Australia," I was excited about it.

"Oh Jim he only has a small place in the mountains it's not much."

"Size doesn't matter, it doesn't matter if he only owns a bloody toilet! It's for prevention of enjoyment of property, sue them! It could cost them billions and it hits them where it hurts!" I enjoyed that.

"Yes, I'll get in touch with him," he said his tone picking up.

"Make sure you do, and anyone else you know, anyone and everyone, I might even sue them myself for emotional distress," I was being serious.

"I'll send you a printout of the report before I fly to Cyprus on Sunday, it's on the web," I told him feeling like I'd done a good job.

"Ok, have a good flight and give my love to everyone."

"Will do and remember, sue the bastards!" I was happy. It felt like a big blow to the Turkish government.

"Yes, yes, alright I will Jim," I could hear the excitement start to spread to my uncle,

"Ok I'll put the papers in the post before I go, take care now."

"You too Dimitri."

That felt like a mission completed. I was riding a wave and I rode it all the way to Luton airport on Sunday afternoon. This visit to Cyprus was going to be different.

Chapter 8

It's a four and a half-hour flight to Cyprus, not long if you find something to fill your time, my thoughts alone were enough to keep me. Reunification, for most of my life, it had seemed just a dream, the possibility of it. But now I really believed that with the changes had come possibilities, which I couldn't believe someone wasn't turning into probabilities, then things would really change. But the biggest changes I'd seen had been in myself. I'd once wondered what would happen to the Turkish Cypriots our Cypriots of Turkish Heritage as I now liked to regard them and that in itself was one of the biggest changes in myself, in a reunified island I was concerned with their safety. Kos and other events in my life had brought me round to thinking that for Cyprus to truly prosper we needed to get out of the perpetuated hatred that exists between Greece and Turkey. Our island is too small for such hatred and Greece, I knew even from my upbringing could not bear to see a Turkish community flourish whilst within its influence. But I'd started to regard these Turks as our Turks, it was all a dream of course but Cypriots first and foremost and as Cypriots shouldn't we now be taking care of each other and ourselves.

Granddad was always playing somewhere on my mind. His past life and the revelations I'd heard about him had now got me seriously believing that there was a motive to his actions. Sending the family to England and allowing the marriage of my parents was just one of them. I'd thought long and hard about how he must have perceived the situation, if he'd travelled abroad even let alone had intelligence training. If my Granddad saw what I could see as far as the hatred went it would start to make a lot more sense. And with the possibility of intelligence training it might also make sense as to why I never remembered him teaching me Greek. He must have done it in such a way for me not to remember, without enforcing it perhaps, but one thing I was now certain of, was that it was because of his death that I stopped. Which led me to another pressing thing on my mind, the news that my Aunt Marie was dying of cancer. It was a bit of a surprise to me as I was told she was suffering when I'd last seen her in October but she'd not shown it, even in her smile. I thought about her smile. It felt so important to be able to tell her I'd carry it with me for the rest of my life, but I didn't even know any of the words let alone string a sentence together. That hurt, I'd found a good reason to put myself out to learn the language for the first time in years, to tell someone I loved them. That was the only sorrow I carried with me on that flight. I felt like I knew why I'd stopped taking in Greek though and I actually felt better about learning it. I felt like I'd been discovering who I was as a Cypriot before taking the Greek language and now the language only had importance because of Marie, it felt strange when I thought of my time with her. I'd not felt as much love from my grandma, it seemed a bit like that same unconditional love that granddad had to offer and the fact that he couldn't talk as I remembered maybe encouraged myself to learn Greek easier. I'd forgotten just how much he meant to me. I was still figuring it all out, those shadows of the past, but they were coming to me.

I landed at Larnaca airport at around nine thirty in the evening and quickly cleared immigration carrying just my hand luggage. I knew that my father, mother and my much younger sister Alex would be waiting at the airport and it was a real joy to see them in Cyprus as I walked into the arrivals' lounge, smiles beaming. My father took my bag and we all walked out to the car park, chatting away as if it had been much longer than the four days it was, since I saw them. I felt like I was on holiday as well which was a nice surprise.

"Food," I said as we drove into Limassol. "I'm starving!"

"Oh there's a restaurant near to the apartment," my mother informed me adding. "We can go there when we arrive."

We parked the car in the apartment block car park and after dropping off the bag walked the short distance to the restaurant. I was pleased to see we were only ten or fifteen minutes walk from my favourite cocktail bar.

"I bet I can't get what I want though," I said as we all sat down in the restaurant.

"What do you want?" my mother asked.

"You really want to know?"

"Yes, I'll see if they can do it"

"Ok, I want capers," I said, "I want guerbegya," which isn't the correct spelling but sounds right, in Greece they're called dolmades, mincemeat, some spices and rice wrapped up in vine leaves.

"And kleftiko," tender cuts of shoulder of lamb in its own sauce.

"Uh, you want kleftiko?" my mother asked.

"Yeah but only the meat mum and the others," I could see my mum wasn't sure of what to make of my request. She knew what I wanted and they might have all been in the kitchen but I'd never been able to get them together on one plate in a restaurant. She looked a bit unsure of herself as she ordered in Greek. It sounded short even though I was eating alone.

"What did you order mum?" I enquired with a smile.

"Kleftiko"

"What with?" I asked already knowing the answer.

"Well I just asked for Kleftiko"

"Just Kleftiko?" I enquired. I could see she wasn't sure if she'd done the right thing.

"Yeah I just asked for Kleftko"

"It's going to come with chips mum," she looked at me surprised.
"No!"
"What do you think it's going to come with!" I was playing with her now and I let my mum know it so she wouldn't feel pressured.
"Well I don't know, salad maybe, some bread I don't know Jim." A bread roll was placed on the table. It wasn't the sort of bread I prefer to eat in Cyprus and not the sort she was expecting to see. I looked at my mum and smiled. My Kleftiko and chips arrived shortly after. I wasn't going to let my mum apologise. I could have ordered myself in English.

I ate my meal, had a beer and chatted with my parents, my sister staying quiet as she often was. After which we walked the very short distance to what was by now their favoured drinking spot a restaurant-bar on the main strip, but next to a car park on a junction so there was a good view of the surrounding area. After one more drink with them I took a pleasant stroll to my favourite bar taking in the warmth, and the feel of the place again, past the now familiar sight in another small car park, the man with his large telescope, 50cents for a peek at the moon. I looked up to my left. It would be full soon, maybe four or five days. That was even more pleasing. I'd always wanted to swim around Aphrodite's rock according to the legend. I was enchanted by it and just the thought that maybe I just might this time, was enough to make the moment that bit brighter. When I'd been here the previous October I'd mentioned it to Bill. It was a full moon, about eleven at night when I put it to him that we should go for a swim. But the lightning that almost immediately broke the horizon as I asked, was enough for both of us, we just looked at each other and shook our heads.

I arrived at the bar to find all the friendly and by now familiar faces that I'd hoped to see there. Took a stall by the near crowded bar ordered a beer, lit up a cigarette, took a deep drag and smiled, it was good to be back. The apartment my parents had booked was on the first floor of an apartment block. It was similar to the one Allen and I had rented, but without the TV, two bedrooms and I was sharing with my father. Fans were essential, it was hot, very hot, 40oC plus on average during the day and only dropping to around 28-30oC at night. I slept well and woke the next morning eager to visit family with family for a change. By the time we were leaving the apartment in the morning it was into the high thirties and I was feeling it. I'd gladly accepted the task of driving the car, relieving my father from a job that he'd done most of his life now being a retired lorry driver. My parents retirement was something that was to come up a lot in conversation, my mother had another two working years and for the first time would open up to the idea of returning to Cyprus with my father. It was something I'd been openly encouraging, as it would give the whole family a permanent base in Cyprus. The sweat was starting to pour before we'd even got to the car, a white four-door saloon. I unlocked the driver's door as I surveyed the surrounding area, and as I opened it, I heard a welcome sound. I looked up in the direction from where it came and simply said,

"I'll be back," and walked. Across a small adjacent car park and through a very small park no more than two hundred metres away, hidden behind a two metre high metal railing fence lined with banana trees, was the source of the welcome sound, a swimming pool. Yes! I knew it would make all the difference in this heat. I walked back to the car with a smile on my face. No one had got in yet, as it was so hot.

"Alex, swimming pool!" I motioned with my head in the direction from which I'd just walked, she looked up at me in surprise, and I nodded with a big smile on my face to show I wasn't joking which brought a smile to hers.

"Didn't you know it was there?" she just shook her head, still smiling. I knew it was going to make all the difference to both of us.

"Well you know what we'll be doing this afternoon," I said and her smile broke into a grin and we both got into the car, my parents already seated and I drove the ten minutes or so to my godmothers knowing the way well. I already knew one of my god sisters was here on holiday with her children and with my godbrother Jim being there it would make it a pleasant reunion. I parked the car outside the gate to my godmothers and we all got out to be greeted by my godfather and Jim who were sitting under an olive tree just inside the garden by the gate. Jim looked sick and a lot older, but I'd heard he'd had a bad flight, which would account for the sick bit, but the grey was certainly taking over. He'd taken his fathers looks as had Spyros, his brother, although they both looked different from each other. They were both of very slight build, but taller than their father. Jim was looking like he needed more recovery time from his flight. They'd both already seen my father, mother and sister, who after saying their hellos carried on to the house. I took one of the unoccupied chairs in the shade of the olive tree. It was a real nice feeling stretching out in the shade, now the heat seemed far more tolerable. Jim had gone off to get me a cold drink. I sat back and studied a plastic container, making out the Greek letters on it into the word 'SUNFLOWER' success I thought. My godfather had just rejoined me as I'd finished it, I was still curious and said allowed as much to myself as to my godfather,

"I wonder why I have so much trouble taking in Greek?" I was talking about my apparent total block to it.

"Your too lazy!" my uncle yelped before he finished off with. "You couldn't be bothered!" I thought about the Thai and Arabic that I'd learnt and forgotten.

"Maybe," I said but I knew,

"I stopped when my granddad died," that I now knew for sure. "Stopped dead," I finished with.

"You remember your Granddad?" my uncle yelped. He often had a tendency to sound harsh and still could, although this time he sounded surprised.

"Of course!" I said. Now more than ever I thought. My uncle made a noise or two and my cousin appeared with the drinks. My father came over to join us and for the next half-hour we chatted. Jim was still exhausted from his flight and it wasn't long before my god sister returned home, one of many sisters, it was all hugs and kisses. Even though she lives in east London, it had been longer since I'd seen her than Jim. But it didn't take long for her children to make the place feel a lot smaller and after a chat to my godmother I felt it a good time to head for the pool. Especially as Jim was, by his own admission feeling too drained to be pleasant company. We left arranging to return the next day for dinner.

The swimming pool was everything one could hope for considering it was an unexpected surprise and not too crowded which surprised me. There was a bar and if there was a shortage of umbrellas the banana trees were perfect and it was under one of these that I settled on a sun bed with my walk man radio tuned into the British Forces station and a newspaper. Pretty much the same as all the other mainly Dutch and British tourists really but it wasn't long before I realised that I was the only one with a Cypriot paper. I found it hard to make holiday talk with the tourists when I was so wrapped up in local affairs like I was. It's their holiday time and their holiday destination, so I'd find myself talking about things that I found of very little interest, but I wouldn't show it. The last thing anyone around the pool wanted to hear about would be missiles or my possibilities and probabilities theory, so I was more than happy to lose myself in my paper and the radio whilst Alex took to her puzzle book. We had dinner in the apartment that night, before I left to go to my favoured bar, which was far busier than any other time I'd been, due to it being mid season. So I only got a chance to say hello to Sergio and a brief talk to Christine.

"Hey Christine, you remember the first time I met you?" she seemed to be thinking about it.

"Do you remember what I asked you?" I could see she never, so I reminded her and of the way she answered.

"Oh don't take any notice of me," she seemed embarrassed by it as she walked away to serve some customers.

"No it was good to hear," we passed smiles and I turned to survey the main strip. It felt good being back, real good. I didn't stay for too long and soon joined my parents and sister for drinks whilst making our plans for the next day.

The next morning Alex and I went off to the pool for a few hours whilst my parents went shopping. We'd made arrangements with my uncle to see Marie before we went to my godmothers for dinner and were to set off around four. I felt terrible about my lack of Greek and not being able to say at least goodbye to someone I loved. I'd decided, since I now knew why I'd stopped learning Greek then I could perhaps open my mind up to it a bit more and start practising, so when I popped off for a packet of cigarettes I figured that would be a good place to start.

"Ena Camel lights paragalo?" All right it wasn't much and it was an obvious effort but I was trying. The Cypriot woman turned to me throwing the cigarettes on the counter.

"Pound fifty!" she snapped and she wasn't very polite about it. I could tell by her tone she was telling me off for trying to speak Greek, when she knew I couldn't and what's more we both knew there was absolutely no need. English is so widely spoken in Cyprus. But to feel like I was being scorned for trying, I was hurt a bit at first, but I wasn't offended, more curious than anything.

Georgio wasn't himself when we arrived which was understandable, we were greeted and went through to the lounge from where the shop front could be watched, coffee was made and we sat. It wasn't a comfortable time. I was summoned to the bedroom after my uncle had fed Marie and given a few minutes alone with her. The sight that greeted me wasn't one I'd expected, if Marie looked ill she was showing it in the way she was laying on the bed and the glazed look in her eyes. Her face had lost that smile and I couldn't help but feel tearful. It was a strong reminder of the last time I'd seen my grandmother after her stroke, I don't even know if she knew I was there. I knelt by the bed and took her hand. The smile that I'd been used to seeing on her face wasn't going to show itself, there wasn't even any recognition. I knew she was on morphine for the pain and the doctors hadn't given her much time. I held her hand and talked to her for a minute or so, knowing that she wouldn't be able to understand me even if she could make out what I was saying. It wasn't long before the food that my uncle had fed her started coming back up. I called to my uncle and tried to help but just felt more useless for trying. We shortly after left for my godmothers, I didn't mind showing that I was upset. But it wasn't so much for the plain fact that Marie was dying. It was that I couldn't talk to her and there was no way I could directly tell her how I felt about her and how she'd touched me with her smile.

At my godmothers we had a family meal which I always enjoyed. The talk was of the Loizidiou land access claim going through. It was myself who'd brought it up, my godmother didn't believe it.

"Marianna it has gone through," I told her.

"We've heard this before, a long time ago but nothing happens!" she said angrily.

"Yes but this time something will happen, the European court of human rights has made a ruling and Europe will be obliged to act," I told her finishing off with.

"If Turkey doesn't pay Turkeys assets in Europe get confiscated," my cousin Jim joined in confirming that action seemed likely. I enlightened my aunt to my actions at home.

"I phoned Yannis up before I left England and told him," my father had heard some information about my grandfathers farm.

"I've heard Azil Nadir's built a hotel on the farm." I'd heard it before whilst here.

"I've told you dad he's just lost a hotel then, bloody cheek!" the thought of the Polly Peck tax cheat who's in Northern Cyprus having built a hotel on my grandfathers' farm was not an idea that pleased me.

"Well it's what I've heard," my father said.

"Well I told you it won't do him no good!" I was already wondering how I'd handle getting to my grandfathers' farm and finding a hotel. I'd only heard the news a day or so earlier, so I was still pondering on it. I'd always imagined to find it abandoned, but I knew that wasn't something that I should have taken for granted. Regardless I felt comfortable about the situation. I hadn't forgotten about my essay and all its content. I just knew that if the invasion of the north went ahead, that it would a very hostile take over and I could understand why. I had to be realistic and consider it a case of what ever will be will be. I didn't actually expect Turkish Cypriots to want to stay. I knew any mainland Turks there wouldn't be welcome with the resentment they would get for partitioning our island off from us for so long. I thought again of the hate filled taxi driver. I knew there would be a few like him and hatred like that when unleashed on a helpless people would drive them away regardless of how I felt.

There were often times when it felt painful not to be able to travel from Nicosia and head North and not stop until I reached the sun kissed golden beaches around Kyrenia. From what I'd heard the beaches were far superior in the north and from the small number of pictures that I'd seen, it looked by far the better side of the island. To have the freedom to take a bike along the north coast, a pushbike even, I longed for the day. I could tell my cousin knew my thoughts, that a day I'd been yearning for was coming and it felt good.

The only concern I had about reunifying the north was over the fact that Greek troops would be used. I didn't think they were necessary if our call up figures were correct and taking into account the reasons that Turkey had partitioned the island, I thought we'd be better off without them. I'd already decided to tell Kyp not to stay in Kos after October as I considered that group of islands to be too close to Turkey for Greece to effectively defend in an open conflict. The more I thought about it the more convinced I was that Jean and Angie on Kos had said what they'd said out of fear. My concern was that if we reunified with Greek troops Turkey would retaliate by attacking Greece, and they in turn could drag Europe into a conflict, which I knew would be a serious affair. I'd watched a parade of Greek troops in Larnaca on Cypriot T.V. and I was a bit disturbed that they looked a little undisciplined as I'd seen more than one, that actually hadn't even shaven for Parade and the dress seemed a little shabby.

The next day I'd promised to drive my parents and sister around the island past Paphos and north to Polis. I was looking forward to showing my mother her own island. We'd already grown a lot closer to each other in the short time I'd been here and I felt it was the way we were relating to each other and it was having an effect on her opinion about retiring in Cyprus. It felt strange, but I felt closer to her here than I have at any other time and I couldn't quite understand why, it seemed to be the country itself, like we were both reacquainting ourselves with Cyprus together. We set off late in the morning but early enough to make it a good day along the main two lane highway that runs a third of the way between Limassol and Paphos. It was a hot morning, but it matters less when you're making some speed. The wind was blowing in through the open windows and the music was on British forces, but low so we could chat. We'd arranged to see Aunt Marie in the evening, which was the only thing on the back of my mind. But I was feeling good, not just good, but like I was opening a whole new brighter chapter on our lives. I felt confident I could talk my mother into retiring here and I knew my father was keen on the idea and the more time I'd spent with them here, the more I wanted to establish stronger links with both the island and them. I'd noticed how well we were communicating here. Just being on the island itself was making a difference to us, it was nice compared to how I used to conflict with my mother in England. I was constantly hearing cars and small boats for sale on the radio at good prices and looking at my father and telling him, I might, if I had somewhere to park them.

After about thirty minutes driving, just after passing through a tunnel. The two-lane highway finishes and you're detoured onto a side road. After turning left at the top of the junction the road meanders down a hill to a T-junction where you turn right and pick up the old coast road. We were approaching Aphrodite's rock. The road breaks through the white limestone rocky coastline a couple of kilometres south of the rocks and as you approach them from some height, you get a good view of them sticking out. The road drops and follows the crescent shaped coastline with the sea to your left. The rock formation is clearly seen and seems to be what's left of a point in the coastline prodding out to sea from the cliffs to their right. As you get closer from this side it's a gentle approach up a slight gradient. You can see the biggest rock clearly breaking over the top of the road, like a big mound getting bigger and bigger in your view. Until the road turns a sharp right round the tip of the cliff and the rock's behind you. I had a warm feeling just approaching it, not just for the strong memories of my first visit, but also my sentiments. I didn't really get much time to take a good look at what I'd thought I'd got a glimpse of on the largest rock as we past it to our left. The bends so tight, that you have to watch the road carefully if your driving, and from the north you only have a visual on it for a few seconds. So I couldn't even check in my rear view mirror properly. I thought about it, it couldn't have been what I thought it was, but it looked like it. My father had the passenger seat I looked at him quickly and asked,

"Was there a flag on that rock?"

"I don't know, was there?"

"I'm sure I saw one," I said. In fact I knew I'd seen one.

"There's a bloody Greek Flag on the rock," I said as much to myself. I continued telling my father.

"It was on the largest rock of the formation facing the road to the north." But no, I didn't really believe it and as much to myself still.

"Nah, it couldn't be," I knew there was something on there. But as I couldn't be certain as to what I'd decided to get a look on our return trip before passing judgement and concentrated on the road in front, wondering which route to take from Paphos to Polis. It was a good day and I wasn't going to let a possible trick of the light ruin it.

By the time we parked the car at the campsite car park on the beach at Polis, the soaring heat had built up a thirst in all of us and the beach bar looked all the better for the familiarity I felt with the place. The wind was blowing from the north-west so it was refreshing facing the sea. In the shade the breeze was the coolest I'd been since I'd arrived on Cyprus without sticking my head out of the car window, air conditioning excluded. I've stood on some beautiful beaches and even though this wasn't one of the best, like the town, it felt relaxed which after Limassol is a real change. The talk on route had been retirement homes and my parents taking one in Cyprus. It actually sounded as if my mother was going for the idea, which she was. It had picked me up no end. My mother joined us at the bar after finding the campsite toilets. There was a good mixture of holidaymakers around, both foreign and Cypriot.

"What do you want to drink mum?" I asked.

"I'll have a shandy"

"I'm not sure if they've got any shandy mum," I said realising straight away that they had to have it. Almost immediately I heard a female voice in a London accent from behind the bar.

"Shandy of course we've got shandy! You want shandy no problem!" I looked over the counter to see the source of the voice. It was a Cypriot girl, possibly a relative of the man that I'd met who run the bar and at that point I thought, God I love this country. There were no hang-ups about the language on Cyprus as in Greece. It was a big difference and I felt so much closer to the place knowing that I wouldn't be considered any less Cypriot for my ignorance of the Greek language and everyday seemed to confirm it to me. I chatted to the young man who run the family bar, a pleasant man who remembered me well from my last visit.

"These your parents?" he enquired. Smiling at them as he asked.

"Yeah I'm kind of showing them around and I couldn't miss this place out, they're thinking of retiring here and I wanted to show them Polis before they commit anywhere." The bar owner took this news warmly and immediately got chatting to my mother, it's only natural to feel some pride in your own area and he knew how I felt about Polis. Part of the afternoon was spent on the beach as a family which was very rare for me as I'd always felt distanced from them, my mother in particular, but not this day. In the late afternoon we strolled around Polis, which I showed them and what joy I felt to see they were actually taking a genuine interest in the real estate agencies getting some information and prices. I told my mother and father plain and simple that I felt the family as a whole would benefit from such a choice and it would keep the younger ones in touch with their Cypriot heritage. I felt good, I told my mother that I knew it was as much for myself and she approved. We were walking round the square when a newspaper headline caught my eye. 'TURKISH WRITER GETS 25 YEARS' Oops! I thought. I walked up to the stand and read a short bit of the article saying a Turkish journalist had been sentenced to twenty-five years imprisonment in Turkey for writing material considered subversive by the government and the military. I wondered how the piece I sent to the Cyprus Mail was considered. It made me think. I'd forgotten that a lot of newspapers in this region were as much government papers, although I didn't have any idea of how the Cyprus Mail stands and still don't, but it did send a shiver through me. We drove back on the more northerly route to Paphos. This way the mountains take you way up, so you can see the coastline for miles. It really is a beautiful view. I pulled the car over to get out and take in the scenery. It was a sight I could stare at all day from the nearby small traditionally farmed holdings on the mountainside, down to the coast, which looked over a thousand metres below us.

"Look there's a caper plant," It was my mother pointing to a bush.

"Is that it?" I went up for a closer look, it was, and not only this one but when I looked around me I found they were growing in abundance.

"Wow this is great, capers everywhere, look at that one!" there was a bush as big as the car and many others, I was ecstatic. It was a delicacy for me but here it was just a common shrub. It immediately got me thinking about my cousin Jim and his complaints that he'd never been able to successfully grow a plant in Australia. I looked at the ground it was almost pure limestone, anywhere the ground wasn't covered by foliage it was bright white.

"It's the limestone!" I exclaimed.

"What?" my mother replied.

"It's the limestone, I bet it's why Jim has had no success growing them, look they're growing in almost pure lime." I looked down at a small plant no more than ten centimetres long growing by my feet and then I got one of my crazy thoughts.

"Mum have you got a nail file or something on you?"

"Oh I think so, what for?"

"I'll show you!" my mother took a metal file out of her bag and passed it to me. I immediately took to the ground and started digging away at the lime surrounding the small plant.

"What are you doing?" she inquired startled and concerned for her file.

"Taking a sample mum, it's alright I wont ruin your file can you put this in your bag," I passed my mother a ten by five centimetre lump of lime, she looked at it in aghast.

"What are you going to do with this?" she asked totally bemused.

"Well your good at growing things mum," I said as I was just freeing the plant that I was digging around.

"And I thought it might help when we get this home!" I stood up with my miniature caper plant in my hand feeling pleased with myself.

We soon set off again down the mountain road to Paphos. I insisted on driving them around the town and showing them some of the sights without getting out. I felt so happy and comfortable which was more important, comfortable about feeling Cypriot. As we left the town onto the road south we passed an army truck and for the first time I was putting together serious thoughts about doing my national service and mentioned it to my parents. I'm not sure if they knew how to take this change in me. But if reunification was going to have to be forced I wondered if I wouldn't want to be a part of it and I felt I did.

We drove past the banana plantations from Paphos on to the coast road south. There are no signs to let you know that you're approaching the Aphrodite's rock formation from the north. There's a drop and a right bend and the rocks in front of you rising up over the top of the road and after a little more than a hundred metres or so the road turns a sharp left and it's behind you again. What greeted my eyes as I followed the road round the right bend was to freeze me in my seat. I stared in disbelief. It was worse than I could have imagined. Right in front of my eyes draped over the largest rock was a Greek national flag and to make it worse, it was positioned so that when the tourists took photos of the rocks, as a few were, they were getting the Greek flag in their pictures. Telling them they were in Greece. I was horrified. I turned the bend putting the flag out of sight but the horror of it over the rock soon turned to anger.

"Bastards! Fucking hypocrites!" I'd thought about our own flag and the life that had been lost attempting to pull a Turkish one down. The rest of the car was silent, I did nothing to conceal my anger.

"Fucking hypocrites! I don't believe it! I just don't fucking believe it! Fucking Greeks!" There was still silence in the car. I looked at my father.

"It shouldn't be up there!" I snapped at him. My father nodded, but I hadn't finished.

"I flew out here two years ago prepared to pull a fucking Turkish flag down and now this, I just don't fucking believe it!" We carried on driving towards Limassol, in my anger I'd increased my speed before taking control. Very little was said for a while and then we pondered certain theories as to who had put it up there, private individual or government which I couldn't believe, I was enraged.

I had to suppress my anger quickly and put the flag out of my mind for a while. Our first stop when we returned to Limassol was to see Marie. This time she was sitting up when I went into the bedroom. My uncle arranged the room a little and we all sat there together, which felt right. I sat on the bed whilst my mother sat at Marie's side and the rest of the family were gathered around. My mother knew what I wanted to say to Marie and I'd told her how I felt bad about not being able to say it myself. I saw a shadow of a smile on her face again and I knew somehow, it would be the last time.

"Mum tell Marie that I'll carry her smile with me forever," my mother passed on my words. I didn't know whether she heard it or understood it but I wished that I'd known her condition in October so I could have made sure she was told when she was more coherent. It just felt important for her to know. My uncle Georgio was always strong about the situation. He didn't come across as a weak man, which he isn't and here he was showing his strength. I promised myself there and then I wouldn't let it happen again. Before we left I was to meet another cousin and her son, a handsome young lad of about six or seven. I said hello and felt like I'd found another reason to learn Greek. I found it more troubling now than ever, neither could speak any English, my own kin and I couldn't even communicate with them. We had dinner at the apartment that night and I had drinks with my parents. I was in no mood to go to any bars or socialise in any way. I went to bed early but even that was to prove pointless, if I slept it was for only the briefest period. I was troubled more than I thought by what had started as a wonderful day turning to anger and then being subdued by grief. And I think what was upsetting me most was the anger over the flag was hindering any grieving that I might have wanted to do.

The morning light found me laying on the bed staring at a small bat that had flopped onto the balcony in the bright sunlight. I pulled the net curtain aside to view it. To my surprise the bat turned it's head and seemed to look straight at me, totally calm despite the bright light and the intense morning heat it was laying in. Only when I stepped onto the balcony did it fly off. The apartment was empty as I'd already passed on the days events an hour or so earlier, before drifting back into my daze. My parents and sister had gone to my godmothers to join them for a barbecue on my cousin's olive grove. I'd considered going but the heat and lack of sleep had made it seem less appealing. I prepared myself breakfast before doing the only reasonable thing I could consider under the circumstances and that was to head for the pool. I was annoyed at my sleepless night. I knew the sight of the Greek National flag draped over our national treasure had enraged me, but I didn't think I was going to have a sleepless night over it. It wasn't so much thinking about it, as trying not to think about it that I thought must have kept me awake because I didn't want to think about it. I passed the day pleasantly by the pool in the shade of a banana tree, between a Dutch family on one side and an English couple on the other side of me, except for the newspaper I was reading I could have been a tourist. So I put the newspaper away and I made tourist talk with the people around me. Whilst observing a Russian looking girl between tanning herself and her occasional couple of lengths to cool off before returning to her sun bed and delicately replacing small leaves over her nipples to protect them from burning. I found myself talking about anything except Cyprus if I could. A week earlier someone had been machine gunned to death in the area which was mentioned, a gang land killing I said as if it was to be expected. A gangland killing it was, but there was a time only recently when it was a real rarity to even hear of such things.

Late afternoon, my parents and sister returned from their outing and to my relief I discovered that shelter was scarce at the olive grove which for myself had justified not attending, we left after an hour or so to take our dinner at my godmothers. As we pulled up at the house I could see my cousin Spyros arriving on his bike, I let my folks enter and waited for Spyros to step off his bike and remove his helmet.

"What happened to you today?"

"Ah, I couldn't sleep last night I would have suffered," I told him. "Sorry mate!"

"You couldn't sleep, why not?" I knew Spyros would ask.

"I don't know, I saw a bloody big Greek flag draped over Aphrodite's rock yesterday and I think maybe it upset me a bit," I saw my his face pull up in disgust.

"What! Nah that's not on," it was all I needed to hear from him. He muttered a few other things but I could tell he wasn't happy about it. I followed him up the garden path and settled in for dinner. The women took care of the serving of dinner and the clearing up afterwards, there's nothing chauvinistic about it and they wouldn't let you help if you tried. Which leaves the men folk to smoke and talk after dinner talk whilst my godfather swatted flies. I opened up about my ideas on the possibility of Russian help which was at first rejected, before I made an argument out of the fact that the political climate between Russia and the west would now allow Russia to partake in such an activity. As I pointed out, no country recognises Turkish northern Cyprus and we had the support of most countries. Russia not only had good reason to help us with our historical friendship aligned with our strong religious links but could also claim the humanitarian high ground. By simply assisting in reuniting our country when no one else could help, due to Turkey's physical strength. And that there would be no love lost between Turkey and Russia as little existed. The argument was thrown in that Turkey would get support from the Arabic states due to the religion, but as I pointed out few Arabic states have any love for Turkey, as they suffered as much as anyone else under Ottoman rule. I thought of Lawrence and took pride in his activities against the Turks in Arabia, which were most importantly, for the Arabs.

The flag on Aphrodite's rock wasn't mentioned in conversation and neither did I want it to be. I hadn't spoken to my godmother or anyone else about wishing to be referred to as a Cypriot first and foremost during the visit either. It wasn't that I felt like taking it back in any way. I just knew it would be a painful subject for myself at least, but especially my godmother. We left my godmothers about nine that evening to return to our apartment. I went straight to my regular haunt for a drink in just my shorts and trainers and my parents went to their bar. Up to then I felt like I had been constantly trying to conceal from myself how I was feeling about the flag. My cousin Spyros was the first I'd mentioned it to and I felt sure I wanted to just forget it. But something wouldn't let go and now I was to test some more water.

"Hey Sergio! Yesterday I drove past Aphrodite's rock with my parents and I saw someone has draped a big Greek flag over the largest rock." Sergio's face turned to disgust as he listened.

"No!"

"Yes a bloody big thing at least fifteen feet across, laying over the rock, like it's theirs or something," Sergio was disgusted. He shook his head as he turned to walk along the bar and loudly hissed,

"It is theirs! They can bloody take it back!"

"Yeah bloody right," I agreed before wondering whether he meant the flag alone or the flag and the rock. I carried on with my drink satisfied that there was more than a little discontent at the idea of there being a Greek flag draped over our national treasure. Christine replaced Sergio at the bar so I thought I'd mention it to her also.

"Chris, I saw a fifteen foot Greek flag draped over Aphrodite's rock." Well it might as well have been the actual rock. She showed her disappointment but she didn't seem too surprised, she leant forward and in a hushed voice said,

"Yeah, this government is a bit like that, Greek!"

"They are?" I responded more than a little surprised. She nodded as she started to walk away. They couldn't be that Greek I thought. No, I couldn't believe it would be the government.

"Christine if I say I'm a Greek Cypriot then it's only to let people know that

I'm not Turkish"

"Me too," that felt sad but true. And it was with that last response in my ears that I walked back to my parents. I felt proud to be Cypriot and belittled by the thought of that flag being draped where it was. I got to the bar where my parents were drinking. My father was in high spirits and they'd got familiar with the bar owner and were now enjoying the perks. I sat down and ordered a brandy sour, it was my father that spoke.

"Jim the bar owner says it wouldn't have been the government that put the flag up there"

"No just some fucking Greek!"

"Jim I'm Greek!" my mother pleaded. I responded firmly but gently.

"Mum you're also Cypriot and times have changed that flag has no place on our rocks, it's not your Greek I'm knocking it's the nationalistic mentality of those pricks in Athens," I told her. "There's Greek and there's Greek Cypriots mum and we have to be different now, Cypriots first and foremost." It was not an issue that I could be moved on.

"Anyway he says it's probably just some Greeks pissing around," added my father. He couldn't have picked a worse way to describe it. I was turning a cocktail stick with a picture of the Cypriot flag on it over in my hand, whilst digesting his words. 'Just some Greeks pissing around' I knew what happened the last time Greeks were pissing about in our country. I looked up at the moon. It was full.

"Fancy a swim Alex?" she looked at me as if to say you might as well be kidding. I looked at the small Cypriot flag in my hand and turned it over before closing my hand around the stick with its miniature flag attached.

"I'm going for a drive," they looked at me with concern, so I comforted them with,

"Just a drive ok, be back soon."

Fifteen minutes later I was heading west with a full tank of petrol not that I needed it and the music low to help me think. I tried to estimate how high up the rock the flag was, better to just get there and have a look I thought. I hadn't committed myself to anything and all I was doing was going for a drive, just to have a look, and maybe even a swim I thought. The moon was full and why not, I didn't have a towel with me but I knew where there was a good one hanging. The drive seemed longer than usual and I was happy to get off of the dual carriageway on to the smaller road winding it's way through the cliffs, I would soon be there. As I approached the rocks they stood out clearly in the bright moonlight and as nice as they looked I was looking out for signs of people. No matter what I was telling myself, I knew what I was going to do, but it wasn't as if I could help myself. There was a driving force behind my actions that night that even I was unaware of. As I got closer to the rocks I kept a constant look out for life. I passed a parked truck on the right, about a kilometre before the rock, but that was all. I drove further and started the gradual climb to the bend that would take me past the rock. It's dark shadow loomed over the top of the road as I got closer and then it was out of sight as I turned the right hand bend. I turned the car around and slowly approached the bend again but this time pulling the car over to the long roadside verge where the tourists had been parked the day before and switched the engine off before sitting there for a moment. I kept telling myself I was only here to have a look, but that's what I was telling myself. I got out of the car, locked the door and put the keys behind the front wheel. I then walked across the road and climbed the crash barrier and slid a few feet down the slope and sat there studying the rock and the offending flag. I could hear the surf and the waves crashing against the rocks, the flag looked a lot bigger and higher up than I'd first thought. I could see a ledge on the rock that seemed to start at about three or four metres up and then run up the side of the rock at a forty-five degree angle, there was a patch of bushy growth along the ledge. The climb itself didn't look that high but just a little daunting when considering the circumstances. I knew I could get to the ledge easy enough and then to the flag. Without another thought I slid down the bank, getting a surprise from it being steeper than I thought. I walked up to the side of the rock and looked up. Heights are actually one of my biggest fears and water at night for some reason. I looked up at the climb I was considering. Standing next to the rock I realised it was about the same height as a waterfall that I used to climb in Thailand, out in the jungle behind the beach where I would stay. If I conquered my fears for the waterfall and it's pleasures, as I had done on many occasions then I certainly would for this. It felt like duty. With that thought I was up the first three or four metres and on to the ledge that would take me higher up the rock.

The sharp jagged edges made for easier climbing but were also scratching my legs and arms, which I simply ignored. I'd considered worse case scenarios and possibilities and the worse thing I felt could happen, would be for me to slip and break a bone an the hard pebble beach. I considered someone seeing me, but what could they say, the flag shouldn't be up there in the first place not that I knew it would matter, the option of me getting caught was not one I wanted to consider. I'd perhaps like to have thought that no one would mind but Cyprus is a country where flag pulling is taken with some seriousness and this was a Greek flag. Even though I was a Greek Cypriot I knew I could pay heavily with a good beating at least if the wrong people caught me and yet cheered by others. But again I put that option out of my mind, for myself getting caught wasn't going to be an option. From the ledge I could see approaching cars a long distance away. From the south the cars could be seen clearly as they drove down the large crescent bay. And from the north it was the traces of the lights that I could see, but for a good couple of minutes as they glowed and flickered until the final bend.

There were three cars approaching that could be seen, two from the south and one from the north. I knew there was little chance of being seen on the rock from the road, especially by any drivers, as they'd need to be watching the road. The only way that anyone might notice was if the flag was being dragged across the rock whilst they passed, or and this was my worst fear, a passing police car stopping to check on my car and having a look around. But I'd decided to deal with that, if or when it happened. The ledge was wider than I could have hoped for and I found I could easily stand on it and walk up the steep gradient climbing to the bushy growth. I was to climb more than walk up the ledge though through fear of slipping and landing on the pebble beach. When I got to the bushy growth I waited for the three cars I knew were approaching to pass. Their lights hardly touched the rock, which spurned me on further feeling safer in the shadow that had been formed on the rock from the car lights and the crash barrier. There were two more cars off in the distance but they wouldn't be here for a few minutes. So I pushed climbing as high as the ledge would take me. When the ledge fell away I paused for my breath and getting a good footing on the rock I rose to look over it to see how far off the flag was. It took me a moment or two to realise that I was closer than I thought. The flag lay out on the rock as far as I could see. It seemed to blend in with the moonlight and actually started not that much more than an arm length away but covered more of the rock than I had imagined. I needed to lean my body over as much as I could to reach the flag's edge with both hands before pulling. It was a hard drag but it was going to come. I fell against the rock to let the approaching cars pass. Then I was up and leaning over the rock again, dragging the flag to me as hard as I could. I knew there was something not right about the force I had to use to drag the flag. It wasn't getting snagged, but each pull I made I had to draw my arms right back with my body weight to get enough force to drag it. I started bundling the flag up to my chest until there was so much of it I had to turn on my side, leaning back on the rock to pull it all over. Somehow I knew my measurements were a bit out. By the time I'd completely gathered the flag up I was lying on my back with the flag bundled up on my chest and thighs. I couldn't get my arms around it, so I threw it down the ledge as hard as I could, which wasn't far. It formed a pile lower down and I started my descent to the flag. Bundling it up again and throwing it further down the ledge, it was too heavy for me to simply throw on to the beach and it was starting to get hard work. At this point it was two thirds of the way down so I sat next to it and pushed my feet underneath the flag and gathered up as much as I could over my knees. When I had most of the flag in my arms I gave it one last heave over the edge onto the beach and without a thought I climbed down and gathered up the flag and dragged myself across the pebbly beach. I was out of breath and gasping heavily but I wasn't about to relax when I was so close to my objective. The flag was down and now I had to ensure it didn't go back up, which meant taking it with me. I'd completely forgotten any thoughts of swimming. I walked around the bank to the road, as the climb up the bank wasn't so steep. But I regarded this as the most dangerous point. I simply had to get myself into a safer situation before the next car came and I would now get very little warning of those approaching from the north. I forced myself up the bank, falling on the flag to keep my footing. It was so big it easily took my body with some comfort. By the time I'd scrambled to the top I was totally exhausted and aware that there was a car coming from the north. I ran across the road with the flag bundled in my arms and got to the start of the long verge where the car was parked and simply dropped the flag behind a bush. The car turned the final bend in front of me before catching me in his headlights' head down and walking empty handed but unknown to the passing motorist totally exhausted. I got to the car picked up the keys and sat in the driver's seat still gasping for breath. I only paused for a moment before I started the car engine and slowly drove along the verge to stop the car next to the flag. I opened the passenger door and leant right across to drag the flag into the foot well of the car, which was quite a struggle, being already exhausted. I closed the door put the car into gear and drove. I looked at the flag bulging out of the foot well of the car and took a handful and wiped the sweat and grime from my face before pushing it down so it wouldn't stick up over the window. I drove back along the road not even thinking too much about what I'd just done, only relieved that I'd done it. As I turned to join the dual carriageway a police four by four appeared in front of me. It was heading towards me at a very slow pace with its blue lights flashing, but just cruising. I felt a shot of fear, hearing the barmaids words about the government being Greek and considered where I might have ended up, if I was on the rock when they passed. I'd still not recovered as I approached the outskirts of Limassol and I could feel my stomach starting to heave, I knew my dinner was calling to be rejected perhaps with the exhaustion. I pulled over about a hundreds metres short of a roundabout, opened the drivers door and heaved. Spaghetti was on the menu tonight and that was now covering the road by my door. I sat up to see if I could continue and at the same time saw a lay by about twenty metres in front of me, before I put my head down again to be sick. I knew if a police car passed now they would certainly pull up curious as to why I'd parked on the road when a lay by was so close for one and the pile of vomit certainly wasn't going to help. I choked out as much as I could as quickly as I could and wasted no time, wiping my face on my tee shirt, I put the car into gear and drove on to the apartment. I hadn't thought about what to do with the flag from this point. I parked the car and looked around. My options seemed limited there was the rubbish skip, but I couldn't. After everything I'd done I realised I was still holding a flag that I knew I couldn't disrespect in that manner. There was only one thing for it. I bundled it up and carried it to the apartment. I was attempting to open the door when it opened with my sister on the other side of it, she smiled not completely surprised. I walked in and dropped the flag on the floor before falling on the sofa and asking Alex to get me some water. My mother came through,

"Oh my god what have you done?"

"Hmmm, well I'm afraid it's a bit bigger than I thought Mum"

"Oh, Shit!"

"It'll make a nice duvet cover," not that I was serious but I was trying to appease her as I knew this was way over her head.

"But they'll miss it!"

"Why?"

"Because it's so big!"

"Mum someone might miss it, but if it's the governments, they'll never admit it, so there is no chance of me getting arrested for this and it wont get to court anyway because" I paused slightly. I couldn't believe the size of it. "It'll be a court case that no one wants mum," I sighed. Then I looked at the brightness and how clean the flag was.

"Look how clean it is, it looks brand new, it couldn't have been up for more than a week or so."

That felt good, knowing that I'd limited the damage that it might have done.

"Anyway I'd be happy for a day in court, not that it'll happen, like I said mum the government will never admit it's theirs, it's hypocrisy! Just pure hypocrisy!" with my father's help I pulled the flag out one way. It stretched about six or seven metres (about twenty feet) and it was big enough as it was but there was something I didn't want to face then. I was stunned. My father could see it. I insisted there and then that it should be folded up and placed in the wardrobe.

"What are you going to do with it?"

"I'm not leaving it here, I only came with hand luggage I'm taking it home."

I couldn't think of what else to do with it. It was off the rock and that was good enough for me for now. I showered and went to bed, as I lay down to sleep that night, despite being proud of myself it was with a tear in my eye. I thought of the altar boy I'd once been in the white robe and blue sash of the Greek Orthodox Church and wondered how or why I'd had to do such a thing, as pull down a flag I'd been brought up alongside. I only knew what I'd done was right, it was just something I should never have had to do.

I slept better that night and a lot happier for knowing that at least tourists wouldn't that day be taking photos of Aphrodite's rock and being left with an everlasting impression that they were in Greece. The next day was to be spent on one of Limassols beaches, which are alright, not golden or anything special in that sense but well catered for. It was just my immediate family and my god brother Jim who accompanied us. Spyros was to join us later. We talked about anything and nothing in particular I remember it well if only for the American Embassies being bombed in Africa. I had my radio walk man on and announced the news as I heard it. Jim cheered at first, which was halted by a look from myself. I could hear from the reports that the casualties would be high. He immediately took it back and I think he may have felt a little embarrassed by his initial reaction, but I understood. There are rumours and always have been that the Americans sanctioned the invasion and partition of Cyprus by Turkey, as they wanted a base of their own on the island, it's said to exist in secrecy somewhere in the north. It's a report I've actually heard from Turkish ex-servicemen. After the beach we took dinner at my godmothers. I'd felt it better not to mention the flag. My parents were constantly keeping a vigil on the news for reports of a big Greek flag being taken off Aphrodite's rock, which I told them to forget about. They'd decided they'd buy a barbecue, Greek style with rotating skewers and so would I, I'd decided. But mine would travel home in a box with company. So that evening as we drove back to our apartment, we stopped off in the old quarter of the city so we could purchase our barbecues. The first shop we went to must have been Turkish as I could hear Muslim prayers being said out the back. My mother had just confirmed to me that the Ottoman period Mosque which stands not a stone's throw away was locked and unused. When I asked why, the answer to which I already knew was, it's Turkish, not that I thought it mattered. But it's understandable with the resentment that partition has caused. It's not been damaged, just locked up. An old Cypriot man came running from a shop immediately opposite, guiding us back to his own. My parents picked out a large barbecue on its own stand and I took the smallest one that was for sale and we had them both packed in a large box about one metre long by twelve centimetres wide and the same again high. I knew I'd be unpacking the box as soon as it was at the apartment, which was what I done. The flag was layered into the box around the smallest of the barbecues. The box was then sealed and string tied around it to make it easier to carry. I was feeling more than a bit paranoid about taking the flag out of the country and it wasn't the official implications as much as the unofficial dangers of my actions. The box was then placed in the wardrobe where it would be out of sight for a day or two, which would take my mind of it. That night I went to my favourite bar for an hour or so. I didn't even want to think about the flag and spoke cheerfully about my mother's complete turnabout as regards to retiring in Cyprus and returned early to the apartment to get a good night's sleep for the next day.

The next day was a family trip with two cars going up to Troodos for the day. We parked up at the car park and all wondered around whilst some of my cousins went for a short horse ride. My father had stayed in town and in our car were Jim, Spyros, my mother and my sister. I felt a lot happier in myself as we walked from the car park. I slowed down to keep pace with Spyros.

"Hey remember that Greek flag I told you was on the rock?"
"Yeah"
"Well it's not up there anymore," I told him. He looked at me a little confused

pulling a funny face.

"How do you know?"

"Because I pulled it down!"

"You never!"

"I did!"

"You drove all that way for that, why?"

"I thought one sleepless night was enough"

"I'm proud of you!"

"Thanks," that actually meant a lot to me.

"Hey Spyros," I called out to him as he walked on.

"What?"

"It's big," he looked at me wondering how big I meant, I pointed from one side of the road to the other. I still didn't realise how much of an underestimation that was.

"At least as big as that" he pulled one of his faces and looked at me.

"You want to be careful you know!"

"I know," I smiled and we walked on and browsed around the tourist stalls and sat in the shade drinking cold drinks. The temperature despite the altitude was still very hot. After a short while we drove on to Kykkos monastery where Makarios first entered the church this being his local area. Passing on route cement mixers coming from and going to, what I assumed would be our new radar station for the expected missiles, there was the odd armed guard standing around to confirm this. From the monastery we drove on to the burial place where Makarios lays and after a picnic in the car park most of the family went up to the tomb of Makarios except for Spyros, Jim, myself and a couple of my god sister's children. I crawled into the boot of the car to lay and ponder about Makerios and what I couldn't understand was how and why did he keep Cyprus independent so long when he was so Greek. Archbishop Markarios, he was born Mikhael Mouskos in Panayia, a village in the Troodos mountains. He entered the church at the age of 13 at Kykkos monastery. At the age of 37 in 1950 he was elected Archbishop of Cyprus and Ethnarch of the Greek Cypriot people and given the title of Makarios the third. I couldn't help but feel that he was Greek in the nationalistic sense, so why the coup, it was all a bit of an enigma to me but it always had been and I really didn't care at that moment in time. I'd liberated one important site for Cyprus on this trip and I was taking the flag home. Satisfied that that was the only thing I could do with it, I was sure if I left it lying around it would go back up somewhere else.

Every one regrouped at the cars and we set off for home, it had been a good day. As we drove I realised how long it had been since I'd actually seen Jim and Spyros together and it felt good to hear them bickering in a similar fashion to days past, a motorist tore past accelerating fast as he did. It could only be

Spyros's voice,

"Bloody people can't wait, only ten years ago they were on a donkey and now they nearly kill themselves trying to get where they're going!"

"I don't believe you Spyros! Your so bigoted and against your own people!" Jim blasted at him.

"I'm not bigoted! It's true ain't it!"

I immediately burst into laughter and giggled as they carried on bickering. After we returned to Limassol we had dinner at my godmothers and it was the usual but pleasant routine. I'd arranged to collect Jim from his mothers in the morning as it was to be my last day and he'd be the one that I'd see the least of, living in Australia. For myself it was to be time to catch up with a brother that I seldom saw.

The next morning my parents and sister walked to do some shopping and I told them I'd meet them back at the apartment later that afternoon. I picked Jim up at around eleven. I'd been looking forward to spending time with him. But he'd only just recovered from his flight from Australia, which hadn't been very pleasant by his accounts. As I've already written he is someone I always felt very fond of and close to. He'd asked me if I could put my flight back a week or so which wasn't possible for me, as I explained to him this trip was on the shortest notice and I planned to return in the autumn. Jim is over fifteen years older than I am and someone that I'd always had the highest regard for. I'd decided not to tell him about my escapade on the rock, not that I was sure why. I thought that some of my relatives might be angry that I'd done it, mainly because of the risk that I knew I'd taken. Although I did think that some might disagree with the principle of it, I just didn't know. The pool seldom seemed to get overcrowded and we easily found some sun beds with lots of space around in a corner. I arranged a couple of large parasols attempting to judge the movement of the sun as best as possible and we settled in. This was a good time for me to talk to Jim not just because of the length of time since we'd last met but unknown to myself even, for the questions I wanted answered about my grandfather. We first spoke of a T.B type infection that had nearly taken my life over two years earlier. I didn't know he knew about it, but it had nearly taken me so I shouldn't have been surprised that he knew. I told him of the pain I suffered when it was at its worst and I also told him I was fully recovered, which wasn't quite true.

We then spoke about his mother and I told him I thought the missile situation was worrying her but I felt there was little to be concerned about, but as he was here, I felt it should be his duty to advise her. I then went on to tell him with some warmth how well my mother and myself were getting on, telling him it's me more than anything. I was relating to my mother in a completely different way whilst in Cyprus and I believed it was the reason she'd changed her mind about retiring here. In England my parents only live around the corner from me and I seldom saw them. I was often very harsh on her for the reasons I gave before, but in Cyprus the relationship had felt completely different. I told him how I felt like I was discovering my Cypriot heritage and feeling proud about it, to which he showed his approval. I revealed to him how I used to feel that my total ignorance of the Greek language was a hurdle which I used to believe would always prevent me from feeling like this, but not any longer. He told me my ignorance of Greek made me no less Cypriot and confirmed for me how I was already feeling but the confirmation felt good. I then went on to tell him how Marie had affected myself and of my intentions to start Greek classes because I'd found a good enough reason to make the effort. As it seems I did most of the talking. Having read my essay Jim knew how I felt about Cyprus. I told him what I'd told his mother about no longer wishing to be referred to as a Greek and that I knew and regretted the fact that it had upset her. He nodded his head as he pointed out to me,

"You have to be careful about how you say things to people as much as what you say."

"I know, I haven't mentioned it since I got here," Jim then changed the subject which suited me.

"When your parents got here they told me you were very angry at me, for not letting you know I was coming," Jim seemed to have taken this news badly.

"No Jim," I told him with a smile. "I did swear but I wasn't angry at you"

"I come off line before I could let you know," he said. I felt like he was apologising which wasn't needed.

"Don't apologise you're here, I'm here, I told you I could make it at short notice, it's not a problem"

"It was just the idea of you being angry at me that I found upsetting, I didn't like it," I regarded that as a sign of how close we were.

"I told you Jim if I was, it was only momentarily, anyway!" I picked up my tone.

"A little anger's not necessarily a bad thing, it's not like hatred or bitterness," Jim looked at me a little confused, I could see he didn't quite agree with my last statement.

"I don't know," he replied. So I thought I'd enlighten him as to what I meant with a smile on my face.

"Anger protects us from the influence of others," I looked at him to see if he understood what I said. He thought about the statement and I decided I'd help him out whether he needed it or not.

"When your angry at someone you love, they can't influence you can they?" he realised what I meant and a slight smile crossed his face, but he still didn't seem to agree as to whether it should be used like that, so I explained.

"When someone you love has pissed you off, or is pissing you off, you need to protect yourself, right?" he nodded in agreement and before he could say anything

I added,

"Love is an emotion, our emotions are often faulted, probably because we're all selfish and dishonest to different degrees, so we need protection sometimes," he looked at me seeming surprised that I was going into such depth, so I enlightened him as to the source of my knowledge.

"Someone gave me a lesson on the concepts of reality and truth," I told him. He now looked more confused.

"Well I took psychology at college but I'd never heard of it taught as a concept"

"Yeah I know, no one I've spoke to has, but Dave was different, maybe it's how he was taught it, because he used to work for British intelligence during the cold war."

I knew Jim would need a quick briefing on my relationship with this ex-agent so I told all about the man I met in a London pub and became close friends to. We became a lot closer as I was there for him when his wife was afflicted with cancer, the illness went terminal and she died. She also died a paranoid schizophrenic and it had caused him a lot of grief at the time. I would be there to take him to the pub occasionally where he eventually revealed his past life to me and an insight into human nature, hence the concepts of reality and truth. He'd also taught me a little about how to use it through conversations. Jim went on to tell me of a truth class in psychology when they had to decide whether a man was telling the truth about being somewhere at a certain time. He failed the test. I listened carefully and when he told me there was a class a week before on the forthcoming test. I told him before he could get to it, that he never paid attention to the relevant information that was unknowingly being passed to the class about this mans destination that would catch the man out. I simply wanted to show that I knew a little bit about it. Jim smiled and agreed he never listened and that he wasn't that good at psychology. I changed the subject.

"You know I've been doing a lot of thinking about granddad lately"

"Your granddad!" he said surprised.

"Yeah, I've just started to realise the effect he had on me when he was alive, I stopped learning Greek when he died for one, stopped dead! Can you believe that?" Jim looked a little surprised. Then told me,

"I spent many hours talking with him, we discussed a lot." What I would have given for those same conversations. Jim went on to add.

"You know he wasn't my grandfather though, I wouldn't have felt the same bond"

"I know," I said before revealing to him. "I've been thinking about some of the strange decisions he made in his life."

"Like what?" he asked.

"Like him allowing my mother to be married to my father for starters," he immediately sprung to my fathers defence.

"Your fathers been a good husband to your mother!"

"I'm not saying he hasn't Jim, not at all, but it is a strange one isn't it, I mean with uncles involved with EOKA and so forth," I said. Looking at him either for an agreement or a reason for it. He looked off into the distance for a moment before silently nodding his head in agreement.

"Yeah, now it was only one or two uncles involved, I don't think they were active but," he was confirming for me just how strange a decision it was and then added,

"Your grandfather was," there was the slightest of pauses. "Sympathetic towards Enosis," Jim said it like sympathetic might have been all he was to it. But what it was I never had a clue. I'd never heard the word Enosis before. I rose and started to gather our belongings to leave. I was feeling good about my last day. I thought I'd mention the flag to gauge a response.

"You know there was a bloody big Greek national flag draped over Aphrodite's rock when we drove past it," he looked up at me not impressed then said,

"Greeks seem to think we owe them something," I sighed more a sigh of relief before saying,

"I kind of got the same impression." Why I never revealed the whereabouts of the flag at that time I don't know. We started arranging our belongings to leave,

"You know they're rewriting history as far Alexander goes," I was talking about Michael woods and his walk 'In the foot steps of Alexander' Jim looked at me with curiosity. Few Greeks can help it when it comes to Alexander. I filled him in briefly on the recent series and we slowly walked along the pool towards the gate. I felt like I was floating, and turned to Jim not caring who heard,

"You know with the changes coming I really do believe there's a good chance we'll be celebrating in Kyrenia next year!"

"I base my conclusions on facts," he replied forever the mathematician but looking pleased at the idea of it.

"Let's just wait and see," I said. "You know what I think," I told him. I was smiling and almost skipping, I firmly believed it was possible. I held my two hands up and clicked my fingers as we walked.

"What a great street party it'll be," I said. Then I took it back to granddad.

"You know the British Army took granddad to the States at some time," Jim put his hands out and firmly said.

"I wouldn't go putting too much into that!" I guessed his concern.

"Don't worry Jim, I'm not going all Anglophile on you, not where Cyprus is concerned," and then added to show how I felt.

"Personally I think they should start paying for their bloody holiday camps, either that or piss off!"

My parents and sister were at the apartment when we arrived preparing to go to the pool. I told them I was driving Jim home before I'd rejoin them. We walked on to the car and started driving towards my godmothers before I continued talking to him about my grandfather.

"The reason I mentioned about granddad going to the States is more because of the effect I know it must have had on him," I filled in where I was going with this.

"Look the one thing I know for sure about granddad is, he was a very tolerant man and he made some strange decisions"

"He was a very tolerant man and he did see things a little differently," Jim confirmed.

"Well that's what I'm saying Jim and if he travelled that would have opened his mind up, he was an intelligent men he would have come back here and seen what was going on and seen it for what it was," I told him finishing with. "I mean the depth of the hatred Jim!"

"Yes it did upset him, that's why he moved the family to England," he said as simply as that.

"Because of the hatred, the depth of it?" I asked to be certain.

"Yes," Jim confirmed. Beautiful! I thought that was all I needed to know. Thank you Granddad I said to myself, I knew you saw it to. I slapped the steering wheel in triumph at being right. It'd felt like since I saw the depth of the hatred that exists between Greeks and Turks and its manifestation on Cyprus and its possible implications, that also if granddad did he might have acted on it. I kind of regarded his actions to reflect the depth of what he saw and I felt like we were seeing the same thing and even coming to the same conclusions.

We arrived at my godmothers house, she wasn't at home so I went into the house and prepared a drink for myself and sat on the sofa to see what was on T.V when she arrived home and appeared at the door upset, she saw me and immediately instructed.

"Dimitri go now to your Aunt Marie's! Now!" she looked at me with some urgency.

"Your aunt has taken a bad turn and the doctors have only given her twenty four hours at the most now go see Marie, and then go tell your mother! Now!" I acted with the haste that was required and as I was leaving my aunt asked me to confirm that I was going to go straight to Marie's and then to my parents, which wasn't needed. Jim drove with me to my aunts and I saw Marie for a brief period. These times are hard enough as it is without the language barrier. But in a moment alone with her in the bedroom I knelt by the bed and took her hand. After a minute or so and with a tear in my eye I told her that I loved her and that she'd be with me forever. Then as I stroked her hair I said a quiet goodbye and gently kissed her on the forehead before getting up and leaving the room. If I let my feelings show on the drive it would have only been in my silence. I went straight to the pool and told my parents the news at which they got their belongings together and left. Leaving Jim and myself at the apartment where we carried on chatting as I showered and prepared my bags for the flight home. My parents weren't gone long and by the time they'd returned I'd given Jim some paper for him to write his home address in Australia on. I also had out the piece of paper on which I'd written my grandfathers details. I showed him the details and told him of my intentions to make some inquiries about him. He looked at it surprised.

"Who gave you this name?"

"Yannis"

"Yannis did?" he said letting his bemusement show.

"Yeah, why what's wrong?"

"That's not how you spell his name! I can't believe he gave you this!"

"What do you mean?"

"It's not Htenary!" he said.

"It's not?" I asked surprised.

"No it's spelt different, it's" he wrote it as he pronounced it for me "Ktenari" and then came another surprise.

"That's not how you spell his first name either!"

"It's not?" That did surprise me, as I knew I was named after him so I thought I'd get that right.

"No Dimitri's spelt with E's not I's"

"It is?"

"I should know, it's my name as well and it's spelt with Eee's," he said. I looked at my parents to see where they went wrong and asked my dad.

"Well how comes my names spelt with I's then?" my dad looked at me a little embarrassed but I could already see the amusement it was causing him.

"Blame the registrar," he said sheepishly.

"What do you mean?" I asked.

"Well we just gave him your name and he spelt it wrong"

"And you didn't check?" my father shook his head with a tight grin. I smiled. It seemed typical of my parents. I finished packing, changed for the flight home and my father brought the car around whilst Jim helped me with the box.

"What have you got in here?" he asked showing trouble picking it up by the string with one hand.

"Just a Barbie wrapped up in some linen," I told him. He raised an eyebrow at the weight. But didn't doubt what I told him, which was more or less true. We arrived at my godmothers and I had my final meal and enjoyed my last couple of hours with the family before saying my goodbyes. I told my godmother I would be back in the autumn, dropped Jim off at his brothers and I promised him I'd keep in touch by e-mail. We both showed our regret at it being so long since our last meeting knowing it might be just as long before our next. We said our goodbyes and I then drove with my parents to Larnaca airport. They were more concerned about the flag than I was willing to admit I was and I knew they were a little worried about me getting caught with it at the airport. I knew there was little chance of that though and comforted them.

"Look if they find the flag what can they say? The worst that might happen is that they'll take it off me," I said adding. "But no way will they arrest me, they simply wont want it in court mum," and there was an amusing side to its size.

"Anyway even if someone looks in the box they aren't ever going to believe it's a flag in there."

There were times I wish I had been caught, if only for a day in court, which I wouldn't have minded and I told my parents so at the time. But I knew the authorities would never want the publicity of a trial if it were a government flag. The idea of that was one that I couldn't accept though. I was a little paranoid at check in as I threw the box onto the scales. I didn't want to answer any questions about what was in there and it weighed in at 19.98 KGs .02 off the limit. I sighed with relief as I watched it disappear down the conveyor belt and I felt another sigh of relief as I passed through immigration and walked through to the departure lounge. The sight of a couple of photos displayed at head height so children couldn't see them stopped me in my tracks. It was a photo of Nikki's cousin at the moment he took the shot to the neck, whilst attempting to ascend the flagpole. Above this was another photograph of his cousin being battered to death by Turkish civilians, it was a sick sight to see. The writing was calling the Turks barbarians and they were barbarous acts. But these photos were good, too good.

Chapter 9

I ignored the flag in its box for the first few days after I arrived home. I felt like I had a hidden secret in there awaiting to be revealed and I already knew what the secret was but never wanted to face it. On the Thursday after I returned Dawn had called around and I knew with her many visits and her links to Cyprus the flag would be of interest to her.

"Here Dawn have a look at what I brought back from Cyprus," I said with a touch of excitement in my voice. I started lifting the flag out of the box in a way so as to keep it in the same fold as when it was put in.

"What is it?" she could tell it was something out of the ordinary.

"What does it look like?" I asked her. To myself the colours made it apparent. The flag was now completely out of the box and on the floor.

"I don't know," she replied.

"Come on Dawn, it can't be that hard, here take this," I held up one side of the flag to drape over her arm, it was going to pull out in the same way it had in Cyprus.

"Now walk down the hallway," she smiled in disbelief. There was a lot of folded fabric in front of us. Dawn backed down the hallway with one end of the flag draped over her forearm as she walked.

"Keep going until it's right out," I told her. She'd backed down about six or seven metres until the full length of the flag was pulled out. Most of it was in a line between fifteen centimetres and a metre wide on the carpet.

"What is it?"

"Can't you tell?"

"No what is it?" she asked excitedly.

"Look at the colours Dawn, it's a Greek national flag"

"Oh shit! It is," she paused slightly. "It's massive!"

I looked at it slowly taking in what I'd not wanted to see in Cyprus. As I was taking it in, the reality that the size of it had just increased dramatically also sunk in and the belief in myself, that this flag, could only be a government flag was confirmed and my heart sunk further.

"Dawn look at the lines on it," my tone was more subdued.

"What about them?" she inquired curiously.

"They're running across, we're holding the vertical," I told her. She studied it for a moment.

"Oh my god! Where did you get it from?" she asked more than a little surprised.

"You know Aphrodite's rock?"

"Yeah"

"It was draped over the largest rock of the formation in line of where tourists were taking photographs"

"No! And you pulled it down?" she looked stunned. I didn't feel very boastful though.

"How do you think it got here," it wasn't said sarcastically. "I drove out in the middle of the night and pulled it down, I didn't realise how big it was, it just shouldn't have been there." I got wondering how I could have misjudged the size so much.

"Shit who do you think put it up there?"

"Look at the size of it, think about the cost of it, and look at the work that would have been needed to drape it like it was." I was visualising it being laid and I found it hard to imagine that it was done at night.

I went through the rest of the week wondering about everything. At this point I should explain clearly the relevance of my misjudgement in size. In Cyprus I'd wanted to believe that the six or seven metres was the horizontal, which would have made its surface area 28 or 29 sq. metres or around 270 sq. feet. Its new estimated measurements meant it was going to be closer to sixty sq. metres or around 600 sq. feet. I believe I'd greatly misjudged the size, because of not only perhaps its height but more likely because of the very low angle of the rock where it was draped. The flagpole needed for this flag would have to be around 35 metres or 100 feet high or ten storeys of a tower block if you like. But I'd seen flags or banners as might be appropriate to call it like this before. But never in Cyprus and not in Greece but on the western coastline of Turkey as you skirt it to get access to Rhodes and a couple of other Greek islands by ferry. I'd always felt like they were rubbing it in when I'd sight one, you can see them from a couple of kilometres easily, but that was the whole point of the size of them.

So I had to come to the conclusion that it was government sponsored, possibly by Greece or our own government and this saddened me a great deal. It was the cause and the root of many of our problems. Greeks and Turks had little in common except for the bitterness and hatred carried on from our history. Cyprus was the only common factor to both the Turkish Cypriots and Greek Cypriots, so both sides as I've been saying had to be totally uninfluenced by our original mother countries policies, not Greek not Turkish but Cypriot. I'd heard our president Clerides anniversary speech calling for compromise and respect although the flag I had, seemed a total contradiction of that. Denktash the Turkish Cypriots president speech seemed so negative and different. He thanked Turkey and said it was with them that his country's future lay.

On Sunday I'd gone to my mother's house for a Barbecue. Of course! My uncle

Yannis had come up from London with his East European wife Eva. She's a very pretty woman and I liked her and was happy for my uncle, she's at least twenty-five years younger than him, but age never seemed to matter. They were both very happy and his children quite comfortable with her. Everyone was in high spirits my uncle in particular and a cheer went up from him as I entered the garden. I didn't feel I'd be able to enjoy the afternoon. I walked across the garden to the lounge. My uncle spoke as I passed them sat on the large swinging garden hammock.

"Hey Dimitri, what do you think Eh?" he asked joyfully. I knew he was talking about the land claim suit, this was the first time I'd seen him since and I gathered his own was going well. No one would have heard the words I muttered, but the look on my face might have shown how I was feeling "all for the greater glory of Greece." I didn't feel like sitting outside for a while and went through the patio doors to the lounge and sat on the sofa, staring at nothing. I didn't want to join in the celebrations right now, at the same time I didn't want to ruin them. I think my father could see how I was feeling, he'd always accepted it must have been a government flag. I was just attempting to come to terms with it. He came into the lounge.

"You all right?"

"Yeah I'm still a bit pissed off about that flag dad," I looked down and shook my head.

"Here your cousin said you left these newspapers in the apartment and she posted them on after she got home," he was talking about my god sister. I'd left the newspapers I'd brought in the apartment but I wasn't expecting and neither needed them sent on, after all I'd read them. As he spoke he produced a large brown manila envelope, which he gently threw on to the sofa. I looked at it and smiled at the idea of being sent newspapers that I'd already read. I opened the envelope and pulled out two copies of the Cyprus mail.

As I opened the papers up I realised straight away that they could have only been brought and left by my father, as they were dated the 11th and 12th and I left Cyprus on the 10th of August. I glanced over the first page of Tuesdays' copy. Bush fires had erupted in Cyprus and the British commanders home had been gutted. I turned the page and most of page three had been given over to another gang related gunning that had occurred on the day I left. I read the related story before turning the page again. I froze in horror at the first column on page four. I was about to go into shock for a day at this news. The bold headline clearly read, 'Greek junta coupist on stop list came freely into Cyprus' underneath this and before the story was the sentence 'inquiry ordered, justice ministry says permit given for business trip'. I read through the piece. It wrote about EOKA b stalwart Vasilis Vintzilaiou the Greek junta intelligence chief and 74 coup conspirator being secretly allowed to not only enter Cyprus, but was for five days roaming freely around the island, with only our justice ministry and our president knowing, to deal with supposed financial matters. I felt like a knife had been pushed into my back and twisted, this man would have been one of the leading Greeks from the 74 coup in our country. An intelligence officer from the Greek coup that threw our country into turmoil was allowed to enter when he was placed on a stop list. I found the word stalwart to considerate for him and preferred the wording of the EDEK political party leader, scum. It felt like leaving a cat in an aviary and trusting it to only drink the water. My mind started processing the information that I was reading and it never took long to realise the very likely link with the government sponsored flag that I now knew must have come from Athens. Greek intelligence coup scum enters our country at around the same time as the anniversary of the Greek coup and at the same time a 600sq foot Greek national flag goes over our national treasure in line of where tourists were taking photographs, this stunk. I called my father back into the lounge and passed him the paper and simply said,

"His flag I think." For me the mystery of whom and why was now over and with our presidents' admission that he knew that the scumbag had been allowed into the country meant he was also involved. It all made sense. Otherwise I was sure some respectable Cypriot police officer might have pulled it down, or would they have, now more than ever I was not only glad I'd pulled it down, but also very relieved I never got caught.

I folded the newspapers up and went outside to attempt to socialise a little before I left. I sat down next to Eva, said a few courteous words and silently ate some desert whilst the revelations were going through my mind. I think she must have known something was playing heavily on me, I could hardly hide it, so I soon got up to leave. I couldn't bear to look anything other than deeply disturbed. In the midst of all this was the growing pleasure of knowing what he put up I pulled down. I got up and said some short goodbyes and headed for the gate, I could hear my uncle joking to my father about Eva.

"Hey Mario you know she almost speaks better Greek than me!"

"Yeah!"

"Yeah she's a fast learner."

I drove straight home. There were more questions I now needed answering. One of them was relating to the word EOKA b. As soon as I got home, I went straight to the P.C. and went on line. I'd never entered any of the Turkish sponsored pages before, only the Greek Cypriot ones but they never ever mentioned anything about EOKA let lone EOKA b, in fact they never mentioned anything about life in Cyprus prior to the Turkish partition full stop.

I already had a complete political section on Cyprus book marked not that I used it much, I'd found it all fairly boring, well all the sites that I'd used. They were well displayed, but they all seemed to say fairly much the same thing and there was one of the causes of my ignorance. I remembered reading a section vehemently attacking Turkey and stating what actions should immediately be implemented as if it was written by someone in power, just to discover it was a readers letter. They all said the same thing but at the same time were telling very little. This visit to the net was to be different though. There was a whole range of Turkish categories for me to choose from, they were informative of our history pre-74, very informative. I ignored the Truth site due to the fact that it had a picture of Makarios with the title of the Angel of death under it, which I simply couldn't pass. I already had a feeling who or what EOKA b was, but now I was to start to understand the meaning of the word Enosis.

I was stunned. This was to be the first time that I was to read in detail anything about the years between independence and the partition by Turkey and I was getting the other side of our history. After independence in 1960 we'd ignored the constitutional requirement for separate municipalities and forced Turks out of the government administration. In December 63 the Greek Cypriots were to revolt against the presence of the Turks and they were forced into their own enclaves, it sounded violent and I thought I could imagine. They weren't prepared to share their new found freedom and indeed the persecution of the Turks had started. I could only imagine the hostilities against them. Things seemed to have improved dramatically between 68 and July 74 when Greeks came by the thousands to finish the job for us. For it was in their name the Turks were being persecuted, throughout this time EOKA b remained active to enforce Enosis, union with Greece. I couldn't believe it but I knew it was true. It's in the blood. We'd got our independence but we wanted more, union with Greece and I knew what that meant to a Turk. My god the stupid bastards, what were they up to.

I could see that when the Greeks came in 74. They were killing Greek Cypriots by the thousands for not being Greek enough as well as Turks. They pillaged and murdered and on one day in 74, three whole villages were slaughtered. They machine gunned the women and children before attempting to hide their bodies with bulldozers before the Turkish army could get to them. The stupid bastards couldn't even do that right and the bodies were found in a mangled state. This was what our present government was referring to as irresponsible people but this was what Enosis meant to a Turk. And what a surprise they came right up to date, to claim that the Russians were now washing a Billion pounds a month through Cypriot banks.

The only positive information I could gather was actually about Makarios. It was a U.N address that he'd made addressing his fears for both the Greek and Turkish Cypriots but it was enough for now I was angry, very angry and I know what I do when I'm that upset, I wrote. The Landlocked Island another good but naïve essay, the title says as much about the essay itself.

The next day I awoke wanting to inform someone involved in politics in Cyprus about the flag. I wondered if perhaps it was not best left on the rock so the hypocrisy would still be displayed. I knew the Greeks had murdered over two thousand Greek Cypriot communist supporters in the coup, but first I phoned my cousin Jim in Cyprus and asked him about the political parties and which ones were which. He told me he didn't know, so I told him about the flag.

"Couldn't you have put it on another rock," he said to my surprise.

"No I couldn't Jim, I don't think you understand what sort of flag it is, I'll get in touch with you when you're at home, I may need your help."

I then discovered AKEL the communist party. I got their telephone number from international enquiries and telephoned them.

"Yes!" the voice sounded harsh.

"Hello," I said feeling right out of my depth.

"What do you want?" Came a harsher response. Nothing like getting straight to the point I thought.

"I'm telephoning about Vasilis that coup scum entering the country"

"What about him?" I knew straight away, this was going to be hard.

"Well I was in the country a week after him and I pulled a flag down from Aphrodite's rock that I think he left." At this point I already knew I wasn't going to get anywhere. There are flags and there are rock covers, this was a rock cover, a bloody big rock cover.

"What flag?" the man shouted almost growling. He sounded like he needed some stress therapy.

"Nothing," I said subdued. I put the phone down. I knew what I felt like doing with the flag and that was to return it to Athens. Then I did something that I would've considered unthinkable at one time. I telephoned the Turkish republic of northern Cyprus embassy in London and spoke to a Miss Dorak, I was nervous at first and felt like I was being treasonous, but soon put those thoughts away as I spoke to the embassy official. I started the conversation telling her about Vasilis the coup scum entering the country, to my surprise she sounded surprised and afraid. The fear touched me. I heard it in her voice when she realised whom I was talking about and she left the telephone for a moment before returning for a conversation during which I told her about the flag. Then the conversation went on to life in Cyprus and she told me what it was like for her growing up in Cyprus pre 74 and this is something I'd heard from many Turkish Cypriots which hurts me. They were made to feel like foreigners in their own country. She told me about an incident when as a child on the beach she had wet sand poured over her head and told to go home. I could relate to that even growing up in England with the Indian and Pakistani migrations, bigots seldom differentiate. One subject we touched and I found no problem in defending was Makarios. She told me that he was issuing passports to Turkish Cypriots so that they could leave the country. I had to be honest and tell her that from my perception of the situation at the time, that seemed a humanitarian gesture coming from a Greek. But I draw attention to his UN address, voicing his fears for both sides of the community. Most importantly from the conversation and I've felt the same from other Turkish Cypriots, it's their love for Cyprus. I couldn't help but feel they themselves felt far more Cypriot than Turkish.

We spoke in length about the situation, during which she indicated that the telephone line wasn't secure which sent a shiver through me. She told me of the very large Turkish Cypriot community living in London, which made me realise that most of the Cypriot population seemed to be living out of the country. After twenty minutes or so I put the phone down feeling a little more enlightened but I was still naïve to the depth of the cruelty that I was to learn had been unleashed on her people.

I did think about returning the flag though and I decided that if I could get some British publicity I might do it. After all it was no ordinary flag. I telephoned the foreign desk at the Independent newspaper in London,
    "Hi, I'm phoning about an incident that occurred in Cyprus recently"
    "And?"
    "And I pulled a very large Greek flag off Aphrodite's rock which I believe one of the coup leaders from74 brought into the country," I tried enlightening the journalist as quick as I could. "I believe it had to be part of," he interrupted me.
    "No we're not interested in any flag stories," with that the conversation was over. I think he thought I was trying to sell a story, but I felt it was a story. Now by this time I'm starting to wonder about journalists.

Later that night I went on line again, it was the fear in Miss Dorak's voice when I'd mentioned the coup scum that had got me wondering. I went to the Truth site. Past the Makarios picture and into the section marked the Genocide files.

I guess the best way to describe its effect on me would be to write of my second visit to the site. The first visit had a big effect on me and I now know I left the site in a state of shock. The next evening I logged on and entered the site and the category entitled 'The Genocide files'. My computer at the time was a little slow. Even the simplest of pictures would take their time to appear on the screen. As the words on the site appeared I knew which picture I was about to be shown. I instantly felt my emotions building up in me. I could remember the photograph clearly from my first visit. By the time the picture appeared on the screen I was looking down. The tears were already streaming down my cheeks. I sat there a trembling mess in my chair. If I'd felt like I'd come to discover my Cypriot identity, then now I was paying the price. Through our consciences we must all carry the sins as well as the glories of our own nations and I'd gone too far to withdraw back to the Anglophile. I wept openly. I didn't care. I didn't care about anything at all at that moment. The one picture in question can not and will not say it all, but it is a good example of what Enosis had meant to a large number of Cypriots. The mother couldn't be seen in the photograph as her murdered children were lying above her in a bathtub and it was the sight of these once pretty children that tore at my heart. They'd been machine-gunned. Blood was all over the place and these three children lay as if they could have been sleeping. I remember I just muttered between the tears,

"God no!"

"Oh you bastards, you bastards, bastards, bastards!"

It was one of the most emotional moments of my life. But there in front of my eyes were the results of the darkest side of any mans nature, indeed the results of what I knew was once being nurtured within myself. The hatred had manifested itself into its most evil form. There were a few other obscenities, all aimed at one race, the Greeks. These children and many others massacred in 63 were slaughtered for one reason, Enosis. It's a word that should be in red, blood red for these people. I don't know if you have been able to comprehend the absolute depth of Greek hatred for Turks. I know how deep it is, I was born to it, even if I was born in England. It was implanted at a very early age and groomed and nurtured. But here it had been unleashed and now I was witnessing the results. They took all that hatred and unleashed it on the only place they could, Cyprus. I still can't believe that you might understand the extent of the slaughter that derived from this hatred and the worst of it happened in 1963 and these poor children amongst the first.

Ten or fifteen minutes later, the tears were still rolling as I simply switched the computer off without shutting it down, risking a failure.

The next day I called on a friend who was in the country for a month's break from his Volunteer work in Thailand. His names David and we were well used to throwing conspiracy theories at each other just so the other could constructively tear them down. I pulled up outside of his house and beeped the horn. He soon appeared. It was the first time we'd seen each other in over a year but he wasn't going to waste any time as he got into the car and slammed the door.

"Have I got one for you!"

"I've got a better one!" I threw that back with confidence.

"Bet you haven't!"

"Bet I have!"

"How you doing?" he asked with a big smile on his face.

"Good you?"

"Good, but I've got a big one for you!"

"I'm sure I've got a better one for you Dave, but you first, please." He gave me a nod for being so courteous. We hadn't gone a hundred metres. All the way back to my house he gave me a run down of his personal theory on the United States of America's control of the funds for the I.M.F. and its ability to pull strings accordingly where loans went, without having to face any of the consequences. Whilst they consume more of the worlds natural resources per head than any other country in the world.

"And?" I asked, as we entered my front door.

"And it's not right," he exclaimed.

"So what are you going to do about it?" I enquired with a smile.

"Don't know!"

"Not much you can do if they're footing the bills, it sucks, but money talks," I said.

"I know but it pisses me off!" he replied knowing there was little that he could do about it. I was going to go straight into this one and I broke in with.

"Cyprus!" I said, setting the mood with my tone, he looked at me and nodded.

"They're going through a big arms build up and this year they take surface to air missiles," I could see he could keep up easy enough. I gave him a run down on the latest news and the Russian connection before going into horrors of 63, for which I knew Turkey had partitioned the island off and back to the possible future.

"And so for all intents and purposes Turkey will believe she is morally right in defending her right to defend Northern Cyprus," I said.

"Ok, but what set you off on all this?" he asked curiously.

"I've been doing a bit of soul searching for my Cypriot identity," I told him as I left the room.

"And I felt like I'd discovered it," I returned into the room with the flag bundled up in my arms.

"Right before I found this!" I dropped the banner on the floor in front of him and stood behind it arms still extended. David stared at it in amazement and then back up at myself.

"Where the fuck did you get that from?"

"Aphrodite's rock in Cyprus, it's our national treasure. It was on the largest rock of the formation," I told him. "In line of where tourists were taking photographs, telling them they're in Greece!"

"I don't believe it! Do you know who put it up?"

"Oh, I've got more than a good suspicion," I threw him the newspaper. "I've got his flag!"

He read the newspaper article at the end of which he gasped.

"Shit!"

"Yeah shit," I said.

"What do you plan on doing about it?" he asked.

"I don't know, I've been writing," I passed him the landlocked island from my desk.

"I'd like to return it to the Greek embassy but I want to find someone to write about it first," I said. David didn't reply, as he was already engrossed in the essay. So I went to the kitchen and put the kettle on and made some tea. By the time I'd returned he'd finished the essay.

"What did you say?" he asked.

"I said that I'd like to return it to the Greek embassy but I'd like to find someone to write about it first, I think it's interesting enough"

"Who?"

"A journalist or something, not just about the flag but I think I've got a bit of a story to tell, it'd make a bloody good book!"

"And what will you say to this journalist?" he enquired mockingly.

"That I pulled the flag off the rock and that scum bag put it up"

"How can you prove that?"

"It's a bit too much to believe it's a coincidence"

"What do you mean too much for coincidence, why?" he seemed to be enjoying this.

"Are you kidding, arms build up, propaganda campaign, possible war perhaps," that wasn't my proof just the background I continued.

"So by coincidence the Greek intelligence officer from the 74 coup is secretly allowed to roam our country for five days and only our government knows about it," I said finishing off with.

"It was around the anniversary of the 74 coup!"

"I've got a better idea for you Jim!"

"What?"

"You write it!"

"Write what?" I asked a little confused.

"The book!" he said, I looked at him surprised.

"I can't do that"

"Why not?"

"I've never written before!"

"What's this?" he held up the landlocked island.

Chapter 10

I thought about what David had said, of course by now you know where my thoughts led me and here is where you join me. I'd considered writing about Cyprus before, but I never felt I knew enough to write a book about the politics of the island. At the same time I had so much anger in me for what I saw was happening as far as the politics went, that I just had to do something and writing is as I've come to discover a great release. I sat down at the P.C. a day or so after my conversation with Dave and started writing. There was a burning rage in myself that had to be released one way or another. In our official history books as well as those of most other countries these massacres were never mentioned individually in any way. I'd just read that during 63-64 we had some inter communal fighting and quite often just regarded it as tit for tat and expecting to be told if it were otherwise. But I was reading of massacres that had never been admitted. But I knew were true if only for this journalists eyewitness accounts.

It all began at 2.10 am on Saturday, December 21 1963, two cars carrying ten Turkish Cypriots, six men and four women drove through the Greek quarter of Nicosia the Cypriot capital heading for their homes in the Turkish quarter. They were returning from Kyrenia after an evening meal and almost at their destination and were inside the Turkish quarter when a group of armed Greek civilians suddenly appeared in the headlights of the leading car and signalled them to stop. Both cars halted. The gunmen ordered everyone out of their cars. The ten done as they were instructed puzzled as to the motives. A crowd of Turkish Cypriots from the overlooking houses appeared awakened by the shouts. Almost immediately a convoy of cars loaded with uniformed Greek Cypriot policemen, brandishing Sterling sub machineguns outside of the open car windows, turned a corner ahead and roared up towards them. The civilian gunmen quickly stepped away from the cars. The first burst of machine gun fire killed two of the women and three of the Turkish bystanders were injured and fell to the ground. The crowd fled, screaming. The civilian gunmen leapt into the police cars and drove off. Christmas 63 for the Turkish Cypriots would be one to remember. Word of the shootings spread and gangs took to the Nicosia streets, apparently they'd decided it was 'open season' for shooting Turks and by 4.am they were tearing up and down the streets of the Turkish sector, shooting from the open windows. In the Turkish sector of Omorphita a northern suburb of Nicosia that same morning, armed Greeks were seen patrolling the streets. Many of them were immediately identified as EOKA members who were not police officers the previous day. A group of Greek police and civilians turned up at the nearby Greek elementary school at Trachonas. A large building in open grounds which overlooked the Turkish part of Omorphita. The group began unloading crates from their trucks and carrying them into the school, it was the weekend before Christmas and the school would be empty of children. Two Turkish policemen from the police station at Omorphita went to the school to make enquiries, they were told the crates contained equipment and costumes for a theatrical performance. The police officers returned to their station to make a report. A short while afterwards Bren guns appeared at the school windows. The siege of Omorphita and its five thousand Turkish Cypriots had began, by Sunday night those Bren guns would be firing on the suburb. Over the Christmas period at Kykkos school 700 Turkish Cypriots were known to have had been taken hostage of those only 550 were returned. I read of the 21 inhabitants of Ayios Vasilios and of the 21 hospital patients that went missing from the Nicosia General Hospital and of the Packard report that appeared in a British newspaper some twenty-five years later. Revealing what had happened to the in-patients, that was a report I remembered reading.

Even this one seemingly minor incident touched me, feeling I knew the bigotry from which it came. From the windows of the British High Commission, the staff watched an old man being pursued across a field by several armed men. The old man was a Turkish shepherd named Kose, who lived near the Cornaro Hotel. When the shooting began, his two daughters asked him to move into a Turkish area. He refused. They rounded up his mixed flock of sheep and goats and drove them away, but still he stayed, making up a little campsite in a dry riverbed.
"The Greeks know me," he told them. "They will not harm me".
Now the watchers at the High Commission looked on as the old man stumbled onto a road panting. The gunmen ran up shooting. The old man fell, riddled with rifle bullets. The young Greeks examined the body briefly, then turned away talking excitedly. Nicosia seemed to have erupted into violence. It read more like our own version of crystal night, only no storm troopers were needed. Of the aftermath reporters wrote some terrible things, all shrugged off by the Greek authorities as unfounded. But I saw it differently, I knew the hatred that went with it, this for myself was Cyprus's secret history. The children who's photographed had grieved me so much were from Kumsal another north Nicosia suburb where 150 were reported to have died over the Christmas period and 150 were taken hostage at Kykkos School. How could we even start to make amends or expect the people of the north to trust us again if we never educated our children about this and now I felt really naïve in being the one offering forgiveness. After five hundred words or so, I read what I'd written, after deciding I not only wanted to expose the hypocrisy and the bigotry but most of all the manifestation and the perpetuation of the hatred on this, my island of love. What I saw and found to my surprise was that I'd written a harsh preface for a book entitled 'I don't speak

Greek' and why on Cyprus I might be proud to say that. I still had no idea of what angle I was going to write the book from, but it was the start of an idea. I read it, then wrote to my cousin Jim before he left Limassol.

Dear Jim,

   How is it I got to my age knowing very little about Enosis, especially with its relevance to Cyprus, with it's relevance to us. I had to look it all up on the Internet, my next task is going to be to confirm that what I'm reading is true, not that I think it's going to be hard. But I'm going to need some questions answered Jim. First I don't imagine any Greek Cypriot would have or could possibly enjoy telling me about the effects it's had on our country. Through my experience of a lot of Greeks I have to say outright, I have found them a very condescending bunch where we're concerned and often found I've had to revert to an arrogant Englishman to deal with them. It actually works, I have for a long time now believed they put too much on their great and very, very distant past and as an Englishman it gives one the upper hand. At least the British Empire only diminished this past century Alexander popped his clogs over 2,000 years ago. I have to say my general attitudes to Greeks probably took a big change 4 or 5 years ago. I'd already taken a few comments from them about my lack of Greek with ignorance of Enosis but knowing that pro-Hellenists had forced the Turks to act. I found myself backpacking around Greece whilst the Macedonian crisis was in the air. I felt sick knowing that a very large number of Greeks actually endorsed their governments ideas to invade another country simply because they were so upset that there might be a Macedonia outside of Greece and all because Alexander was Macedonian. Can you seriously try to comprehend such an attitude, only pressure from every country in Europe made the Greek government see they wouldn't get away with it. Can I know your thoughts on all this, I don't suppose I'd be so upset but I thought we'd learnt. I never even realised we had such an openly Hellenistic nationalistic government, Clerides has even got blood on his hands, shit we could be going for reunification with a government like that, but this is the worst part. I believe that reunification is going to mean expulsion for our Turkish Cypriots if it happens. After reading their papers they are actually scared Jim, and the propaganda, it's all so transparent I just thought Turkey were bad, but now, I have to ask certain questions like why does our government not mark our side of the buffer zone so people don't walk in by accident? A good suggestion is to look at ourselves before we throw too many criticisms at others and I'm not having a go at our people. But how could so many say 'we use to live all right together' with our Turkish Cypriots whilst whenever Enosis rears it's ugly head, hundreds of them got slaughtered. As well as any Greek Cypriots that weren't quite Greek enough. Too often I was told there's nothing to tell. I'm a bit pissed off Jim, I've been scouring both their sheets and ours, theirs scare me. We've got easily confirmed mass slaughters on our hands and consciences, even if because we've ignored them. My response to them is just about right. No, as I wrote before I won't have a Greek telling me as a Cypriot what language to speak. What pride is there in being Cypriot if we have to carry the burden of our own form to ethnic cleansing, and at the heart of all this is Hellenistic nationalism. Can you imagine what that does to me knowing some of their attitudes to us? How will the world judge us? If my worst fears are realised and our government forces reunification we might have a good party to go to, but what sort of questions are going to be asked of us. I'm sure you can see the hypocrisy of it. I have always been telling people we have a strong desire to live with Turkish Cypriots in peace and I'm sure you must have said the same. I know you and I aren't Hellenists in the nationalistic sense and I don't believe most of our country is. I don't know how far it'll go but I may have started a book on the subject. If all my fears on reunification are realised, the Cypriot government doesn't realise the repercussions in Europe. We will be forced to make account for our actions. The Turkish Cypriots have not been helped any by Denktash and Turkey's aggressive nature but what were they seeing that we couldn't? The Turks are playing a losing game and it will affect the way the world perceives Turkish Cypriots but only temporarily. As the people of greater number on the island if we're really serious we should be able to reach out and say enough already. It should be us genuinely holding out the olive branch but the situation has only served to push us towards anyone that we feel will help. Oh! Thank you Greece, haven't you always been there for us. The irony for me may be that that Greek woman on Kos could be opening her door to a Turk, there's little doubt in my mind that if we reunify now, they'll do it. Anyway that all rests on a few possibilities which may be far away but all the talk seems to indicate that there is a possibility. I believe we could make it look like Turkey started it. The talks already started i.e. Turkish tanks are in attack formation in the north as Clerides points out, what is the best form of defence?

I'm going to send you some of the material I've been writing in the form of letters etc. I would appreciate feedback a.s.a.p. One issue I should pursue is the Makarios UN address on his fears for the Turkish Cypriots. The most that the Turks have against him is the fact that he was quite happy to issue passports to Turkish Cypriots so they could leave. It's almost impossible to say he was pro-Enosis when the Greeks invaded and he was the first Cypriot the Greek's overthrew. I believe he saw the real consequences of Enosis and that genocide comes with it for Turkish Cypriots. And forever that Greek Cypriots will carry the consequences. He must have died a very sad man, for he died on a truly divided island. As I've said, I'll send you some of what I've written, even wrote a preface. The thing I'm going for is a complete change of thought, no small task I know. The one message we've been trying to send is that we are an independent nation. Our past is what it is and our future can be whatever we make it. If Greeks felt so much for Cyprus, why have they brought so much shame on us?

Last but far from least, can you please try to explain to your mother. I know she may have been a little hurt when I told her I didn't want to be known as a Greek Cypriot. As much as I love Cyprus I'm just not Greek enough for them and I've seen what they've done to Greek Cypriots in the past for not being Greek enough. Can you believe I even fear my own people knowing this is how I feel write soon,
Take care,
Love Jim

My paranoia at the time was starting to show but it reflected what I was reading, as did my fear and the whole time I had the unnerving presence of the flag in whose name these massacres had occurred now in my hallway, in a cardboard box.

I was on the crest of a wave as far as writing went and I was angry. Although at first I still wasn't sure of what I was going to write. But the sights and reports of some of the 63 massacres alone and the anger within me were enough to spur me on. I sat down and typed not knowing where it was going until after thirty minutes or so, when I stopped and read what I'd written. No one would have been more surprised than myself, for that's who and what I was writing about, to expose not only the bigotry and the hypocrisy, but also the perpetuation of the hatred on Cyprus, myself, my own story. It may not surprise you, but I sat stunned. A week or so later I saw David again, he wasn't surprised the book was under way and after he read the opening chapters, he gave me the confidence that was to spur me on further. I was pleased with myself, pleased and determined.

Over the next week or two I wrote vigorously with a passion, fury. It wasn't easy for me with so many emotions boiling over. I was sure my cousin would be impressed with the results and I was getting so much good feed back from my friends. I was soon to telephone my godmothers to see how they were and to find out where Jim was. To my surprise my godfather told me he had just telephoned from his home in Melbourne to say he'd arrived home, I went straight online and e-mailed Jim telling him how hard I'd been working.

It was an unusual time for me, I'd actually gone to the trouble of finding out when the next Greek for beginners class was going to start at our local regional college. Despite the book and the title I actually felt far more open to the idea of learning the language, and firmly believed that much of the block that I felt I'd put up had been pulled down. Like, I don't speak Greek but I'm learning, but for my own reasons. The main reason for myself to learn was to be able to talk to my uncle Georgio and my country cousins. I promised myself I'd never let anything like what had happened with Marie happen again. Never was I going to let another relative pass on without being able to tell them how I felt about them, I soon received a reply from Jim

HI Jimmy,
I just got back yesterday and I have got a terrible flu or some exotic bug so I won't say much right now. Having read your notes that you sent me in Cyprus I cannot be anything but a little disappointed. In general, you are re-iterating the same old propaganda that the British and Turks were touting for generations. Before you seriously begin to write your book, you should look at the history of the occupation of Cyprus and what were the causes of the current situation. I'll try to be more explicit when I feel better, hopefully in a couple of days or so.
Regards
Jim

Before I seriously consider writing a book! I knew he had no idea of just how serious I was. I sent him an immediate response. I was a bit pissed off as I thought I was addressing the causes of the present situation. I really couldn't see any reason why Cypriots couldn't live together if they regarded themselves as Cypriot first and foremost. It seemed to be the Greeks and the Turks that were having a problem. I was getting a good idea of how Jim stood on this one, but his comment about 'Greeks thinking we owed them something' stuck in my mind. I replied straight away to his e-mail telling him I'd been sick myself lately and ended it letting him know what I thought of the propaganda quote.

'I flew out in Oct 96 because I was pissed off at the Turks and I wanted to demonstrate, Your mother wouldn't allow it. I told her my feelings and she became more adamant and I couldn't understand. I wouldn't have gone with your mother, not with what I had in mind, perhaps one of the few times I have had a fatalistic approach to life. I told your mother if I got hurt it would make world news. I was serious I knew it would have. Maybe I may have to fly out and ask your mother why not, but is there a need. It would have made a pretty picture to look at every time she departed from Larnaca airport along with Solomou and his cousin.

Propaganda; Organised propagation of a doctrine by use of publicity, selected information, etc, sorry but I think it has to count, and what parts of their propaganda don't you like. Would it be the child pulled from a shallow grave with his hands tied behind his back or the three villages we couldn't quite dispose of properly.

I asked a couple of intelligent unbiased people lately, who'd remember 74 well,

what they really thought of Greek Cypriots and I don't want to walk forward with the brand of hypocrite that Athens will give us. If I write as a Cypriot, it is as a Cypriot first and foremost. When your ready I'll start mailing parts of the book, I should have a good hour or so reading for you.
Take care,
Jim

I wasn't to wait too long for his response, entitled 'History is the guide'.

Hi Jimmy,

I hope you are feeling better; I'm still pretty weak. My stay in Bangkok was a big disappointment as I was not able to do what I wanted. The place was flooded most of the time I was there.
Now, let us talk about History: For more than 5 thousand years Cyprus has been predominantly GREEK. Throughout the various occupations of Cyprus by the Phoenicians, Assyrians, Egyptians, Persians, Greeks, Romans, Byzantines, Venicians, Turks and British, Cyprus has been predominately populated by Greeks. During the Ottoman Empire, Greeks and other nationalities were forced to
speak Turkish and in 300 years the Greek language almost disappeared. In 1878, the Congress of Berlin placed Cyprus under British Administration and in 1914 Britain illegally annexed it outright.
There are basically two things to consider in order to understand the current situation of Greece, the Greek people and Cyprus:

1. The constant erosion of Greek Culture and Land as witnessed by the territorial claims of the Turks, Slav Macs, Albanians, Bulgarians and the British.

2. The interference of Britain and the US with their political games.

Helenistic nationalism is not a concept of conquest or force but a union of Greek language and heritage. It is there to counter the forces that are trying to undermine us and take away what is ours.

Just as I am proud to be a Cypriot I am proud to be a Greek. One does not make me any less than the other. Of course, many mainland Greeks feel that Cyprus is part of Greece and historically they are right. It is only through the "divide and rule" attitude of the British that denied Cyprus Enosis. One of the tactics that the British employed during their occupation was to raid Turkish Cypriots homes and villages disguised as Greeks and kill hundreds. This was to set Turk against Greek and prevent Enosis; what Turk would live under Greek rule if he thought that Greeks would be killing them off. Up to that period, Enosis was a foregone conclusion, (the small Turkish population did not object) but the British did not want to relinquish control and to the present time they still occupy so called "Sovereign Bases" in Cyprus. The British drew up and planned the current partition of Cyprus during the 1950's struggle for Enosis.

There are many more facts you should consider before you take a swipe at the Greeks, but I am tired and lack the ability to chronologically list the events. Many of the facts have been documented and verified in many books and films. The approach I feel you should be taking is one of neutrality and look at the British and US interference; the Cypriots were betrayed by their political games.
Regards
Jim

I felt I was being neutral. Here I expected the five thousand-year history bit, which I had to say I now thought sucked. For a number of reasons, one being that I could think of a number of occasion's when ancient Greeks had gone slaughtering ancient Greeks, and five thousand years ago, shit, that was a long time. But the main reason was that we actually took different routes nearly a thousand years ago. I knew what still linked us after five thousand years. Well there was the obvious one, language, the importance of which is not to be underestimated. But to be honest except for that and the religious link I couldn't quite get Jim's point we still had a population difference and that is a fact. I tried to think of anything that should hold us so close to Greece. There is the food of course, but I found out on Cyprus that they don't have capers in Greece, I smiled when I was told that, I just thought it was like gurbegya and dolmades. National pride in my capers!

We had to join them on this hate thing all because of our common language, heritage and a five thousand-year history. I felt like I was tearing at our Hellenistic roots, my roots even, which I was and yet at the same time when I looked at the history and the amount of times we had been occupied. It was the Greek line, our Greek line that had run through the heart of Cyprus for those thousands of years. I couldn't help but feel I was tearing at myself as much as anyone. It was a very painful period for me. But I still wondered why we should carry on hating with them when our paths took such different routes so long ago.

What he'd said had got me wondering though. Well unlike Jim I went to church quite often even if I wasn't religious and perhaps took a bit more notice of them. Maybe it was for the architecture but anyway. I knew I'd never seen a church ruin in Greece or Cyprus apart from the ancient temples of course. But I'd actually seen one or two churches in very good condition from the pre-Ottoman period. I remembered one a delicate little church no bigger than my bedroom. This part of Jim's history had been a bit deceptive.

If I'd had of known anything about the Ottoman Empire, I'd have known that it was through the regional religions that they administered their empire, it's a canny way and it worked well. Which would obviously mean that the language part wasn't quite true, although the language was degraded a lot under Turkish rule. As it was more the administrative aspect of the Church that the Turks were concerned about, having said that it would strengthen its administrative powers. By nature the Turks are migratory and by their own description will encompass any people that wish to call themselves Turks, which would cause some problems when trying to force that concept on Greeks.

The constant erosion of Greek culture and land, as witnessed by the Slav Macs, Albanians, Bulgarians and the British. Well here I thought he was attempting to justify the Macedonian affair. I didn't believe they were making any land claims. They just wanted to call themselves what they felt they were, Macedonian. What upsets a lot of Greeks is that the majority of people that live in what's known as the country Macedonia are not the same as those from the province of Greece known as Macedonia. They settled in the region a long time after Christ, but what Greeks get most upset about is that the flag that Macedonia chose to symbolise their new country, is a certain star more commonly associated to the Greek side. It does seem a piss take, but that's all. I couldn't believe he was attempting to justify Greece's aggressive response to it all. I didn't see it as erosion of Greek culture and they were religiously connected to us being eastern orthodox.

He'd also written Hellenistic nationalism is not a concept of conquest or force but a union of Greek language and heritage. It is there to counter the forces that are trying to undermine us and take away what is ours. I had to giggle at that one. It seemed a little paranoid. Like who's trying to undermine us. But his next paragraph made it clear that there was a very big difference between him and myself.

Just as I am proud to be a Cypriot I am proud to be a Greek. One does not make me any less than the other. Hardly surprising Greeks felt like we owed them something, where was his acknowledgement that we'd long ago, regardless of the reasons, took very different routes.

At this time I was getting my P.C. upgraded it didn't stop me from writing, but it put a hold to the e-mails for a week or two. I really felt that Jim was actually avoiding the main issue. To myself at least the constant perpetuation of the hatred for whatever reasons simply isn't healthy to any civilisation. By this time I'd found a letter that was sent from Makarios to the Greek president a couple of weeks before the coup of 74, but not just any letter. This letter highlighted the changes in the man himself, which would also be reflected in the country. I didn't need to be there to understand the turmoil that the Cypriot people were going through. Makarios was once the staunchest supporter of Enosis, but by his actions and this letter the man had changed dramatically as had the country. He had changed for the country. The letter was sent to the Junta president and it gave me far more freedom to write what I felt. For myself it was a sad letter to read and I've just used relevant paragraphs, as it is such a long letter.

'I am sorry to say, Mr President, that the root of the evil is very deep, reaching as far as Athens. It is from there that the tree of evil, the bitter fruits of which the Greek Cypriot people are tasting today, is being fed and maintained and helped to grow and spread. In order to be absolutely clear, I say that cadres of the Greek military regime support and direct the activities of EOKA B terrorist organisation. This explains also the involvement of Greek officers of the National Guard in illegal activities and in conspiratorial and inadmissible situations.'

He'd shown he knew where the evil was stemming from and of course he knew how it was manifesting itself in our country.

'The National Guard, with its present composition and staffing, has deviated from its aim and has become a breeding ground for illegal activities, a centre of conspiracy against the state and a source of recruitment for EOKA B. It suffices to say that during the recently stepped up terrorist activity of EOKA B. National Guard vehicles transported arms and moved to safety members of the organisation who were about to be arrested. Complete responsibility for this improper conduct of the National Guard rests with Greek officers, some of whom are involved head over ears in the activities of EOKA B.'

And this final paragraph from the letter, he's shown me that he understood, as I did, that to be Cypriot we had to be different. Because we had to live with Turks, accepting that our two country's had taken such different paths. I was filled with sorrow and anger, at the same time. Sorrow for the fact that I now knew how much of a broken man Makarios must have been when he died. And angry because I knew that with his leadership we not only had a chance, but we were turning a bitter hatred into something more positive. He would have made many of us proud.

'The National Guard is an organ of the Cyprus state and should be controlled by it and not from Athens. The theory about a common area of defence between Greece and Cyprus has its emotional aspect. In reality, however, the position is different.'

I sent an e-mail to my cousin. By this time I was up to chapter six as far as writing the book went and I found that writing chapter four had had a serious effect on myself, with my memories of church no less.

Hi Jim,
I appreciate your response I've been off line for a week, my book is still going, 30,000 words plus. Now I understand what you are saying, and already in the book I've discovered the depth of it all. But these days I have to confess if I declare I'm a Greek Cypriot then it would only be to enforce that I'm not Turkish. I don't know as a Cypriot whether that's a bad thing or not, I don't speak Greek but I will stress that if I had children I might ensure they are taught Greek, just as I might also encourage them to learn Turkish. For Cypriots speak many languages now.'

I went on to tell Jim all about my feelings as regards to the Macedonian affair and the effect it had on myself. Before getting back to what I felt was the heart of the matter.

'Here is a truth for you and I still find this astounding I knew nothing about Enosis until you first mentioned the word in Cyprus. I never would have looked it up and this I will point out, that perhaps there is a part of our history and a very important part that has been concealed if you like, from many, myself as an example. So much damage done in 74 why couldn't they leave it alone Jim, please believe me that this has not been an easy path for myself, but why couldn't they leave it be. As a majority in an independent country would we have been any less Greek. I hear what you said about the British and I see that some of it might have been Britain's doing. But even if we split it fifty, fifty you've still got a very sad letter from Makarios to ponder. We forgave our Turkish Cypriots for the treatment of Greeks under Otto, my next question is, has Greece? A Greek in Kos told me to forget our north, from where I feel my roots are, because it's gone, we lost it, did we do that Jim?

It is not our ancient history that now concerns me, but our present and our future. I still believe next year I'll be able to walk across the line freely. I don't know how proud I'll feel about it though. As for the book I'll send it in its complete form after it's finished and as I said all I can honestly write is to say how this has all affected me and it's what I'm doing. It's something we all should have the freedom to do, its called self-expression.
Take care,
love Jim.

The Makarios letter was more than enough to appease my mother I left it with her and she finally understood why we had to be different. Now I have to point out here that what I was doing was troubling my mother a bit but Makarios has that effect on a lot of Greek Cypriots, he was worshipped. But I knew she too had been ignorant of the truth.

Soon I was to find the infamous Akritas plan, I read it, and the way I was feeling at the time I didn't like it one bit. I couldn't actually believe it and had to have it confirmed, it was a little baffling although it seemed like an attempt to mobilise the general population, by making it appear as if there was a genuine need. There's far more to it than that, it seems to read like it's not only a long-term plan but it also seems to get one wondering who's read it and who's actually living to it. Indeed I even found myself asking the question should I be living to it. By my first impression of the Akritas plan it seemed to take everything into account, even the partition of our island on the path to Enosis. I read it and spent a long period of time confused by it, I threw it on to the sofa sat down and just stared at it. Not only confused but a little bewildered as to how anyone could write such a piece. Not so much for any sinister aspect it may have, but it seems open-ended and doesn't take into account any progression by the people as Cypriots first and foremost. It was published in a Greek Cypriot newspaper for the world to see in 1966. I could see the Akritas Plan would be considered a formula for genocide if you were a Turk. No date was given for it but I could see the aim of it was to ensure that Enosis was brought about. I was later to discover it to be what the Greek Cypriot's were apparently supposed to be working to in 63.

I was laying in bed one night thinking about what Jim had written about the British army. Now even if he were right about the divide and rule part, which I knew was possible not that they'd have had much trouble dividing the two communities, especially with what I was reading. But the idea of them killing hundreds in Cyprus, it wouldn't have made sense with Granddads actions, not that I was assuming he would have known, but it got me thinking some amusing thoughts, so I e-mailed him again. I couldn't help but giggle at what the stereotypical Greek looked like.

Jim,
If as you say the British were rampaging around Cyprus dressed as Greeks killing off Turks so that the Greeks would get the blame. Then why did my grandfather an intelligent man allow his only daughter that I know of, to be married and I'm told it was with his blessing to my father. Who at this time was a sguaddie in Cyprus and therefore a possible participant in these actions it sounds hard to swallow Jim.

I can't help (please forgive me) but giggle at the thought of asking my dad to tell me all about his possible night time activities in Cyprus,
"Dad you know when you was in Cyprus?"
"Yeah"
"Well did you or anyone you know go out at night with thick bushy moustaches and baggy trousers and maybe big loose black waistcoats and a bit of colouring on your face and kill hundreds of innocent Turks, just so that the Greeks would get the blame.'

At this point I was having trouble typing I was giggling so much.

'Maybe the British were using special forces to try keep it all a bit quieter, possible otherwise I think my dad may have heard something but I'll ask some others just in case, S.A.S perhaps all hand picked for their natural thick bushy moustaches and their fluent Greek.'

Here I suddenly lost touch with the funny side of it all though.

'I'm sorry Jim but what you are saying seems a bit unreal ' by the hundreds' I don't know how comfortable anyone of Turkish heritage might have been with Enosis. We Greeks and I know what I'm saying on this one. I think we have no love for Turkey or anything that ever spawned from it, from the animals from the east, for they have been the cause of our forefathers misery and we'll make our forefathers proud.'

But where is Alexander?

And where were the bloody Spartans when we needed them?

It's history Jim it's all history, a great history, a very great history but history never the less, we can no longer claim to be the cradle of democracy we once was. There's a bitterness Jim, a bitterness at what we had and what we have, and we both know we should have got western Turkey back, it seems so recent. Even going to Istanbul, although I didn't stay it felt like a bit of bitch when you always feel that if justice was done it might still be Constantinople, what a wonderful name. I have always myself felt cheated by Turkey, but it's the perpetuation of the hate, it's the perpetuation, time to say enough.'

Here I was thinking of the good work that Makarios was doing, I knew he too along with many other Greek Cypriots had seen the hatred for what it was and was building from the ashes something positive. As I wanted us to once again.

'Too much misery has gone into building platforms to justify history as you said let history be our guide but let us be careful of where it guides us, less we be blinded by it, rather than led by it. From my perception to turn such hatred into something positive is one of the greatest things a people can learn. I think I know what it means to be a Greek Cypriot.
Love Jim

His response wasn't far away. It felt a little hostile at the end but it was a very informative e-mail.

Jim,
if as you say the British were rampaging around Cyprus dressed as Greeks killing off Turks so
that the Greeks would get the blame, then

How did the Greeks and Turks dress? Not much different from each other: it was more clue-leaving like speaking Greek and wearing crucifixes etc. Some Turks helped the British kill their own people.

Why did my grandfather an intelligent man allow his only daughter that I know of to be married and I'm told it was with his blessing

I am not sure that this is true, Grandma gave a different story.

to my father who was at this time a sguaddie in Cyprus and therefore a possible participant in these actions

If your dad was in Cyprus at the time, he was certainly not privvy enough to know what was going on.

Denktash himself admitted in a program televised by the BBC (or ITV) some 15 years ago and repeated here in 1989 or 1990, that he was involved with others (implying the British) in terrorism against his own people. He personally bombed the gate to OLD NICOSIA killing 30-35 Turks.
These details were not for public consumption, or else there would have been an outcry from all over the world, particularly from the Turks.

sounds hard to swallow Jim, I can't help (please forgive me) but giggle at the thought of asking my
dad to tell me all about his possible night time activities in Cyprus,
"Dad you know when you was in Cyprus?"
"Yeah"

These were secret operations if one sguaddy was to know, then there would be a risk of a leak and the operation would have failed.

and kill hundreds of innocent Turks just so that the Greeks would get the blame."

maybe the British were using special forces to try keep it all a bit quieter, possible

NOT just possible, but PROVEN.

otherwise I think my dad my have heard something but I'll ask some others just in case, S.A.S perhaps all hand picked for their natural thick bushy moustaches and their fluent Greek,

AS ABOVE.

"Well did you or anyone you know go out at night with thick bushy moustaches and baggy trousers and maybe big loose black waistcoats and a bit of colouring on your face

This sounds a little stereotypical if not racist remark. First, many Brits at the time spoke Greek and nearly all Turks did as well. Second, you must be naive to the extreme if you think that ordinary sguaddies (even Generals or ordinary senior military personnel) would know of it

I'm
sorry Jim but what you are saying seems a bit unreal and I don't know how comfortable anyone of Turkish heritage might have been with Enosis,

Before the 2nd world war, the British were negotiating with the Cypriot leaders, to facilitate Enosis; some of these leaders were Turks. The negotiations were going ahead to the point of details of implementation when WW2 started. The British then asked the Cypriots to co-operate (help) them against the Germans. During WW2, a large percentage of Cypriots died helping the Brits. The condition that the Cypriots gave for this help was the successful implementation of Enosis after the War. The Brits delayed and then reneged on the agreement seeing the problems that were developing in Palestine and Suez. This is when EOKA started to fight for Enosis and that is why the Brits did everything to maintain a presence in Cyprus: By setting Greek against Turk, Britain forced a situation where Cypriot people (Greek and Turk) would never unite against British occupation. When Cyprus became independent, Britain imposed an unworkable constitution and system of government, and claimed two areas of Cyprus as "sovereign bases".

In the early 1970's Cyprus was getting its act together and the Brits saw this as a threat. The Americans wanted a Base in Cyprus and asked Makarios 5 times to be allowed to put a base in Cyprus and 5 times
Makarios refused. The Brits and the Americans then collaborated and asked the Greek military regime to send Sampson to overthrow Makarios. The rest is history. The Americans have a (supposedly) secret base in the North of Cyprus. Photos were circulated around the world at the time and many countries questioned the American involvement in the overthrow of Makarios.

Early this year, the American secretary of state and the special rep (commissioner) for Cyprus apologised to the Cyprus government for their past mistakes and involvement; referring to the Sampson overthrow of Makarios.'

My cousin without doubt is a great source of information. I enjoyed the one about Denktash and I had to believe it, as it came from the horses' mouth so to speak. He then went on to say

I don't pine for another Alexander or the great ancient history to repeat itself but history has to be known and understood before judgement could be made. Greece is the cradle of democracy, nothing can change that but our democracy now depends on third parties. He then added that, bitterness is no use, only compromise and understanding can be our salvation but it takes more than one party to compromise. Don't confuse ancient Greek history with modern Cypriot history.

He then finished with a comment that was to stick in my mind.

If anyone asks if I was Greek or Greek Cypriot, I don't say I am a Greek Cypriot, I say I SPEAK Greek.
Regards.
Jim

That was a lot to take on board, I enquired around and discovered that it might have been very possible that the S.A.S. could have and most probably would have been used in such operations as they were based there for much of the time. Britain's divide and rule and tactics are something that no one I'd met would deny, indeed historically it is a British trait. I e-mailed my cousin and told him as much I saw It was possible, I never saw how we could prove it. I felt like I was being scorned a little as well. The British were as I was to discover make some sinister decisions in Cyprus. But I felt sure that he was trying to imply that they were the main causes of the present problems. With the hatred I wondered if it would be needed, but I never considered that meant they never used it. As for the clue leaving I don't think wearing a crucifix or speaking a language can be described as clue leaving, they may be clues, but nothing was left. Other than that I still didn't feel at the time he was even coming close to offering me help on understanding our present situation not that I needed it, he seems to leave me with more questions. The answers I would discover for myself.

As for the cradle of democracy, I regard a cradle as a support, which it is, as much as the birthplace. I simply could not justify that Greece still is that support, whilst many Greek Cypriots are so ignorant of their recent past. And for the remark about my parent's marriage, it had come from my grandmother I'd already started to consider the big differences between my grandparents and he was to set me off on a bit of a mission.

I could feel a strain between my cousin and myself and it wasn't something that I wanted, but I could feel it anyway. As for the British I started to recall a T.V. documentary that I could remember and it was all about EOKA (The national Organisation of Cypriot fighters). EOKA weren't just fighting for independence. Unknown to myself they carried on after independence under the name of EOKA b. When I think back to the time, it makes so much sense. The campaign during the EOKA b era was against Turks, seen after independence as the only obstacle to Enosis, Which is why the name of Grivas stopped being mentioned. During the fifties it was a fierce campaign against the British and it was this period that the T.V. documentary related to. It started off telling of some of the tactics used by them and showed some ingenious little matchbox bombs and other assorted goodies if you were so inclined as EOKA were. Much of their campaign was waged against British servicemen and their spouses. Now here I have to say that even recently I've found that some documentaries can distort the truth to an horrendous degree, but I don't for one moment doubt the truth behind the testimonial I was to remember from this documentary. Colonel Grivas as he was known, was EOKA's top military man. When I first heard his name mentioned by relatives it was as a hero in the fight for independence and then I'd hear very little of him at all. His fame had turned to infamy by the late sixties and now I knew why, it was because he carried on with his ideas through EOKA b. One of the most wanted men on Cyprus as far as most British were concerned, only most though. Here my mistrust in the British government's actions increased dramatically. After seeing the results of some of Grivas work the program showed an interview with an ex-British intelligence officer on Cyprus during this time. I remembered it well, the man got increasingly upset as he described how time and time again he would track down Grivas and time and time again he would make a request for permission to either pick him up or take him out. He was always refused permission to do either. The next day Grivas would be out killing more British army personal and their spouses. He and the programs makers were to assume it was so he wouldn't be made a martyr, but that would have only happened if he were killed, this officer was sure he could have had him either way. Grivas was to be banished from Cyprus after independence as a proviso, by whom I'm not sure, but he would return in early sixty-four.

Here I think I should write a little about the man Nicos Sampson, born Nicos Georghiades in Famagusta in 1935, not much though, he's not worth it from my perception. During the fifties he was an EOKA hit man. In 1953 he took a course in journalism in London and it seems an English surname. He seems a contemptible sort because apparently he used to shoot his victims in the back and then be the first to the murder scene to report on it. He was arrested in 1957 and sentenced to life imprisonment and released in 60. He boasted of his killings in his own newspaper after that called Makhi (meaning combat) he really isn't a subject worth writing of, merely to say he enjoyed killing it seems, not just Turks, but Turks, British and Greek Cypriots.

What Jim said had said about my grandfather went totally against everything I believed for more than one reason. The most important to myself, was my personal relationship with him. The love that existed between him and myself was the strongest thing I could remember about granddad, that I always felt I was the apple of his eye, even when he was surrounded by grandchildren and I never really knew why. I couldn't believe that I was the result of an unwanted marriage as Jim was suggesting and it was now in contradiction to what he'd confirmed in Cyprus at the swimming pool. I believed that either Jim was lying or just as likely now my grandmother was.

I was round my parents' house shortly after and soon to have an amusing conversation with my father about his marriage to my mother.
    "Dad what made you decide to marry mum?" My father just hunched his shoulders.
    "I saw her and said she'll do"
    "Is that it?"
    "Yeah," he said seeming a little embarrassed.
    "And granddad approved?"
    "A far as I know I wasn't told otherwise"
    " Jim says that Grandma told him that Granddad wasn't really happy about it."
    "Did he?" my father looked genuinely surprised at that.
    "Can you think of any reason why he might have said that?" My father shook his head.
    "No"
    "As far as you know granddad was quite happy about the marriage?"
    "As far as I know, he seemed quite happy."

"You never felt any animosity or anything the first time you met?" I wanted to be sure.

"No none at all"

"I didn't think there was, Jim's suggesting there was, but he said it come from grandma," I'd been considering the differences between grandma and granddad.

"They were very different weren't they?" I said. My father nodded his head emphatically. Yes very different I thought. I felt like Jim had pushed me on this one and I was determined to prove him wrong. I went round to see my sister Gina for tea about this time and the subject of the conversation. Naturally, I took it there.

"You know I've been communicating with Jim about this book?" I'd told her all about my book project although I don't think she took it seriously.

"He says that grandma told him that granddad wasn't happy about mum and dads marriage," Gina looked at me surprised.

"Really!"

"Yeah I don't believe it though," I added.

"No nor do I," she said.

"There were a lot of differences between him and grandma weren't there?" Gina looked at me as if that was an understatement.

"Do you remember the arguments they used to have?" she said.

"I do now, shit! They were bad weren't they!" Gina nodded as she dished out tea. If she remembered them like I did, then they were fierce. If granddad and grandma were in the flat together, I'd be in a side room with granddad, it was as bad as that. There was often such bitterness in the air that they'd be apart from each other as much as possible.

Chapter 11

By this point I was in turmoil and much of it was about my grandfather and my memories of him. My last conversation with my sister had reminded me of so much anger that used to exist between my grandparents. It was to also leave me considering what I'd been thinking about him. I had an idea of what it was like to be in a bitter relationship and I had to admit that there was a lot of bitterness in theirs. I wondered how much he even enjoyed life then, being in his mid eighties with what I knew was going on in Cyprus, aligned with the reasons he left, I couldn't imagine him being very happy at all. I knew he saw what I could as far as the hatred went and no matter how much I tried to get away from the idea. I couldn't help but think that he may have known that if he'd taught me Greek and passed away whilst I was still young, I would have been left to fall completely under the influence of my grandmother. I thought of my mother and her two full brothers and of some of the horror stories my mother would tell me, which I knew come from my grandmother.

Being brought up Greek is to hate Turks and as I was always being told, my grandfather was a very tolerant man and that was to Turks, so different to the people I'd been reading about. I knew it couldn't have always have been like it, otherwise he simply wouldn't have done what I knew he did, so I knew we must have lived all right together.

Then there was the British Army taking him to the U.S.A. Why take him there at all and remembering that at around the turn of the century to WW1 this would have been a long voyage, why? I couldn't think of anything other than intelligence training and still can't. I had enquired with British Army records but they said that because of the years involved it may be a fruitless search and have since confirmed that. But there is no other sort of training that I could think of that would necessitate taking him completely out of the country. Intelligence training could mean a complete change of perspective. I knew this for sure from my friendship with the ex-British intelligence officer. I considered what he taught me and how it could be used. It has actually changed my whole way of thinking in some respects and in some very strange ways that I may not even be aware of. I started to consider my sponsor child. I chose an orphan for a specific reason and he's six years old. Through my gifts and my messages to him he will know that I love him and that's important to any child. It might be the only real love he may feel, although I hope not. Regardless here I have the ability to influence this, my sponsor child, a great deal even from afar. Love really can be that powerful. For

Christmas I'll be sending him a flute and a puppet along with his writing tools, and of course my love, I'm nurturing him. It's the love he'll remember all his life and yes I hope to influence him in many ways, not a bad thing, if it's positive.

I was writing one night when I considered the stance my cousin was taking. I could feel myself getting upset about it, I knew he, like our government, wasn't acknowledging the Christmas 63 massacres and I felt it was putting a terrible strain on our relationship. I felt distanced from him already and there was so much going through my mind about my own past at the same time. I'd spent nearly two years in Australia and New Zealand myself and the most annoying part about his stance was that he was ten thousand miles away from it all way down under. It was a very emotional e-mail and it was to let a lot out, but it was all building up in me.

'G'Day,
You know that's still a term that I use with a lot of affection. I try not to think of Oz these days, I really don't know if I'll ever get back. But it's nice to feel I saw some of the best parts of it even though I never got to Ayers rock, three days on a bus, no way, but I would've flown. I wept when I last left Sydney, had my head against the window to hide the tears. I hope you appreciate the country and the people, I never really understood them until I went back of beyond, found myself on a sheep station rounding up sheep and flushing out tiger snakes with a rake. Grubben Gullen, they call it a village but it's just a pub and one house. And the snowy mountains, those Brumby's are good horses, although I had to get a stick to get the best, doesn't mean you use it, the horse sees it and he knows and I haven't even mentioned the ocean or New Zealand. Those kiwis know what they've got and they're right to be proud of it, they're always telling you God made the world in six days and on the seventh he created New Zealand. And exploring such a beautiful country and watching whales swim past from the shore whilst albatrosses glide overhead one could almost believe it. Nature, I call her my true mother and you've got so much of it untouched. I could've settled with an Ozzie girl, but it wasn't love for her, just the country, so it wouldn't have been honest. But boy I miss it, maybe it's because it's been the only place I could really escape from people, just myself and nature but at least nature gives one a chance to find oneself. Got to change the subject, got a tear in my eye, I'll get back.'

Here I could feel the strain building within myself and I wondered how our different feelings towards being Cypriot would affect our personal relationship and as much as I was angry with him I was also starting to fear him, for simply knowing I was writing the book. I got back to the PC and asked him.

'Jim are we still brothers I've got a couple of more tears in my eyes now'

I broke down under the strain and left the P.C. for a while. I could feel the difference between us and it was those same differences I knew Cypriots must have felt in 74. I went back to it a few minutes later still distressed.

'I plan to fly to Cyprus soon to see your mother and hopefully I'll be taking my brother, as he is showing more of an interest in Cyprus, maybe because he's getting to an age where perhaps one might ask, who am I and I will show him the answer. He is Cypriot even though we were born and raised in England to an English father, the only family we really know are Cypriots, not only Cypriots, but also Greek Cypriots and I will hopefully be able to convey to him some of that. I'm going to night school tomorrow to start learning Greek, why?

Not only is it part of my heritage but far more important, is that for the first time in years I've lost someone I've loved very much and never been able to tell her, because Marie spoke no English and I spoke no Greek. You wouldn't have known it, but I felt very close to Marie and I have to be honest in saying that for the short time that I knew her. I felt more love from her than I'd felt from many others in a lifetime. It can have a big effect Jim I know. I don't know who'd believe me and I don't care because the last few months I've realised why I put a block up to Greek. Your mother speaks good English, the relevance of this, it's love, I remember grandma in my younger years and I also remember her and grandfather were very different, shit tears again.'

By this time I just couldn't stop typing and even through the tears I just had to let it out.

'I did not have a happy early childhood Jim, in fact, it was very miserable. I can remember as a child counting my hours of happiness as the hours I could be away from home. I never felt that anyone else seemed to miss granddad as much as myself back then and I can remember resenting the fact. Yep, if I remember back I did resent it and no matter what, you could have dragged me to church a hundred times as I probably was. Or told me off as much as anyone wanted, boy writing brings it out, but no matter what, I wasn't going to forgive anyone for not missing granddad as much as myself or for perhaps not seeing how much it had hurt me. I was a child Jim, and children need to feel love, unconditional love and at that time I only ever felt it from one person and he was gone and no one seemed to care, whether it's true or not it's how I remember it.

They say genes skip a generation and we are products of our grandparents, I also know we like to hang on to things that we hear and like, someone once told me I had a very strong resemblance to my grandfather, such a strong influence. I feel like I've been in conflict with you Jim and I don't want to. Chess would be easier.

I'll write,
Love Jim.

Before I only knew when I stopped taking Greek in, now I knew why. I never received a reply to that e-mail and that would be the last time I'd communicate with Jim for a while. I shut down the PC and went to bed and wondered that question are we still brothers, I couldn't believe it was all so deep.

Despite everything I was excited by my first Greek lesson, it felt like a new era for me. It was also bloody hard, but I left determined although confused, confused as to whether I'd ever use what I was to learn. It was at this time that I realised what effect writing this book might have on my life, I brought my textbook though and remembered why I was doing it. To talk to my relatives and for myself, if they weren't good enough reasons then there was another, for all the times Cyprus had been invaded I understood that the one thing that really held that link to our great and distant past, was our language and our religion.

It was about this time that someone asked me what I was really hoping to achieve from writing my book, I said what I'd written, but he pushed me further and asked me what my best hopes might be. I told him I'd like to give the people of Cyprus a book they could identify with, but unwittingly I exposed the divisions between Cypriots themselves, and my cousin and I, I feel, are as good an example, as you will get. I spent two years in Australia, I knew Jim wouldn't see what I saw of the country and probably never wonders far from a PC. I say this only because there's a great pleasure that one can draw from nature. When you find yourself surrounded by nothing but nature, maybe for myself it was the pleasure of feeling at ease with her. She may be harsh at times, and she may often seem unfair. But she is never spiteful, never bitter, she has no pride, she just is. And down under they've got so much of it there and it's a land that I believe makes Australians what they are. For all his words my cousin makes his home across the world, away from our problems.

I returned to my writing feeling guilty about not recognising the Turkish republic of North Cyprus, but as much as I was reading and writing I still couldn't accept the partitioning of my country. I regarded it as a problem to face, I knew that there was no way they'd allow Greeks to rule over them. Whilst writing though, I'd been hit by a realisation of why it's 'better to say your Greek'. I was even angrier that only Greeks and Turks knew it and more so that it had already affected my life on my visit to Istanbul. It was the only reason I could imagine there being a difference and it was that Greek Cypriots were the only ones being held responsible for the massacres in Cyprus. I was infuriated by the idea that this had happened, but found it to be the only possible reason why 'It's better to say your Greek' if you went to Turkey. What I really couldn't understand though was, why? Most of it was Greek and not purely Greek Cypriot resentment at Turkish Cypriot's being a block to Enosis. So how and why did Cypriots get all the blame? Now I was really pissed off at my cousin! I felt the likes of myself, my godmother and even Georgio and Marie were being branded as butchers for the actions of others, others like my cousin perhaps. I was angry, bloody angry I sent a short note with some promised photos to him and told him that I was angry, but not so much at him, just angry at the difference and at how the difference was defined.

I went over to visit my parents about this time. My mother had by now got used to the idea of my writing the book, not that I knew whether she understood what was going on, my mother left Cyprus when she was fourteen and by the age of fifteen was married to my father.

Here I want to say that my parents are very happily married although there was a time when it wasn't so happy. I always had the impression and believed that my mother resented the fact that she was simply married off to an Englishman. She really believed that no one cared where she went and it was a resentment my mother would grow up and live with, something I may have felt as a child, she was twenty one when she had myself, the fourth of seven children. On the basis of what I'd been reading and had been told, I firmly believed that my father fitted well with my grandfathers thinking. I call it a plan but maybe more of an idea, not one of those sinister ones, unless of course you consider me sinister. But yes, I believed that I could have been the result of a little idea my grandfather had. It's the depth of it all. It really is that deep. I've heard people relate it to Protestants and Catholics often. But I think you'd have to literally go back three to four hundred years to find a time, when even for them, things were as bad as in Cyprus in sixty three. Now hatred for Turks is a Greek trait, it's as simple as that and by the time my grandfathers idea might have been formulating in the fifties, that hatred would have seriously started manifesting itself. Even according to my cousin's facts, in the only place it could, Cyprus, with almost one fifth of its population of Turkish descent, enough to consider a threat but never enough to be a real danger. But if there were those that wanted to consider them a threat, there would be many to listen, on top of this they were the only ones now blocking Enosis. The resentment starts to spread, my grandfather realises its possible consequences and acts accordingly by first moving his family to England. His sons are married but he has a daughter. Now he could have found a Greek husband for my mother, he had a dowry, instead he allowed the marriage of my mother to my father, and now I felt I was sure as to why. It was of course all just a personal theory based on what I'd been told but it was the only explanation I could think of for allowing the marriage, as it really is that unusual. Neither of my parents could be described as very intelligent. But I'd consider them of their time, my father a WW11 evacuee and my mother with very minimal education and her rural Cypriot upbringing. In my younger years I'd have to read for her. I sat down on the sofa next to my mother who was eating some Greek chicken soup, my father was sitting across the lounge.

"Mum I want to talk to you about granddad," she was sitting comfortably but this was a touchy subject.

"What about him?"

"You know I'm writing a book, and you know I've been coming to some conclusions about him," I paused slightly, before continuing. "And so far they've been right."

"Yeah," she was listening to me whilst eating and watching T.V.

"Mum you really think that granddad didn't care who you married?"

"He couldn't care who I married!" then she flipped. "A black man! A yellow man! A bloody red man, he couldn't care!"

"Mum that is a load of bollocks!" I lost it but immediately then went in to save the conversation. I calmed my tone down.

"Look mum it just doesn't fit in with who granddad was, I know it may sound strange but I think he would have not only been happy about dad, but thrilled with the idea," my mother seemed bemused by all this. I thought about his will being a last testimonial.

"I'd would love to have a look at his will," that was a bad subject with my mother. After we'd been told that he left his land to myself my brothers and sisters, some relatives had come down from London. My eldest sister was awake to hear my mother apparently being pressured into signing some papers, it was after that we were told it had all been a mistake. It was something I'd mentioned to her a couple of times over the years, but she'd get upset and say there was nothing to tell. She thought I was enquiring along those lines again.

"I don't care about the bloody land Jim!" she said angrily. But then she said something that would silence me.

"There is no will! He didn't make a bloody will!" she spat some food out. "Your grandfather gave it all to Yannis before he died!"

I sat in silence. It wasn't what I wanted to hear. I suspected someone had been less than honest with me and about my grandfathers' will of all things. Yannis had confirmed he had the will and my mother denied he ever made one. I considered he was just agreeing he had the papers. I looked at my father, I could tell he wasn't sure what to make of it all, but I had a good idea. I stayed away from the will subject and I told them all about what had been going on in Cyprus and the effect it must have been having on my grandfather. I finished off with a comment about 74 as I left and my father said something, but for some reason I never really took it in, although I heard what he said. I was thinking about the contradiction I'd heard about the will. It was all too much for me. I went home and settled in front of the T.V. to vegetate for a while, watching the Saturday night game shows. A few things were coming back to me and I didn't want them to. Little traces of things I'd said to my grandfather and he'd said to me. That's all my memories of him really consisted of, traces here and there. In an emotional outburst I went to the P.C. and wrote. I never knew what I'd written at the time. I was just very upset. The most prevalent thing on my mind was the bitterness that existed between my grandparents and how unhappy he would have been with everything. I went back to the Saturday night television without reading what I'd written. There seemed so much that I wanted to forget.

I spent that Sunday night at some friends in London and Monday morning I found myself in Bedford place at the door to the Turkish republic of North Cyprus embassy, as I knew I would. I had to. I was actually surprised that they had an embassy at all, as no country in the world recognises them. The constitution of the T.R.N.C, which was approved by themselves in May 1985, actually goes back as an administration to December 1968, the state of the T.R.N.C. is only recognised by Turkey. The building was a large Georgian terraced house, the door was locked. I saw the bell with its fitted surveillance camera and buzzed. At this point I have to comment that I was extremely paranoid not only about writing the book but also having anything to do with the T.R.N.C. I buzzed the bell again and felt annoyed at being kept waiting. I looked at my feet and by my left foot saw a small bell button, presumably for the embassy staff. I pushed my left foot against the bell two or three times extending the final ring for a good ten seconds. I couldn't believe I was annoyed, not at being kept waiting by anyone, but to be kept waiting by the T.R.N.C. now if that sounds silly it is. I was annoyed at them for keeping me at the door waiting whilst their Turkish army hadn't even bothered to ring when they invaded Cyprus, I know it's silly but it's how I felt. A middle-aged woman opened the door and without saying a word let me in. I followed her through to a waiting room along the hallway and on the right. The room would have been about eight or nine metres square with some workspaces partitioned off by the windows where she was sat. I entered the room and stood in the centre when a young woman entered and asked if she could be of assistance.

"I'd like to see a Miss Dorak please"

"Miss Dorak's not in yet, but she shouldn't be long," the woman was polite.

"I'll wait," I said.

"Would you like some tea or coffee whilst you wait?" the woman asked.

"Coffee please."

I hadn't even made an appointment. I realised I was being a little arrogant. The woman went off and left me standing in the middle of the room staring at the holiday posters of northern Cyprus. I was in awe.

"Where's that?" I asked pointing to a poster featuring miles of golden sand. The middle-aged woman looked up.

"It's the Karpasia peninsular," she replied. It was just as I'd imagined. It really is the best part of the island. Then I saw a poster of Kyrenia with the mountains in the background.

"It's beautiful," I said as much to myself. "They really are that colour," I said allowed. The Kyrenia Mountains have a colouring in our oil painting that was hard to believe, but the poster confirmed it. I walked to a poster of Kyrenia harbour. It looked busy, but it seemed to have lost some of its character. I sighed at the sight of it, taking in the scenes when my coffee arrived. I sat on a sofa and wondered again, why?

"Miss Dorak is here now would you like to follow me please."

The woman who'd brought my coffee announced. I followed her up a flight of stairs to a large office, presumably the ambassadors' where I was asked to take a seat on one of the large leather sofas. If this was the ambassadors' office then I could only presume that the elderly man sitting behind the large desk sifting through the days' papers was the ambassador. There were two large flags either side of him, one the Turkish national flag and the other, the flag of the T.R.N.C. I had no idea as to why I'd been left with him but whilst in his company I had to confirm one thing.

"Excuse me are you Turkish or Turkish Cypriot?" I asked. The ambassador looked up seemingly unsurprised by the question.

"Cypriot," he replied.

I nodded my head as an acknowledgement and I thought about what an ignorant pig I was being, but I knew that I couldn't help it. Miss Dorak arrived shortly after and politely ushered me into an adjacent office. It was a nice spacious room and I immediately felt a little more comfortable, slightly embarrassed about my behaviour perhaps and certainly a little paranoid.

My present host soon made me feel more comfortable when she pulled some cigarettes out, at least I could smoke without feeling bad, we both lit one up and went into a deep and long conversation on a subject close to both of our hearts, Cyprus. She knew about my escapade on the rock already and we broached almost every subject except for land rights, but with my missile theory it seemed irrelevant at first. I got up and paced around the room a little walking to the window and looking out over the square through the net curtains. Cyprus seemed so far away, yet all its problems seemed to be so close to me now, even two thousand miles away, not something that had happened before. During the conversation the phone rang, she spoke for a few minutes answering some questions as she spoke. When she put the phone down she informed me it was someone enquiring about buying property in Northern Cyprus and cautious because of the National Service, as if it was a real problem. I felt gutted, a very large proportion of the Turks living in Northern Cyprus are recent immigrants' from the Turkish mainland. Something I know Cypriots from both sides of the community resent after being told about the way land prices had increased because of it. At that point I wanted to talk about land claims but how could I when I felt that there was so much being denied by our side. Every time I threw Russia into the conversation though Miss Dorak would get excited.

"If Russia messes with Turkey, Turkey will invade her," I knew that was an off the cuff remark. I smiled.

"I don't think so, Turkey is not going to invade Russia, Turkey's not that stupid." It wasn't said mockingly although she could see I knew there was no chance. I thought of the exploits of Napoleon and Hitler, then considered that some in Russia might welcome it. A war they know that they'd win. At times of economic gloom it can be a boost to the economy. I also knew that Russia would get world support. Perceptions, Miss Dorak had a book on her desk with this title.

"You know the worst thing that Turkish Cypriots have going for them?" I asked her.

"What's that?"

"It's the name........ Turkish." I looked at her and she looked at me but I knew she knew that I meant. Their human rights record isn't very good at all, in fact it's appalling, but I thought I'd make it easy for her.

"It's the name......Turk, well every one's seen Midnight Express."

"But they have prisons like that in America!" she threw back defensively.

"They might, but no one's ever made a hit movie about any of them."

We talked on and she gave me some books on the situation and the Turkish position and a copy of The Genocide Files by Harry Gibbons, I was surprised there was an actual book of the title. Makarios was mentioned again when Miss Dorak described his actions as ethnic cleansing, at which I threw her a look to show how I felt about her choice of words to describe a man giving out passports. I browsed through the books she'd given me reading texts as we talked.

In April 1966 a local Greek Cypriot newspaper Patris publishes The Akritas plan. I held a copy of it in my hand I wondered how long it would have taken before my granddad read it. I knew it must have broken his heart. The main architect and the chief of operations Akritas, was a man called Yorgadjis who is now dead. But I would soon be incensed at one of its more minor apparent architects, our present President Glafco Clerides. I looked at Miss Dorak.

"He can't be still working to this?" she never responded. Either way it's something to be left to the individual to decide. Things had been calm and stable between sixty-eight and seventy-four, then the forces of the Greek junta acted. Makarios must have seen it coming hence the letter to be placed on file followed by the UN address. I remembered saying aloud in a moment of silence. "Twenty thousand!" said to be at least the number of Greeks and Greek Cypriots on the rampage on behalf of Enosis in our country in 74, which was where I was now focussing. Over the night of the 14th of July hundreds of Greek mainland officers are secretly flown in to Nicosia and driven away by the National Guard who numbered well over ten thousand bolstered by thousands of EOKA b members and The Greek Army contingent based on the island. They're equipped with thirty-two T-34 Russian built tanks with artillery in the form of twenty-five pound guns and over a hundred armoured vehicles. All in all, said to be well over twenty thousand.

July 15th 1974 Code name IPHESTOS (VOLCANO)

8am the Greeks attacked the Presidential Palace, the offices of the Cypriot Broadcasting Company, Nicosia International airport and the archbishopric inside the city walls. Despite taking a pounding the presidential palace was fiercely defended for several hours. Makarios supporters are being dragged on to the streets and shot, others are fighting for their lives. The Presidential palace is destroyed but Makarios escapes.

11am Cyprus State Radio announced the death of Makarios. Without giving details the announcer shouted, "Long live the National Guard". The National Guard with its contingent of Greek mainland officers backed by thousands of EOKA b fought on against Makarios supporters, various left wing groups the Reserve Force and the Police. In the middle of the afternoon Nicos Sampson is declared president. Something that must have drove fear into any descent citizen, especially any Turks. Many Turkish communities are surrounded and taunts are being thrown! Makarios is dead and your next!

But before the days out the voice of Makarios is heard on Cyprus Free radio calling his supporters to fight. The call was answered and Cypriots all over the island rallied by the call from their leader fought bloody pitched battles with the Greeks. It was heartbreaking to read, but now I understood why Makarios is where he is now. Fourteen years after the birth of our nation he and his supporters are now fighting Enosis to the death. The Washington post quoted a Greek University student who had seen the bodies of Makarios supporters dumped in graves four at a time. At Kykkos his supporters are rounded up and slaughtered. Greek Cypriot member of parliament, Rina Catselli wrote in her diary "Everybody is frozen with fear, they all listen speechless to hair raising details; the small child who after being killed accidentally was taken and buried in a mass grave. The old man who when he asks for the body of his dead son was shot on the spot, the tortures and executions at the central prisons. In the Nicosia General Hospital they prevent the doctors from taking care of the wounded just because they belong to the Makarios faction. The presidential palace destroyed to cover up the fact that it had been looted. Works of art were plundered from the archbishopric by the henchmen of the Greek junta. My god everyone is frozen with horror and is silent. Nothing is sacred to these people and they call themselves Greek! In that case we must not keep that name longer."

The morning of the 20th July Turkish Phantoms attack pre-selected targets. The Turkish amphibious Forces land on five-mile beach some five miles west of Kyrenia. Paratroopers and commandos are air lifted in. At 2pm, the Greeks launched a counterattack against the Turkish forces from Kyrenia to the east and Lapithos in the west, three T-34's are destroyed and the Greeks retreated. The Turks successfully formed a bridgehead and a land corridor to Nicosia. The fighting continues but after the landings by Turkey things get bad for the Turkish Cypriots.

Hostages were taken all over the island and the National Guard burned out the Turkish quarter of Limassol. A few days later after enough forces had landed, the Turkish military pushed out across the island. Some retreating EOKA b members in the Famagusta bay area slaughtered the three hamlets of Maratha, Sandallar and Atlilar before the Turkish regiments could get to them. According to some sources Greek Cypriot National Guard documents were apparently captured in the following weeks, revealing plans to wipe out the entire Turkish population of the island.

The last twenty minutes or so I'd started to become increasingly uncomfortable. I was considering the effect the Akritas plan might have had on my grandfather, it must have broke his heart and the bitterness between him and my grandmother. I was also remembering what my father had said on Saturday on my way out of my parents' home. He was reminding me, but how could I forget. My cousin Jim and my godfather were in Kyrenia at the same time in July 74. It sounded like a war zone before the Turks invaded let alone after, but he'd told me nothing of this. I was thinking about the differences between my grandparents and the way they fought and I was thinking of how much of a different person I would possibly be with my grandmothers' influence if I spoke Greek. I was now thinking of all the hatred that we'd been brought up with just unleashed on Cyprus again and the ugliness of it. The two thousand communists that they murdered were all Makarios supporters. As I'd dare say the majority of the casualties were. I couldn't believe my relatives had let me get to such an age without letting me know the depth of it. I couldn't believe with all the information that I'd got from my cousin, he'd told me nothing of this, but then his words. "If anyone asks if I was a Greek or Greek Cypriot, I don't say I am a Greek Cypriot I say I speak Greek" went through me with a shiver. Of course, now I knew what he was doing in Kyrenia in the summer of 74. I was considering very strongly now that my worst fears might be true. I was pleased to leave there. I needed to get out. I had some possibilities running through my mind that I didn't want to face. At the same time I felt an urgency to get home to read what I'd written in my emotional outburst on the keyboards Saturday night. When I arrived home a few hours later very upset. I sat there stunned and a little confused at what I saw under the heading of personal notes.

I lost someone who once knew how to love a child and a light was gone from my life whilst the world carried on. Did anyone else really care I didn't think so at the time and put a block up to all that these people would give me. For I never saw no loss in them, the day my granddad went away from my life and love was gone from me for many years. Over two years have passed since I lay on a deathbed of my own. A painful bed full of thorns and through the pain I pleaded to go but it wasn't to be my time and I returned knowing the one lesson that I could only learn from such an experience. That if there is one thing worse than living with regret, it is surely dying with it and I went in search of what I once lost not knowing why I put such a block up to all I am and who I am. I returned to Cyprus seeking out the spirit of the one who loved me most, only to find the love again and at the same time discover the reason why I put up the block. Love is stifled in Cyprus, stifled by it's secrets and I brought back with me that that stifles love on Cyprus, from a rock I love to a box in purgatory.

It's the same colour as that that I refused take for all these years, the Greek without the love. For that's what I was brought up with the Greek without the love and the one that taught me was without love and when we lost him, I lost more and now I know the reason. I have it in a box and the reasoning being better in a box than on a rock in Cyprus.

I heard your message grandfather I sought out who you were, I heard your message and I believed and I wonder if you knew that I would be the one, or did you ever wonder I'd do as well.

Did the gas switch slip or was it turned, for I remember the day you taught my sister to count, it was you who told me the alphabet first and numbers next and this is not for you, so I played alone and waited my turn which never came. Did you know that whilst you lived you would teach me that that I think had hurt you most, the Greek in a Cypriot.....

Chapter 12

I now knew the flag and language were linked in a way that I'd never imagined. I also now knew that my near death experience with the TB had a bigger effect on myself than I had ever imagined. Come Wednesday I knew I wouldn't be able to face Greek classes. There was a terrible possibility in what I was thinking that I didn't want to face, but I already was. I telephoned my Greek, Greek teacher at her home and told her that I couldn't attend that night's class and didn't even think I'd be able to attend the rest of the beginners group at all. I was very upset.

"Suzi?"

"Yes"

"Hi it's Dimitri I started your Greek beginners class last week and I'm just phoning to ask if there's another course starting later in the year perhaps," I was just managing to hold it together.

"No there's not, is there a problem?" she asked. I really didn't want to explain anything.

"I've just been having a bad time recently," I told her.

"What is it dear what's the matter?" she could tell I was distressed.

"I wanted to learn Greek so that I could talk to my relatives," I was holding back the tears.

"And why can't you? What's wrong?"

"I just can't at the moment I'm too upset Suzi," I told her. I knew I wouldn't be able to hold back much longer.

"Nonsense of course you can," she replied. I knew she wouldn't, couldn't understand the thought that was going through my head.

"I can't Suzi not at the moment," I couldn't hold back any longer so I let it straight out.

"I think my grandfather may have committed suicide," I said. Tears were rolling now.

"No you mustn't say such a thing."

"I can't help it, I just can't, not now, it's the deceit," this was to my Greek teacher who I hardly knew. I was now weeping openly.

"What is this about Dimitri?" she asked concerned, I took a deep breath.

"Cyprus!" I let it out with a burst as I pulled myself together a little. "I just can't Suzi, not at the moment."

"Do you want to come over and talk about it, I have a friend she's Cypriot I can call her?"

"Maybe," I paused slightly. "Can I get back to you," I was taking control of myself now.

"You do that, if you want to talk then you come over and we will talk," she told me before we said our goodbyes.

Whether my grandfather actually committed suicide I will never know. But I have to say I believe that there is a strong possibility that he might have, I just imagined how unhappy he must have been. It was the language. I'd gone too far to turn back now, I found myself halfway through a book I'd rather not have started, yet I knew I had to finish. I now remembered the reason I was playing when my grandfather was teaching my sister and I to count. It was because my grandfather had started teaching me the alphabet first as we agreed. Alphabet first numbers next. I wanted to finish the alphabet of on that day, but instead he started teaching us to count, which wasn't what we agreed. Up to now I felt I'd been reading my grandfathers messages as I called them, fairly accurately and even now this one I try to put away, although I know there is a good possibility of it being true.

The language unites us. I think my grandfather took a look at what he was doing and what was happening in Cyprus and possibly realised that at eighty-six he might have been able to teach me the language as he was. But what guarantee that he would make it to ninety and or long enough to teach me how to use it. To pull me aside one day and tell me to hate no one, not even a Turk considering its implications on Cyprus. The realisation that my cousin was in Kyrenia during the time of the Greek coup made me see the difference it might have made personality wise. I grew up during the Vietnam War and remember the pictures vividly. All that my cousin told me he saw was Turkish phantoms bombing our villages. He told me of the black smoke that indicates napalm and I would hate those deemed responsible accordingly. The seeds of my hatred were given a good bed to grow in. Nothing did he tell me of Greek Cypriots being slaughtered by Greeks and Greek Cypriots but why should he. For by his own admission, he is a Greek and that's a language I just don't speak.

If you have underestimated the depth of the hatred then let me tell you. Yes, it is so deep that if I take my grandfathers other actions into account, then I do believe it's possible. This seemed a far from ordinary person in far from ordinary circumstances, in sixty-six the Akritas plan was published in a Greek Cypriot newspaper. That alone, after 63, I knew would have broken his heart. Cyprus remained in unrest until sixty-eight, by that time I think if my grandfather had decided to do it, he would have already made his mind up and he'd never have seen the changes that came after his death.

All I could say with honesty is that if he had of lived, possibly another three or four years then I know I would have taken enough of the language on board not to turn back. I even wondered if he knew how I would react to his death. I would have most probably joined the National Guard at some point as to my grandmothers' wishes and I dare say I would not be the same person I am today. Many people scoff at the suggestion, but I know it may be true, I know the importance of the language. Especially if I take into account the news reports that he might have been reading. I now realised that I would have a problem learning the language for any reason and would find it hard to even attempt to take it, knowing the symbolism of it on Cyprus and this is one of the saddest aspects of the situation I found myself in. I wanted to learn Greek to speak to my relatives but found the hatred that exists around them too much to absorb with it. At this point I was immersed in the Turkish propaganda. I was also deeply involved reading about the 74 coup whilst at the same time attempting to analyse what happened around Christmas 63 to the beginning of 64. So I felt I was very much trying to relive both periods, particularly 63, it was the massacres that concerned me and the Gibbons book was very informative. I knew that the massacres were committed by a very small minority, so I was trying to understand what the general majority must have been feeling and all from the notes of an eyewitness and our greatest critic.

I couldn't help but feel the language had been choked from my heart in the first place by resentment and just as I was discovering the most important reason to learn the language again. My love for my relatives, I felt the barrier that I put up way back as a child would still be there, living as I was in my work. I couldn't help but feel resentment, to what I felt was being offered with the language, and soon I knew I would return to Cyprus and face those I loved, to tell them.

I went to visit my Greek teacher. I felt I had to. I needed to know how all this could happen. I couldn't and didn't believe we were knowingly so hateful with such terrible consequences and talking to her I could understand how it all got so bad. If you asked me about British history I could give you a fair account of both its recent and distant past. As for Cypriot history, well there I had only the basic facts but I had a very reliable source to some of the relevant background for myself, which was my grandfather. My grandfather was born only three years after the end of the Ottoman rule in Cyprus and from his tolerance alone without his actions. I do not believe that he grew up hating Turks for any vengeful reason. If he'd been brought up with the hatred, I knew he would not have been the man he was. So when was the next big event in Cypriot history, along comes WW1.Granddad would have still been in his prime and Britain was at war with Turkey and so Cyprus was annexed by them, stolen according to my cousin, but annexed sounds understandable under the circumstances. This is the only time I can think of that my grandfather's intelligence training assuming as I am, now, that he was trained in that field might have served the British army. Unless of course there are those that might consider him a traitor to the British, but why? Divide and rule wasn't necessary at this time, the Cypriots would have been easy to rule. So I considered it likely that he possibly and probably spied against Turkey, if he was spying on Turks it was even possibly disguised as and living as a Turk. It made so much more sense. If he had lived with them, to spy on them, he would have lived as one of them, understanding their ways would account for so much.

I arrived at my Greek teachers' house and rang the doorbell. Thinking back it seems so long ago now but it was merely a month or so. Suzie let me in and we went through and sat in the conservatory where she brought us coffee.

"Firstly let me say that I think the Cypriot people should be free to decide there own future," she told me letting me know straight away that she would be as impartial as possible.

"I know Suzi, it's not you, but there are many others that just won't allow us to make our own choices," I thought I'd enlarge on that.

"They lie to us Suzi," I told her. "Look at this, it came out last year how am I supposed to look my relatives in the face knowing that they may be a party to keeping all this concealed." I passed the Genocide files to her. She'd never seen it before. I told her about the Akritas plan and of my other revelations, then I told her about my grandfather and my final conclusions, including the one I never wanted to face.

"I know what I said to you on the phone sounds incredible but I actually believe it could be true, I really do." I was glad for someone to talk to about it. I continued telling her.

"He never hated Turks Suzi and he was so different from the rest of my family, completely different. It's the timing of everything, it makes so much sense now," I said. I was upset and my smoking had increased. I lit up another cigarette before continuing.

"I really do believe that he may have committed suicide," I paused slightly I wanted to get off the subject but couldn't.

"The massacres would've broke his heart Suzie, and I don't think he could help but teach me what I know must have hurt him most." I was thinking of my personal notes. I snapped out of the emotional slide I was taking.

"No you shouldn't say that," she said trying to reassure me that he wouldn't.

"You know my mother thinks he didn't care at all, about who she married," I wanted to hear her opinion on that one. She snapped it back immediately.

"No I don't believe that's true Dimitri," she said sternly. "No I can not believe that at all! It's not their way!"

"I know that's what I've been telling her," I figured I'd tell Suzie more.

"Let me tell you what I know about him, " I went on to tell her what I knew about his life. Of how I believed that he was happy with an English husband for my mother because he wanted to find a way out of it, for at least some of his grandchildren. I then went on to tell her about the great differences between him and my grandmother. How I thought it was a last throw of the dice for him so to speak. I also told her how much I think he knew the language might have made a difference and I used my cousin as an example. Suzi knew of the slaughter of Greek Cypriots by the Greeks and Greek Cypriots.

"All he told me about was Turks napalming our villages, he never told me anything about this, no one ever has Suzi," I told her keeping it together.

"Can you imagine what that did to me and how much I hated them for it, the Turks."

"Greeks are brought up hating Turks," she responded gesturing with her hands that she herself was. Then added. "There's Constantinople," Suzi confirmed to me what I already knew.

"Yes! That's what I'm saying in twenty three Greece and Turkey had a big population shift, Orthodox to Greece and Muslims to Turkey," she dropped her head a little when I said it. No Greek like's to be reminded of that affair.

"We never Suzi we still lived with Turks, our paths took a very different route," I told her. It was an obvious difference. Suzi then went on to tell me about her school years. She is fifteen to twenty years older than myself.

"When I was at school in Greece every morning we would say a prayer for Cyprus," she put her hands together imitating those prayers.

"We would pray for the pearl," she revealed.

I looked at her filled with a sense of horror and at the same time I think she realised as I did, that they would, unknowingly, be praying to rid us of our Turkish community, with which we'd lived in peace with. And at the same time realising where such sentiments could lead.

"That's what I mean Suzi!"

Under Ottoman rule the Greeks were made to suffer like everyone else. After WW1 Constantine was restored to the throne but Constantinople wasn't returned and nor would it be. Only a few years previous in 1915 Greece was offered Cyprus if she entered WW1 on the side of the allies, she declined. Now although this part of history might seem to have little relevance to Cyprus, it should be mentioned due to its effect on the Greek people for one, but perhaps the most important reason. Is that historically, it is only just being recognised by most countries as the first genocide of the 20th Century. Between 1916 and 1921 over 3 million Christian Armenians and over a half a million Greek Orthodox Christians were massacred by the Turks in Asia Minor, the Turks new homeland, which might give some reasoning for what happened next.

In 1921 the Greeks invaded Turkey from Eastern Thrace and they did well at first and struck deep across much of Anatolia, but it was too deep. The Turkish forces pulled back tactically allowing the Greek lines to thin out. When the time was right, Attaturk attacked, dividing the Greek forces and pushing them all the way back to Smyrna. Which they then ransacked and burnt killing around 30,000 people. Many were forced to swim for their lives to the nearby moored ships, from which they watched Smyrna burn. Turkey would soon displace all the Greeks by religion from that area over to Greece, most of them in 1923. Over 1,500,000 in a population exchange by religion with around a half million Muslims, going to Turkey.

The effect of this is not to be underestimated. For the Greek people it was an absolute tragedy. With a large percentage of the population being removed from what was once, a treasured part of Greece. At this time as much as any, through our religion, language and history these mainland Greeks were still our people. The British government probably knew that in 1923 with the population exchange they had a stick of dynamite just waiting to go up. Light the blue fuse paper and all that hatred would have just been unleashed.

Here I have to be honest about something I feel is rather important. I'd never known about Eastern Thrace and the failed invasion of 1921 until this point in time. Well I've never studied or gone into modern Greek history with any depth at all, I could see now, how I'd simply been regarding Cypriot history. When I realised what happened I simply thought, Shit! Soon afterwards I went on my P.C. atlas and looked at the area concerned around Izmir. As I took it in I was attempting to imagine how it must have felt. Not getting Constantinople back but having Smyrna and eastern Thrace returned. Only to launch an attack against a country whose population was four times greater and well capable of addressing the situation. I couldn't believe it. I was absorbing our history there, both modern and ancient realising that that area would have kept its Greek heart throughout the occupation by the Ottomans, of course it had, it had been Greek since a long time before Christ. Then I couldn't help but be drawn to our related history in the area and the campaign of Alexander against the Persians. This campaign would have drawn Greeks from all our Ancient States together and the Greeks of Cyprus had gained their freedom from the Persians after giving assistance in the campaign at Issue and Tyre. After that many more would have joined him to continue the campaign against Persia. But it went way beyond that. It was the sheer depth of our history there. I leant on the desk with my elbows to rest my head in my hands and just stared at it all absorbing how long and how far back Greek history went in that area and thinking about what a disastrous move the invasion was. It took me a couple of minutes before I said to myself quite clearly and deeply.
"You stupid bastards!"

Back to Cypriot history. In the thirties Greek Cypriots rioted against high taxes.

The Turkish community never partook in the riots, which wouldn't have looked good for them. These riots were extremely serious at the time and a lot of damage was done, with British troops being recalled to address the situation. I'd heard a few people say that this was the start of the troubles between Greek and Turkish Cypriots, but when I did some basic research it wasn't hard to discover that the Cypriots were revolting against a high tax levy imposed on them by the British. Which sounds about right, it reminded me of the poll tax riots. And the American war of Independence was something to do with a tax riot. Well they do seem to be the most serious types of civil disorder. And all this time one still has to remember the rising bitterness that would have been felt for not only losing Thrace to Turkey. But resentment at the total upheaval of nearly one and a half million people from a land that they'd have inhabited for thousands of years, many of these migrants would feel resentment in their own country. The Cypriot people are a very religious people at heart and our church like the Greek Church has a character of its own. This funny enough would be strengthened due to the nature of the Ottoman rule as it ruled through regional religions, so ours thrived in that sense and its power increased accordingly. That's why I found there to be nothing unusual about our first president being an Archbishop. It seems perfectly natural. I could also start to understand what happened in sixty-three and on into sixty-four. As bad as it felt, I could understand it. I could also see how most people would have got wrapped up in it.

From fifty-five to fifty-nine, EOKA were fighting for Enosis, union with Greece and nothing short of it. We were so taken by the cause, in the schools, children in Cyprus as well as Greece would have been brought up to believe that it was not only our destiny, but also our right. We were fighting not only for our freedom, but also for the right to be unified again with the people with which we had such a long history. No one could have, or would have considered the consequences of such a cause alongside the resentment that would have built up in the Greek people over Thrace and we were of the Greek people. Except perhaps for the British. Even during the cold war, as good as the U.S.A may have been at gathering information, quite often when it concerned global affairs they'd bring it to the British for analyses, drawing on their experience from centuries of colonial rule. And I couldn't believe they weren't considering the possible consequences.

There seemed to be a lot of truth in what my cousin had said about British games and what games. They would have known that one day we would take the calling of and for Enosis. During the late fifties the terrorist campaign was fierce and the British knew that concessions would have to be made. The campaign would have gone beyond independence, as that wasn't what EOKA was fighting for, it was Enosis and nothing short of it. But there was the obstacle of our Turkish community. They would now block it any way they could.

But there was one important point that it took us a few years to realise. These weren't just Turks. These were Turkish Cypriots and they were home, as much as we fought them in the struggle, which I could now understand, they weren't going to leave. It meant a whole new ideal had to be incorporated that of an independent Cyprus with both communities, which had to be worked for. My grandfather wouldn't have known that things improved immensely in 68, the year of his death. But things settled down towards the end of the sixties. I could really understand now why Makarios is on top of the mountain. It would have been that hard a job leading us out of it, especially after Christmas 63. EOKA b became the cause of resentment by the late sixties not just from Turks, but also and possibly more so, from Greek Cypriots. I remembered that time well. We wondered if we could make it as a country, but we were giving it a damn good go. And there in those few years I saw something that made me proud. We were as a people trying to push back the bigotry and hatred that had been unleashed, to allow Cyprus to grow. I considered the consequences that the 74 coup had and I wondered if that was as much to blame for people not talking about any of it. The fact that Turkey partitioned our island was a bitter blow to most Cypriots and would have drawn all the people together and I could understand that. I knew it was harsh of Turkey to say the least, after the effort and change of the previous eleven years. I considered what a burden some Cypriots must carry. And the hatred is just perpetuated.

I left my Greek teacher glad for the talk. Now I could understand how it all got so out of hand, not that I liked it anymore. From my perception Enosis had to of become the force it was from the mid to late fifties onwards. I'm not saying the idea never existed before then, because it did, but not like it emerged in the fifties, then it had EOKA. It wasn't the union with Greece bit I was so concerned about. It was what had brought such a deep hatred. No matter how I looked at it, it was all history and so long ago, except now and our partition. I could understand a little more about how the bitterness would have naturally been there from the loss of Smyrna and I could also see the importance of the religious link. I had to now consider the nature of our religion.

The church is as much as any establishment, anti-Turkish and in its own way a little militant, which I found more disturbing, but I understood. Crete got its freedom from Ottoman rule soon after the British took over the administration of Cyprus. But towards the end of Ottoman rule in Crete the Cretans put up a fierce struggle for freedom, which would always be brutally put down by the Ottomans. Cretans and Cypriots were I knew very closely linked since our ancient past and the Minoans. I knew that after the earthquake that's believed to have seriously damaged their civilisation on Crete many migrated to Cyprus and were part of our history. Those strong links would have been cemented again and again and strengthened right to this day by long years of Byzantine union, indeed our history walks hand in hand with that of Greece. The strongest link throughout this time to present date would have been our language and religion despite our church being ecclesiastically autonomous.

I could now see the link between all that and our present problems. Our links were strong, very strong and with Enosis I believe had come the desire in some, for revenge, not just for Smyrna, or for three hundred years of Ottoman rule, but for anything any Greek ever had against a Turk.

Greece had taken a battering as far as its integrity had gone, over the previous five hundred years in particular. I'd heard Cyprus called the pearl of Greece before. As a child I'd look in an atlas and see how far it was from modern day Greece and that it was quite a way. On a bright summers day my grandfather would have been able to see the mountains of Turkey. I knew, as a child there was trouble going on in Cyprus. But as a child there would be little I'd be able to make out of it. But between 68 and 74 things were quite peaceful, which is why 74 came as such a shock

I may have known we were independent but I knew many, even here in England, considered her to be Greek as I did, but not one of the Greek isles as such. A typical conversation as a child would be.
  "Where are you from?"
  "Cyprus"
  "That's one of the Greek islands isn't it?"
  "Is it?"
  "Yeah it's Greek isn't it?" I'd know it was Greek but it wasn't a Greek isle in the same sense perhaps as Crete, as I felt was being suggested.
  "Yeah but it's a long way from Greece," I'd say. Trying to point out the obvious.
  "Yeah but you're Greek aren't you?"
  "Yes."
  "Yeah that's what I thought, it's Greek."
I wondered how much damage such thinking had done.

Now at this same time I'm building up a number of pictures in my mind of the situation both in 1963 and 1974 and of one man in particular, Makarios. One of the problems I could see I was having was that the author of the majority of the material I was using was so biased against Makarios, in most cases, I considered it blind bias. So why was I using it? For one, the author Harry Gibbons was very much on the scene in 63 and it would seem 74, but his depiction of Makarios the man in 63 and 64 confused me, his depiction of Makarios the man in 74 disgusted me. He genuinely expected the reader to believe that Makarios and the Greek Junta were fighting each other to see who would go on to exterminate the Turkish Cypriots and lead a new Byzantine Empire. It would make extremely uncomfortable reading for any Turkish Cypriots knowing Gibbons regards their extermination as being so important. But this propaganda wasn't aimed at the Turkish Cypriots, but more the Turkish general population and of course anyone that would pick up a copy of his book outside of Cyprus of course. If that wasn't ludicrous enough he was even suggesting the end purpose of all this was to invade Turkey and retake Constantinople, I'd never read anything so pathetic. The fighting was between Greeks and Greek Cypriots against Greek Cypriots. No Turks were touched before the landings and after the landings it still seemed the Junta's forces taking hostages, although I could imagine others doing so in fear of the Turkish army. After the Turkish Army pushed out EOKA b gunmen wiped out the three hamlets, but the slant that this author was putting on it was appalling. At the same time I'd been able to feel so many things about the calling, as I now put Enosis and the emotions and even the fear that would surround it. I was also coming to understand much of what happened in 63.

If I was feeling for anyone it was Makarios. The changes in the man between 1960 when he was the staunchest supporter of Enosis and 74, when he was its main obstacle were incredible enough. Yet throughout this period he was damned by his critics for being responsible for all that had happened. Something I felt I'd managed to do was understand some of the emotions surrounding it, the fear being one of them. It was the same fear I felt towards my cousin and godfather even, knowing that I would return to Cyprus and my cousin knowing I was writing this book. A fabricated fear perhaps. From the time I'd spent engrossed in our darkest moments, but it was a real fear. I was starting to get a feeling about Makarios in 63 now and I was certainly thinking he too felt that same fear. Let me tell you about the fear. When I first started this book the most prevalent emotion was anger and somewhere along the way I touched the fear. It's the fear that many lived under so many years but few can touch. Yet once touched, you know the fear. I used to tell people I was not anti-Semitic but against the Israeli state for its abuse of the Palestinian people. Whilst writing this book though I touched that fear from which I can only imagine Israel was born and now I understand. It's the fear of your neighbour, the fear of the unknown stranger that might be standing next to you. It's the fear you feel when you know your life has no meaning to some, to those that might feel that their cause is so great that your life has lost all significance in comparison. Now I truly understood what it meant to be Cypriot first and foremost. That's the sort of fear that Enosis invoked not only in the Turkish Cypriot community but far more so in the Greek Cypriot people. The statistics said it all. Harry Gibbons was too biased against Makarios to get anywhere near to the truth. This was important to me for more for than one reason. The main one at this point seemed to be that he was quite wrongly damning forever, a man he neither knew, nor could he possibly understand and that had far worse implications.

Even the situation, I knew, would be beyond Gibbons' comprehension. He neither understood the Greek Cypriot people, or how they would have reacted even, to the idea of a Turkish uprising. Nor the effect that Enosis or the feelings surrounding Enosis would have on a Greek or Greek Cypriot. The most important reason the Gibbons book mattered though is because Makarios is where he is. On the mountain and as far as most Cypriots are concerned a Patriarch of the island and I could see why. I was also starting to realise that one effect of his book, was that it would make it totally unacceptable for any Turk to consider a unified island, ever, Makarios was very wrongly being touted as the truth site suggested an Angel of Death.

Throughout this time I'd continued writing simply to bring the book up to date. And at the same time as I had this going through my mind there was my own family and my grandfather still to consider. I decided to telephone my father to talk to him about my mother and ask how she was feeling. He let me do most of the talking.

"Dad how's mum?" I asked.

"She's alright."

"Dad I know some of the things I've been doing and saying lately may seem strange and I know it's upset mum a little but it's helped me to understand a few things," my father was just listening.

"Can you imagine the low self esteem mum must have, thinking that granddad really didn't care," I told him. As hard as this may have been, it needed saying.

"She did everything she was supposed to and then thinks she was just fobbed off." I didn't consider how my father may have felt about this but I knew he understood.

"Dad I know what I'm saying sounds strange, but I think you fitted well with granddads thoughts at the time I really do," my father was still listening.

"You know I think he might have turned that gas tap himself," I said.

"No I wouldn't have thought so, he seemed alright."

"That's not what I'm saying dad, it's just the way things were in Cyprus in the early sixties and then the Akritas plan gets published," I sighed. "It would have broke his heart."

"Yeah but he wouldn't have known about it, would he," my father replied. He was thinking of the quiet man he knew. After everything else he did I found it hard to believe he wasn't keeping in touch with the situation at home. I remembered waiting for him on the steps of mountain house. I replied cynical to his suggestion.

"I don't know dad, the British press would have been full of it," I was thinking of how he'd disappear a lot of mornings. "So tell me where was it he used to go for a few hours most mornings?"

"For a walk," my dad replied. I found that idea amusing.

"Dad he was over eighty years old, eighty year old men don't go for walks for two or three hours." I think my father could see what I was saying. I felt sure he was smiling.

"He was a very shrewd man," my father muttered.

"He needed to be dad," I was smiling now.

"Dad one last point, mum says granddad never made a will and when I asked Yannis if he had the will and the papers for the land, he said he did," I paused. "One of them is being less than honest with me," I just had to ask.

"Can you tell me which?"

"The latter," my father replied.

"Ok thanks," I put the phone down and pondered what he told me for a moment. So was my father saying there was no will or what, I wasn't quite sure I pressed the redial.

"Dad that last question never answered anything for me," I was going to be more direct.

"Look I know what's done is done, but we know that some relatives came down from London after granddad died and mum had to sign some papers, what papers were they?" I asked.

"I don't know," he replied. This is what we'd heard too often.

"Well why did she have to sign then?"

"So they could get the land," he said it as simply as that.

"What do you mean dad?" I wanted more now.

"I don't know, there was no will and they said it goes to the youngest don't it?" my mother was the youngest.

"I don't know does it?"

"Well it's what I was told," he replied.

"I'm taking it for granted that you were left out of it"

"Yeah"

"Dad I don't know of any such reason as to why it should go to the youngest," I didn't know whether Cypriot law covered it. I knew under British law it wasn't true.

"I don't know, it's what I was told," he said.

"Maybe in Cyprus, but not here, I don't know, either way it's not nice to think about dad."

I put the phone down. Overnight the realisation would sink in, that my mother would have signed away at least my grandfathers' home, if not his farm that night. Something she could never admit to us. I considered what I'd already heard as far as my family went. I didn't know which, whether it was the farm or the house as they were on different plots or both. Nor would my mother as she could neither read nor write at the time. I now felt very sad for my grandfather indeed.

Whilst all this was going on I was still considering Gibbons interpretation of 74 and more importantly the symbolism attached to it. Makarios lies high on the mountain, as a symbol to the island and I now knew he deserved to be there. But Gibbons was building up a picture of him both in 63 and yet again in 74 as some kind of demon, like some sort of Anti-Christ. I wrote a letter immediately to the T.R.N.C. I was angry about the Truth site and at the same time I was drawing more conclusions. I wrote personally to Miss Dorak, as it was them that had supplied the book in the first place so I regarded them as being the influence and responsible for the web site. I told her that I took extreme offence at the title given to Makarios and at the same time I considered the man was very much misunderstood by them. I also told them that he was a platform that I myself might fight for. That was not something I wrote lightly.

I was so far through a book that I'd written more about myself, I knew, but in anger at the perpetuation of the hatred on Cyprus, by Greek Cypriots and Greeks and despite everything, all I could really feel towards Greeks was nothing more than annoyed. Especially those that were involved in the 74 coup, which I now felt sure, had to include my cousin. I wondered how many of the missing 1600 men that were lost back in 74 were lost to Greek hands. Heroes to our island and our flag, yet lying in unmarked graves because those responsible would feel too ashamed for bringing the Turks. It felt hard to justify what they did, but it was a loyalty to a different Cyprus, a Greek Cyprus, like Crete perhaps. Fighting so many who were Cypriot first and foremost. I would have fought my cousin for that difference in beliefs, to the death if need be. Yet it would have always been our affair and the worst I could feel towards any of them was still simply, annoyed. I'd started to understand how most Greeks felt about Cyprus. I felt I could also understand what the majority went through in Cyprus in 63. I'm not saying the massacres never happened, but nearly all Greek Cypriots I knew were ignorant of them, to most, I guess, it would have been a last throw for Enosis, for many a rally of force against the rebellious local Turks. When I read of Turkish flags going up, I had to smile, now if that sounds sick, then it's not. I had to envisage myself back in Nicosia in 63, there're people fighting Turks all around me, I would have been ignorant of the massacres, but remember we've just had three years of unbroken peace and suddenly there's fighting. All this continues and then some pillock goes and fly's a blood red Turkish flag. Now I hope to be the mildest of men, but I know seeing that flag go up would make me reach for a gun. I don't know what it is, but I knew that most would feel the same way and as soon as I knew that Turkish flags were being risen, let alone being risen over some historical Byzantine monuments a short time after the troubles' started. I knew that many, like myself, would have been reaching for a weapon. I hardly found it surprising it got as bad as it did, particularly with Greek mainland troops joining in and the influx of mainland Greeks. I'd certainly stopped pointing the finger of blame though. Even the Greek hatred itself, I now knew to be more of a terrible bitterness born out of a deep resentment that we had for the Turks.

What was upsetting me most though, was that Makarios seemed to be wrongly getting the blame for just about everything. When it was him the people followed, yet despite 74, the worst I still felt towards Greeks was annoyed. I could tell by now that we'd been partitioned for 63 and perhaps for our failure to acknowledge the terrible incidents that occurred and I guess that's what I felt most annoyed about.

I soon telephoned the publishers of the Genocide files, Charles Bravos. I'd already contacted them to ask for permission to use material for reference and spoke to Zeki a Turkish Cypriot who worked there. I was familiar with him and he was aware of my writing project, as I so often referred to it.

"Hi Dimitri I passed your request through for you," he was talking about the copyright request. Now I like Zeki, he is soft spoken and as angry as I was I never wanted to take any anger out on him.

"Thanks Zeki, I'm phoning about that," I said before telling him what I was feeling. "Zeki I don't agree with Harry Gibbons interpretation of people and events in 74, especially Makarios"

"You don't have to" I already knew that but I guess I wanted some feedback on it.

"Zeki it's his portrayal of Makarios," I told him. "As if him and Ioannides were really fighting to lead some new Byzantine Empire, that's bullshit!" Zeki knew I wasn't angry with him. I continued.

"It was his people fighting Enosis Zeki, my people, our people even!" I was getting emotional but I continued.

"Your people weren't even touched until after the landings," I let Zeki respond.

"I know, I know." It is undisputed that nothing more than taunts were thrown at the Turkish Cypriots before the Turkish military landed. We went on to talk a bit more about Cyprus and how much different everything could have been or should have been, it's always a heartbreaking conversation to have and felt no better this time round.

Shortly after this I went over to see my parents not mentioning the conversation with my father or anything about the will. I just wanted to be close to my family for a while. I spent a bit of time there and whilst leaving, my sister arrived in her car. I stopped my car and let my window down so I could talk to her.

"Hi Gina I've been talking to dad about the land," she knew what I meant.

"Oh yeah."

"He's told me Mum did have to sign papers for them to get the land, don't mention it though, mum will probably get upset about it."

"Ok," she replied.

"You know I'll never know why he wouldn't finish the alphabet off with me that time, I guess he must have thought you'd finish it with me," I told her. Thinking that would have put my mind at rest. My sister looked at me a little surprised.

"I couldn't have"

"Why?" I asked.

"I didn't know it!"

Chapter 13

Writing this book has been an amazing experience for myself, amazing and painful. Much of the pain I've kept to myself. So often feeling that I was writing a book that was going to be so critical of my own people. When all I really sought was an end to the bitterness and the hatred for these very same people. I never realised the strength or the importance of the first book of the Genocide files, Peace without Honour, re-released in this trilogy in 1997 and I've tried starting this chapter many times such are the emotions that it invoked in me. I guess the only way to do it is as honestly as I can, as I've attempted to be every step of the way on my passage, not caring who I would have to write against, just as long as it wasn't to damage the status of Makarios. I actually felt certain that I'd have to write at least a few bad things about him, but despite any faults he may have had as a man, I come through this to be his strongest supporter. Now here I have to point out that as much as I know that I'm coming into contact with a lot of propaganda and that so much about Cyprus is propaganda. I do not regard this book as anyone's propaganda, this is a journey for myself and I've been writing this book on the longest part of it.

At this point though I really couldn't work out why I'd written the book. I'd actually written up to chapter twelve and all I felt was annoyed, yet I knew that my book had some sort of purpose but I just never knew what it was. So I went back to reading the Gibbons book, Peace without Honour, for the second time, but I must point out here the first time was in haste and quite plainly the man was starting to piss me off. I mean really starting to piss me off, more and more. But contained in his book were so many intriguing facts that I'd never heard or considered, nor had anyone else I knew. Like I said this man was on the scene particularly in 63 and it was these facts that I was interested in. To myself they were starting to lead to something. I wasn't sure at first where it was all going but like I said, there some very intriguing snippets in the Gibbons book, revealing even. His last book of the trilogy 'The Genocide files' itself, I knew was so off the mark that I'd written to the T.R.N.C telling them what I thought about it. In the first book though, Gibbons' interpretation of Makarios is still blindly biased to be polite, but the facts he details were leading me to an intriguing possibility based on his facts, and you know what I'm like about possibilities. Before I got there though I got somewhere else. Someone was having a bloody good go at defining the difference between a Greek and a Greek Cypriot. And I did not like the difference one bit. To say it pissed me off is a complete understatement, stuff it, I felt like kicking the S.O.B to death. I've calmed down a bit now, although I still feel like giving him a good kicking at times. I probably will whilst your reading this. But here's the ironic part, I actually wrote to Gibbons via his publishers. A nice letter thanking him for so many details, boy was my head somewhere else. I hadn't realised at that point what he was doing and what book I was reading.

This is to Harry Scott Gibbons you couldn't return my letter could you Mr Gibbons, because according to your book, I don't exist! I am a butcher! A butcher of women and children! A tormentor of Turkish men, women and children! I can only do evil deeds to these same people and that's all I will ever do, as will my children and their children according to Harry Gibbons. His book damned my entire race and myself forever. It may not be important these days when it seems anything can get published. But it was very important where and when Gibbons had his book published, I got so pissed off I went straight to the back page and was horrified. His book Peace without Honour was refused publication in Britain in the late sixties, so he took it to Turkey, where coincidentally, he'd been working those past few years. Harry Scott Gibbons, Fleet streets best known Middle-Eastern reporter. It may not have had a major effect on the politics although if it affected the people it would certainly affect the politics. But it wasn't so much the politics I was after at this point, it was the perpetuation of the hatred and I'd found one of its main sources. Harry Scott Gibbons, may your name be damned on Cyprus forevermore as you damned my race to every Turkish heart that read your publication in the late sixties and the early seventies.

Almost three months since my last visit I find myself returning to Cyprus on the 17th November, again it was booked at short notice. I thought at first to finish the book in the company of my own people, but of course it wasn't to write at all. I was returning to Cyprus to live these last chapters. To my final conclusion and to the end of my own personal passage, not only into our history but also within myself.

I flew out to Cyprus on an Air Malta scheduled flight with a decent sized travelling bag, but the only clothing it contained was a change of shirt, a few pairs of socks, some underwear and a book, there was little room for anything else. The flag that I left the country with in a box in August was returning with me in a bag. The flight left Heathrow around mid-day. I caught my connecting flight in Malta and found myself sitting alongside an elderly gentleman that I'd sat next to on the Heathrow flight. It now felt safe to assume he was Cypriot, at the about the same time as he would have been making the same assumption of myself. After that it felt easier to strike up a conversation and I told him of my book and that as much as I was writing about myself, I was also writing about Cyprus. Until now I'd never considered that my lack of Greek and the fact that English was my native language might discourage people from saying what they felt about our problems and their opinions.

"You know the British are to blame with their divide and rule," he said in a resentful manner but without anger only forcibly, which wasn't needed.

"Oh I know," I told him. That's one thing that's become clear. I now, more than most, know how much trouble they've gone to, aiding in the partitioning of Cyprus.

I landed at Larnaca around 8pm and nervously waited for my bag. Just recently two Israeli spies had been caught spying in a very sensitive military area of Cyprus. Israel has a defence pact with Turkey which also includes the exchange of information and the arrivals hall was desolate and with my in bound flight arriving from Malta, it made the possibility of a stop and search at Customs far more likely. My large Kipling travel bag appeared on the carousel. I didn't wait for it to come round to where I was standing I walked round and hauled the heavy bag on to a trolley that I was using. I then proceeded to customs not knowing what to expect. As I turned the corner I could see it couldn't have been worse and knew that I'd at least be stopped. Normally there may be one customs officer, perhaps sitting back on a chair; tourist flights from England wouldn't get much attention. This time there were three uniformed officers there, two of them emptying the contents from a brief case of a respectable looking middle aged man onto the counter, the third officer, at sighting me, immediately approached me in a manner which simply made me think, Shit!

"Where have you flown from?" he asked sternly.

"Malta," I quickly realised that was the wrong response. "London via Malta."

"Passport please," now as much as I didn't want to get into trouble, I couldn't help but feel amused. I was imagining his expression if he discovered that just about all I was carrying in my large bag was a Greek national flag. He glanced at my passport catching my first name.

"Where you from?" he asked. I knew what he meant by that question.

"Ayios Amvrosios"

"Ayios Amvrosios eh?"

"Nai," I replied in Greek to which he continued his questioning in Greek. I immediately but politely broke in with,

"I don't speak Greek"

"Where are you staying in Cyprus?"

"In Limassol with relatives"

"Ok," he said as he handed my passport back and motioned me on at the same time. I took it and joyfully proceeded through the hallway. My spirit was soaring but I never started skipping until I was out of sight.

"God I love Cyprus," I said aloud. And skipped all the way to the taxi rank.

I arrived in Limassol earlier than expected and it was all hugs and kisses with my godparents. My godfather seemed particularly warm. I wondered at first if he knew about my book or whether it was the twelve-year-old Scotch Whisky that I'd brought him, although I knew he was just pleased to see me. It didn't seem to matter though. The book had taken somewhat of a change in direction. My main concern was now the truth. I felt I'd been merciless about where I was looking and how I was looking, but I now knew the direction it was taking, as sure as I knew its purpose. I told my godmother that I would be getting a hire car the next day and going around to Polis for a few days, returning on Sunday to catch up with my cousin, Spyros. The night was clear and I sat up late on the balcony after eating a prepared meal that my godmother had made. It was a beautiful starry night. I thought I was going to be entertained by the expected meteor shower but I never saw one. I went to bed late and when I slept it was deep, it just took me a long time to get there.

I had so much going through my mind. I started this book out of anger at the perpetuation of the hatred in Cyprus thinking it was all one way but I now found myself a victim of it. As angry as I was though I'd brought the Gibbons book with me and was continuing to make my own personal analysis of the 63-64 period. I had come to some sort of an understanding, not just to many events of 63-64 but to the people and the situation even. The majority of people fighting in 63 would have been fighting for what they considered a just and noble cause, now that may sound too much for some and I understand it. But I also understand why in 1960 Makarios still held the ideal of Enosis, union with Greece, I've started to understand that calling, I've even felt it. Now it was during the second half of the fifties the campaign turned to violence. This violence was aimed at the British and anyone that was known to be collaborating in anyway and that would include washing floors for them. This would be enough to be considered a legitimate target, now as harsh as it may sound, it was a terror campaign, it had already proven successful elsewhere in the world and now it was our turn.

I knew what the Turkish politicians wanted by now, and I know what British attitudes are like when it comes to giving up certain possessions. The two sovereign bases on Cyprus aren't mere military installations, to the British Forces they're part of their institution, like a possession, nearly three hundred square kilometres of Cyprus, wouldn't like to give it up. Up to nineteen sixty (and even in nineteen seventy-four) more Greek Cypriots were killed than British or Turks put together during EOKA and then later EOKA b's campaign. These are major considerations to consider where I'm going. I'm considering Britain's options when Suez fell and considering the Russian-Egypt link, Cyprus and the listening posts on Troodos would have been of even more importance to the British. Now they are fighting a civil war in their very last foothold in the whole area. Gibbons states that Cyprus lost its strategic value to the British after the fall of Suez, I only assumed my father was in Cyprus because I knew that he was in Suez, he never did go via Cyprus though. These bases are just regarded like possessions. Well before this time Britain would have already returned a number of Greek islands to Greece and with their own experience in Cyprus they would have more than a good understanding of both the Greeks and the Turks.

So they're fighting a civil war that they know they will eventually lose, it was inevitable. One man that was going to ensure this, Makarios. Now I'm not much of one for fanatical religious leaders, which is how I know some people regard him. Makarios may have been just a fanatical clergyman to some, but that same clergyman, would have for well over the last fifteen hundred years, and that's a gross underestimation been the real power behind the Greek Cypriots. No matter who, thought, they were in control of the island, since the Byzantine period, the real power behind the people would have always been the church and that power would only be strengthened by Ottoman rule. So particularly after the EOKA campaign his role as leader of Cyprus would be a natural one to the people. Having said that I believe Makarios was as good a statesman as one could get on the world arena and considering the strength of the religion in Cyprus, who would have been better placed to lead us, he was a man of his time. I think he got conned though, as did most other Greek Cypriots, myself included.

Ok, the British banish him but to no avail. But while he's away Kutchuk, who was at this time the Turkish Cypriot leader, submits a plan to divide Cyprus in 1956 and then in 57 the T.M.T or Volkan or Volcano as it translates had established itself on Cyprus. Now I didn't know too much about this before but their purpose from Turkish sources were to,
1: To fill the gap in the Turkish defences.
2: To unify all Turkish underground forces.
3: To co-ordinate their activities and to form ties with sympathisers in Turkey. All this was to achieve,
4: To Inspire confidence in the Turkish Cypriots. These silly sods became known as the fighters and also to join these ranks would be British trained Turks who were used against the Greeks in the EOKA campaign. I was starting to get an understanding of the resentment to the fighters as they were called. These men were being described from 1963 as being the Turkish saviours. I can't help thinking now that they brought it on their own people.

Well set the scene, Cyprus 1957 and your EOKA happily fighting the British to get your freedom and that is how Enosis was regarded. The Turks were simply asked to step aside and to stay out of it, but you look over the road and a year after Kutchuk submitted his plan to partition Cyprus, there's the Turks starting their own militia for no reason, except for the four given above perhaps. But when you haven't caused them any problems and considering the nature of your own campaign, I think the division's well and truly started, worst than that though. They wanted to partition the island off for themselves and that would have been so badly resented and yet feared at the same time by the Greeks, considering the strength of their Turkish kin.

The whole time this would have been going on the British would have been working on their own possibilities and probabilities and their own agenda.

So Britain's fighting a losing war. What to do, what to do to secure those bases. Make a deal? The Macmillan Plan, of course! In June 1958 in the absence of Makarios the British Prime Minister Harold Macmillan proposed a seven-year partnership scheme of separate municipalities, the Greeks rejected it outright claiming it to be tantamount to partition, which it was. But by December 58 it was to lead to Greeks and Turks (not Cypriots) talking about an independent Cyprus for the first time. Makarios was brought back into the talks, which would eventually lead to the treaty of Alliance and Guarantee and for the British their Treaty of establishment, by which they'd keep their bases. Makarios only went along with these talks in the first place in exchange for the abandonment of the Macmillan plan. That might do for starters, but the only problem with deals is that they can be broken and guarantee nothing. So, one solution and one possibility I'm seeing arise would be to make a deal and formulate a plan on the basis of what's known.

What are we working with here, we've got eighty-three percent of the population making a demand that the British already knew the other seventeen-percent of the population are against. But also take into account that this seventeen-percent minority have a very powerful and friendly ally, of course Turkey, only some eighty kilometres away.

Now Makarios is condemned because as he's going through the process of signing this treaty he is also proclaiming all the way, that not only his aim, but the hearts desire of the Greek Cypriots, was still Enosis, loud and clear he's shouting it out and that's a fact. So the Makarios government from day one denounced this treaty as unworkable. So why did he sign it? He later states to stop the bloodshed and when you consider that most of the bloodshed during the 55-59 campaign was Greek Cypriot that might be a good enough reason. Now when I looked at the situation closer I could see it might be unworkable. Most of the Turkish places in the municipalities couldn't be filled through lack of education and the right to veto could have been seen as good enough reason to consider the treaty totally unworkable. The treaty allowed for a Greek president and a Turkish vice-president who both had the right of veto, now I only said could be seen as a good enough reason. That's exactly what I believe the British wanted.

The treaty of guarantees allowed for any of the three participating states involved, Greece, Turkey or Britain to act to ensure the independence, territorial integrity and the security of the republic of Cyprus by preventing 'direct or indirect Enosis or partition or annexation' by any of the three guarantor states.

I'm trying to work things out. In 63 things got bad, as much as I can understand the time, let me tell you things got bad. Most Greek Cypriots would have had no idea of the atrocities, yet something was going on and it all seemed to be under British auspices. They knew, they knew all about the massacres and the atrocities. It was the three years of total peace beforehand that did it though. I knew they'd made a deal by 1960 with Makarios to allow him to act in 1963, which would include the treaty of establishment for themselves. But a two faced deal. With one purpose, but two directions, their one purpose would be to keep the Sovereign bases. They would then be able to achieve this if Enosis was ever brought about or more likely if Turkey partitioned the island off, either way the results would be the same for the British. They'd made too many mistakes as far as I was concerned for it not to be true; I could imagine the conversation along the lines of.
"Your Beatitude (as they called him) we know you desire Enosis," and this is the crutch. "Of course we know Cyprus is Greek." Yes I could imagine the conversation going along those lines.
"But we do have a problem, we seem to have been left with these damn Turks," nothing meant. Now if you're thinking that's bias, no I don't think so. They'd know Greek attitudes and Makarios was Greek. So Makarios says,
"What do you suggest, they are getting a bit loathsome, that ugly man Kutchuk wants to partition our country, damn Turks!" he does actually look like Herman monster.
"Why couldn't they go home when the rest of the Turks went?" meaning the population exchange.
"Well we're British sir! We couldn't be seen to be partaking in anything like that, but we do have a plan for you." It certainly is my theory.

Now in October of 1961 Makarios wanted a fully integrated Cypriot army. But Kutchuk the Turkish leader refused and used his constitutional vote to do so, as he favoured separate military companies which doesn't read well at all for a united island. After that time the Turkish TMT and EOKA went back into training, during which time the Turks were known to be importing weapons for whatever they intended. Now by Easter of 63 it's well known that Makarios has started training for Christmas. This is one bit I don't understand, they start training and preparing for Christmas as early as Easter yet the British show no sign of acknowledging what is going on, I really can't believe that. We are talking about something that a large number of the general population were involved in and one reason I can't believe the British never knew is because of their close links to the Greek Cypriot community. It also fits in nicely with some later developments. A big consideration to take into account was Greece, big setback perhaps, on November the 23rd Greek Prime Minister Papandreou stated that his government had no intention of overturning the Zurich and London agreement (That was the treaty of alliance and guarantee). Why though I don't know, as it seems totally contradictory to what he does after Christmas when he'd be pouring troops in to the country to do exactly that. Which gives me the impression that they, as well as the British were playing games. Now on the 30th November Makarios puts in his 13point plan to amend the constitution, things are bugging me. Patterns were building up which were leading to possibilities that I had to consider. They're the sort of things that were keeping me awake, I felt like I was sifting through so much.

The next morning I awoke late, I went straight outside for a cigarette. My godmother was in the kitchen.

"Kale mera," I said brightly as I strolled past.

"Where are you going?" my godmother enquired.

"For a cigarette," I replied.

"No you're not!" my godmother was ruthless. "Get back in there and have a wash first! Then you'll have some breakfast! And then you can have a cigarette!" I had a big smirk on my face all the way to the bathroom. I returned after washing and ate some toast washed down with coffee before smiling at my godmother and telling her,

"Now I'm going for a cigarette."

My godmother brought me some more coffee outside and we started to chat, funny enough the first topic of conversation was my uncle in Australia. Now this is my mothers' full brother and the relative that came down from London after my grandfathers' death to encourage my mother to sign over whatever she signed. I actually like the man very much, as I do all my uncles, but my mothers' two full brothers are both close to us. I'd already decided that there was probably little wrongdoing as far as the will went, or if there was I wasn't too concerned now, at worst I figure they'll be someone else donating towards my parents retirement home. I told her about my book and to my surprise, she never seemed surprised.

"What are you writing about?" she enquired.

"Myself, Cyprus," I didn't quite know how to explain it.

"It's about yourself?"

"Yes," I replied. My godmother made a slight face not showing her feelings either way, but an autobiography can hardly be commented on.

"Why are you back so soon?" she asked.

"I said I'd come back around now anyway I like it here off-season," I told her. The conversation progressed more. I'd phoned my godmother up before I arrived and told her that I wanted to pay a revisit to the tomb of Makarios, I hadn't considered the next suggestion but it was to make me think of staying there a little longer.

"If you want, I can telephone the monastery and book you a room for a couple of days?" it's normal for people to stay at the monastery, especially Kykkos with its mountain air.

"Maybe, it's a good idea," I told her. "But if I do, I'll go on Monday, so I'll decide on Sunday," there was no need to commit myself this early.

"Ok, you want to get a hair cut before you go?" she asked. That was right out of the blue.

"No," I said a little surprised. It wasn't so much the haircut that concerned me. I'd been thinking about it, but the prospect of it being cut on Cyprus did nothing to thrill me.

"Why not?" she asked. I didn't know what was getting into her.

"I don't mind having it cut but the girl that cuts my hair is in England," I told her. Nikki had returned home before heading off to Asia. I think my godmother took that as a hint that I'd let anyone cut my hair.

"I can do it now!" she said excitedly. I could see how she felt about the prospect, she opened her hands out as if to say why not. I hadn't seen her like this for some time although I found it amusing.

"I know. I've been thinking about it, but not now," I said, but not sternly enough.

"But you should if your going to drive around Cyprus, people will think you are a spy or a drug smuggler or something." Now I knew my godmother was being serious here. But I didn't think about it for long, I wasn't carrying any illegal substances and I couldn't imagine many spies driving around with nothing in their bag but a Greek flag twice the size of the penalty area of a football pitch in their bag. I was smiling but I'd decided.

"I don't think so," I said it sternly. "No, no way!" she seemed amused by my response. She knew she could push me where I wouldn't let others.

"Why haven't you got married yet?" she asked. I really wasn't expecting that, now she'd got a little more serious.

"I don't know," I told her. "I guess I've just never met the right person at the right time."

"You never met the right person before?" she asked surprised.

"Oh I've met the right person before," I said with a smile. "Just not at the right time, it wouldn't have been right," she saw I was thinking back a little.

"Ok!" she said as she shrugged her shoulders. I enjoyed this side of the relationship with my godmother. As old as I was it was nice to know she would still be concerned with such things as my hair, my smoking and of course marriage. I went off that afternoon to get a hire car that was to cost me fifty pounds for a week. Returning shortly after, passing on route my favourite bar which was getting a refit as many seemed to be at the time, so I was quite pleased about my plans to go straight round to Polis. The rest of the day was spent around the house and on the veranda. The weather was beautiful for the time of year being in the mid-twenties every day. That night I slept a little earlier and woke eager to be on my way but in no rush to leave, if you can understand that. I washed before appearing for breakfast, which I ate before taking leave for my cigarette.

"That's better for you it isn't it?" my godmother said. She was commenting on the pre-cigarette routine. I nodded my head, as I had to agree with her. My smoking had increased dramatically whilst writing at home.

"Where are you going today?" she asked already knowing the answer.

"Polis," I replied.

"Ah, you like Polis?" she already knew that too.

"Yes I do, it's nice and quiet compared to Limassol," I told her. My godmother held a finger up and went into the house before returning with an old map of Cyprus. I could see the date on it was 1974. She looked for Polis which was quickly found, she laid the map out on the table and immediately started to reminisce on an island tour she made herself before partition. Taking in Kyrenia and Nicosia, before going on to Paphos.

"It was wonderful," she declared. Going all dreamy. I seldom saw my godmother talk like this, she gently threw her arms out as she carried on with her tale.

"I felt so young and free, it was really beautiful," she told me. She spoke of the strangers she met along her way that soon became friends and I was enjoying hearing her recall with affection her memories of both the people and the land. She turned the map over and started reading some Greek literature on the back. She seemed surprised at what she was reading.

"I didn't know it tells the history of Cyprus on the back!" she said reading little bits out to herself as she went.

"You know on Crete they speak the same dialect of Greek as on Cyprus?" she asked me seeming surprised, I wasn't.

"It doesn't surprise me," I smiled shaking my head. Of course many Cretans were on Cyprus in 1974 fighting for our country and few would have given so much for us. By this time I was standing and leaning back on the low wall.

"You know if you want to go north Dimitri you can," she said finishing with. "You have a British passport," I wasn't expecting that, but I'd made my mind up there.

"No Marianna, you know I want to go," I told her. "But I'll wait, I'm not signing the Denktash agreement, not now not ever." I now knew why my uncles resented Denktash so much. Not only was he a force behind the Turkish fighters. He'd been banished from the island in 64 to return a few years later to help form the administration that they now call the TRNC. I knew what I'd been thinking so I told her,

"Maybe I'll cross over at Dhakelia in the spring," she seemed more bemused than surprised. The border with the British sovereign bases isn't patrolled like the line.

"But you'll get arrested, they'll put you in prison!"

"I know, I don't care," I shrugged my shoulders. "It wouldn't be for long," I said.

"I don't understand, how will you see anything if you get arrested?" she asked.

"I'll see enough," I smiled. "I'll look south to the mountains and north to the sea, that'll be enough for now," she thought about it for a brief moment then said.

"Ok, more coffee!" changing the subject immediately.

"One more before I go," I told her. I drank my last coffee and set off with my bag.

I stopped by on my uncle Georgio before heading off proper. He didn't seem too good. Not unwell, just as one might expect to find someone after they'd said goodbye to their lifelong companion. It had been three months since Marie's death and it showed that he was missing her. I thought of the tales I'd heard about whales, swans and albatross that pair up for life and when their partners are lost, they too often find themselves lost and soon deteriorate, perhaps in a quest to join their loved ones. It seems natural to myself, sad but natural. I stopped for some early lunch. I couldn't help but show my happiness at being around such loved ones, the language was still a big problem though. After lunch I was on my way around the coast to Polis via Paphos and of course past Aphrodite's rock. It was such a pleasant day and I'd felt fortunate enough for the sunshine and the warmth, but I had an even warmer feeling for just being back in Cyprus. I parked up on the road near the rock and walked down with my camera. I thought about climbing it but decided not to, it would have been easy enough, but I was thinking about getting to Polis with plenty of time and happy to just walk around the base. The idea of the flag being there hardly bothered me at all now. "Stone of the Greek," I said allowed as I looked up. I guess it's a sign of how much the Turkish propaganda has changed me. At the same time I found myself asking if I'd do it again and I knew I would. It might be in our history but I can't help but think of Greek flags over Cyprus as an impediment on our future.

Gibbons was getting everywhere. One thing I saw early though was that the British showed complicity to the massacres of 63, which lead me to ask more serious questions of them. The British schoolteacher who witnessed the Kykkos School massacre, where 150 of the 700 hostages were shot on Christmas day. Was flown out straight away by the British High Commission. The author Gibbons seems to find nothing wrong with requesting her to come forward, as he does through his book and web site. He really is that stupid. The question I'm asking is why the British High commission doesn't have her necessary details to forward? They took a report and flew the woman out, after she'd witnessed the massacre and the removal of the bodies, yet have no records available to enable anyone to trace this woman.

This sort of thing would have terrible consequences and I have to write of it as it must be brought up. So let me quickly tell you what I know about them. 150 of the hostages were from Kumsal and 550 of them from Omorphita, taken to Kykkos School from what I can gather by Greek mainland army trucks. Christmas day 150 of them were picked out and shot and the bodies removed and hidden. If suppression of the truth and if massacres of this nature were allowed to go unchallenged by us as a democracy. We could never be rightly considered that by a percentage of what we now accept would be a part of the population of Cyprus, the Turkish Cypriots. Yeah I'm not giving up on this Cypriot bit, I'm suppressing a very angry Greek but I'm not giving up. I knew the British would take that as a consideration when they decided to conceal the truth. I can't help but believe though, that if that was the case and the facts are facts, then what else would they do to make the situation look so bad.

The same day as this massacre took place Orek who was representing the Turks was in a meeting with Clerides at the British high Commission to discuss a cease-fire. When it seems Turkish air force jets buzzed Nicosia and the High Commission at 200 feet, that was such good timing, they were soon to be joined by Makarios and the Commissioner. During this meeting it's revealed that the hostages are at Kykkos School and it's then announced that the Turkish mainland contingent that was permanently based on the island had moved onto the Nicosia-Kyrenia road. All this would rattle the Greeks a little and here a cease-fire is agreed on, but only on principal, because Orek needs to confirm it with Kutchuk, the Turkish Cypriot leader and the islands' vice president. Now here's another bit of interesting insight. When Orek and Kutchuk discuss it the same day they decided to postpone any cease-fire until after the hostages are returned. It's not right! I thought about it, there's fighting all over the area and they will not call a cease-fire until hostages are returned. It's going to be a lot bloody harder to get the hostages released whilst everyone's fighting around them as opposed to calling a cease fire and getting them out, something's not right.

Straight after that meeting at the British high Commission, Ankara Radio (Turkey) announces a cease-fire. Adding that, the Turkish and Greek mainland contingents would be placed under control of General Peter Young from the

British Sovereign bases and would jointly supervise the cease-fire. Now apparently the BBC had been making cease fire announcements right through the Christmas period, the BBC is as much a tool as any. It doesn't seem right that the whole place is going up and not only the Turks are taking their time over agreeing to a cease-fire but the British are constantly announcing them. What I'm noticing now, is that the only ones that are doing what they should be doing are the Greeks. I know what some of them were doing isn't very nice, but at least they are doing what everyone knows they are doing. I can't say that of either the Turkish politicians or the British.

Now that's going to be thrown in to the air, that night Makarios does something strange. He went to the Nicosia General Hospital and pleaded to 29 Turkish nurses to return to his home at the archbishopric. They went with him after much pleading and after he'd confirmed their destination with the British High Commission. It was Christmas night nineteen sixty-three, all over Nicosia people were dying, mainly Turks, fifty-nine at Kumsal, Omorphita was under siege. I wrote myself that it sounded like our own version of crystal night. Yet whilst all this is going on Makarios goes to the Hospital and persuades a large number of Turkish nurses to return to the palace with him, telling them. His words "There are a few irresponsible armed men about out there," his first words when they arrive are,
"We're safe here now," and. "No one can harm us." It seems he's just as scared as anyone.

Now nothing seemed right. I've got the British announcing cease-fires whilst the situation was not only deteriorating and couldn't be further from the truth and they haven't been agreed. But whilst they're doing this, they know about the massacres and are doing nothing except suppressing the information on them. Then we've got the Turks who wont agree a cease-fire until they get back what was then a large unknown number of hostages. Now if that doesn't make sense we've got Makarios who the Turks tout as the angel of death going to the Hospital to rescue Turkish nurses. It gets more intriguing. Gibbons has some revealing facts, facts and interesting conversations that I'd never have been able to get elsewhere and the fact that he is our biggest critic. They are facts I will rely on. I'm not surprised his book wasn't allowed publication in Britain in the sixties though. It would have brought into consideration some very serious questions that would have been asked of the Foreign office. Now this is the important bit, that same night Makarios goes into conference with the representatives of Britain, Turkey, Greece and the U.S.A. and at three a.m. returns Cyprus to the British unconditionally, completely, his quoted words later that morning to Gibbons are;
"This island belongs to Britain!" when asked what he meant he said.
"I have asked the British to take over, Cyprus is once more British," when he

was asked more he revealed that, and these are direct quotes.

"As from three o'clock this morning I have handed Cyprus completely over to the British. The island is no longer my responsibility."

I felt sure he was attempting to cleanse himself and the people of the massacres, some of which he must have known of. Ioannides the 74 Greek junta leader and Sampson our psychotic wannabe leader first met during the strife of 63. Ioannides was serving with the Greek mainland contingent. It was during this period that they both put a plan to Makarios to exterminate all the Turks of Cyprus. Makarios turned it down.

Few people know about Makarios returning Cyprus to the British that night. Because they turned it down. With full knowledge of the situation they turned it down. The British decided to word it a bit differently.

"The government of Cyprus has accepted an offer that British, Greek and Turkish forces stationed in Cyprus, which have been placed under British command, help its efforts to ensure the maintenance of a cease-fire and restoration of peace."

Pretty much the same line that was fed to Ankara Radio presumably by the BBC a day earlier. Now there's something not right here at all and even more sinister is that the Turkish politicians were present and knew that Makarios had returned Cyprus to the British. They knew and never kicked up a fuss when it was reworded. In fact they aren't saying anything. Now if I was Turkish at the time I think I'd have strong preference, a very strong bloody preference.

Why the fake cease fire announcements in the first place and why conceal the Kykkos school massacre and most importantly why not accept the return of Cyprus. How could Orek and Kutchuk claim they cared for their people when all they are doing are delaying cease fires, whilst they know their own people are being attacked and why, and this is the most important one that does it for myself. Why when they must have known that Makarios had returned Cyprus to British hands completely, they don't even seem to be bothered about them declining the offer. I would be bloody well demanding that they run up the Union Jack again! Turkish Cypriots are being attacked left right and centre!

I could understand Makarios resenting the British so much after 63, knowing that the situation would never have got so bad if they had of taken control as requested. Gibbons seemed to get everywhere, he bumped into Makarios whilst he was dropping off the Turkish nurses that he'd rescued and told Gibbons what he'd done earlier that morning, hence the quotes, it's a conversation Gibbons had. The British never told Makarios to his face that they were going to decline his offer, with the Turks beside them, they accepted it. Which surely meant they must have discussed it with the Turks before making their decision. Afterwards they were to make a big fuss about getting the hostages back, when they could have simply called out British soldiers, there and then and got them out, less the 150 that the British already knew about of course. I know for a fact that the British had enough Special Forces in the form of the parachute regiment and the S.A.S. on the island if they wanted to use them for this purpose. But I think they were otherwise engaged. I couldn't believe the deceit of the Turkish Cypriot politicians knowing all that was going on around them. But although they knew that Makarios had attempted to return Cyprus unconditionally for their benefit, as much as his, they kept quiet whilst their own people continued to suffer.

Just as deceitful though were the British. After the press release Gibbons approaches Sir Arthur Clarke and confronts him about what Makarios had said, it seems he was a little embarrassed about it. He confirmed Makarios was telling the truth and then said, and I quote.
"Well this is the way we have decided to word the statement," Gibbons uses this comment against Makarios by taking the, we bit, as meaning Makarios as well. I just had to give you an example of how blindly biased Gibbons is. I couldn't believe it all.

I drove on to Polis getting there early teatime and took the same room as I had a year before with Kaloo the friendly elderly Cypriot woman, whom recognised me instantly and coffee soon followed. Which I drank before I drove down to the beach to watch the sunset behind the distant hills to the west. The beach bar owner was there as usual and I got another coffee, whilst we had a little chat and I took in the views again.

That night I had my evening meal at a fish restaurant in town before having a walk around and reacquainting myself with the place. I noticed something that I'd seen before but had taken little interest in, a Cabaret, and this was Cyprus. I looked down the steps it seemed quiet. 'Nah', can't be I thought and continued on my way before returning to my room for a very peaceful night's sleep. I was feeling far better within myself, my sleep pattern had taken a big change whilst writing and I knew that I'd been writing very much out of passion.

Friday morning I woke up late, feeling fresh for a good nights' sleep and had a shower before going to the small square and eating a good breakfast. I then drove down to the beach and took a leisurely stroll to Latsi pronounced Latchi, it was a pleasant sedate walk, I couldn't help but pick up litter, but I was pleased to see there was very little to collect. Latsi is the home of the baths of Aphrodite, I'd seen it many years ago but it was the beach that I was taken with this morning.

Despite the weather, people were very few and it's a clean and natural, blue flag beach, not built up in any way except for the unimposing bars and restaurants at the western end.

I stopped off for a Cypriot coffee at Latsi before strolling back along the beach. Getting settled along the way for an hour or so to just pass the time and enjoy simply being. The last three months had been so hard for me and I was feeling relieved to feel I'd gone through the worst of it, but regardless of how hard it was, I was glad everything had happened. I soon returned to the beach bar to chat to the Cypriot bar owner that I'd got acquainted with. I never expected to be able to talk openly about this book with Greek Cypriots, but I did and chatted away happily with him.

"You're writing a book eh!" he confirmed.

"I seem to be," I said. "It's about myself and Cyprus, a kind of personal passage sort of thing." I've never been sure how to describe this book.

"When I first started writing this book I asked an English woman if she thought we were hypocrites," I told him. "She said yes and now I've told my cousin I have a book I can give her." It is an actual conversation that I had. I also thought we were being hypocritical flying so many Greek flags only to discover that, it's not that we are hypocrites, rather that we are forced to live in hypocrisy.

"Hypocrites!" he was disgusted at the idea.

"Yeah bloody English eh!" I said, enjoying this.

"I go back to our worst time in 63-64 and then the 74 coup," he was looking with interest.

"So I find out for myself the hard way that 74 was an internal coup," I said revealing.

"EOKA b in my own family," I told him as I put my hands out. That summed it up in one way. I was smiling by this time. It wasn't so much that I found the idea amusing. Let's just say, I now find myself sympathetic to it all. He smiled at the same time shaking his head, I could take a guess that he too like many Cypriot families have got their own lurking member or should I say ex.

I returned to Polis and my room where I read a little before eating at the same fish restaurant as the night before. After which I took a short stroll to a local bar. The same one that I'd drank at the previous year where I sat with a Cypriot guy and chatted as we watched some T.V. It felt strange seeing the streets and the square so quiet. We chatted about the present situation a little before I'd finished a couple of large scotches and a beer and took my leave. That night I lay awake for a while before I slept and I knew then that I wouldn't return to Limassol the next day. This was all too peaceful for me.

Of course after the Christmas cease-fire the situation never improved at all.

There weren't any more massacres like Kykkos School but the fighting continued. Here's an example of the British helping to maintain the peace though, they knew the situation, they knew what sort of things were happening, but the day the cease fire's announced, Greeks are attacking the village of Aghirda in the north. The Turks informed General Young, his quoted response.

"I'm sorry I have no authority outside Nicosia." What a bastard was all I could think. Not only is he refusing to help but in the same breath is revealing that no help could be expected outside of Nicosia. Now that really pisses me off. They would have known the intensity of the resentment that would have been unleashed and how it was being unleashed and they weren't going to do stuff all to stop it. This was not something that had been going on for years, it was only a few days old and the Turks of Cyprus were never suppressed in any way like this before. The fuse paper had been lit and they were going to watch the firework display. Makarios had made it quite clear to them the day before that they could have the power to do everything they wanted. But the British, the long time friends of the Cypriots felt that they didn't have the authority, what rubbish! It'll be no surprise for you to hear that the fighting would soon increase outside of Nicosia. I slept not happily just more comfortable knowing that it wasn't just Greek resentment for the Turks that was to blame, it just wasn't that simple.

The next morning I was drinking coffee and enjoying the moment with my elderly, but happy hostess when a young couple that had been staying the night came down with their packed bags. Kaloo tried tempting them for a coffee, which they declined, as they were leaving and they wanted to make Troodos their next destination early. I'd spoken to them the previous night and I was interested because the girl spoke English with what sounded like an American accent, yet I also knew she was Cypriot.

"Where do you live?" I asked her.

"Larnaca and you?"

"England," Kaloo came over and started chatting away to me in Greek as she often did, I smiled and informed the girl I never spoke Greek, she looked surprised.

"You don't speak Greek?" she said it in an enquiring manner. I guess I felt obliged to answer, not that I minded any more.

"No, I'm actually writing a book about it," I told her. "I think it might have had something to do with the troubles here in the sixties," I revealed. "It seems I stopped when my grandfather died and after that I just wouldn't take the language without the love." I don't think anyone could have expected such a response. I also knew how sad it sounded and I wasn't surprised that she changed the subject.

"That's a nice necklace," she said. I was wearing the piece that Marie had made for me on Kos.

"Thanks," I acknowledged the compliment.

"No really, it's nice, I know I make my own jewellery," she was saying this as she was leaving with her male companion.

"I know," I said as much as saying goodbye at the same time. There was an affectionate smile on my face thinking about the necklace. The nicest thing about it is that I always felt it was made with love. Marie and I communicate very little due to the language barrier, but I knew we said it with smiles.

I had breakfast. Then phoned my godmother to tell her I would be staying another day before taking to the car. I considered heading towards Paphos until I looked at the map and decided to head east to Kato Pyrgos, which is about as far to the east along the north coast as you can go. I topped the car up with petrol and drove along the coast road.

It wasn't long before I realised the land here takes a dramatic change as the limestone gives way to the brown sandstone hills east of Polis, I knew I was in for another treat as far as scenery went and I wasn't to be disappointed. This is the northern edge of the Troodos mountain range. I suppose it's always easy to think you've seen it all, it's usually when that happens that you find out how wrong you are, when that something new and unexpected appears. The road follows the coast for some twenty kilometres or more before you lose the good shouldered road and it turns into little more than a tarmac track. Undaunted by this unexpected change I drove on along the hills and the low mountains. The recent rain had encouraged a coating of tender grass shoots to carpet the landscape. To myself it was beautiful. You're soon made very aware of the rural background to the area by the lack of people and the herds of goats easily seen, scattered along the hillsides and occasionally on the road. There is another aspect to this area that soon becomes prevalent though, and that's the increasing number of Greek Cypriot army posts along the route, along with a scattering of abandoned and ruined dwellings. I was aware that I was driving towards the line but I knew I was a fair way from it, the road followed the line of a hill on my left, round and towards the sea when a sight that I wasn't expecting confronted me. Directly in front of me some three hundred metres or so away, was the blood red flag of Turkey and the flag of the T.R.N.C. flying from an observation post. Now I hadn't seen any signs, but I really didn't fancy taking any chances especially after having my head deep in their propaganda for the last couple of months and facts are facts. The snail picker was picking snails and that was all. He may have been in the buffer zone, but only just, by about 5 metres from what I could remember and he was hit three times, in the back. These are Turkish mainland troops that man these posts, they have no respect for and get none back from Greek Cypriots. I stopped the car and gazed up to my right, where there was a Greek Cypriot army post and to my left, where there was a U.N observation post, I could see a UN soldier watching me through a pair of large tripod mounted binoculars. I knew he had a very clear view of me even in the car, so I simply held both hands up, as if to ask where now. I could see him making some arm movements of his own, but they weren't good enough for me. I drove on to the small UN camp and parked the car just inside the drive knowing that someone would come to give me advice on the road in front. Two soldiers soon appeared from some buildings a little below the drive and sprinted up to the car.

"I'm going to Kato Pyrgos and I saw those," I said as I pointed over at the Turkish flags that were flying.

"No it's alright just follow the road," one of the soldiers replied. I looked at the road and I could see it followed another hill round to the right.

"I see it," I said. I still wasn't sure where I was though.

"Just don't get out and walk ah?" not that I intended to.

"No it's ok just keep on driving"

"Thanks," I reversed the car and returned onto the track and slowly followed the road round to the right, realising as I did, that it could only be the Turkish enclave of Kokkina. I passed more abandoned mud brick homes, a whole village even, this area was to see the brunt of the trouble in the summer of 64. I increased my speed and continued along the road, past dwellings both inhabited and abandoned, through Mansoura and into Kato Pyrgos. With the heat it felt like summer, better than the last British summer that's for sure, but it was around mid-day and Kato Pyrgos was quiet. I hadn't really known how far along the road I was going to go when I left Polis, but I knew this was where I was heading. I wouldn't say Kato Pyrgos is the most warming place at first sight, but just after you reach the eastern edge of the village is possibly the reason why, the road ends abruptly with a gate across it manned by a single soldier. His stop sign wasn't needed, end of the road I thought. I could make out the name Kyrenia in Greek on the gate, but I knew it was still the end of the road for me.

I put the car into reverse and made a U-turn before slowly cruising through the town. The most prevalent thing on my mind was the weather. It was so much nicer than the previous October. The temperature was in the mid-twenties. As I drifted through the small town I was looking for somewhere to get a drink and perhaps some conversation. I thought about my chat with my godmother though and didn't think I'd go down to well the locals, it just seemed that sort of area and it was so close to the line, I accelerated deciding to try out one of the tourist restaurants just outside of town.

Now so much has happened this year that simply seemed destined and if that's the case I can't believe that the next place I stopped at wasn't written in. I found myself at Mansoura and an unimposing fish restaurant. I say unimposing because I never noticed it at all when I drove past it the first time. I saw the Coka Cola sign by the road but not the building, which from the east can be clearly seen with its large palm leaf roofed balcony that served as an eating area. I took a guess that they'd still be open as the chairs weren't turned up. I turned the car onto the dirt car park, which sloped, all the way down to the beach, it was a steep gradient but I didn't bother turning parallel with the other car that was parked there. Instead I left it parked on the slope that lead down to the sea. As I turned the engine off, in the silence, I suddenly realised how beautiful the whole place was. I left the car and entered the restaurant building where I saw a middle aged Cypriot woman sitting on her own.

"Hi," I said taking a guess that she'd speak English.

"Hello," she replied.

"Can I have a can of sprite please?" I asked.

"Certainly." The woman went to a drinks' cooler and took out a can of sprite, whilst I placed my wallet and camera on a table before she passed me the can.

"Thanks," I said.

"Your welcome," her English was fluent.

"It's nice here," I said. The woman nodded her head in agreement. I gazed out through the glass doors before I placed the can on a table and walked out and onto the balcony taking in the scenery, I felt drawn to what I was seeing. Now I've seen some beautiful beaches in my time and they aren't all golden sand and coconut trees and nor was this one. The beach is some seven or eight metres below the height of the road, which most of the time is about a hundred metres back from the beach, but follows the low cliff line in places. The beach itself was pebbly and the surf made more than enough noise to cover the sound of any passing cars, as rare as they were. I walked east looking across Morphou bay but focussing on the near coastline, it felt magical and I wasn't quite sure why.

The coastline was so different from anything else I'd experienced in Cyprus, I glanced up and down after passing a light blue freshly painted upturned boat, the blue was a shade of blue I was familiar with and it felt good to see. I continued walking on to the beach. There was something special about it and I wasn't quite sure what it was, I felt entranced by more than the sheer beauty of it. I ambled along the shoreline past some rocky outcrops picking up any stones or pebbles that caught my eye. There was nothing to disturb me. I was feeling a peace that I felt I'd been missing for so long. I wouldn't have been aware of the odd vehicle that drove past behind me as I sat on the beach, out of sight of the restaurant and took in the splendour of this newly discovered place. I realised it was the seclusion. I looked left, nothing but nature, I looked right and it was the same, nothing but nature. I couldn't see the road, any houses or people even. There was nothing there to disturb me. I closed my eyes, the sound of the sea, music to my ears. I lay back and felt completely at ease. It was then that I realised that since starting this book, I'd not felt at peace with myself until this moment and I was cherishing it for what it was, a precious moment in time. I hadn't even taken my cigarettes with me, didn't need them. The sun was warm on my face, the breeze fresh, the ambience felt sedate and for the first time in months I felt all the sadness that I'd been shrouded in, being blown away like pollen in the wind, to leave me in a state of total tranquillity.

When I realised what Gibbons had done, I'd gone into a rage, a rage that tore so deep at me I knew it could have easily drove me up the mountain wanting to take it out on anyone. A Turkish border guard would have been perfect. But at a range and looking down the sight of a rifle, a target is a target. I was so filled with anger I might have taken it out on simply anyone. I'd never have had to look closely at the body, to inspect the corpse and witness the damage done. Nor to face the grieving relatives to tell them it wasn't me, but the rage. The Gibbons book and what I believe the British had been doing really did have that effect on me. For the first time since I felt that rage I'd found a place and a time where I could shed a tear for knowing that I too could have and may still be, a victim of the hatred. But I'd come a long way in the last few months and the only thing that kept me off that mountain was this book. I lay back, on my own, in the comfort of nature and shed a tear for the man I knew they'd have made me.

After thirty minutes or so I walked back along the beach to the restaurant and ordered some kalimari and salad to eat, at least my diet had improved. By this time the middle aged Cypriot woman, I'll call her Maria had been joined by her husband Andreas whom I drank coffee with and chatted, soon to be joined by John, their youngest son who was about thirteen. They'd returned to Cyprus after living in London for some years and had set up a family business in an abandoned Turkish residence. There was nothing unusual about this, my uncle had done the same after being made a refugee from our own village. Maria's own family was in the same situation as they also had property in the north. She told me of her concerns, of feeling insecure about the situation. But I'd assured her that the same thing was happening on both sides and that no one would return for this property, without her being returned to hers. I didn't feel it was advice that should have been needed, but it seemed to help. I chatted to Andreas for a while and drank coffee and I knew that if there were anywhere that I wanted to spend the rest of my time on this visit, it would be here. I made my mind up there and then and told them before I left that I'd be back in the morning, knowing I would drive on to Limassol early afternoon to get some time with my cousin Spyros.

Now I could skip the night bit in Polis here but....... Well I went back and ate at the same restaurant, as before, it was a good meal about half a kilo of fresh fish and salad. On a table over the other side of the restaurant was a lively but elderly Cypriot gentleman. I'm having a giggle thinking about him. A wonderful chap, perhaps in his mid to late seventies with a bottle of Zivounir chatting up two

German women that he'd known for some years, who were about half his age. We'd got talking across the restaurant after he poured me a glass of Zivounir and I went and joined them, before we departed to continue drinking elsewhere.

Here seems a good a time as any to tell you about this Cypriot moonshine or mountain firewater or even firewater as it's most commonly known. The effect is a bit um' well I can normally walk on it and I can talk on it, I'm very happy on it and I'm hardly ever sick on it. But after a few glasses that's about all I can do on it, so who was I to argue with my elders when the German women left us on our own and he took me to the local cabaret. Well here, I am glad to say that walking, talking and being happy were about all I was capable of doing. It cost me fifty pounds talking to a Romanian girl and yes, sex would have been cheaper but I didn't care. I was feeling very cynical about the world I'm living in and this seemed honest compared to how some people behave in life, I knew the price and I was happy to pay it, it did mean I was on a tighter budget for the rest of the trip though.

The next morning I awoke bright and early. Yep the Zivounir can be that good, had a shower and made up some coffee, it was another pleasant morning. I was putting my morning cigarette further and further back. On the way to the shower, which was across a very short external hall I saw a familiar local chap walking up the stairs with a length of four by two timber over his shoulder, he'd disappeared when I come out. I heard some banging as I dried and dressed myself, before taking my coffee out on to the veranda to take in the air.

"Sorry if I woke you," I heard from above. I looked up and saw the local chap about my age leaning over the roof with a cigarette.

"No, not at all, I was already awake," I told him. He went on to tell me how he was doing work for Kaloo and we chatted for a while about what I was doing. It was a pleasant conversation and I couldn't work out why it felt so strange until I realised much later on, that we'd had more or less the same conversation under similar circumstances the year before. It's so nice when you feel as familiar with the people as the place. I'd even noticed the contemptible Cypriot who I'd spoken to about the National service, but he never seemed to recognised me, not that I wanted him to. I had a final coffee with Kaloo telling her my destination and after getting her best wishes I set off for Kato Pyrgos.

I stopped off again at Mansoura, which was my destination and met Andreas and Maria's eldest son Andy, who was there working on a friends car. Everyone was so friendly and they all spoke good English, although my ignorance of Greek still bothered me. I took a walk on the beach telling myself I'd be back in the morning and little would change. It was a short walk as I was aware of the drive ahead of me and I wanted to spend a little more time with Andy before I left. I realised

Maria hadn't heard about the land access claim against Turkey, so I gave Andy the details and returned to the restaurant promising everybody I'd be back the next day, before heading off across the mountains to Kykkos, Troodos and on to Limassol.

My godmother warned me to remember to beep my horn on the corners on these mountain roads, I said I would, as I do. But I'd never been on this road before, from this the Tilliria area of Cyprus to Kykkos. You see roads, on the map and think, they'll do. Well it was about five kilometres along this one before I realised what sort of road it is, I was horrified, I'd pushed it time wise but this was no road to make any time up on. It was narrow and well surfaced but it was very new surfacing though and the road was smooth, with a coating of sandstone in places making it slippery and the crash barriers were still to be placed. I drove most of the way leaning over the steering wheel on whatever side of the road felt safe. I wouldn't wear my seat belt in case I drove over the side and even considered turning back. I actually got an attack of vertigo at one point, fantastic views though. It took me a little under two hours to drive the fifty or so kilometres to Kykkos and I was just happy to get back on to a road with barriers on. When I got to the monastery I drove slowly past and on up to the tomb of Makarios. I parked the car in the main car park, took my camera and walked up the hill to the tomb. I wasn't feeling tearful and neither expected to as I turned to gaze upon the tomb, for the first time. There were a couple of young German tourists behind me taking some photos, I waited for them to leave before I went on one knee said a prayer and crossed myself. Now I know I've said I'm not religious, well I just don't trust any religions with my soul, like establishments, they're ruled by men. It doesn't mean I don't believe. I left the tomb site before walking up to the small chapel nearby and taking in the view south to Olympus where you can see the British forces listening post mounted on the highest point in Cyprus. I returned to the tomb area and taking the step, walked onto the mound immediately above the tomb. From there I looked north across the mountains where I could see Morphou in the occupied area. I could almost make out the whole of Morphou bay. Just out of sight and behind the mountains would be Kyrenia, it was gazing out across there, a tear filled my eye.

The drive across the mountains had taken my mind off things for a while. After the uprising of Christmas 63 and the following events, Grivas is coming back. Only this time he is anything but a friend to Makarios. They may both still want Enosis, only they have a difference of opinions as to how to get it. Makarios simply wants to rewrite the constitution by majority consent. This was about the time he was giving passports out. Grivas wasn't the bureaucratic sort. Makarios didn't bother to attend the peace talks that were to start in London in mid-January, he sent a man called Kyprianou who is still a politician in Cyprus and Clerides.

But nothing is going to be resolved. Now it's not the demand for Enosis but simply that the Cypriot government wanted Cyprus to be ruled by the majority of the population. I'll quote Makarios here, just because I can.

"The main cause of the friction between the Greeks and the Turks and the root of the evil is in the Treaties of Guarantee and Alliances. The treaties were not the outcome of free will by all parties." This is where he states that he signed the treaty to end the bloodshed. It might sound like Enosis and it might have even led to it, but not for any sinister reasoning. Remember how small Cyprus is and remembering its history, 83% of the people who are a bloody good majority simply wanted something they'd always regarded as their eventual right, self-determination. Beginning of January Makarios is requesting a UN presence, but by the end of January a NATO force is being proposed, Makarios rejected it outright saying that the British peace keeping force was helping to create conditions favouring the Turkish demand for partition. I can see what he means and whilst all this is going on a Greek General Pantilides is announcing in Nicosia the establishment of the 'National Guard'. That was nice of him. The Greek government was now getting heavily involved. Let me give you an idea again of the situation for the private individual in Cyprus at around Christmas time and beyond. Lets imagine you and myself are both Greek Cypriots and we've been watching this entire fighting going on. Now remember by this time many Turks do seem to be revolting in one way or another, I do say seem but many actually were. Gibbons is constantly running into Greeks whilst on his crusade around Nicosia and even though he still suggests that all the Greeks wanted was to kill Turks, he's constantly running into scared armed Greeks hiding in shop doorways etc, he's just so biased. They're flying a Turkish flag over St. Hilarion castle for starters that's an ancient Byzantine monument, one of the most famous in Cyprus, and ours. Gibbons doesn't appreciate the symbolic meaning behind something like that. To myself it's like Greeks holding the Blue Mosque in Istanbul. The British may have fixed bayonets in Nicosia but it was all for show. The Greek community took the piss out of them, they'd still be able to carry on attacking where they wanted, the British would get there, often get bullied about and have things like Enosis slogans scrawled on their armoured cars. I found that amusing, well it's the sort of thing I might have enjoyed, painting graffiti on an armoured car, takes the piss. Remember that Greek Cypriots would have known that there was at least intent on behalf of the Turks before this to take their own part of Cyprus. And after Christmas 63 Makarios knew just how real that threat of partition was. A lot of Greeks and Greek Cypriots simply never knew. Things' progress now though, on February the 4th the U.S. embassy is mobbed because of the NATO proposals (it's shortly after bombed) and it seems a new ally has stepped on to the scene, Russia. The Russian ambassador in Nicosia is assuring crowds of the Soviet support for the Cypriot 'Struggle for independence' lovely. I've got Russia back on the scene again. So its 1964 Makarios is getting the

British sussed out and he's making friends with Russia, stuff it, it's only the middle of the cold war, why not.

It sounds like anarchy is going on. But by the end of February Makarios is setting up his own 5,000man police force and Russian arms are making there way into the country. At this point I have to say that if Makarios has complete control of this police force, it's about all he would have complete control of, the reasons for me saying this will become apparent. On March the 4th the UN agreed to a resolution for a UN force in Cyprus, but that's all they did. These are far more acceptable to Makarios than a NATO Force and he wouldn't have known how useless the UN could be back then. In Cyprus nothings changing, so by mid March Turkey prepare an Invasion fleet and seems ready to invade Cyprus unless a cease-fire is announced or the UN make a move on the matter. The UN goes into session to debate the crisis and the invasion's called off at the last moment by an announcement that the UN will be sending Canadian troops. Now here's another strange turn. Whilst the Turkish invasion fleet is being prepared the US 6th fleet is moving to the area. When the news of the invasion being called off hits the newspapers, it seems the British dropped a totally untrue claim that Russian submarines were heading for the area. Making it appear that the UN troops were sent to Cyprus to avert an East-West confrontation. At first I was wondering what was going on, it seemed that the USA and Britain were now appearing to be protecting Cyprus from partition. It wasn't for Cyprus though. It was because the powerful Greek Lobby in the USA were already making itself felt on the president, who had his own war going in Vietnam. This it seems would be enough for them to put pressure wherever they could to avert a Turkish invasion, but there were other implications of their pressure on the US government which would become more apparent in the next few months. The Soviet submarine claim would also give anyone the impression that Makarios had some real influence with the Soviets and vice versa. And remember, this is 1964 and the middle of the cold war.

I turned around, took a pine from one of the trees growing above the tomb and walked back down to the car, sat in the drivers' seat and took a drink of water before smoking a cigarette. Five minutes later I was driving back past the monastery and down to join the main road. At the bottom of the hill from Kykkos the road comes to a T-junction, it's a right turn to Pedoulas and on to Troodos. But I was looking at the dirt track that started immediately over the other side of the road clearly marked by a tourist sign which read, 'EOKA headquarters 1955-59'. I drove straight across the road and followed the heavily wooded two-kilometre track past a solitary flagpole from which the Greek national flag and the pennant of EOKA flew, to the end of the track. I parked the car and got out before having a quick look around to survey my surroundings. I could see the foot track to the hideout clearly marked through the trees of a heavily wooded hillside. I closed the car door and locked it before taking to the steep hairpin track, up to the hideout. I was a little disappointed at first when I got to the hideout, not that I knew why, but I discovered how small it was or appeared to be. There was a grey stone entrance to the underground burrow, which would also constitute its underground walls. It looked like they'd hollowed out the ground before building the stone surround to the hideout and covered it over again. It all looked so, not sad, but lonely. I imagined the place to be a hive of activity in its hey day and recalled some of the photographs I'd seen of EOKA fighters sitting around such wooded areas, clutching their Sterling sub machine guns and smiling. I got down on my knees and crawled through the entrance, not far, but far enough to allow my eyes to adjust to the dark and see what was in there, it was musty, dry and dusty. I twitched a few times holding back a sneeze. I could see the back wall about a metre and a half in front of me, the entrance was at one end of the burrow and when I looked to my left I thought I could make out a wall, a little over two and a half metres away. I took in what I could and crawled back out. I took a step back and thought for a moment and returned to the car. I wasted no time when I got back, I opened the boot and pulled my bag around so I could unzip it and pulled out any extra contents on to the boot floor before zipping the bag up again. I then took one quick glance down the dirt track and pulled the bag up and over my shoulder by its hand straps, so as heavy as it was, the weight was close to my body and held by my upper arm. I wasted no time ascending the track and out of breath and in a sweat I returned to the camp and threw the bag into the burrow entrance, as I took to my knees and pushed it all the way in, following behind it. Sitting on my knees in the middle of the darkened burrow getting my breathe back, my eyes adjusted much better and I could see that my first estimation had been about right. I pulled the bag out in front of me and completely unzipped it revealing the bright blue and white flag that had started this all off for me. I pushed my hands underneath it and ceremoniously lifted it out and placed it behind the bag, before pulling the bag out of the way. I never had this planned at all, but it felt so right. I turned the flag so that I could unroll it down one side of the burrow, like a bed, which I did. It was looking good, one half of this new bed was blue and the other half was white, split perfectly down the middle. I unrolled it to about a bed length and easily had enough fabric left to form a comfortable pillow. I brushed my palms across it for no particular reason, gave it a nod of approval and crawled back to the entrance, stopping only briefly for a final glance before pulling myself back and grabbing my empty bag as I did. I brushed myself down as I took to my feet again and threw my bag over my shoulder as before and wasting no time, descended the hill not even bothering with the hairpin track, but deciding to take the more perilous but direct route. I kept on my feet by almost falling towards different trees. Before taking a hold of one near the bottom of the steep slope and using it as a brake to slow my descent and simply released it, as I passed it at not much more than a fast walking pace. I walked around to the car and extracted the keys from my pocket and pushed them in the door lock. It was at this point that I realised that no matter who my grandfather was, or whatever his thoughts might have been on all of this. He never knew what I did and I am not my grandfather. And I knew then, this wasn't his story as I'd so often believed. It was mine.

I was looking up the hill at the unseen camp and thinking of how they must have felt when they were fighting for Enosis............moments of freedom, probably. I thought about how sad it was that the flag that they'd fought so proudly for, had been abused by so many to follow. I released the keys took a step back and came sharply to attention and raised my right hand in salute, I couldn't believe I was doing it, but I was.

"To times past!"

I said it clear and I said it proud. Now they may be times past but let's get one thing straight about this. It wasn't union with Greece that these men were fighting for. It was Reunion!

I got into my car reversed around and drove back up the dirt track and set off towards Troodos. I didn't feel like I had to explain my actions to anyone at this point. My grandfather might have been upset about the situation in Cyprus, but I knew he wouldn't have known the truth that I knew about it. I got to Troodos a little later than I expected and I wasn't sure what time I'd make Limassol, but from there, the drive was a pleasure all the way down to town so to speak and I arrived with great timing. Five minutes after I'd walked through the door I was eating dinner. I'd had a great day. I got a little telling off for not phoning though, which was fun, even when I tried explaining all the public phones at Troodos were out of order, which they were. I was told I should have asked a shopkeeper. After dinner we sat out on the balcony and smoked cigarettes, drank coffee and talked. My cousin told me about his new video camera, which he'd never managed to get working. It was fun throwing in my share of the banter over that one. He'd had it for three months and still hadn't been able to work out the instructions. The serious conversation was to come later.

I'd been sat up alone with my godmother for about a half an hour or so watching TV before I finally got around to asking her what I wanted to know. Not that I was trying any earlier it just seemed to come out at the right time.

"Marianna can I ask you about my granddad?" I realised how long ago it was. It seemed like a lifetime.

"What do you want to know?" she asked hesitantly.

"Anything," I told her. Anything and everything I think I meant.

"I'm not really the best person to ask," she said. I felt then I was going to be disappointed but I knew she'd know the details that I wanted.

"Why not?" It was a curious reply. My godmother then stammered a little and slowly said.

"I don't like to talk about your grandfather it upsets me." I knew than I wasn't going to like what I would hear, but I'd gone to far to turn back. My godmother then told me about a brutal stepfather who resented my grandmother's children from her previous marriage, which meant her and most of the uncles that I knew, including Georgio. She told me of how he'd make them eat olives instead of cheese whilst complaining about feeding someone else's children. She told me of hard hours of labour on the farm and being sent away to work whenever he could send her and of one night in particular when she was working long and hard. It was harvest time, she was very young and she hadn't slept much at all, when she was sent back to fetch some things from the farmhouse, she collapsed with exhaustion when she arrived, only to be woken up by the pain of a mule switch across her back. I could tell it was painful for my godmother recalling the details for me. She told me of how she used to lay awake with a migraine headache and listen to my grandfather abusing my grandmother. Whether he struck her, I don't know, but so many things started to sink into place. When I asked why they'd married, my godmother said it was for my grandmothers' land, I did get defensive there.

"But he had his own land," I said. I couldn't believe he'd married out of greed. My godmother only thought about it for a moment before seeming to agree.

"I suppose they must have loved each other when they met," she sighed. I felt sullen.

"I always remember him so differently," I told her as I put my two forefingers together and looked at her. "I just remember being so close to him."

"Oh your Bompapa," her tone picked up as she said it.

"Yeah," I said nodding my head.

"Yes! You were his! His grandchild!" she said with a smile. I knew then that most of what I remembered of him and of the time and my reasons for not taking the language were right. Just that the reasoning for the differences between my grandparents were my speculation which wasn't to say I was wrong. As for the suicide theory, I still couldn't rule that out considering his main source of information at the time would have been the British press of which Gibbons was a very active part of. He would have read much of it in very much the same manner as I first did, when I was angered enough to enter the truth site, sensationalised. He'd have never known the truth that I knew though. My next question came a bit harder, I wasn't sure how to ask, but I needed to know.

"Umm," I paused slightly. "Every one emphasises how tolerant he was," I said. My godmother looked at me, I could see she wasn't sure what I meant.

"Well the tolerant bit," I felt like I had to spit it out. "It was towards Turks," I said. My aunt only seemed a little surprised, but I think more because I asked. She smiled again.

"Everything was so different then, it wasn't like today, we all just got on with our lives, no one cared," she told me. It seemed to me then that my grandfather was just like many other grandfathers, or was he.

"Yeah but I got the impression that he well," it sounds silly but I wasn't sure how to say this and I can't help but feel it's a reflection of the damage that's been done.

"I got the impression that he liked Turks," my godmother laughed a little, not a sneering laugh.

"Like I said it was very different then," she told me before thinking for a moment and nodding her head.

"Yes your grandfather did have a lot of Turkish friends," she said. "We never had any Turks living in our village but he always used to bring them home from other villages." It was said as if he was particularly friendly.

"Turkish friends," I said. I simply wanted it confirmed.

"Yes Turkish friends."

Now I knew that there might be a possibility of some or even a lot of truth to my speculation, but from that day on, one I hoped to be able to lay to rest. I have to add here, my grandfather might have been just like many others in one sense, although I haven't mentioned it, it wasn't uncommon for Turkish Cypriots to be godparents to Greek children and vice versa as is the case with a couple of my cousins. The main difference with my grandfather would have been his intelligence training and myself.

My mother told me an amusing story as to why there were no Turks living in Ayios Amvrosios. My first thought was something sinister, but it seems no such thing. A Turk stopped by one night and slept out in the doorway to one of the municipal buildings and had a bad dream. That was it, he had a bad dream telling him to leave Ayios Amvrosios forever and not to return and after that night, no Turk ever came to live in the village. The next question I asked, was about my mother,

"So what about my mother and fathers marriage," I asked. "How did that come about?" my godmother only thought about it for a moment before a smile came over her face and she told me the amusing story of a younger sister that simply couldn't be controlled. Sent to England when she was fourteen to live with my godmother and extremely rebellious, she was constantly running away. So under the circumstances and considering my mother even regarded marriage as some form of freedom, my father was found as the first possible suitor. The documents were altered and my mother was married to ensure that nothing worse could befall her, as might have been possible considering her age and the unfamiliarity of her surroundings. It was as simple as that. I couldn't help but find it all amusing. Although my grandparents were in some disagreement about it at first, they knew that there was little else that could be done and afterwards, no, my grandfather didn't mind whatsoever, but I already knew that. So it seems my mother had been a lot less than honest about her younger years and in turn my grandfather, which I found extremely sad considering she is my own mother. I smiled. I thought I'd now tell her about the flag,

"Marianna I want to show you something," I said as I got up and went to my room and returned with a photograph of the flag. I started explaining my actions as I passed it to her. She never even seemed surprised.

"Who took this?" she calmly enquired. Asking about a photograph of myself holding a corner of the flag up.

"A friend" I said. I wasn't expecting this response. I could tell she wasn't angry about it.

"It was on Aphrodite's rock when I came out in August and I drove out and pulled it down."

"I know," she said calmly.

"You know, how?" I was surprised.

"Your father told me," I should have known I thought. I then went on to tell her how I started writing a book, in anger at first, at the flag and certain revelations, after telling her I no longer wished to be referred to as a Greek. A book all about myself but at the same time about Cyprus, and how through it I felt like I truly discovered my Greek heritage. She asked me how I was getting my background information to the Cyprus problem.

"I've got some books to read"

"What books?" she enquired.

"Oh just books, ones quite a good source, direct from an eye witness," I told her.   •

"What eyewitness?" I think she might have been concerned so I thought I'd give my godmother my final assumption.

"It doesn't matter Marianna, look, the way I see it, Denktash has got what he wants," I said. "The British have got what they want and they think we'll be happy with what they've left us," I looked at her to emphasise my final point. "I don't think so," I finished with. She nodded her approval although I know this book says more than that. We weren't to chat for much longer. I apologised to my godmother for bringing up my grandfather and went to the sink to get a drink of water before returning to the sofa and picking up the photograph of the Greek flag. As I got to the hallway door, I stopped and turned to my godmother who was stood at the sink.

"You know Marianna, up to fifty-nine," I held the photograph of the flag up. "This was the only flag most Cypriots had," she looked a little confused and stammered slightly when she spoke.

"There was the British flag...........the Union Jack," she replied.

"No Marianna," I said. "That was a flag of occupation."

With that I bid my godmother goodnight and went to bed. It was then that I realised how I'd once regarded the British occupation as little more than a transition period as I am sure others do. When to many like my cousin and indeed myself now, it was just as much an occupation as any that had come before, only its long-term effects were a lot worse. I slept well that night, my sleeping had improved somewhat as I was less troubled about my writing this book, I felt like I'd come a long way and learnt a lot about myself and my country in the past few months.

The next morning I joined my godparents for breakfast. I was feeling bright and cheerful and looking forward to driving back to Kato Pyrgos. We'd already said our greetings and I was eating a bowl of Corn Flakes when my godmother spoke slowly and clearly.

"Jim, After Cyprus got its independence, EOKA became EOKA b," she pronounced the b like a v as it should be, I looked at my godmother lightly humming an acknowledgement as I was sipping up the last of my milk. There was no need to ask what they were fighting for. This was a conversation I should have had years ago. I nodded for her to continue.

"And they were around until 74 and now some of them are in government," she told me. I smiled at her.

"I know," I said. Getting up to put my bowl in the sink, still smiling as I took my coffee, not looking at my uncle.

"I'm going for my morning cigarette," I told them. I guessed they must have talked about it at some point in the evening and decided to talk to me in the morning. They'd opened themselves up to questioning, but I felt I knew any answers that they could give me and of course neither of them were here in 63 so they would have only read the British press reports. I'm not just taking it for granted my cousin and godfather were EOKA b in 74. But it will be up to them to talk about it. I can still be annoyed at them occasionally for being so irresponsible, but only occasionally, they never knew the truth and the coup failed anyway. All I can say here is that I'm glad neither of them were in the Famagusta area where the three hamlets were wiped out. I was driving my godmother to the bakery before leaving, when she brought up the subject of so many Greek flags being flown. It's a conversation that was to stick painfully in my mind.

"You know sometimes I get confused about why there's so many Greek flags also," she said. She really was surprising me now.

"You mean because of Makarios and everything?" I replied. It is one of the reasons why I wondered.

"Yes, yes, I talk to people about it and they say it's how it must be, while our flag is broken." That sounded so sad.

"I understand," I said. Which I do, broken, how true it is. But I couldn't help thinking we were given a flag whilst those that gave it to us were in the process of destroying the ideology of it. I thought I'd ask a question that I already knew the answer to.

"This book I'm reading Marianna, the man says that we are a breed apart from Greeks," I told her. I was talking about the Gibbons book.

"We are," she replied without hesitating. That's something that most Greeks and Greek Cypriots accept.

"Not like this man means," I said as solemnly as it was felt. I couldn't tell her how Gibbons has defined us as opposed to Greeks. I had a coffee with my godmother before leaving, whilst she got the same map of Cyprus out to see where Kato Pyrgos was.

"There it is," I said pointing it out. Her eyes lit up immediately.

"I love that area!" she said as she put a finger on that area of the map. "Right across here and to the north is my favourite part of the island," she told me. As she slid her finger across the map, along the same lines as the border with the occupied areas. It was a sad silent moment for me. I soon said my goodbyes and departed for Kato Pyrgos by way of Paphos and Polis, stopping off at Paphos for some food supplies.

It took me the best part of three hours to get to Mansoura. When I stopped at the beach side restaurant everything was so peaceful for me again. The place seemed desolate amongst the backdrop of the hills, scattered with the ruins of the past. Yet to myself it felt like paradise and I know where paradise is, in the heart. Marie was the first to welcome me back. She seemed surprised as I appeared.

"You come back!"

"I promised I would," I said cheerfully as I sat down. Almost immediately a coffee was brought for me which I drank whilst chatting with Andreas and John. They'd already told me that they could find accommodation for me in the area, not that I thought it would be a problem. John had asked me if I wanted to go fishing with him and his father, to which I agreed as soon as I'd arranged a room. We soon set off for nearby Kato Pyrgos and the Pyrgos bay hotel, myself following them by car. As soon as I pulled up at the hotel the proprietors appeared from the reception and I was introduced to the elderly couple who run the place and instantly I felt ignorant for my lack of Greek again, but John was making up for it, telling them who I was.

"She wants to know where you're from?" John asked me inquiring for the elderly lady.

"Ayios Amvrosios," I told him. To which her eyes lit up as she spoke in Greek.

"She say's it's beautiful there!" John informed me excitedly.

"I've heard," I said with a slight but sad smile.

I took the keys to my room, which was seven pounds a night for bed and breakfast, but never bothered looking at it. Opting instead to go fishing with John and his father. I followed them in my car a couple of kilometres or so back towards Mansoura, where we left the road and followed a dirt track that led out onto a low point and down onto the beach. Here a layer of very flat bedrock formed numerous small rock pools, which surrounded the beach around the point. Further out the waves were just rolling over the edge of the bedrock keeping the whole system of pools fed by fresh seawater. Before we could fish we had to catch our bait, which turned out to be as many small hermit crabs as we could find. After which, John, Andreas and I sat out on the beach, whilst they snatched whatever fish would take the bait. No weights, no float, just a rod, a fixed line, a hook and of course a hermit crab on the end. Any fish, big or small, from the size of my finger to the length of my hand, they'll taste good

It was a pleasant afternoon. I sat back and decided that I'd made the right choice. As the sun set John announced that they would be going to Latsi to have dinner with his brother Demetre who worked in a hotel there. I told him I'd see them the next day and I returned to my hotel. It wasn't necessary to enter the reception to get to my room, the door of which opened up onto a small balcony and overlooked the small car park at the front. I took whatever I thought would be needed for the two nights that I would be staying and found myself very pleased indeed with the room. The hotel was situated on the eastern side of Pyrgos bay, the area was very unspoilt and from my room I had a beautiful view of the bay, which started directly below the hotel. I could see a large balcony below me, which would have led from the dining room. The bay itself was crescent shaped and broken up in the centre by a long finger of flat rock that pointed out. At about the same point to the left was a beachside restaurant mounted on a low sandy cliff that surrounded the bay and from there was a slip way down to the beach. I could see a life guards chair, not that it was now needed as it was well off-season and everything was deserted and the restaurant closed. For myself it couldn't have been better. I had a shower and a shave before preparing something to eat from my supplies and settling down to a terrible book for a couple of hours.

By June 1964 conscription had been imposed in Cyprus raising a large number of young conscripts for the new National Guard. Kutchuk immediately put in another request to Turkey to partition the island off. The Turkish army would have landed on Cyprus on the 5th of June but the USA put extreme pressure on them not to take action. Greece is taking a more active role in the affairs of Cyprus pouring thousands of troops in and Grivas with them, with the rank of Brigadier General in the Greek army. The UN was unable to do anything to address the situation; of course they never had a suitable agenda. The attacks continued. Now this is where Gibbons reveals more of the plot. It was about this time that an Anglo-American action plan was prepared and proposed as a basis for a Cyprus solution. It reasoned that

'The continued independence of Cyprus was not feasible on the grounds that the initiatives that Makarios (not mentioned by name) had taken had made Turkish military action likely, had jeopardised the south-east flank of NATO', and that Makarios. 'Had strengthened the influence of the USSR and local communists to the extent that the prospect of it becoming a Mediterranean Cuba must be taken seriously'.

I think it shows where their main consideration was, there was no way that Makarios would have been in full control at this time and remember that fear I told you about, Makarios would have known it by now. But it seems the British and the U.S. are stating that they no longer want to see him in power simply because he's made friends with Russia.

The following events only go to confirming that Makarios was not in control back then. By July the main area of confrontation had moved to this, the Tilliria region and the Turkish villages of Mansoura and Kokkina and a few others were to spend part of the summer under siege. Although it may have seemed that the Greek troops were here at the bequest of the Cypriot government, it seems that they had very much their own agenda, as had the USA and Makarios would never have known. By August the troop build up is at its peak and there is reputed to be near on twenty thousand Greek mainland troops on the island and a lot of hardware in the form of twenty five pound guns and Oerlikon 20mm guns, mortars and armoured cars. Many of the UN posts in the area were attacked and overrun and soon after over two thousand of those Greek men were directing their fire towards Mansoura and the surrounding Turkish villages. August the 7th the Turkish air force flies four f-100's over the area and fire warning rockets into the sea, to no avail. Makarios can't stop the fighting because he's not in control over it. The rift between himself and Grivas is such that they are now, as much in competition with each other. It's during the next attacks by Turkey that Makarios threatens to call the Greek Cypriots to attack Turks all over the island, if Turkey attacks again. Makarios has this power over the people. But it's only in Tilliria that the Turks are being attacked and he is not, to my mind, in control. Makarios might have been winning the campaign to rule the hearts of the Cypriots but Grivas has got a bloody big contingent of the Greek army under him, many of which were now fighting in this region. In the early hours of August the 8th around 200 Turkish women and children take refuge at the UN camp here in Kato Pyrgos. That same day the Turkish airforce struck blasting Greek positions in the hills and destroying a Greek patrol boat as it fled the scene. And the situation was soon brought under some sort of control. But here are some interesting memos that were being passed around at the time. This is where Gibbons is once again so helpful to us, some of these were secret and have only recently been made available.

On August the 18th Ralph Murray the British Ambassador to Athens told the foreign office that Greek prime minister George Papandreou had proposed to the United States, through the American Ambassador to Greece.

"That Greece should cause a coup d'etat to be carried out in Cyprus before agreement with Turkey and that this coup d'etat should include an immediate declaration of Enosis." Proposing that the US and Britain "Should assume the task of restraining a Turkish reaction and that after this Enosis, Greece should come to terms with Turkey".

That same evening, the British cabinet sat to discuss the proposals, a note of the meeting said.
"It was suggested that the removal of the Archbishop Makarios might be a precondition to any settlement of the Cyprus question," it then went on to say. "It was conceivable that the Greeks could build up Colonel Grivas as his successor, it would be useful to establish contacts with Colonel Grivas, preferably overtly, so that we could be clearer where he stood." As if they didn't know how he stood. Little things like this would have always got the Greeks thinking that the British were with them on this Enosis thing. Makarios knows though, he knows all too well what the Turks will do, and he also knows the British wouldn't stop them.

Now here the plot thickens, a telegram sent from the British Embassy in Washington to the Foreign Office dated August 25th said.

"As you will have seen from the full page articles in the New York Times recently, the Greek-American lobby is getting very active and president Johnson is in no position to throw away votes. I do not suggest for one moment that anyone in the (US) Administration would encourage the Greeks to act, but they would find it hard not to be relieved if Papandreou had the gumption to go for Enosis in spite of Makarios and the Turks," it finished with. "One danger that the Greek government will have inferred from its most recent exchanges with the American, that they are favourable to Enosis. If the Greeks then have the courage to act unilaterally, the Americans will not stop them. Nor will they physically prevent a Turkish military reaction against Cyprus, but, for congressional reasons, the administration will not avoid taking action (non military) against the Turks by cutting off aid etc if the Turks use United States equipment."

At this point I can't help but feel that the only thing keeping Makarios in power is the threat of a Turkish attack. Now we've got the USA in favour of Enosis to please its Greek lobby and also to get rid of Makarios who's built up ties with Russia. The only thing that the Americans don't know is that no matter what they or any one else does, if Enosis is forced on Cyprus, nothing would stop a Turkish invasion except direct military conflict and remember the British must have already had a deal going with the Turks. So here's the British warning the U.S.

"Please tell Mr. Ball that we see grave dangers in pressing for Enosis now without prior Turkish agreement as to conditions. Her Majesty's government could not in any case associate themselves with such a move or take part in trying to persuade Turkey to agree to it."

George Ball was the U.S Secretary of State for Foreign Affairs at the time. Britain would have known the whole time that Turkey would show no hesitation in partitioning the island. Such dirty double-dealings going on behind Makarios's back. The Greek government planned to make amends with Turkey by giving it a few Aegean islands when I read that I simply thought you bastards! Kos was one of those named. Piecing the events of Christmas together with all this I had to come to the conclusion that partition was always the British preference. There was simply too much suggesting it now. They'd allowed the situation to slide too far and the fact that they knew so much yet did so little and then these final dirty dealings. Of course the British government could not allow to see it partitioned then because of Britain's commitment to the USA and their commitment to Vietnam. Johnson wasn't going to risk losing that all-powerful Greek vote at such a crucial time for him. Vietnam was all that was saving us though. The British were in favour of Grivas and they knew what Grivas was like. The British government obviously likes Grivas a lot more than Makarios. They locked Makarios up and threw him into exile for leading his people, for taking his role. But Grivas, he's been killing whoever he wants and the British government like him. The differences between him and Makarios after 64 were the same as my cousin and myself. I would have fought my cousin to the death in Cyprus in 74 if I were ten years older and him EOKA b. I can see now, how the British had done a bloody good job of dividing the Greek Cypriots as well.

Here's what I felt the British were doing for starters. They planned to keep their bases through partition and I can't believe that they never did a deal with the Turkish Cypriots. Appeasing the Turkish Cypriot politicians whilst more of their own people got killed. Just as I believe that they did a deal with Makarios to allow him to act in the first place and to get the bases secured. The Turkish Government showed a lot of restraint and trust in the British at first and they never acted in the way that the British might have wanted or expected them to over Christmas. The British were flying reconnaissance operations over the Turkish coast watching for an invasion force at the time. But Makarios wasn't the bloodthirsty devil he's made out to be and attempted to return Cyprus to Britain unconditionally. Meaning that they would have had to address the situation. But the touch paper had been lit and it was a display the British intended watching. Things never improved for Cyprus under British control (which sounds like a sick joke) or under the UN who were working to the same agenda. Now here's the last quote and what a quote it is from Alec Douglas Home the British Prime Minister as a final response to the Americans and this would be the one that would also stop any Greeks DEAD in their tracks in Cyprus.

"It looks to me as though the present constitution is unworkable," he stated adding. "It seems likely, then, that any constitutional conference will end in dead lock and that the only solution will be partition. If things turn out that way, there will be no need for Guarantors and our presence on the island, would be superfluous."

I think would 'seem' superfluous was the word he should have used, they were useless from the start. Of course, they know our history. The British would have known that if we were partitioned we would never relinquish our land to Turkey, I mean never, absolutely never, that's what Thrace was all about. Our history is with the land. They knew we'd never rewrite our constitution if it meant partition hence they keep their bases via the original constitution, which was the whole idea.

After 64, the situation eased off tremendously and Makarios might have made it. But in 1966 the Akritas plan gets handed in to an anti Makarios newspaper no less, damning us all as if we'd never stop our quest for Enosis. I can't find the architect for the Akritas plan. I know who it's supposed to be, but I don't believe a single man wrote it and President Clerides only ever acknowledged it as being genuine. You see after that got published the Turkish government would have believed that whatever we did, whichever way we did it, could simply be interpreted as applying to the Akritas plan, that's the way the plan works, it's never ending. If there wasn't a British hand in writing it, which I find very hard to believe, I knew it had to be a British hand passing it to the newspaper, hence the omissions in it. I believe the omitted sections would have perhaps revealed dates or details that would have shown it for what it is, a relic of the past. Instead even today I could be working to the Akritas plan, if I wasn't writing about it that is. The last section uses the fear that EOKA would have invoked in Greek Cypriots, against themselves. Makarios was attempting to make the most out of a constitution that even the British Prime minister was now saying was unworkable.

After I read for two or three hours I sat out on the balcony and watched the beautiful night sky, unpolluted by any unnatural lights. The stars appeared as crisp and as clear as anyone could imagine them. I was just wearing a pair of shorts so I sat out with a blanket wrapped around me feeling so sad about it all. I knew there was nothing that could have been done to save us after what I'd read. The USA would have given approval for the 74 coup just to keep their Greek lobby happy, let alone the military aspect. They were prepared to risk partition then though, as they never had a friend at that time in either Greece or Cyprus. To them the NATO alliance and the cold war was their most important concern. The British on the other hand would have known that partition would inevitably follow any attempt to force Enosis. After all, they knew far more about the situation than the Americans. The only difference to today, that they wouldn't have taken into account, would be Cyprus now being able to accept Russian help.

I could see a car pull up in the restaurant car park. They were a lot more noticeable by the fact that it was the only unnatural light I could see. I watched some men getting out of the car before a lantern was lit, then I could make out there were three of them. I watched them walk down to the beach and follow the waterline towards my hotel. I stood up as they got closer, so that I could watch them through the trees with their buckets and nets crossing over the beach onto a rock bed, where they started searching around and I lost interest. John had told me that large octopus and crabs were easily caught in the rock pools at night. I sat back for another minute or so and decided to call it a day.

The next morning I awoke bright and not too early to the sound of the surf, which was bliss for me. The sun was shining and the view looked even more spectacular in the morning light. It wasn't so much that the area is some kind of Eden to look at, the hills, which have few trees, had just a hint of green to them. But what made it so appealing was the lack of any sort of developments. It was just so natural. I took my time getting dressed and went out into the reception to have some breakfast. The elderly Cypriot man greeted me and indicated for me to go down the stairs to the restaurant. I was a little surprised to be getting bed and breakfast, as I was sure that I was the only person staying in the hotel. I happily sat there though and made a meal of some cheese and toast washed down with coffee. I never took much notice of the view from here as a tree rises way above the balcony on this level. With breakfast soon done, I'd decided I'd take a walk on the beach and never returned to the room. I followed the road around to the restaurant overlooking the bay and walked down the slipway on to the beach following a similar line to the men the night before. Their footprints only just visible in places either softened by the wind or washed away by the slight tidal movement. As I approached the hotel I saw some steps leading from the hotel balcony to the beach, I realised I could have come straight down from there, although I took a guess that the balcony door might be locked. I gazed up to count how many rooms there were at the same time taking notice of the fact that they all had their curtains drawn. Giving me the impression that the hotel was empty, except for myself. I wondered out on to the rocks and was to soon lose myself, between my thoughts and the rock pools. I found this place stunning and could only say it must have been for the tranquillity.

I potted about the rock pools making my way as I was went. Looking for anything and nothing in particular. Hermit crabs and shrimps and lots of winkles, whose shells the crabs were usually occupying. I realised it was the first time I'd done this in Cyprus, found some rock pools to simply discover. I was quite close to a spit that stuck out a little here when I noticed some form of trench system dug into it. As I got closer I saw a wooden shuttered aperture about 50 CMS long and about 15 CMS high in the side of a low mound that I was approaching, indicating that it had been used as some form of an observation post. The sandstone spit wasn't steep at all and easily ascended from the direction I was walking. I had a pretty good idea of what I was going to find before I got to the small trench, which run between two observation points looking out past the bay to Mansoura.

In the summer of 64 the fighting was taking place here and around Kokkina. Kato Pyrgos gave me the impression of a troubled village when I drove through it and I now knew that they'd seen their share of the troubles. The majority of which would conclude on these beaches in August 64 when the Greeks heard the British Prime Minister Alec Douglas Home's statement that the only solution to Cyprus would be partition. That would quiet them all down a bit. It's something the Greeks learnt when they lost Thrace, when Turkey takes land it is for good and all too often it's Greek land. That would put most Greeks off the idea of forcing Enosis on Cyprus, I say most because Grivas stayed around until November 67 when he flew back to Athens in exile. There was another invasion threat around then from Turkey but on top of the pressure that Johnson applied again there was a big political change in Greece to consider. Now here's the problem I'm having at the moment and it is that I don't believe the U.S. version of history on Cyprus. In front of me they are stating right through that Grivas is here at the bequest of Makarios. I don't believe that one bit. As early as 64 they are proclaiming their differences and I knew from then, even before the US and British memos about overthrowing Makarios for Grivas. I knew that those differences would be the same differences as between Greek Cypriots in 74, as between my cousin and myself. Greek Cypriot Grivas may have been, but the Greek was deeper in him than the Cypriot, he run his own little one man terror campaign against the Turks. The total toll for the Turkish Cypriots between Christmas 63 and 68 is really quite low though, and these are Gibbon's figures, 205 missing most likely dead and 273 killed, not counting the missing. It seemed Kykkos school was a one off. I felt sorry for the fact that it hadn't been confronted. But here I must point out that I'm not giving the Greek casualties during the uprising and there would have been many Greeks killed as well as Turks. It's the sinister acts like the Kykkos school massacre that really concerned me. I'd dare say Grivas must have seemed like a bit of a joke to many Turks. He would have been in his late sixties by now, a bitter relic from the past. He even took part in the failed Greek invasion of Turkey in 1921. Grivas would return to Cyprus in September 1971. To form the EOKA-b organisation and one of the names on his death list would be that of Archbishop Makarios. Even by the beginning of 64 though, all that Makarios wanted was to be able to make the constitutional changes that were deemed necessary for it to work. If that sounds like Enosis by another name, it's not. He wanted to achieve his goals democratically, if then, the people decided on Enosis then so be it. I think he knew that Cyprus would never return to Greece after Christmas 63 though. Which left him caught between the British games and a cause even he would now, come to fear. I made my way from the mound thinking about how so much damage had been done in so little time, only eight months. I wouldn't say there was no resentment after that, just a bit of bigotry on the beach perhaps (sic joke) please allow me one at least.

Off in the distance I noticed a small grey motor launch being trailed by another a few hundred metres from the coast coming from the direction of Kokkina. I carried on walking across the rocks deep in thought. The sad point to all this for myself was that I knew that most Greek Cypriots actually do regard themselves as a breed apart from Greeks. Why though I don't know, I like to think it's because we just have to be different. I certainly knew that the Greek Cypriot people held no real resentment to the Turkish Cypriots. There wasn't any violence between the two communities before they got stirred up and we actually blame the Turks for partition, not the Turkish Cypriots, even though it's their politicians that are more to blame. I already knew that most Greek Cypriots were willing to make an effort. I just knew it would be so hard to establish any trust between the two communities now, even writing this book I couldn't see any Turks believing me. Yet I couldn't help but hope. We are so fragile as people are and there seemed to be so much damage done. The Cypriots it seems are nothing more than a powerless majority, if that makes sense. I still firmly believed we, the Cypriots, are a majority on both sides, but on both sides we are pulled or pushed to taking sides. I could see one of the real problems that would have existed then and possibly still does today is a misunderstanding of each other as a people. How strong our sense of history can be and how weak we are to it. Gibbons says that when the Greek Cypriots took on the Turks of Cyprus they simply stepped out of their class. He's such a fool. I know that most Turkish Cypriots would simply say that Cyprus was their home. I got to wonder about how we should perhaps start initiatives with the Turkish Cypriots and I meant the people and not the politicians. Partition was still to myself an unacceptable situation. I thought about a proposal I'd seen put in by a Greek Cypriot suggesting the establishment of a new Turkish Cypriot city in the north and some Turkish troops being allowed to stay to encourage confidence. It sounded good but I knew he had no idea of how the Turkish Cypriot politicians would feel about it. More amusing to myself was our governments' response that any settlement must be made according to the UN's resolutions on the matter. The total inability of the UN to act in Cyprus both in 64 and 74 was part of our problem as far as I could see.

I caught myself wrapped up in my own little daydream as I walked under the trees below the hotel balcony and onto the beach. I took a gaze at the two grey boats that were just west of the bay, when I noticed something that caught me completely by surprise. I was almost stepping over them as I saw them, fresh footprints. Someone had been on the beach whilst I was on the rocks. As soon as I saw them I thought about taking my shoes off as this woman had, at about the same time as I saw the ever decreasing circle they'd formed, some six or seven metres up the beach from the waterline. My first thought was 'Right, I'll catch you out!' I stepped over the footprints and carefully walked across to the far side of the decreasing circle, stopped and turned to survey the situation. The circle itself was close to four metres in diameter and the woman had made four to five revolutions before getting to the centre. Now I'd done this myself before and as far as I knew there were only two ways of doing it. I knew there were no footprints behind me so no one had jumped that way, but what I was actually looking for was a second person. The reason being I'd already noticed whoever she was hadn't taken a big leap of any kind. The prints stop in the middle where the woman simply seemed to stand on her toes and the sand hadn't been disturbed from the mould they'd made. So I assumed that she'd tip toed out before leaping to a companion. To my total dismay there were no other footprints on the beach whatsoever, except for my own and these. I knew then that she could have only walked out backwards which I really wasn't expecting. I looked up to see that they'd come from the direction of the hotel steps, which were about ten metres away. Only appeared though, as she'd walked through the sea about five metres in their direction and I couldn't see any footprints between the hotel steps and the sea. I wasn't expecting this. I leant forward with my hands on my knees and surveyed the prints. The main reason I wasn't expecting her to have walked out backwards was because she'd made so many footprints walking in. They seemed about five or six in size (U k) most certainly female, and most likely young due to the way that she'd been putting most of her weight on her toes and she seemed light on her toes. Only leaving the faintest of lines to show where her heel had gone. She'd taken such small steps most of them seemed to be no more than 10 to 15 centimetres in front of the hind toes, and the way she'd taken them, lots of weight on her toes but there was something else about them. The angles that some of them came down at were giving me the impression that she might have been waving her arms about or something. This whole time I was also realising that every print I was looking at was perfect in that none showed any signs of disturbance after they'd first been made. Now I even had to consider the time that it would have taken someone. Not one of the many footprints that I looked at showed any sign of disturbance. The harder I looked the more apparent it seemed that she'd not walked back, but I knew my mind could not accept any other conclusion. I looked up at the hotel and shouted aloud at the hotel and at anyone who could hear,

"Someone's having a bloody laugh!"

With that I simply turned my back on the footsteps in the sand and continued walking towards the slip-way. Noticing as I did that the two boats, which had just passed me weren't flying any flags of any description. I considered it safe to assume that they were Turkish.

I returned to the hotel room, collected my car keys and drove over to see my new found friends at Mansoura. When I arrived, I parked the car, waved at Andreas with some of his family from the car park and went straight onto the beach. I took a deep breath and felt like I was in paradise again. I took my time strolling along the beach, studying stones and pebbles again as I walked and waving a long dry grass straw in my right hand, stopping occasionally to let it catch the breeze and rise a little before I'd walk on. If the sound of the sea in my ears, a warm and gentle sun on my face and a fresh breeze that I could smell as well as sense all over my bare skin weren't enough to fill my senses, I found the view beautiful. As I walked down the beach with the sea on my left and the hills on my right and the road unseen over its ledge I felt totally and pleasantly smothered by nature. It was a little while before I ambled back to the restaurant for a coffee. Regardless of how I was feeling, this was to be for myself one of the most pleasant days I'd had in Cyprus for a long time. I think the more the day rolled on the more pleasant it simply felt. I started the afternoon off with a very large Cypriot coffee that Andreas had brought me and was to pass much of it in conversation with Andy and Demetre, the two eldest sons of Andreas and Maria. If I said Andy was in his mid twenties, although maybe a little older. With a two or three year old daughter and a wife who were both present, then Demetre would be around his early twenties. Marie was around and John was at school for another hour or so. My accommodation was quickly brought up as a subject.

"How do you like your hotel?" asked Andy.

"Oh, it's lovely," I said showing my approval with a smile but wanting to show I meant it.

"The view from my room is fantastic, the beach looks beautiful and I can hear the sea, which I like." I would have gone on longer about it, but I knew they could see how happy I was.

"Are you the only one staying there?" he asked.

"As far as I know, well I haven't seen anyone else," I'd forgotten about the footsteps in the sand until then.

"It must be quiet?" asked Demetre, as if the solitude would be a fault.

"It is," I said with an almighty grin on my face.

"You prefer it like that then?" he asked. I knew that was an unnecessary question, but I got a lot of pleasure out of answering it.

"I do right now, its bliss! It really is!"

"What did you do last night though?" he enquired. He would be at the sort of age where the solitude might be considered a big fault.

"I read a book for a while," I wasn't going to tell them which one. "I really enjoyed sitting out on the balcony and watching the stars, that was nice, it feels like it's been years since I'd seen them so clearly," I told them.

"No lights uh."

"No, no lights," I confirmed with a smile.

We chatted on and Andy. Who has a hair recession problem, told me how it all started after he moved back to Cyprus and how he discovered the possible cause.

"This girl I met told me it's the lime in the water," he revealed. "And not to use conditioner," he said feeling his hair.

"Right," I said taking that one in. Andy had obviously got that information a little late, I had noticed mine seeming more brittle. Marie sat down to join us and I told Andy in front of her to ensure she got in contact with a solicitor to enquire about lodging a suit against Turkey for non access to her land. I felt great about telling, I thought they'd have known. But it was like I was watching another 1/4 million pounds going out of Turkey's purse, so it was with extreme pleasure. I thought I'd ask about the Turkish enclave of Kokkina as I'd spent part of the night reading about it.

"How many people live in Kokkina now?" Andy slowly shook his head, I thought he was going to say he didn't know but said.

"I think it's just the military now," he looked at his brother. "There's just soldiers at Kokkina now isn't there?"

"Yeah just soldiers," Demetre confirmed. He seemed knowledgeable on the matter as he'd recently served a long stint in the National Guard.

"How do they get supplied?" I enquired.

"By boat two or three times a week, Tuesdays and Thursdays I think," he said. "I'm not sure about the other day," he looked at his brother. "Sunday I think," it was Tuesday today.

"So I guess that was them I saw this morning," I informed them. "I saw two small launches not flying any flags."

"Yeah that's them," they both confirmed at the same time. Demetre then went on to tell me how they once past close to him whilst he was fishing. They could see he wasn't sure what to do, so they comforted him with a few words, told him there was no need for concern and asked how the fishing was.

We talked further about how we regarded Turkish Cypriots as opposed to the Turks and let me tell any Turkish Cypriot readers. This is a common conversation. We do save any resentment we've got for the Turks of Turkey and perhaps one or two of your politicians Then Andy told me about his fire fighting exploits in the summer bush fires that struck Cyprus.

"Well they come around looking for volunteers and I thought it would be a laugh, well not a laugh, you know what I mean," he said slightly embarrassed by his choice of words."Yeah, like a new experience," I added.

"Yeah," he agreed before continuing. "Well I had no idea we were going to be fighting fires in no mans land," he revealed. I was showing my interest.

"So we pull up with our fire engines and all our equipment and everything and at about the same time we got there, fire engines and men from the other side started turning up," he told me showing his bemusement of the time.

"From the north?" I confirmed to myself. Then enquired. "What happened?" I was eager to hear of any contact with Turkish Cypriots on Cyprus.

"We had a great time," he said. "We were all chatting away, laughing, they were joking with us, it was great," he sounded excited as he spoke.

"Really," I replied wanting to hear more, after what I'd been reading that sounded fine. I liked the thought of it, fighting fires side by side in the only place they could. He seemed to have enjoyed the experience. But what he told me next was to sadden me and remind me perhaps of the worst aspect of our situation.

"Yeah but whenever these," he made hand motions indicating to me military lapels and confirming it with. "I don't know Generals or something, they had these fancy lapels," I knew he was talking about the military.

"Well whenever one of these would get close to us, they'd just shut up!" I wasn't expecting that.

"No!" I said surprised as I was.

"Yeah, they just went silent," he informed me. "Well when they started talking again, I asked them, you know, why they went quiet so quick." I knew he was going to tell me but I was eager to know.

"What did they say?" I asked totally engrossed. Andy seemed to be thinking of the conversation whilst recalling it for me.

"He said they treat them like idiots, they look down on them," with those words my heart sunk. That drove home a harsh reality about the situation in the north. The main threat to the Turkish Cypriots now comes from Turkish mainland migrants, who are simply Turkish and that's it. That's bad enough but I know how many of these Turks feel about us. Before I read the Gibbons book and whilst writing mine, I asked a middle aged Turkish Cypriot that knew about my writing project. 'What's the difference between a Greek and a Greek Cypriot in Turkey?' he seemed confused as to why I was asking. Yet I knew from my visit to Istanbul that they knew the Gibbons definition, as do many Greeks. I recently read another sad story about a Turkish Cypriot who committed suicide whilst doing his national service in Cyprus, he was in his late teens and although no reason was given. I read that he'd lived in Australia until he was 13, I really felt sorry for the poor sod having to come from Australia to that.

John arrived home from school, at which time I could see food being prepared for dinner, so I put in a timely order for some pork chops. After dinner, Andy left with his wife and child and I sat and chatted to Demetre about this, that and life. His father had pointed out some photos of some large fish that they'd caught and Demetre told me about how much he enjoyed fishing and being on boats, saying he was born for it, and John asked me if I wanted to go fishing again that afternoon. I gave my head a couple of short emphatic nods letting him know what I thought about fishing and told him I'd follow him and his father in my car. John liked to talk, which I didn't mind at all, he'd been brought up in Highbury in London so I knew we had a lot in common. I finished my conversation with Demetre and we both left in our own cars to go to the fishing spot, which was on a different beach. I already knew which way to go, but I never knew how far I could go. So when I started to drive my hire car, a Subaru, down a rough looking dirt track, which I knew would take me down to the beach some six or seven metres below. I wasn't surprised to hear Demetre blast his horn to warn me not to go any further. I immediately slammed on the brakes and put the car into reverse and almost thrashed the poor little thing to death. But even with Demetre pushing it wouldn't move. I think we had the same idea at the same time though and he stepped aside to allow me to drive forward a few metres on to a flatter length of track, before putting the car into reverse and flying back to the top. I parked the car in front of Demetre's and we had a laugh as he showed me just how rough the track was, as we walked down to join Andreas and John on the beach. I spent a bit of time investigating the nearby rock pools, which always seem to attract me. Demetre never stayed and I shouted my goodbyes and it wasn't long before I returned to sit and watch the fishing. As I settled in making myself comfortable against the sandstone cliff, whilst keeping a little light conversation with John going. I thought about just how happy I was at that moment. I'd come to the end of my search as far as my grandfather went. I was disappointed with my mother for being far less than honest with me. I already knew why I'd put up a block to the language and I felt that that was confirmed, during my conversation with my godmother. I just knew the suicide theory was mine. I couldn't help feeling my life was an epitome of Cyprus in some way. But as I sat there absorbing the beauty of the coastline, looking east in the fading light, I let all my troubles drift away again. The distant coast had taken a lovely orange hint to it. I felt spoilt. I was starting to feel another one of those perfect moments that seem so rare in life. I was watching John and Andreas interacting in a way I never did with my father. I'd learnt so much about myself and Cyprus these past few months and if I felt sad for anyone, at that moment, it was for that six-year old boy, who lost so much that went unnoticed.

Chapter 14

I guess this is more or less the journey home. I awoke bright and early, on this my last morning and wasted little time in washing and packed my things in the car before I paid the bill and left the hotel feeling good about getting home and finishing this book. As I pulled away from the hotel I saw a soldier hitchhiking and thought, why not? I pulled the car up and told him I was going to Polis, he jumped in and we left Kato Pyrgos. I stopped off at my newly discovered friends restaurant and home and left a note telling them that I'd be back in the spring. It was a lovely day. The air was fresh and clear, very clear. My new travelling companion sat upright in his seat as if at attention, looking straight ahead. It made me feel a little uncomfortable. Now I pick up hitchhikers for what I suppose might be the same reason as most others, to be helpful to a fellow traveller and for a little conversation. Well I wanted a conversation.

"How long have you been in the army?" I asked. Suddenly feeling conscious of my hair length.

"Sixteen months," he replied. His voice was stern, slow and very direct and his unused English thick. Now straight away I realised he might be thinking I'm a spy or something. I'm serious, it's Cyprus and he didn't even know if I was Cypriot.

"My godmother lives in Limassol, she told me I should get my haircut or people will think I am a spy or something," I said getting two things out of the way. I just wanted to chat.

"People with long hair are a minority on Cyprus, it's true!" I did not like the way he said that but I smiled. I knew what he meant. I felt like I was breaking a little ice. I was looking out at the hills.

"What do you think of it here?" I asked. Taking in the beauty of it.

"I hate it, it's barren!" he replied. Now as passionately as I may have loved it, he did seem to hate it.

"I don't know, there's not many trees, but there's a touch of green after the rain and I think it's beautiful," I said. I had to defend the place. He seemed to find my concept of it amusing and I noticed he was smiling a little as he turned his head for the first time and said,

"There's nothing here!"

"I know!" I said with some joy. I then went on to tell him I was writing a book about Cyprus and myself and as we were passing one of the many water taps that the British had built along these roads, adorned with the crest of the British crown I told him,

"They're the ones that have done the most damage to Cyprus though!"

"Yes the British have been the cause of much misery to the Greek people," he replied. You should meet my cousin I thought.

When I first entered the truth site I sat in this chair in shock. The second time I entered I wrote of. I was a trembling mess thinking I was looking at the manifestation of our resentment. Those three children and their mother huddled together in a blood stained bath. It tore at me so deep. Around that same time whilst visiting friends in London I was watching some scenes from Kosovo on the television in a sandwich bar, with the horror that such scenes should summon in a man. We've watched it lately in Bosnia and then Rawanda and now it was Kosovo, it just seems to make good viewing these days. Someone asked me if I didn't think we were getting immune to it. I looked at him and became even more cynical to the human race. I told him that I would never allow myself to look on at such scenes without feeling for the pain of those that I'd be watching. Even from the comfort of my armchair a thousand miles away. I felt just as much for these three children and their mother Mrs Ilhan.

The description given in the Genocide files Book one, Peace without Honour, seems to be the original Gibbons text. As the P.C. word program he's used to overwrite the book has not been used on the original transcript, you can tell by the P.C. correction marks. Anyone using a P.C. word program will know what I mean. The Ilhan massacre was different from everything else I was reading though. The account by Gibbons, it just never seemed right, if I said out of context with what I was reading you may not understand, but it was. It always seemed to have that, I've got to say it, professional touch to it. I'm supposed to be reading about an armed rabble, I couldn't work it out, Mrs Ilhan a Turkish army officers' wife was having dinner that night with her three children and five family friends, her husband was on duty. They lived in Kumsal a suburb of Nicosia, supposedly attacked by 150 Greeks that Christmas Eve night 1963, I say supposedly for a reason. It's not that I'm denying Greeks attacked Kumsal that night, over which a hundred and fifty hostages were taken, and nine killed. But I've always wondered if these were Greeks that killed these people. Gibbons gives his account of their murder both on the Internet Truth site, and in his book 'The Genocide files' on page 124. It was Christmas Eve night.

That evening, Hasan Yusuf Gudum, an elderly Turkish landlord, was visiting one of his clients in Kumsal.

With him was his wife, Ferideh, his neighbour Mrs. Ayshe Mora with her one-year-old daughter, Ishin, and her married sister, Novber.

They were paying a call on the family of Major Nihar Ilhan, the chief medical officer with the mainland Turkish army contingent. The major was on duty that night with his unit, His wife, Muruvvet, was with their three children, Murat, Kutsi and Hakan, aged seven, four and six months.

The nine were having supper in the dining room when one of the Greek private armies, augmented by workers from the Severis flour mill who had – willingly or under coercion – joined their ranks, crossed the dry Pedieos river bed.

The conversation around the dining table cut off abruptly when bullets began to spatter the outside walls, sounding like heavy rain.

The group rose hurriedly, the women dragging the children, and Gudum ushered them to the back part of the house.

They all, four women, four children and one man, went into the bathroom and closed the door.

The landlord's wife suddenly changed her mind, left the bathroom and went into the separate toilet where she locked herself in.

Mrs. Ilhan, the major's wife, stepped into the bath, and holding her baby stood facing the door, her other two children clinging onto her legs.

The two other women and Gudum crawled terrified into the corners beside the door. Mrs. Ayshe Mora held her baby close.

There was a crash as the front door burst open and a continuous roar as machinegun bullets spewed through the house.

Footsteps came to the locked bathroom, an unknown hand impatiently rattled the knob, and a voice called in Greek,
"How would you like Enosis?"
Then a hail of bullets tore through the wood and Mrs. Ilhan and her children, caught directly in its path, were lifted off their feet and dumped on to the bottom of the bath.

The killers smashed the door lock and jumped inside. One of the major's children moaned and was scolded into permanent silence by a short peremptory burst. Then the raiders saw the others huddled on the floor. They played their guns on them like impatient children forced to water the garden flowers. The three Turks were all wounded, some seriously. A bullet struck the foot of the baby Ishin. These were the ones that survived, it just didn't seem right to me. One of them at least wasn't even seriously wounded and at such near range. When I say these guys are good though, it's because they seem too professional and Gibbons accounts are good, he's just very bloody biased. Now when I say these guys are good, remember this is an eyewitness account. Next

'The locked door of the toilet drew the gunmen's attention to the landlord's wife. The door was beaten in by machinegun butts and the woman dragged out whimpering. A pistol was placed to her head, one shot was fired, and she slumped to the floor, dead. The killers whooping and jeering, charged through the house, machinegunning cupboards, smashing furniture, slipping and sliding on the dark red blood that crept out of the bathroom.'

In this report even the idea of a Greek shouting "How would you like Enosis," before opening up with a machinegun never sounded right. He shouted it in Greek, but "How would you like Enosis," I couldn't quite imagine a Greek shouting that out. "Turkish dogs," yes but not. "How would you like Enosis," and I was wondering about the survivors when they'd seemed so professional with the whimpering woman and even the child in the bath, with the short peremptory blast. I tried to imagine myself there so many times. They were using Sterling machine guns and would've most likely emptied the clips on the three cowering on the bathroom floor. These machine gun clips only last a couple of seconds when the triggers pulled right back, hence the short burst to the child in the bath. They would have emptied their clips before they could have been sure the Turks were dead. Yet they reloaded fresh clips to shoot up the furniture. It just all seemed odd. I thought at first that they were possibly Greek mainland troops with their efficiency but they weren't. The Turks can differentiate, as they often are in Gibbons' book, even from what was shouted here, they should be able to, the dialect is that different. And the Turks like to say when they hear mainland Greeks and anyway I knew that the Greek mainland contingent was at Omorphita that night. But oddest of all for myself was the silence before they shot the woman. They simply dragged a whimpering woman out of the toilet. Then they silently and I'll emphasise this 'Silently' put a pistol to her head and shot her.

There were survivors hence the running commentary. Three people survived and watched this. I was troubled that these men were supposed to be a rabble. In other places they don't seem to know their tit from their toe according to Gibbons, but these guys were good. You know how the mere sight of Mrs Ilhan and her children in the photograph that was supposedly taken three days after the massacre affected me. But something always troubled me about this report. I knew that 150 hostages were massacred at Kykkos school but I can't help but regard the Christmas troubles as an uprising, more typical to Omorphita, where five thousand Turks were put under siege and casualties were fairly low. They weren't completely under siege though. There was an exit left to Mandres or Hamit Koy as the Turks call it, which the Turks took advantage of and most of the five thousand escaped to that hamlet, 550 that stayed were those taken hostage at Kykkos school. The Turks seem surprised that the Greeks never gave chase to pick off the helpless refugees, I wasn't. They were leaving and I knew from what I was reading that that was the whole point of the siege. They weren't going to leave Cyprus though. Like I said I've tried to imagine myself at this massacre a dozen times. It was the shout and then the silence before the shot and the way they executed the whole program. I was already convinced these weren't part of any Greek rabble.

So I'm sitting at my P.C. last night just closing down to go to bed. Looking at the Gibbons book, Oh! It's a good book Gibbons, I am genuinely so pleased I've got it. Last night I'm looking at it thinking how I couldn't quite believe how stupid Gibbons is, with his interpretation of the times, so I thought I'd pick it up again, just to confirm what I'd written. It must have been fate. I opened the book on page 150 and read.

'Peter Bostock walked up to me. Peter was the R.A.F information officer in Nicosia. During the Christmas fighting, I made full use of his unusual attribute-- for an information officer, that is. He actually delighted in giving reporters information, from the part of Nicosia where he lived. I had kept up to date on the movements of the Greek private armies, the police, the Cyprus army and the mainland contingent, as well as what the RAF was doing.

Peter gave me a photograph. It showed a woman and three children in a bath, blood splashed over the white tiles. It was the scene of the Kumsal massacre.
How Peter got it he refused to say. All I knew was that it had happened somewhere in the Turkish quarter.

I suspect that the photo was taken by one of the RAF residents in the area, several of whom stated later they had seen Greeks entering the house and heard the shots.

But with nothing to identify the pictures by names, time or place, I could not, send it to my newspaper. They would have demanded a caption to go with it, and Peter just didn't know anything. Two days later my Daily Express colleague, Stan Meagher, photographed the death scene himself. His picture was syndicated around the world and did nothing to enhance the Greek Cypriot cause.'

I can think of a caption but I won't do it. Gibbons gets so much in between that it never occurred to myself before when I read his book, but this was Christmas day at the British high Commission. Just after the cease-fire talks, where the Turks decided it would be better not to call a cease-fire until their hostages were returned. Spaced twenty-six pages apart from the massacre. By now though I'm familiar with the story so I knew this was the very afternoon after the massacres occurred. Gibbons seems to believe that overnight, one of the nearby RAF residents to Mrs Ilhan nipped over to her house and got a snapshot of her and her children in the bath. Whilst the place spent much of the night under attack. I'm sorry if I seem callous but I've had my head in this for the last few months. Weren't they concerned about being mistaken for a Turk and perhaps getting hurt? 150 hostages were taken that night from Kumsal. Such considerate neighbours. My how brave they were, but lucky they took their flash with them and such a quick photo development. Only the British could turn out photographs that quick in Nicosia on Christmas day 1963, thank you Harry. Of course, this is the stuff I told my cousin we could never prove. Here's the part I find amusing though, Gibbons, printing all these little facts as he has for analyses, when he hates us so much, his bias has blinded him. He is good with details though and he likes to boast about how he knows everyone. He seems to get up the nose of a lot of them.

RAF information officer in Cyprus for the Christmas fighting, this is only a few days after it began. My how quickly he became familiar with the world's press. They show Gibbons the Middle-East's best known reporter with a respected London paper, a photo that the world's press would take another two days to get. Lucky Gibbons had Peter to keep him and the other reporters informed, good old Peter, the RAF information officer, he's the man, gives you all sorts of help, worth the odd drink occasionally. Gibbons doesn't stop to think of any psychological aspect of it. Those gunmen left survivors. "How would you like Enosis," should have been more like. "Ere we go, ere we go," I think. And then Peter comes out from his darkroom with his own latest snapshots, wonderful work Peter!

It was the shout and the silent shot at first, but this confirms it for myself. British Special Forces would have their own breed of psychopaths for this sort of work. The type that might find some pleasure out of putting a pistol to a woman's head and pulling the trigger. And the type that would probably ask those poor children to "Smile please" before taking their photo to be handed to an information officer. I used to have this problem, like others, thinking the British wouldn't do that, even though I always knew they would.

But now putting aside what the British have done here already, something far more sinister has happened. Present day in Cyprus, the Turks are now claiming the photograph syndicated around the world was a montage, suggesting improper conduct by the press, but this is not true at all and they're hiding something. Major Ilhan never knew about the slaughter. He couldn't have known or even had any idea of what had happened at Kumsal and nor would he for at least three days. Otherwise, he, like any man, would have returned to check on his wife and children. Which meant the Turks, his own people, had not informed him. And far worst, I believe his politicians had kept the mainland Turkish army contingent to which he was attached, on the move outside of Nicosia and away from the fighting for at least two or three days, so that he wouldn't know. Gibbons never took the Ilhan photograph as Peter may have wanted, which meant the British and Turks had a problem. One of their best propaganda set-ups would be wasted. Unless they could insure that all the bodies, including the woman shot in the head, lay where they died despite eyewitness survivors, until the press could find them or get shown them another two days later, as was the case with John Starr of the Daily Mail. The bodies were definitely still there, as other journalists also saw them at the same time and to do this would have meant keeping Major Ilhan the Chief Medical officer with the Turkish contingent away and in ignorance of the facts, away from any casualties even. Which would have been made possible by first moving the Turkish Contingent to which he was attached out of barracks on to the main Nicosia-Kyrenia road, which was done the day after his wife and children were murdered. And then the next day on to Ortakoy where they made camp, until I assume they were brought under British control. This has got to be one of the sickest and most sinister pieces of propaganda window dressing I have ever heard of. My apologies to the then Major Ilhan I have felt for you from the first time I saw the photograph, but I can only believe the Turkish Cypriot politicians had your family targeted by British Special Forces for this part of their sick campaign.

Now I find myself asking another question about the 150 shot at Kykkos School. The British now seem to be involved in the Kumsal attack and nothing will convince me otherwise. Now there's another coincidence that must be taken into consideration. I had considered the numbers before, but there wasn't anything linking them, but there is now, the British. 150 taken from Kumsal to Kykkos School to be joined by 550 from Omorphita where 150 were separated from the others and shot, after which the bodies were concealed. Too much of a coincidence there I think, considering the British knew about it and kept it quiet. I can only believe now it was insidious Englishmen who shot these people and concealed the fact, knowing the future implications it would have on us as a nation, and it seems far more than possible now. They'd have done it that I do know.

So I'm thinking this soldier would get on well with my cousin, and it would be about then that I was noticing for the very first time that off in the distance to the

North, I could see the coast of Turkey. It was the first time that I'd seen it from Cyprus. I kept casting my eyes over to it until the road took a turn and was heading north at which time I was to look to my right.

"Shit!" I exclaimed loudly. "I've got to pull up!" I shouted. It was the Kyrenia mountain range. I had never seen them so clearly. Almost straight away I saw a place to stop off the road on the right and I parked the car and got out and took a few steps closer, as if it would help. The mountains seemed to loom up clear and sharp in a way that I'd never seen them before, their jagged points and ridges showing up in the clear light.

"I've never seen them so clearly!" I was talking aloud to the soldier as well as myself. The soldier responded.

"Beyond those mountains is Kyrenia," he said in his thick English.

"I know," I simply stared in awe for a couple of minutes before silently returning to the car and whilst I attached my seat belt, I took a last glance before putting the car into gear and moving on. It was another sad moment for me but it wasn't long before I spoke.

"My godmother said I should go if I want to, but I won't sign the Denktash agreement."

"That's good," said the soldier. I thought I'd change the subject.

"So Cyprus will be in Europe soon," I said cheerfully. It's something that most Cypriots are looking forward to.

"I don't know," he replied. It's amazing how many Cypriots don't keep up with world affairs. In fact most don't have much regard for national politics for that matter.

"Oh for sure," I confirmed.

"I think Europe is very beautiful," he said. I smiled. He said that with some warmth.

"It is," it's getting bloody big as well I thought. I dropped the soldier off at a junction in Polis and I drove on into the town centre, where I parked up and walked to the main square to get some breakfast.

I was sitting at the same restaurant in Polis as a few days before, eating the same breakfast. When I noticed something that seemed to have slipped my attention before. Someone had painted a central building in the blue and white fashion that I'd associate most with Greece. I hadn't noticed it before and I have to confess, I liked seeing it. I believe it was a throw back to WW11 when the Italians controlled many Greek islands, so the locals would paint their homes to show loud and clear who they were. I felt that our traumatic past had caused some sort of identity crisis within many Cypriots. If I write from a personal perspective then I have to say that those same colours on any Cypriot building might have caused some offence in me only a few months previous. Symbolism seems so important in the world we live in. I find it sad but true. I can't help feeling that unless we reconcile ourselves with our past then, others after me, will ask the same questions that I know I found myself asking which left me not only doubting Makarios, but also my own country. Gibbons says that when he saw Greek flags on Cyprus the swastika would be more appropriate, the way that events unfolded in 63-64 and in 74, I have at times found myself agreeing with him. It was in that flags' name, that Makarios was being hunted down in Cyprus in 74 and his supporters were being slaughtered. There are many of us that regard ourselves as Cypriot first and foremost, I know I'm not alone. Even though our flag may be broken it's still our flag and to myself it is our duty to repair the damage that's been done to it. This journey that I've been on, has left me feeling different to the Greek flag though, fonder of it, it's part of my history.

I know many Greeks will understand how I feel, and I know I'm not alone. We celebrate 'Ochi day' with Greece as if, it is, genuinely something significant to Cypriots. To those that need informing 'Ochi day' or 'No day', as is its translation, is where Greeks and some Greek Cypriots celebrate the day in October 1940, when Italy demanded that Greece allow Italian occupation of strategic locations on Greek soil. Greece's firm refusal plunged her into WW11, but also improved her self-esteem tremendously. Now that is Greek history and not Greek Cypriot history, there are differences. I can't help but think of my own 'Ochi day' or 'No day', and it is a day in history that happened. It is also a day that every Cypriot will one day read about if he or she is to take any genuine interest in our history. That was the day in 1915 when Greece said 'No' to accepting Cyprus in return for her participation in WW1. Only six years before Greece decided to launch her own fatal invasion against a country whose population outnumbered hers, by well over four to one, the results of that disastrous invasion Cyprus has felt in some terrible ways, more than once since.

I knew it wasn't Greece's fault that so much resentment was unleashed on our island in 63 and 64, the division of the Greek Cypriots had already began. I couldn't help feeling that Britain imposed an identity crisis on to the Greek Cypriots and then we fell into a bigger pit, which would have suited the British well, by not talking openly about our recent past. The secrets that stifle love on Cyprus also make it a lot harder for the truth to be revealed. Even though we were and still are of the Greek people, we've always been the Greeks of Cyprus, just as Cyprus has always been Greek. I could imagine the shock in the Greek Cypriots when they discovered that Britain was actually discussing with Turkey and Greece what to do with Cyprus, as soon as our independence campaign turned to violence in 1955. No Cypriots were even invited to the talks and Turkey made its interest clear by bombing its own consulate in Salonika in Greece. By 1964 the world had a definition for Cypriot self-determination and horror stories from the likes of Gibbons and massacres like Kykkos School to help define it. 'Enosis,' I knew it would forever burden our country with the threat of partition. If, ever, we were to attempt to progress from a constitution which gave half the power to 17% of the people whom never showed any interest whatsoever in the constitutional affairs of state, only thirty years earlier.

After breakfast I drove through Latsi looking to see if I could notice Demetres' car at whatever hotel he worked at, thinking I might stop by and say hello, rather than goodbye. I couldn't see it, but there was another destination on this same road that wasn't on the itinerary but I couldn't resist it, and wasn't to be disappointed when I arrived, the baths of Aphrodite.

Aphrodite, the Greek goddess of love, beauty and sexual rapture, and to myself, more so now than ever, one of our islands most precious national treasures. Aphrodite loved, and was loved by all, mortals and Gods alike, what a woman. I was quite surprised when I got to the baths. I noticed some workmen erecting some railings on the path that leads to them and then I got to the bath, I remembered seeing it in murkier days, it was beautiful. The bath is a natural pool fed by a fresh water spring in a small open cave with overhanging foliage. The water was clear and enticing, I could imagine wanting to slip into it in summer, even now it looked appealing. There was a notice asking people not to bathe in the water and another asking people not to adorn the tress. I thought the area looked tidy. I know it may sound silly to some, but we still pay homage to Aphrodite on Cyprus. I'd never thought about it too much before, so I guess I may have taken it for granted. We'd have continuously paid homage to her now for around three thousand years, it's the continuity, the power of faith that I was thinking about.

Moments of madness, I'd felt a few since starting this book. I was gazing at the pool and for the first time since my conversation with Andy and Demetre thought of the footsteps in the sand on Pyrgos bay, I'd flipped. They just didn't seem possible. I thought about driving back to Kato Pyrgos just to get a photograph of them. They were footsteps in the sand though. I knew even a photograph wouldn't prove what I was seeing. Someone had seemed to have danced to the centre of the circle in small steps before standing on her toes as if reaching up and that was pure and simply where all trace of her vanished. I'd flipped when I realised that even if she had of walked back, which I regarded as near on impossible. It could have only been through the sea to the rocks that I'd walked from and I knew I'd seen no one.

I soon set off again taking the high north road to Paphos. I knew where my next stop was going to be and yes it was planned, for the book and for myself. I'm reacquainting myself with my heritage and loving it. Tomb of the kings and they weren't just kings' that were buried here. It didn't matter that the Romans were here, when they were. They would have just been ruling us like the British, happy to let us get along with our lives whilst they got along with whoever they were conquering. I'd come to be close to my ancestry. After everything I'd been through these past months, I knew who I was and I wondered amongst the tombs feeling proud about whom I am. I walked into one of the partially enclosed tombs and sat down in the shade, and smoked a cigarette whilst thinking about what I'd been reading and my god brother.

The Colonels of Greece took power on the 21st of April 1967 to rid themselves of their corrupt government. A good job too, these colonels don't seem as bad. Gibbons donates his second book of his trilogy completely to them, I thought he was creeping myself. They recalled a lot of the Greek mainland troops from Cyprus, and by November Grivas had gone and Makarios would be able to breathe easier. Makarios had known how real the threat from Turkey was since1964 if not a week before, many others simply weren't regarding it as so real. I could hardly blame them though if they were being encouraged by certain country's to act. In 1964 it would be the Greek Government with U.S. and British encouragement, until the British Prime Ministers warning speech and it was a warning speech. In 1974 those very same governments were doing the same thing again. But by then most would have forgotten that warning speech, but the Turkish threat would be greater than ever. One of the reasons I considered it to be greater than ever was because of the Akritas plan being published and of such incidents as the Kykkos School massacre. Which was why I was so disturbed that the British concealed the truth about it and more disturbed to consider that it might have been them that did it. They would know the importance of reconciliation, by another name its called forgiveness.

The 74 coup was an internal affair. That was the worst part of it. My cousin has started communicating with me again now. I believe he stopped because he knew I'd realise he was EOKA b in 74. But I wrote and told him I knew about it and that there is no realistic approach other than to show complete and utter unity until we can return to the land of our forefathers. I sat back with the last of my cigarette and tried to imagine myself being ten years older and in Cyprus in 74. This was perhaps the saddest aspect of that time, I knew if I was here, at such an age, I might have found myself in conflict with my god brother to the death. I thought about it and I knew that the difference we felt, would be enough for myself, to defend my own country's leadership against any outsiders, which Greeks were then, regardless of our history. I would have fought my own brother with such terrible consequences. I sat back and a tear filled my eye again. We'd have stopped fighting each other as soon as we knew the Turks had landed, but that would have been too late. They came in with crack paratrooper and commando regiments and we wouldn't have been prepared for such a conflict. Whilst HMS Hermes was anchored taking off British Citizens, only a few miles away the Turks were landing troops in a full scale amphibious invasion. Leaving us to defend ourselves from the might of the Turkish army, we knew we didn't have a chance.

My cousin says for five thousand years. I could say three to three and a half thousand years, but its somewhere in between and I could be more accurate, which sounds crazy as I can get it more precise, but I feel it. I don't know whether that's enough to make the difference between my god brother and myself. But reading the Gibbons book back in England. When I realised the games that the British had been playing along with the Turkish Cypriot politicians in 63 and 64. Using Greek resentment to force Turkey to partition our island, forever. To realise that 74 was the achievement of that goal. I looked back. It was so strange. I was in such turmoil. I couldn't describe the emotions I was feeling. I looked back with the horror it deserved. Before I'd only seen or felt my grandfather looking on at me. But when I looked back, then, in that rage. After I realised what they'd done and how they thought it would be, I saw them all. Men and women, my grandfather was looking down and behind him stood three and a half thousand years of ancestry, my ancestry and there were many, there were so many and so many of them were angry, I looked amongst them and I looked to them. My grandfather stood insignificant amongst the gathering looking down. The warriors amongst them were demanding, no words could I hear, just their anger could I feel, it was terrible and so real. Some looked down as if not knowing what to tell me, I felt helpless. But one looked at me, not with the anger of the majority, nor the helplessness of a few. She looked at me with a knowing eye.

I spoke to Zeki today. I'm still waiting for copyright permission from Gibbons. I asked Zeki, is he Cypriot or Turkish first and foremost and he seemed confused by the question as are many. He told me of the horror of Nicosia in 63 which he lived through, I said I will tell of those same horrors. But I told him I can never accept a partitioned country and asked him again how he stood as being Cypriot went. He told me perhaps the Cypriot would be for the future and then proudly told me of his forefather who came to Cyprus from Anatolia two hundred years ago. I felt so sorry for him. So recent and not understanding of the call those same lands have on us. We talked on about Christmas 63 and I told him of the British deceit I'd found and he agreed that it was there and then he said something that I wasn't expecting.

"You know when the British went wrong?"

"When?" I asked.

"In nineteen twenty-three," he told me. He was talking about the population exchange. My first thought couldn't be helped, although I kept it to myself, he was telling me he thought his elders should have been returned to Turkey. It would have saved us all a lot of misery. I asked him,

"Zeki, do you know what sort of difference Russian help will make?"

"Let me tell you something about Russia," he said. "With Russia, if you give her a hand, she'll take an arm." I smiled considering the crisis we're in today and told him,

"That sounds a whole lot better than the present situation Zeki."

I can't help thinking if the hand that reaches out to help, can pull us high enough, who is it that say's no. Aphrodite answers to no man and will reach where she pleases.

Gibbons writes as if he is an Englishman although he was born in Scotland and claims to be of Irish ancestry. He doesn't know where he's from, but I know about being an Englishman. You're extremely lucky if you can say any of your forefathers fought at Waterloo, or any famous battle. It was always something that I took for granted, but never considered like this before. We all know the famous battles as gatherings for our forefathers. I should imagine I had forefathers at Salamis but I know with certainty my forefathers marched alongside Alexander at Issue and Tyre and then on to destroy the Persians and all who stood in their way. These same forefathers would have stood amongst the gathering along with the shepherd.

I told Zeki, what I would tell Gibbons here. My cousin may say for five thousand years but I know for myself, I know my forefathers have been on that land for over three thousand years. Three thousand years and I will not let any future generation go by without remembering that.

Today is December the 15th. It's been said that the missiles leave Russia today, but nothing is confirmed. This year, next year, they will come. They will have to.

My next stop was to be the Byzantine Museum in Paphos. It was on the itinerary for the book and for myself. I passed the Pine Mansions hotel and drove around the centre and behind the hotel and parked up on a quiet street knowing that the museum was nearby. Before I found it though, another museum of a different kind caught my attention. The Ethnographic museum as it's called, but perhaps the Museum of Folk tradition and cultural heritage, might be more appropriate and I couldn't resist it. The museum itself is housed in a strange looking house to myself for a Cypriot folk museum, in that the building looks perhaps more Mexican to me from the outside, but I think that's my ignorance of Cypriot architecture. It's actually a noteworthy example of late 19th century Paphos urban architecture. It's a large villa type house with a red tiled roof and a very large lower level, which can't be seen from the outside. Its three arches, which are a faded light reddish colour with the high metal-railed fence along the front veranda, gave it its Mexican appearance to myself. The main entrance is through a wrought iron gate and up seven steps leading you straight into the main hallway. From the moment you walk in you know this is a museum with a difference. From standing in the main hallway you immediately get an unexpected impression of grandeur, that the house may have once seen, with lots of large ornate furnishings and red velvet around the place, it seems genuine enough. There was a table on my right as I walked in, displaying a number of different publications, to my left and in front and prominent by it's positioning a large high backed armchair. On which a Cypriot woman in her late fifties was sitting talking to what might easily have been her daughter who was just leaving. They said their farewells and she wasted no time in coming to my attention.

"Good afternoon sir, would you like to look around," she was direct but very polite.

"I do, how much is it?" I asked.

"It's two pounds entrance fee and two pounds for the brochure," she said as she walked over to the table. I'd already taken the money out of my wallet by the time she'd turned to give me a brochure, after which she immediately went into an extremely fast unexpected verbal tour of the museum.

"The museum is spaced over two levels there is the," she went into a set routine and spoke so fast and so direct I almost switched off as I flicked through the brochure thinking it would do. I showed an interest in what she was telling me was where. I got a complete rundown of over half a dozen different rooms and their mixed contents and various aspects of the museum, in a set piece that was so fast as to leave me exhausted attempting to keep up.

"So if you go down to the lower level first and afterwards I will show you around the upper level," she said, holding her hands out. "The staircase downstairs is outside and along the balcony," she motioned through the doors as she informed me.

"Great thanks," I said with a bemused smile.

"Sure you'll be ok," she called out as I was leaving.

"I'll be fine," I called back with a smile.

I made my way down a staircase at the side of the building to the backyard and the lower rooms. I walked through the corridor taking in the contents of the rooms as I did. The bedroom with the barbers' chair and the room opposite filled with such working tools like the olive press's and a cotton gin. The walls in some rooms were adorned with costumes and in others with shepherds tools and skin bags, that would have been used by those shepherds. I made my way out through to the backyard to explore outside. There was no one else around and the sun was warm, as I ambled about taking everything in. The yard held so much history, ancient agricultural tools, a small cave tomb in the outside wall from the same period as the tomb of the kings and a very small ancient chapel set in a cave. Ancient pots and other assorted antiquities, it was very much a living museum. I slowly made my way back to the corridor and through to the room that I'd saved for last. The villagers' bedroom, which held the iron four-poster, with its crocheted lace covering and mosquito net coming down over one side. Before I got to the bed though I passed the barbers' chair, but not without taking a seat in it. I sat upright and leant back to explore the table in front of me, with its loose scattering of barbers' tools, before being drawn to the mirror in front of me. The past few months had been such an emotional roller coaster with so many twists and turns. I was now thinking about Kose the shepherd. Wondering whether he'd really been a victim of Greek resentment or simply camped in an appropriate place to be observed by the High Commission staff, who watched him being chased down by men who I now knew, could well have been British. I thought about how the British were handling the media and started to wonder just how much chaos they'd caused over that Christmas 63. All the treachery and deceit that I was feeling, covered over by our resentment. I understood why we couldn't answer for so many of the crimes. We didn't believe them. We'd never been told of them from our own sources or by the British in Cyprus. Yet I could see the Turks would be living with them every day and we'd never see what they saw. I was in so much turmoil. I sat erect in the chair with my head up and took a few deep breaths as I explored the man I was now looking at in the mirror. It felt like it had been so long since I'd studied my own features. I explored my face first. It didn't seem to be showing any signs of the stress that I was feeling. I brought my eyes to gaze upon their own reflection. If I was showing what I was going through at the time, it was only in my eyes. I gently closed them and let slip a tear, before opening them again looking across the tabletop, but feeling so distant. I brought myself round and I gazed across the room and over the bed before letting my eyes roam the peasant costumes and the rooms' furnishings. Like the living museum, this felt like a living bedroom. I realised that most of the items placed around the room would have been familiar to both cultures in Cyprus. The bed was made and with its lace covering looked evermore appealing. A part of me was feeling totally drained. I slid myself off the high barbers' chair and first sat on the bed feeling the fine lace for a moment, before slowly resting my head on the pillow. It never took me long before I brought my feet up and brushing the dust off my footwear, I lay back putting my hands behind my head, and explored what I could only imagine to be the history of the both communities. It felt so sad knowing the damage that had been done and no one ever knowing how. Yet I was somehow soothed knowing I was looking at relics from a time, when we were all so innocent of it, as I gazed, I started feeling that the Turkish Cypriot people could never see what we were saw in their politicians. Nor could they have ever known how we'd react, and the sort of forces that are invoked, when it comes to that defence of our land. I couldn't help thinking about Gibbons remarks of how

English the Turkish Cypriots are and how British the Greek Cypriots appeared to be, before he redefined us and I dare say a lot of it may have rubbed of on us under colonial rule. But Gibbons pays scant regard to even British history. I'd forgotten the Anglophile within me. But I remembered what it was like to feel proud to be British and for myself, being working class, it came from feeling that few people had suffered more at the hands of the British government than the lower classes, of their own people. Why should we have expected them to have any more regard for us. I slowly felt my Cypriot dream being eaten away by the ignorance of the likes of Gibbons, and the deceit of the British, until all we had left was fear and loathing.

I got off the bed and brushed the lace with my hand before gazing around the room once more. I left with a last glance at the mirror and went straight to the stairs and ascended to the veranda, entering the main hallway to the museum to explore the upper rooms. The woman who'd given me my verbal tour was about to entertain a tourist with the same lines, leaving me free to roam at will. There wasn't as much to interest me on the upper floor. Three rooms were immaculately laid out, one as a study and two sitting rooms with ornate furnishings and fittings. There was an elderly Cypriot man wondering around, whom I assumed to be living with the woman in the two front bedrooms. In the hallway there were a few wooden chests and a few display cases with some folk art and one full of coins and paper money, which I gave a little time before making my way to the entrance. Where the woman was just finishing giving another tourist a verbal tour, I was so pleased I'd had the downstairs to myself for those brief moments.

"Did you enjoy your tour of our museum," the woman called out to me before I reached the door.

"Yes very much so," I said turning to talk to her. "It's been very pleasant," I thought of my spell on the bed. •

"Would you like to write something in our visitors book," she asked. Writing anything was the last thing I wanted to do at that moment.

"No I'm fine thanks," I said. "I've been here before," I lied.

"Oh when?" she asked.

"About ten years ago," I said. Not knowing why I'd lied in the first place.

"Have you noticed much difference," she enquired. I thought there must be a difference or she wouldn't have asked and at the same time I wasn't sure if she knew that I'd lied. I took a guess at the brochure being over ten years old.

"Not much," I said.

"Oh, there's much more dear, much more," she said proudly. "Are you on holiday?" she enquired.

"No not really," it never felt like nor was it a holiday. "No I've come out for a book that I've been writing," I told her as her husband walked to her side.

"Your Cypriot?" she enquired with a knowing smile.

"Yes"

"Of course you are, as soon as you walked through the door and I saw you, I thought this man is Cypriot for sure, I know you are Cypriot, yet I talk to you in English," she said seemingly bewildered by her own actions now.

"That's all right," I told her. "I don't speak Greek, its kind of what I'm writing about," I informed her.

"You're writing a book about yourself?" she asked.

"Sort of, my grandfather has been a bit of an influence," I still wasn't sure how to explain it. "I discovered that I put a block up to the language after he died and I think it might have been related to the troubles here in the sixties." I told her. More so now than ever do I think of how the press would have affected him.

"Where's your grandfather from?" she enquired.

"Ayios Amvrosios"

"Ayios Amvrosios, ah it's beautiful there," she turned to her husband. "Isn't it beautiful there," he was nodding his agreement.

"I know "

"Have you been there?" she asked.

"No" I replied with a grim smile showing I wasn't going to let it get me down. She may have realised and quickly broke in with.

"And your book! Is it about your grandfather?"

"Kind of, " I said slowly. "And myself and Cyprus." This seemed to interest her more.

"And what's your name," she enquired.

"Dimitri Jordan," I informed her as I started politely backing out of the hall.

"And your book, what's it going to be called?" I was surprised at the interest.

"I don't speak Greek," I said. She seemed approving and nodded.

"You don't," she replied making the title seem natural.

"No," I said humbly as I turned to leave.

"You know if your grandfather is with you, you will know!" she called out assuredly.

"And one other," I said turning round and holding a finger up. "Of that I'm sure," and in the same breath I said goodbye.

I told a lie and a pointless lie and I'd never been able to work out why. I'd never been to the museum before in my life. I find it has been so long since I had a need to lie to anyone. I'll seldom do it to save the emotions of others.

I walked from the museum and the short distance to the Byzantine museum, which is at the bishopric in Paphos. The building houses a lovely collection of icons, wall paintings, bishop's stoles and cloaks, manuscripts and books. A lot of religious history, perhaps, but I think it says something about the people. The building is like I said, in the ancient bishopric. A well kept building that would have always been of the greatest importance. If you look in the Cypriot history books, it might say the Byzantine period 330-1191 AD. I'd already started to regard things differently before I flew out. Gibbons regards our Lusignan Period as being Cyprus's most brilliant period, when I read that, I just thought, you prick.

It's not that I've never known about it, but it's never felt like this to me before, our history, to myself. Through Byzantium we would continue our links with our past. It's the continuity associated with it. I couldn't help but feel it, that continuity that through countless invasions has always kept that constant thread that links us from who we were, to who we are today.

The Lusignan's or Franks were here for nearly three hundred years. They tried converting us to Catholicism and we wouldn't take it. It wasn't who we were. To myself, now more than ever the church isn't just a religious instrument in Cyprus. But more the thread that leads me to my distant past.

They've already started rewriting our history. Only twenty-four years since partition and already Gibbons has started rewriting Cypriot history, for the Turks. Gibbons seems to think there was a Turkey and even a Turkish People some 7,000 years ago. From where he will say the first settlers arrived, with a new wave of Turkish immigrants around 2,500 BC. My Cretan kin are by now nothing more than refugees and victims of suppression, who made their way to Cyprus sometime in between then and the 9th century BC, insignificantly, it would seem. Gibbons doesn't even mention a Greek connection until he's bringing up Greece declining Britain's offer in 1915. Gibbons has no idea whom or what the people of Cyprus are. Now more than ever, do I understand our churches hostile attitude towards the Turks. Our country and our people were degraded under the Ottomans and now they want our land, but they let our religion flourish. More fool them. I studied the wall paintings and the icons for a while but I have to be honest and say, that having had a religious upbringing, it never seemed like history. I was soon to get on my way.

The Colonels of Greece were to lose power on the 25th November 1973 to the incoming Junta. I must point out though, even these Colonels it seems were willing to partition Cyprus and do a deal with Turkey to rid us of Makarios, I found that very hard to believe of any Greek, I assume that's why Gibbons liked them so much. George Grivas died of a heart attack in a Nicosia hideout on January 27th 1974 at the age of 75, worn out and sick with cancer. This would have given Makarios a bit of a respite. There'd already been a failed assassination attempt on his life and in April he outlawed EOKA b. He would not have been able to take this step whilst Grivas was alive, both were highly regarded by their own followers. Hundreds would soon be rounded up and in my cousins' words, he was getting his act together. On July the 1st he lowered the length of national service from 2 years to 14 months, on July the 2nd he sent his letter to the Junta president General Dimitrios Ioannides. No matter what Makarios did though, it would be to no avail, he'd made his bed so to speak. Cyprus was saying no to the US and Vietnam was in the closing stages. No doubt the Greek Lobby in the US would have been applying more pressure and the coup was on, now nothing could save us. It's no secret that the British government of Harold Wilson was supportive of the Greek coup and they knew its consequences. Even as a guarantor power, the British foreign office were then claiming they had no right of intervention, which makes me wonder what their so called rights of establishment was ever for. This must also bring me to the defence of George Grivas and I find myself asking whether or not the British weren't always using him as a tool, encouraging him, as they could have. I find this hard not to believe, when they were in support of Nicos Sampson.

I've paid scant regard in this book to the Turkish partition itself, indeed even to any Greeks that may have been killed by Turks in 63 and 74 and there were many. The three Turkish hamlets that were wiped out, there were around 180 of them in all, were taken by EOKA b gunmen after the landings. They knew the Turks were coming. I have to be honest here and say, that if I had been in Cyprus, at that time and ten years older, that I too may have taken Turkish hostages and told them the same thing. Your troops come, you die. We'd known the Turks for a long time by now and we knew their nature. Turkey takes, she migrates they're a migratory people. It's what they do. We'd learnt that a long time ago. They weren't going to take the whole of Cyprus, but they took what they might regard as their share. Makarios left our fate in the hands of the UN Security Council, knowing there was little he could do about it and with Ecjevit's words. Turkey showed the world that, "Might is Right."

I don't think the British were done though, now we get back to Gibbons. So a short while after the Turkish partition they find Gibbons so called Genocide files, to which he titled his book. These ridiculous files are the Turks main defence for partition. Even today they still use these files against us as if they really are credible. Fools fodder I think Gibbons. Let's have our own look at these Genocide files from Gibbons' accounts shall we. File No. 216/5/296, no that's not a date, it's a file number. It's apparently dated the 7th March 1974. The file number gives the impression that there were a lot of them. Now Gibbons only has a very small set of these supposed Genocide files that were "Captured," so we'll never know what file no. 000/00/01 says, will we. I'm smiling because after what I know the British have already done, I can only believe that these were planted files for the Turkish propaganda machine. They were supposedly "Captured" in the weeks after the failed coup. Very vague isn't it. Captured, that's a word, no they weren't found on anyone. The files themselves were just "Captured" placed more like. They implicate the Cypriot government and are pretty much in keeping with the Akritas plan, as this file number states that the Greek Cypriot population was to be organised to assist the National guard in the slaughter of the Turks, good to know we're so consistent Gibbons. You see the plan behind these Genocide files, was that after the Greeks had taken power and overturned our government, they were going to mobilise the and I have to capitalise this, as it is amusing. The ENTIRE Greek Cypriot population to take part in this, the final solution. I couldn't help thinking what jerk wrote these. So the Greeks are going to come into our country and after overthrowing Makarios of all men. They are gong to reunite the Greek Cypriots as a people, for our favourite sport, because as Gibbons says, we just want to kill Turks. Yep that's all I want to do in life Harry, it's Christmas day today and I'm dreaming of Christmas 63 Gibbons. When we had lots of Turks to kill, I could find my new friend Tony the Turk and give him my seasons' greetings. This is such a sick game and I don't like it. The files themselves go to even more pathetic lengths, because after the Greeks have taken over our government and reunified our people, because they'd have to be reunified after having to fight them. This is the sort of thing we are going to do. Now let's take the Turkish town of Lefke and four other villages. We are going to. "Attack at night, silently, without using lights, as quickly as possible for the cleansing of Lefke." Of course it must be silent, so as we can surprise the Turks. It would be nicer if we could get to the 4,000 Lefke Turks before they wake up, wouldn't it Harry and they wouldn't know it was coming. Well if we left it a week or two after the coup they might think everything's all right again. Sampson would be in power and every one continuing their business, Gibbons just doesn't see how pathetic these files are. They actually contradict themselves with Lefke, you see after we've attacked the Turks at night or during perhaps, Lefke was going to be wiped out with artillery fire. Which would either be totally pointless after our late night attack, or just plain stupid, what Gibbons offers us here just doesn't make sense. Gibbons claims that these files show how long and how much work went into the planning of the proposed Genocide. Claiming that it was on the scale of the Normandy landings, or even a moon landing such was the precision. If that was the case could I ask why files describing the training of combatants involved in the coup almost a year earlier were included with these plans? This was file number 330/110/43287 dated August 7th 1973 now that is a long number. Why take training files into combat? And even the numbers themselves seem more than a little confusing considering the dates given them. Pathetic as they may seem it's the files themselves I'm concerned about and why the British planted them and I can only believe it's them, not that I don't know why.

I was soon to arrive at Aphrodite's rock again. I parked the car at the nearby restaurant over the road and walked through the tunnel that takes you out onto the beach. I wanted to climb it this time. It was to be a lot easier than I imagined, although you have to know which way to come down as a couple discovered as I was making my way up the first time. I went up twice because I forgot my camera and so glad I did. In his book Gibbons uses conversations to trap people, which was one of the reasons his first book Peace without Honour was so damning of us, he used this sort of tactic against Makarios. Gibbons had heard a rumour that Makarios wasn't in complete control of the situation in 63 so he asks him if he is in control of his people. Now we are talking about a country's leader and a newspaper hack, of course he tells Gibbons he's in charge. There, well done Gibbons, you nailed him to the cross for your Turkish readers. Damned for everything that's happened because he said himself he's in charge. If I seem to be emphasising his first book, it is because it was that important. And anyone reading his whole trilogy will know that the Turkish servicemen, who were leaping out of their hospital beds to get to Cyprus to save their Turkish kin in 74, knew the Gibbons definition. On p. 22 of his first book he relates the story of Ferruh Djambaz. Ferruh was five when she watched her father being killed by EOKA gunmen and it's her account that the Turkish reader got. You get a couple of pages of rhetoric from this woman who's describing her father's death. She gets to tell the reader how she'll never live under Greeks again and what lies we still tell, as we'd never lived all right together. Her father stepped out of his home in 1958 and a gunman walked up behind him and calmly shot him through the head before walking off, and why was he shot? Let's see shall we, in Ferruh's own words.

"First he was a Turk, and Greek Cypriots hated the Turks and still do. Second, he worked for the British, and Greek Cypriots hated the British, and perhaps still do. And there was one more thing. During the day my father served the British. At night he worked for the T.M.T. he carried arms to enclaves of Turks so they could defend themselves against EOKA. The Greeks found out and executed him."

Execution is the word Ferruh, fair game for my uncles I think. You were five years old and this was in 1958, your father was fighting EOKA, what did he expect a discounted price on our land. Can I also ask what enclaves? It is 1958.

So I'm going back to the top of Aphrodite's rock and I couldn't help but look where I climbed only three months earlier on that August moonlit night. I was standing on the ledge looking up at the bush that I climbed past and thinking, shit. I knew I hadn't dragged the flag over the bush, but had gone past the bush, which was why I couldn't believe where I was looking. One slip and it was at least a fifteen-metre drop straight down onto the pebbly beach. I stood there for a couple of minutes looking at the unnecessary risk that I'd taken. I just shook my head and said to myself with a faint smile.

"You stupid bastard."

I then followed the track up to the summit. What a beautiful day it was, the sun was shining and the wind was fresh and I looked down at Aphrodite's rock, still thinking, one day. There were a couple of tourists on the summit, a father with his teenage daughter. So I thought I'd ask them if they could get a photograph of me with the rock in the background.

"Do you speak English," I asked the girl.

"Yes," she replied I could tell straight away that she was English.

"Would you mind taking a photograph of me with my camera?" I asked holding it up.

"Sure," she replied.

"I want to get one with Aphrodite's rock in the background," I told her.

"This is the rock isn't it?" she asked.

"No it's out there," I said. Pointing to the rock.

"I'm sure this is the rock," she replied.

"No that's it there, I'm pretty sure it is. I'm writing a book about the place," I said. Which was partly true. Then I thought about the myth and how that had to be the rock, as the one that we were standing on couldn't be swam around.

"There's a myth that if you swim around the rock three times under a full moon at midnight," she finished it off for me.

"You'll meet your true love."

"No I think it's said you'll live forever," I told her. She seemed disapproving of my interpretation of the myth.

"I don't know if I'd want to live forever," she told me looking over the edge.

"I don't know," I said. "Under the right circumstances it might be nice," I thought about her interpretation of the myth and decided it didn't seem right, as Aphrodite wasn't monogamous. Her father had joined us and I discovered he was with the R.A.F in Cyprus (funny enough) and we soon entered into a conversation about the rock.

"I was out in here in August and pulled a 600 square foot Greek flag off it," I told him.

"I saw that," he said.

"You saw it?"

"Yes I stopped because of it, just up there," he was pointing to the spot from where I'd seen tourists taking photographs.

"I took a photograph of it for my other daughter, she's got an interest," he told me.

"You might have been one of the tourists I saw," I said. Thinking about calling him a tourist.

"I just thought it was a bit strange," he replied referring to the flag.

"You thought it was strange, I was bloody furious about it," I told him. "And so were a few others, I drove out in the middle of the night and pulled it down," he looked at the rock.

"Braver man than me," he said.

"Nah just angry," I told him before revealing.

"I took it home and wrote a book about it," I then realised how that must have sounded. "I brought it back and put it somewhere less hypocritical."

"Where did you put it," he enquired.

"In one of the old EOKA hideouts," I told him.

"Oh which one?" he asked that a bit sharp.

"Why do you ask, your not going to pull it out are you," the idea of a British serviceman touching that flag where it lay, was not one I liked.

"No! We're told to stay out of Cypriot affairs," he said. I looked at him knowing that he may be told that. But the British have had the wrong hand in Cypriot affairs for far too long.

"It's in the old headquarters at Kykkos," I told him. Still not trusting his reasons for asking. As far as I was concerned that flag lays to rest in the heart of Cyprus, and it's Greek, it's just not our flag anymore. I already felt the British had tried to choke the Greek out of the Greek Cypriot people. Let's see how they continued it after partition. Shall we go to the Packard report, I remember this report, the British would never have released it whilst Makarios was alive. He would have had them over the coals for it. This report appeared in the 'Guardian' a respected English newspaper a year after his death and twenty-five years after the 21 Hospital patients went missing from Nicosia General hospital. There was no substantiating information in this report at all for such a damning statement. There were no headlines to go with it. It was simply quoting a 'hitherto secret report'. Naval Commander Packard, who was based in Malta, had been sent to Cyprus to trace missing persons from Christmas 63. This is it.

"One of Packards first tasks was to try to find out what had happened to the Turkish hospital patients. Secret discussions took place with a Greek minister......it appeared that the Greek medical staff had slit the Turkish patients Throats as they lay in their beds. Their bodies were loaded on to a truck and driven to a farm north of the city where they were fed into mechanical choppers and ground into the earth."

Now according to Gibbons this was to the Akritas plan. The Akritas plans say nothing about even killing Turks let alone making fertiliser out of them. I can't help but ridicule it because a report is all it is, a centimetre or so in an English newspaper, my how the British like to use their press. It seems that most of the Turkish propaganda comes from them. Take another look at the report, isn't it just a great one to quote, as I'm sure it often has been. Let's see what Gibbons tells us happened in the hospital that night. Yes he does. Thank you again Harry P. 113.

Nearly a hundred pages away from where he put the Packard report.

That same afternoon, Christmas Eve, the 21 Turkish in-patients in Nicosia General Hospital disappeared.

An eyewitness, a non-Cypriot nurse, said later that a group of armed Greeks went through the wards asking for the Turkish patients.

Many were recovering from surgical operations. The gunmen pulled back the blankets and sheets and ripped off the bandages.

While the patients screamed or fainted, the newcomers blandly remarked that they were acting on information that the patients were concealing weapons beneath their bandages.

The 21 were taken away and never seen again.

That's a bit of a different story isn't it! So why the report four years after our partition and twenty-five years after it happened. Taking into account their involvement in Kumsal and that the British had kept the Kykkos School massacre quiet, well there's 150 missing persons they weren't concerned about, which would mean no reconciliation. It seems the British like Gibbons would leave us damned to keep us parted from our land.

That's a loathsome thing to do to my people.

Back to my conversation on the rock. He told me he knew which hideout as he mentioned it to his daughter. I told him about the Gibbons book that I was using for research and I told him of my final conclusion to my book.
"The British get damned with their divide and rule!" he looked a little sheepish at that one, but it wasn't about divide and rule, it was divide to partition.
"You know who was in the country when the flag went up don't you?" I asked him, he looked none the wiser so I told him.
"The Greek intelligence guy from the 74 coup," I thought he'd have an idea of what I was talking about. I looked at him and continued.
"Our president Clerides knew he was here, arms build up, missiles from Russia," I think he knew the picture.
"Did you know he flew with bomber command during the war," he said.
"And got shot down over Germany," I finished with and looked at him as if to say, so what.
"He's still Greek," I said and continued with. "Russian planes getting lost over Cyprus," he looked straight at my chest before moving away a little.

"Why not," I said. "Incentives are right on both sides, even the financial ones," I was rubbing my thumb and forefinger together letting him know what I thought.

"It's sad," he said meaning why should the money matter.

"Hmm, it's not that bad," I replied not feeling too guilty about it.

I soon drove back to my godparents in Limassol and I changed for my flight home and spent a little time relaxing with my godmother before taking my hire car back and getting a taxi to Larnaca airport with one very cheerful taxi driver. I got to the airport and planted myself down with a can of lager in the near deserted departure lounge, a few hours early, feeling totally exhausted for the emotional roller coaster I'd been riding.

I was slouched over the seating in need of some conversation so I couldn't help but talk to the tourist sitting across the isle. Him and his wife were the only people about.

"Nice holiday?" I asked.

"Lovely," the man replied with a big smile and a Scottish accent.

"First time out?"

"No," he turned to his wife to confirm how many times they'd been, then turned back to me and said,

"About our tenth time," I burst into laughter. It was far more than myself.

"You like it then," I said with a grin.

"Ooh aye," he replied with a wink and a smile. We got chatting about how nice the place is and how warm the people are. There is without doubt an affinity that the Greek Cypriots in general feel with the British people. But I can't help but feel that that affinity and trust that the Greek Cypriots have shown the British government has been abused. Last night I lay in bed thinking about the changes in myself in the last few months and even the last six weeks when the changes have been the greatest. I was thinking about a couple of e-mails that I'd sent, one to a Slavic Macedonian and another to a Turk. They weren't e-mails I could have written before I started any of this. It simply wasn't me. Last night I worked on chapter seven and I couldn't believe I wrote it. I actually feel much more aligned with my cousins' way of thinking. It's real. This call, it is so real. I don't know if some Greeks know how bigoted and racist they may seem at times, that's not a criticism. I understand where it comes from, now, more than ever, for myself, if it wasn't for this book I wouldn't even attempt to explain it, as I'd either not know how to, or I wouldn't be able to, or perhaps I wouldn't see it in myself. I realised then the true extent of what I was writing. If the British psychological warfare department know how we feel and I have to assume they do, as I know they're not stupid. They could have planned the partition of Cyprus along with the Turkish Cypriot politicians as early as 57 or before and played it as a long-term plan. They know our history and how weak we are to it.

As I walked through to the departure lounge I noticed straight away that the information board had been rearranged. It was far more informative and the photographs that had been up in August had been replaced with more suitable newspaper clippings. I stooped to read a government propaganda leaflet. I was impressed with myself. I had Turkey drawing up the partition plans in 66 because of the massacres of 63 but on publication of the Akritas plan, the leaflet said 65 so I guess no one wanted to deal with the Akritas plan, which I understood, as they wouldn't know how to.

I do actually consider Turkey to be a bit of an innocent partaker in this affair. Britain knows the Turks like we do. They're migratory and if they can, they will migrate and it's as simple as that. Britain got her migratory instincts going. I believe they were even telling Turkey what they had a right to by giving the Turks 30% of the constitution in our treaty. The only part of Cyprus the British got defensive about in 1974 was Nicosia airport, threatening the Turkish military with air strikes if they attempted to take the airport. I can't help but thinking the British were just making sure that the Turks played the game right.

Someone put a posting on the Cyprus newsgroup recently stating that DNA testing of modern Greeks and Turks had shown that they were exactly the same. I replied to the author and told them, that over the years, with even the smallest amount of cross breeding that that might be so. But there's one very big difference between Greeks and Turks and it exists, and it is real. I can't describe how real it feels for myself. That is our sense of history, but to say it is nothing more than a feeling would be diminishing the strength of this force.

As I browsed through a gift shop in the departure lounge I came across a little pocket book on Cyprus for two pounds and brought it, to read everything I should have read years ago. I've known for a while that there have been other publications suggesting that the British encouraged Makarios to dismantle the 1960 treaty that Christmas 63. As for myself I'm not only saying that, but also much more. Take into account Peter our RAF information officer from 63 and his snapshots of Kumsal and Kumsal itself and the Kykkos School massacre. I read in this little two-pound booklet that some politicians have requested that all sides open up and be honest about what they have been up to. As for Cyprus and all Cypriots it would be the best solution, I feel pretty sure then that I'd be going to Kyrenia next summer. It can't happen though. I should think someone at the British Foreign Office would be spilling their tea on their best suit over the thought of that one. I've often heard of Cyprus being called an emotional problem and it is, because the British have been manipulating our emotions, both the Greek and Turkish Cypriots. Whilst using the mainland people of both cultures.

I not only strongly believe that the British encouraged Makarios to dismantle the constitution but my main suspicion now, is that they may be lying to more of our politicians. To stop us from taking our own course of action when they have been the cause of our misery. Non reconciliation as Makarios would have known being an archbishop, means no forgiveness, that has much greater consequences on a community and the Turkish Cypriots will always remember it. That would go along to making it near on impossible for us to live together. We've got the TRNC punting Makarios as some sort of anti-Christ, which is going to piss a lot of Greek Cypriots off and I know why now. Gibbons had already damned us in Turkey by 1970, but fortunately his latest effort is so pathetic, not just with his fools fodder, but his bias has blinded him. In a less intelligent person he would most certainly leave the Greek Cypriots damned forever, which is what worries me about the average Turk in Turkey.

I want a peaceful solution to the Cyprus problem, we all do, but we need it now, we've suffered enough. But I know it will not happen or is likely to happen with the way things are progressing.

I can't believe the timing of this book. I find it hard to take in everything that has happened to me in this last year. I find myself writing this at almost the exact time that I've been most concerned about in 1963, that Christmas Night and Boxing Day morning. Makarios at this moment would have still been showing the Turkish matron around his home and in a few hours time he would be handing the deeds to Cyprus back to the British. I can't help but shed a tear for him knowing that and it feels like I've been there for so long. Thirty-five years ago today was the last time the Greeks of Cyprus stood united as a people, now I do have a tear in my eye. When Makarios returned Cyprus to British hands, even though they never told him to his face that they weren't going to take it, it was the end of a dream for our people and no one knew that more than Makarios, but many simply never knew it. Makarios sounded so happy in Gibbons' account, talking to Gibbons after returning the Turkish Nurses that morning at the High Commission. Before the British had told him of their rejection. Gibbons wrote that Makarios looked positively enraptured as he was gazing around at the trees and the buildings and the scenery. Which gave me the impression of a man that felt relieved from a heavy burden. How crushed he must have been later. He most likely knew about Kykkos school and he would have to carry it himself, for the people and at the same time he would have known what the British were attempting after that.

Here I think I should write a few words in defence of our President Clerides. As Greek as he is, I think he's just being conned and tricked along with the rest of us, or, and this is not a nice one to consider, he is conning and tricking the rest of us.

I find absolutely nothing to justify the Turkish propaganda about him. They attack him like they would any of our politicians. So his EOKA code name was Hiperides and he's never stated that he has ever quit EOKA, so what. I spent much of my time writing this book thinking it was going to be an attack on him and his government. But as my journey progressed I discovered the true purpose of this book was to get to the truth and as I got closer to that truth, I felt more defensive of these same people. I was perplexed though as to what use the first few chapters. I read them now and find myself even amused at the man I was so recently. I even find myself agreeing, in a way, with the old Cretans. Although I know my grandfather would not be ashamed of me, and if I had of taken the language I feel for sure I wouldn't have been able to write this book. So perhaps it was meant to be, but the block was real, I had a choice and I wouldn't take the language without the love.

Final words I can't believe it. The news headline for myself on the 24th December was 'Positive' resolutions meet conditions for missile cancellation'. It seems we are going to go along with the latest UN resolution proposals to cancel the missiles and perhaps avert an event. More useless bits of paper, probably drawn up by the same people that caused this problem. I've been concerned for Greece through the last part of this. But I know that's how they're holding us now and our government takes the bait and flies more Greek flags. I know that Turkey have been threatening Greece if things go badly for them in Cyprus, so Turkey must be thinking that things could go bad for them in Cyprus. I feel very suspicious of this present situation. Especially with the recent increase in Greek nationalism on Cyprus, which I simply don't understand. I know that was a government flag I pulled off the rock. The question I find myself asking now is did our government know about it? If they did, they shouldn't be in power, especially as I know that Mr Clertdes was in control of propaganda during the EOKA campaign and would know its implications. Let me make it simple, Christmas 63 and the world was led to believe we were slaughtering Turks for Enosis, union with Greece. In 74 the world watched our coup and even though it failed the Turks had Gibbons so called genocide files to hang over us, again this was supposed to have been for Enosis. Now we have an impartial hand reaching out to help us and it is a hand that can help, Russia, but someone has been draping Greek National flags over our national treasure. I think we've been fooled again.

The Cypriot people as a whole are suffering constantly in this crisis. My people in general do not know how the Turkish hearts feel towards them and are tearing themselves apart hoping for reconciliation. Denktash's response to the cancellation of the missiles is to demand the recognition of his self-declared state the TRNC. We'll squeeze the life out of that bitch you call your Turkish Republic of Northern Cyprus, the squeeze has started, and we will keep squeezing. But the truth is, whilst we squeeze our end fate becomes ever more imminent with the influx of the colonists. They're migrating. The desert is dry, but foliage still grows.

I can't help feeling for myself that there are two major mistakes the British made with their games, and the first was not seeing the end of the cold war and Russia's ability to exert pressure in the region if need be, if we have the courage to take it. Britain keeps her bases because we live in fear and we still hold that vice presidents seat open for a Turkish Cypriot. As if it will happen in this generation or the next with the likes of Denktash and no doubt they are bringing up a new generation of Denktash's and Kutchuk's, to continue their own cause. This is the situation that Britain has left us in, holding a useless constitution and a broken flag and even worse a partitioned country for her rights of establishment. The reality I see is that the game they started over forty years ago is ongoing. The British are actually making confident long-term plans in Cyprus whilst the Cypriots suffer every day. The psychological games that they started so long ago are still going. Which is why I think we should stop flying Greek flags or we might find ourselves more concerned for Greece than our own reunification, which is what the British want and nothing changes. With all the deceit and treachery we've been shown by all, it's time we took our fate into our own hands.

The second mistake they made was underestimating the strength of our ancestors. I've felt so many strange forces whilst writing this book. I've questioned my sanity many times because of it, only to know my sanity was not in question, but the integrity of others. I couldn't work out why the force was so strong though, when I was writing against my own people, as I was at first, even though the whole time I knew I was only writing for these same people. It was a very hard time for me, but of course, I would never have gone to the TRNC otherwise and then I fulfilled my destiny and here I give Cypriots the truth. I told the TRNC after my very first telephone conversation with them not to abuse Makarios, as the dead can talk. You just needed to look the right way, at their actions and their deeds whilst they were alive and their voice will come at you, like words on a tombstone. And they gave me a book full of conversations with him. Thank you for the book, but that's all I'll thank you for.

I have to request that the international community takes note of the Gibbons book to understand the deceit and the depth of the problem, but they must also understand, that Cyprus is being torn apart by this problem. Not that we'd tell the tourists, meaning we suffer in silence, but I think I've come to tell the world, we can not suffer much more. We are trapped in a nightmare that is tearing our people apart and not of our making. The world may see the line that partitions our island as just that, a line. Then let me tell the world, to the Cypriots, to myself, it's like barbed wire wrapped around our hearts.

For myself my last words are my daydream in Kato Pyrgos. My friends have been worried about me lately, I told them about the footsteps in the sand. I've told a couple of people Aphrodite danced for me on Pyrgos bay beach whilst I daydreamed. I'll return to that hotel in spring and enquire about whether anyone else was staying there, but I know there wasn't. I don't care who believes me, the footprints are in my memory and she dances in my heart. I was thinking of what I'd like to see being done for the younger Cypriots that are going to follow us and I saw a large yacht in full sail out over the bay. Crewed by none except Greek and Turkish Cypriots in whatever proportion wanted to participate and blown by nothing but the wind and I'd call her, 'The spirit of Cyprus'.

The change between this and my very last word can only reflect what I feel we're faced with to get to that dream. My last words have to go as a response to the last words of Harry Scott Gibbons whom I assume to be living somewhere in the Kyrenia area, most likely on Greek land. He knows how my book has turned since I wrote to him and I've been taunting him on the Internet. He'll alter his web site accordingly as if it will help him after this book.

These are the last two paragraphs of his book, The Genocide files, Gibbons and the TRNC's final solution to the Cyprus problem. After he writes about how the TRNC should be allowed to function independently under Turkey's wing, partitioning our island forever. He is the one now stating the course that our national struggle should take. I have to tell the world their final solution is not one we can accept.

And South Cyprus, Greek Cyprus, can have its own dreams come true. Entry into the European union, and union with Greece which appears to be the hearts desire of every Greek Cypriot.

You be damned Gibbons! You know who I am and you know my heart, and now I know you. Water your flowers but don't go making any long-term plans in Cyprus, even burial! You know nothing of the Greek Cypriot people and that has been your main problem since you started this quest of yours, you lack any understanding of us. I blame you for my grandfathers' death Gibbons, yes I do believe he committed suicide, I read your news reports and I knew he could have, as I might have in his position. I damn you Gibbons as you damned each and every one of us. The child grew up.

Gibbons finishes with; I am aware that this solution will be sneered at. But I am being realistic. I have been to Turkey often in the course of writing this book. I know how the politicians and the military think. And I can say this without fear of contradiction from them. Neither Greece nor Greek Cyprus will ever get control of Turkish North Cyprus. Not without going to war with Turkey.

And winning it!

Then so be it, I beat the drum Gibbons. I beat the drum that marks the end of your time in Cyprus, for you, Denktash and that bitch you call the TRNC. We'll choke the life from you. I wonder how much of the real truth you actually know. I wonder if you'll be able to look Zeki in the face again and it's him that I'll leave you with, and the end of our conversation from chapter twelve, before I even felt my ancestors. Zeki will no doubt be in touch with you.

"Why do they hate so much, do they not know it's unhealthy for any civilisation, and why do they hate us so much?" meaning Greek resentment for Turks, I was surprised.

"Do you not know Zeki?" I asked.

"No tell me!"

"You really don't know?" now I was surprised.

"No please tell me!" he pleaded.

"Do you not know our history Zeki?"

"Oh Alexander the," I interrupted him.

"No Zeki! Our History! You've settled on the land of our forefather's! And that's a land no man should rest on when the Greeks are gathering!"

Footnote to 14

I finished writing that over a month ago. And I'll start this footnote with a speech made to the British Parliaments House of Commons by the hon. Major Legge Bourke the member for the Isle of Ely in 1954.

"I wonder why the hon. Gentleman and some of his friends opposite object so much to certain actions of Soviet Russia? To what do they object? Here is the principle that where military security is concerned we have the right to occupy a country, whatever its national ownership may be, to disregard all plebiscites or elections, and to tell those people that it is good for them to be under our rule. I wonder whom we think we are deceiving? Whom do we think we are taking in with all these ridiculous announcements and this talk from the other side? I wonder who will be deceived by the Minister's statement about all the good we have done for Cyprus and how we really want to give them self-government - but of course, not to let them do what they want to do. Oh no - we give them everything else and deny them what they really want. This has been going on for a long time. We have been told by those opposite that Cyprus had never been under Greek sovereignty. It happens to be the only one of the hundreds of islands of Greece, which is not part of Greece proper. It is not part of Greece proper because Disraeli swapped it with the Turks in 1878. It became part of Britain in 1878, and believed that as a colony of Britain it would get independence, but it is as a result of being a British Colony, that it has been denied the independence and Enosis which have been obtained by every one of the Greek islands. To the Cypriots we say,

"It is all for your good. We know you better than you know yourselves."

There are some 10,000 Cypriots who have come to Britain and have their own ideas about this. But we know better than them. Even when under the great influence of this Metropolis they remain obstinately convinced of their grievance they feel Greek; they are Greek - even then hon. Gentleman say,

"No, no, gentlemen - with time and trouble we shall teach you not to be Greek."

How often in our colonial history have we said the same thing? It is an ironical fact that we are starting the trouble in Cyprus on the same day as we have the ignominious end of the trouble in Egypt. May I say to hon. and right hon. Gentlemen opposite that this retreat from Egypt is a scuttle. Hon. and right hon.

Gentlemen replied,
"We shall be tough. We shall not give way. Where our national security is concerned we stand firm."

And 18 months afterwards they crawled into the conference room.

My family and many others would soon join the 10,000. It was a very strange feeling knowing that I was actually writing parts of my country's history as I was learning about it. I was just analysing the facts with the emotions involved, as I learnt them, on the tail end of a book that I was actually writing to stop the missiles and found myself calling for them. The final decision can only be up to the politicians. I can't take back any of the forces I felt during the writing of the book or the strength of them. I've promised myself I wouldn't, I've told myself I couldn't, they were real, so real. It's been foretold in Cyprus that in 1999 the Cypriots will be free and I couldn't help but feel I was in a way releasing them with the truth that I'd found. I couldn't believe I had such a destiny. So many times I'd wondered whether this could all be real considering my life was so different only a few months ago, before August 98 and even knowing it was so real, I found it hard to believe. To know I was writing such an important book. I lay in bed one night whilst writing the final chapters and in my turmoil I demanded a sign, a physical sign from the forces I felt. I demanded one before I went any further because of the implications of the book in Cyprus and instantly I was given the blocked out memory of the footsteps in the sand. I know what I saw on Pyrgos beach and at this moment in time those footsteps in the sand are my anchor and no one can tell me they never existed. I remember being angry with myself at the time. I'd recently been reading about Socrates and I knew he would have been staring at those footsteps until they blew away, having said that they would have probably blown him away. I just had so much on my mind.

But with what I know I am up against now, I needed such a sign. I feel I've just revealed the acts of a very desperate country, but it wasn't just a desperate country, it was much worse, it was a desperate establishment, a bad machine. But it goes on to this day and I would like to say enough. Even today in Cyprus, we have Clerides writing to the UN and asking if the recent resolutions are going to be enforced, and stating that he will freeze weapon purchases, to allow the UN to implement resolution 1218, which urges disarmament on both sides. From Ankara, there's no response, and from London we have David Hannay saying, "Manoeuvring for tactical advantage of this sort, saying I am the good boy, I have accepted, they are the bad boys, has not frankly moved the Cyprus Question from ground zero for 35 years." He wants us to recognise the rights of the Turks on Cyprus. Their right to our country that is and I think he must be referring to the London talks in January 64 after the Christmas uprising. When we stated we just wanted a constitution that worked. Now we just want our country back. The problem we have here is that my side, the Cypriots don't want to talk about Christmas 63, so we can't respond to such comments, because they don't know what went wrong, yet! They will when they read this and they are not going to be too happy about it. It's only because of the likes of Kykkos School and Kumsal that they don't want to talk about the uprising they all took part in. As for the Turkish Cypriot politicians, they are claiming that 17% is not a minority, as opposed to 83% that is, but I think they must be going on the British based idea of possession being 9/10's of the law.

I look at the world around me and we've still got so many wars being waged for all the wrong reasons. Not that I think we should be fighting them at all. But what sort of world should we expect when arms sales seem to be one of the strongest driving forces of commerce, along with oil the pharmaceutical and just as recently the nuclear industries. Well let's go back to Vietnam when I was a child. That was to me a financially motivated war. Certain companies made billions and I honestly believe a Nation lost a good President for that war. There's conflicts being fought all over the world, but it's well known that it's big business now and money has become a new religion to too many people in the wrong places and power corrupts. And all the time our stolen land on Cyprus is being settled on and our Churches being turned into anything between mosques and cattle pens. I think that's a sign of what intentions the Turks have and where the intransigence lies. Denktash himself is now laying claim to the rest of Cyprus on behalf of Turkey and he has a son who seems to have the same idea. I know that Europe has been making some very positive moves to attempt to bring about a just and peaceful solution with actions such as the land claim suit. But behind our backs the British government I know at least, are already writing off hundreds of millions of pounds of Turkish debts, which seriously offsets any political gains made on our behalf. And now the British Tax-Payer will have to donate to keep this hypocrisy going and I can't believe the U.S. and the German governments aren't considering the same thing. I feel that Europe on the whole wants to help us. But who can, or will, undo the evil that has been done.

One of the problems I was having towards the end of the book is that I could find absolutely nothing against the Greek Cypriots. I'm not surprised they built up certain resentments towards the Turks during their independence campaign. The Greeks of Cyprus were not used to such deceit. They said they'd kill anyone associating itself with the occupying powers. It might sound harsh but it was honest. The British were known to take EOKA members to the Turks for disposal during the 55-59 campaign. Can you imagine what acts like that did to the Greek people as a whole.

No! Our present situation cannot continue and I know our politicians know that. But I know they also know that if we act for ourselves, in a hostile manner, Turkey will strike Greece in retaliation, Greece will have to strike back for her land, and rightfully so. But what pressure is put on Turkey not to take this course of action. None, Sorry, Gross Hypocrisy.

Just as Cyprus has always been Greek, we are the Greeks of Cyprus. We are at a point in our history where we must make a monumental decision regarding the fate of our island. I know what I will tell my forefathers on my judgement day. But as I said, this is just a book and books in themselves change nothing.

I do want a just and peaceful solution, but I'll emphasise the just. I think it's as much to do with the questions we ask and I think the Cypriot politicians have some very serious questions to ask of themselves. The truth is so often hard to come by for more than one reason. Mostly it is because people are less than honest. Sometimes it is just that the truth is not something we can bear to face. So we in turn, become dishonest with ourselves, to save our own emotions.

Right now the British and the U.S want us to rewrite our history books. I imagine with regards to the 63 massacres and as we haven't been able to prove in any way it wasn't us until now, that would partition us forever, the games go on. Our politicians have the serious decisions to make. For the Cypriot politicians I'll leave them with a quote from Socrates to ponder. No one could say he was a man of war or violence, more of wisdom. Socrates believed that virtue was knowledge, hence his famous assertion that 'No one does wrong willingly,' he also believed that we should live in harmony with and listen closely to nature.

> "If one had true knowledge of virtue,
> Of what is right and good,
> One would appreciate the necessity,
> Of acting in accordance with one's knowledge,
> And act accordingly!"

Chapter 15

I wrote my life seemed an epitome of Cyprus, well now I find myself in the same situation as Cyprus. I too have a past that I might not like to talk about, but must, because of this book. So now I will write more about myself, before certain people attempt to take advantage of what may be seen as my past and slaughter me in the press, as they have done in the past with Cyprus. The footnote and this chapter are the only parts of the book the British Establishment don't know about. I feel certain they've seen the rest via a leaked source, which is why I am writing this chapter. When I realised I had to write this though, something happened. The strength of the book-increased tremendously and kept increasing until it became a message to mankind to reveal a prophecy fulfilled. Indeed the greatest prophecy given to humanity which is why I make no apologies for so much detail. You are about to get a complete rundown of my mainly adult life, as I don't intend answering any questions after the release of this book.

I was born at seven minutes after seven on the seventh of April 1962, the fourth of seven children on a London over-spill council housing estate. At 11 the child went on to earn a scholarship to public school. Most parents would have been delighted by such a feat. Mine weren't and I got no guidance at all so I went to the local state run comprehensive school. I suppose I might have had a bit of an attitude towards authority during my education although I didn't think so. Beatings were common place at this school, at this time, it was how they kept you in line and they beat you with a stick. The first time I was given what I considered an unfair detention I asked what the option was and I was told it was a beating, so I smiled and said I'd take the beating as it was less intrusive on my time and the pain would pass. It actually happened like that. They knew what I thought of their beatings. At 15 in my last year of school during my mock exams, I finished my maths exam early. So I pushed my paper and desk as far away from me as I could and took a book from my bag and read. It was an autobiography. I was quite open about what I was doing and making it clear that I'd finished my paper, and with over an hour to go I was not going to sit fiddling my thumbs. The teacher on duty took the book off me and told me to collect it off his desk after the papers were in, which I did on my way out. Before I got to the exit the teacher confronted me and asked me, what gave me the right to take the book back and I told him I was acting as he instructed and by every right it was my property. He told me to hand the book over to him so he could confiscate it. I refused point blank on the basis that it was my own personal property, which was now causing no offence to anyone, his actions were now nothing more than spiteful, this was supposed to be education. He took me to the headmaster, who asked only once for the book and I refused. I was suspended indefinitely. At the time I was on probation. I got arrested for burglary. A friend took me to a social club and we entered through a window that he'd left open as his father worked there. I'd recently read a letter to my parents telling them that bailiffs were coming within a week, so I took full advantage of the situation and unknown to my friend I took enough money to cover the bailiffs. You'd have to understand how I felt towards bailiffs. So my probation officer at the time told me I had to return to the school, no matter what conditions were set. I was allowed to return only on the basis that I forfeit my exams and this was acceptable to the probation service. I felt like my whole education had been wasted and I left school at fifteen without a grade to my name.

By this time I'd been up in front of a High Court judge on my own. The charge was robbery. It was a smash and grab. I'd gone out with my much older cousin's husband and two others not knowing that they were going to commit the crime. I just thought they were going out for a drink and the next thing I knew we were pulling out of a petrol station without paying and I knew then that the night was going to be different. I'd actually fallen through the window when it happened, it was quite amusing but everyone got arrested and when it came to judgement day, the others took it all the way to Crown Court then pleaded guilty, which I should have expected, but wasn't. I went not guilty on the grounds that I was an innocent partaker of sorts, basically I told the court my cousin was carrying everything. Which wasn't quite true, but at the same time it was a daunting challenge that as a fifteen-year-old schoolboy, I took well, not guilty after a five day trail. I was good in the box and the judge was to despise me many years for it. I learnt that Barristers could find themselves being questioned though. As happened on at least one occasion when I gave evidence and watched a man get an 18 month prison sentence, for the thoughts in his head.

A year later at 16 I was sent to a detention centre for three months on charges of criminal damage and attempting to obtain money by deceit. A car was kicked as it nearly knocked some people over as it sped out of a youth club. I never kicked it and the police knew I never but they picked me to arrest for it. With the deceit, it was a court expense form. I was giving evidence for a friend and I never told the unemployment office I was unavailable for work. My solicitor of the time will swear to this. That I was not sentenced so much for the criminal damage or for the deceit, but more for being 30 minutes late for the court case. The police sent me a letter telling me my court time had changed. I discarded the letter and turned up at the given time, which was thirty minutes late. My solicitor was frantic about it and he told me if I pleaded guilty I would get three months or if I pleaded not guilty I would get six months. But no matter what though, he knew, I was not going to be allowed to walk away from that court a free man, simply because I was late and they'd been waiting. I trusted him and took the 3 months.

British youth detention centres were terrible places for children to be sent to. Short, sharp, shock treatment combined with military style discipline, which included drill. I took a couple of beatings but every day I'd watch children as young as young as 14 getting beaten by certain brutal officers. It's the establishments as much as it is the people. During this experience though I was touched, touched with a hand of warmth and kindness from a Prison officer and his wife and I promised myself, it would be that touch that I'd remember. Three weeks after my release I was sentenced to another six months detention centre for robbery with assault. That hurt. People I had been out drinking with, a whole year earlier gave a man a beating, but I went nowhere near it and kept others away telling them to have no part of it. There was a co-defendant who was guilty and the judge who despised me told the jury to find one as you find the other. I got six months on the basis that I was simply in the area, as the court transcripts will show. I was gutted. Here I passed my only two academic grades that I hold, Maths and English. I got the highest grades possible without even studying. But apart from that I learnt that time inside was simply a waste of time.

A week after I was released I was picked up with eight others by the police in a Ford Anglia car. I was in the boot of the car with a friend, coming home from a punk concert. Nine of us in a Ford Anglia, a small early seventies English saloon car, it sounds funny enough but it was to turn out to be a night that would have a devastating effect on my life. I only got around to being able to talk about it last year. It was over 19 years ago and I was 17 years of age. At the Police Station I was separated off from the others and told to strip to my waist. I was then told to stand with my hands in the air and face the corner of a detention cell, which was facing the desk. And I spent between two to three hours taking beatings off whichever officer of the three on duty happened to be walking past and wanted to beat me. Sometimes it would be just fists, sometimes a truncheon with a towel wrapped around it, whatever they wanted really. They thought that because I'd just got out of a detention centre I'd sign a false statement saying we were carrying car tools to fight locals with. I asked them at the start if I could use the toilet and they told me to get stuffed, so I timed the situation out as best I could and just took whatever they had to give me. I took it for two to three hours then I told them that I'd sign a statement for use of the toilet, a cigarette and a cup of tea. I used the toilet, drank my tea and smoked my cigarette, whilst I took the five minutes rest which was what I really wanted. They in turn eagerly wrote a statement out, which I refused to sign on the basis that it was a pack of lies. I got dragged over the desk and beaten more. But after that, they realised it wasn't going to happen and they let me lay down on the cell floor but with a high powered beam in front of my face and if I turned over, I got kicked. It wasn't that night that broke me at the time though. It was watching those officers smirking at me in the court when the charges were dropped, that hurt, I was witnessing the total and absolute failure of the establishment. But I learnt how precious five minutes can be.

After the court case I returned to a friends house and they started to prepare themselves hits of barbiturates in syringes and asked me if I wanted to indulge. I'd been around drugs for a long time by now. Since I was thirteen, when my eldest sister had given me some amphetamines or speed after I'd walked into her bedroom, whilst her and her boyfriend were indulging. She never told me what it was or what affect it would have on me. I was confused as to why I couldn't sleep all night and I spent most of it talking to a young Tawny owl that I was rearing. The owl died soon after as a friend brought me some dead mice, which I fed the owl before I discovered they were dead because my friend had picked them out of a poison grain box that farmers use, I was on my own poison that night though. But this was four years later and I was very much aware of my own personal morality and had always regarded injecting as taking things one step lower, hence, I'd always declined or been able to walk away from the situation. Sitting there in that chair, that day though, I asked myself a question that I'd always asked but always had an answer for, Why not? And at that point in my life sitting in that chair after what felt like a lifetime of abuse. I didn't have a reason at all and I wouldn't find one for four years.

It was around this time my grandmother asked me to go to Cyprus and do my national service but I think you understand and over a year earlier that I'd enquired about the British army, but the burglary offence stopped that. It was also around this time when I was arrested for carrying a bag of these same barbiturates. They weren't classified drugs though and therefore not illegal to be in possession of. But because I'd said that I paid money for them and me being me, they charged me with aiding and abetting the supply of drugs. Thereby forever being able to brand me as some form of drug dealer. My solicitor can bear witness to this and the earlier matters, as I will ask him to, Neil Davidson a man worth mentioning.

It was also around this time that one of my mothers' friends started telephoning me and asking me if I could get her a video recorder. I told her the first time and the second and the third time, "No!" but still she called back. At the same time I had two friends who happened to be selling a video recorder, a stolen one. The woman had interfered in my life so much I told her I would send them around and she said, no. I had to bring it. I'm just too trusting. I got there a half-hour early and she wasn't expecting me to arrive at all. She made me leave with the video recorder and I was arrested around the corner from her house. When I got to the police station I was told that the doors were open and if I told them who stole the video recorder I could walk straight out without charges and when I asked them the alternative. They told me five days in a cell and a stitch up in court. So I asked for a newspaper as I take my friendships seriously. The woman got off a shoplifting charge. End of June 1980 after spending two weeks at the Stonehenge Free Festival when it existed, I was in front of the judge who despised me. I got 6 months to 2 years Borstal training.

Wellingborough was a category A. Borstal. At the time there was film around supposedly based on the same place and perhaps was. The movie was called 'Scum'. After two Detention Centres I wasn't expecting a holiday camp. I remember sitting in the medical centre waiting to be examined a day after I arrived and I watched a man walk in after being hit in the face with a shovel. I decided there and then that the first man to push me would be the man that I'd lose two weeks for. It took a couple of months but I was expecting it when it came. The silly sod wanted me to go into the toilets to fight him. He never got to finish his sentence off when he was challenging me. In full view of everyone in the dining hall I went from the extremely quiet trainee, that I'd been up to then, to a lion. I was leaning back on the window when he approached me, with four or five friends behind him to ask me if I wanted to step into the recess with him. My response was three straight jabs to the nose to put some stars in his eyes and all the time in the world for the right, which came with all my body weight. It was quite amusing to watch him literally take off backwards. They took us both straight to the cells and I extended a hand to him before we were locked up, which he barked at, but bark was all I knew he'd ever do from then. The next morning instead of the usual Governors report for fighting, I found myself on a minor report. One of my section officers witnessed the incident and took care of it. I thanked him and he told me that he'd watched the whole affair and he knew that I had to do what I did and I felt a mutual respect was built up that day. I just wanted to get through it as quickly and as quietly as I could and even the officers would ask why I was in a borstal. My first cellmate was doing the same sentence for seven armed robberies. I got a First year City and Guilds in Motor Mechanics, whilst making their best ever grades. I spent the rest of the time working on my own in the chapel as chapel orderly. The chaplain always surprised me as he witnessed the start of the fight I had, when I elbowed the man involved, who was at the time sitting behind me and digging his toes in through the back of my chair whilst at church. Although I think he saw me ask him very politely to stop first. I was sitting in front and the chaplain was playing guitar. He only missed a beat. I lost my job once because I told them there was nothing to do whilst the Chaplain was on holiday. He not only made them give me my job back, but a week off my sentence for doing it so well, as he thought I hadn't been rewarded enough time off for good behaviour. One of the panel thought my good behaviour was all for show. So I could get out as quick as I could to commit more foul crimes in the world, as I knew time inside was a waste of time. It should be on file funny enough. He was strongly opposed by my record and two good Section Officers. I was always the one who they'd let out of the cells to make them tea on Saturday afternoons. It meant I'd be able to sit and talk with them for a few hours. There's good and bad everywhere and most of these were good men. I'd got into an in-depth conversation with one officer one night that he started, which led to Lawrence of Arabia. His face was a complete picture when I corrected him on a point and told him that I'd just finished reading the unabridged version of the Seven Pillows of Wisdom. Lawrence was a great man and a dreamer all right but he was very wrong about destiny and nothing being written. I served around eight months and my best company was a couple of Small Owls, which were quite rare and probably rarer now. They used to call to each other and play on the volleyball posts outside of my cell. One of my cellmates told me once that he wanted to commit suicide, but he never knew how. I told him a way with the toilet door and a sheet, but asked him not to wake me up. I know this sounds callous, but some people really can make you feel like that. It was all two man cells and the wrong cellmate can drive you crazy. The Prison Officers told me that only one in ten never went back inside and it was that tenth man that made them proud. I'm glad to write of them being that one in ten and I imagine the chaplain liked me because I actually polished the memorial plague for a deceased Prison officer.

I was now nearly 19 years of age and in a sense very much a non-conformist. I think you can see why. Here three major influences were to enter my life. Mandie a woman I was to spend the next five years living with. Steve or Custer as we used to call him due to his long golden hair, who I'd first met at Stonehenge the previous June and Rudi an Austrian Optician, although it would be a couple of years before he actually made an impact on my life. I recently went to a concert with Mandie and she asked me where she fitted into my life and I told her that she was the balance I needed at a time when I needed it and that is so true. She was also the first woman I felt like I'd really made love with. Steve was wild, wild young and free and we got on well with each other. He used to ride the country on his 750cc Yamaha motorbike running drops for a chemist that was making methadrine, it's a high grade amphetamine, speed of a sorts and as it was an influence on his life, so it was on mine. I remember the time well. I was living with Mandie and her three-year-old son Craig and I was happy. Mandie is five years older than myself but at the same time she was never smothering in the sense that she allowed me to do fairly much what I wanted. It was like she knew that she was going out with a younger person and was going to let them grow, in their own way, unlike many relationships I see where often one will sooner or later seem to dominate the other. We lived in a two-bedroom council house opposite my mothers. Steve died in a van crash at the age of 23 in early 1984 I was 21, it was around the same time as my grandmother and five other friends died, all within six months of each other, but his death was to have the biggest effect on myself. I decided after he was cremated that I was going to stop injecting as I was and taking drugs in the manner that I had been. I went to bed where I stayed for two weeks in some form of a daze, with Mandie constantly nursing me.

It was shortly after this time that Rudi was to make an impact on my life. He was an Austrian Ophthalmic Optician, very proud of the fact that his father was a Colonel in the Nazi SS during WW11. He would often boast of how he had two thousand Jews under his command. His words not mine. It took me near on two years to work out what exactly he meant by lampshade time, as he often used to call it and yes he was a loathsome creature. But he offered me a job and it wasn't factory work, which was about all you could get in my hometown if you didn't have the grades. Plastic and rubber factories are prevalent here. I worked in one for three and a half days. I couldn't understand how people could choose to spend one third of their lives in there. But when poverty's a kin of slavery, the choices seem less. I chose a wayward life for a while and I do not regret it one bit, I do have three shoplifting charges against me though.

Rudi gave me a way out of all that and I took full advantage of the opportunity. I was working for £60 a week in the workshop of an optical practice that he opened that spring in town. The money was no good, but it wasn't so much the money that I was concerned in. My first day at work I arrived nine o'clock prompt. Rudi soon telephoned to tell me to take ten pounds out of the till and pick up some amphetamines for him and have a hit waiting for him for when he arrived at the practice. I felt sick. He used me and I used him. That's about the best I could say about the situation. But within a year I was ready to move on to another company in the same profession and to take advantage of the start that I'd been given. I knew Rudi's time was up though, when immigration came to tell him he was an illegal immigrant. I had to lock the toilet door and sit on the floor for ten minutes holding my nose so no one could hear me laughing. I started another job and he got deported.

At 23, I went to work at a branch of Norville Optical. They were at the time and most likely still are the biggest wholesale optical company in England. With a head office and a large factory in Gloucestor and branches all over the country, supplying optical lenses uncut or fitted in frames to opticians. This was just at the start of the days of the one-hour service outlets in England. By now I had my driving license and a car and pay had started to improve, but most importantly for myself this was a good company to go on and continue what I regarded as my training which I did. In fact it was a very good company to work for and I learnt a lot whilst there. It had a good workshop and I got on well with my colleagues, the eldest technician also had plenty of time to pass his skills along, which he did well and within a year I was ready to move on again. As good as they were I knew that I wasn't going to get where I wanted with them and at 24 years of age I moved on to Cambridge Optical, where I was given a good break by an ex-employee of Norvilles. Who was at this time, the production Director of this the second biggest optical wholesalers in the country and I was at head office. I found it boring at first, almost on the same detail every day. Until the second month when the director took me aside and asked me if I'd establish a new department in the coming month, to continue in the new building that the company was soon to be moving into. I was on top of the world, I'd been noticed.

Before then though around Christmas 85 I went to see my doctor, as I was concerned. You see even though I had more or less stopped taking drugs, it was the more or less bit I was concerned about. I told him that I was in the habit of injecting occasionally with friends and he told me that if I never had any problems, addiction wise, and I was happy in my life, then there was no harm in what I was doing. It wasn't what I wanted to hear. The actor Rock Hudson had just died. I remembered reading as a child about how many Sparrows would come from one breeding pair, in ten years, if each and every one of them was successful and I was concerned. Over the next year I would stop completely and at this time it wasn't once a month. I usually got collared by a couple of friends in the pub because I had a car and temptation would follow.

It was that spring 86 that Mandie who had an evening job two nights a week at a cosy boat marina restaurant asked me if I minded if she worked five nights a week. I told her with my better job and the pay to match, she needn't work the extra days and it would affect our relationship. She took the extra days and started coming home from work later and later and I took another girlfriend but I never did it the right way. Helen was too beautiful to resist, and I, like anyone else could resist anything but temptation. I gave her a lift to work one morning and she told me she'd just finished with a friend of mine, so I asked her straight out. Although I have no regrets at all about my relationship with Mandie, it should have ended a year earlier for myself, when I met Helen. We had stolen nights on the beach and dreams that we'd share, that I've never forgotten. I've just never felt forgiven for what was to happen.

Christmas 86 was due and I was a rising star in my company, but my home life could have been a lot better. I never knew where things were going to go with Helen, but I knew things weren't going well for Mandie and myself. Around October though I felt a change. A week of night sweats and I knew that my body was telling me that something had happened to it. It only took me until November to go to a doctor and I asked him for an Aids test and he sat back and laughed at me. He regarded the idea of me thinking I might have the virus as amusing, even though I'd shared needles and he told me to go away and think about it for two weeks then to come back and see the nurse if I still wanted a test. Meaning not to bother him I think. Two weeks later the nurse was refusing to take my blood due to what she regarded as the absurdity of it. Me thinking before them. She called the doctor and he told me the same thing. So I sat on a chair and told them that I regarded an Aids test as my right, and that they had to take my blood and test it by that right, and I wasn't leaving until they did. It had caused quite a scene but I didn't care. Two weeks later I was sitting in front of the same doctor with a grin on my face. No, I wasn't happy. I was in shock. I'd just driven home from work in shock. I'd found out my test results from the nurse by phone. I was looking at another total failure of the establishment telling me to look on the bright side, as I had three years to live. It should be on file. Mandie tested negative and I never had the heart or the strength to tell Helen. She was 18 and I simply never wanted it to affect her life in any way. By Easter I was living alone and glad to be giving up my job to do, what, I never knew. But I had another job offer from the Production Director of Cambridge Optical to help him and a partner establish a new company that following autumn. I got a 35% pay rise from Cambridge Optical that year and I'd found myself looking forward more to my company car than I was to the coming Spring, my favourite time of year. In a sense I've long since been glad it happened. Later on in life I would look back and regard the period of my life before my positive diagnosis as my most selfish time, when I never gave others in my life the consideration they deserved. For a while after, I was simply in shock. I was the only known HIV+ person in my hometown, which would go on to have the highest P.P.C of known positive cases in England, second only to that of Edinburgh in Great Britain. I don't feel and never have felt resentment about my condition, even though I feel completely let down by the establishment because of it. The same establishment I've found myself reliant upon because of the virus. The reason my status has not been mentioned earlier in the book is because it has absolutely no relevance to Cyprus or that aspect of my life whatsoever. Indeed, when it comes to Cyprus, it is, as if I have had two very different lives and even though I know the time I've actually spent there is very little, it has almost been, as if I'd found a completely new identity this last year. At 24 though my life was now just about to begin in a sense because of the positive test.

I watched on T.V recently that another Simian, a Chimpanzee this time is now being cast as the possible cause of the HIV virus. Let me tell you what I read about it in a journal in my dentists' waiting room of all places. It was a few years ago now and I was simply too embarrassed to take the journal. But I read about an American medical scientist working on a 'Live' cell vaccine for polio which he was manufacturing from the kidneys of a Philippine Monkey, that was much later found to carry the actual virus, not a similar virus, but the exact same HIV virus. Whether the monkey is in existence today I wouldn't know. I'd dare say that if the story has any truth to it, they would have most likely been wiped out by now. Apparently this scientist first took his 'Live' cell polio vaccine to Africa where it was used extensively during the late fifties. About twenty years later in the seventies, the same scientist, would use a variant of the same vaccine for a Herpes treatment that he administered in the San Francisco area to gay men. I believe he was once a Harvard professor and the U.S. Food and Drug Administration have never looked into it at all. If there's any truth in these claims whatsoever, it not only shows the failure of the medical scientists to control themselves. But also a total and absolute failure of the establishment to control the same system that are now cloning and are endangering our natural balance with genetic modification, as if nature really needs modifying. In the UK they haven't even started counting the cost of the beef contamination with B.S.E. or C.J.D the human variant of mad cow disease. I heard a spokesman on TV recently say the crisis was past. He wouldn't be saying that if it were he watching his grandchild dying a babbling mess, not even knowing that they are afflicted with this terrible condition. And these are the people to which we are forced to entrust our future wellbeing with.

June 1987 and I took off for Greece and very much an Englishman with Greek heritage. I would return for the job that I was offered and over the next year I took some time in investing in myself. I got my B.S.A.C. diving licence and it was also about this time that I'd met David in a pub behind Oxford Street. He was running a counselling service in London once a month for positive people and we became very close friends. He left the British Intelligence Service because he was HIV positive and he taught a group of us the concepts of reality and truth during a group counselling session, but we just went into greater lengths about it in our private conversations. He was a wonderful man.

Spring 1988 and I brought a two-year-old horse called Searan Opal-Tek and along with the horse come Tracy. I met Tracy in a pub in early 88 and at that time I had a yearning to learn to horse ride, perhaps for a distant desire the child once had. Tracy had the use of two horses at that time, one a horse on loan to her and a friend's horse. The loan horse had to go back and I had a taste for it. I also saw an easy way of keeping a horse and told Tracy that if I saw the right horse, at the right price, I would buy it. She was selling her saddle the day I saw his picture go up and that same day we decided to keep the saddle, for the horse we'd just brought. I gave Tracy a half share of the horse repayable over any length of time, on condition that she looked after the animal and we went halves on the upkeep of him. I was earning good money by now and I brought Searan from my travelling savings. Buying him meant I went to Australia a year later, but he was well worth it. Searan was born on the 4th of July 1985 and on that day a light walked into the world for me. Late spring 1988 and I found that light and I discovered a whole New World with this horse, that I taught, as much as I learnt on, in those early years. He was a fine animal and worth much more than the £900 I paid for him. A week after we brought him Tracy went on holiday and I spent the next two weeks lunging and long reining him, constantly learning about him, as I learnt with him, it was a beautiful experience for myself. I told Tracy I wanted a fast horse that could clear a five bar gate to escape the haughty land-owners who claim to own what they merely tend and I wanted a horse with spirit. I got a first class champion. Three quarter thoroughbred, a quarter Arab he stood over 16 hands and was as much a friend to me as an animal, although he was certainly no pet.

September 88 came a big employment change when I left the Production director and his new company, mainly because I considered his partner such a despicable character. All he cared about ten years down the line was retiring with his brand new BMW and other materialistic possessions that he desired, he never had any consideration for other people at all. His attitude to myself also took a big change when he found out about my status. It was a move for the better and I still keep in touch with the other director, Paul Kelly. I went into retail optics and it completely changed my life. I now really enjoyed the job although I'd never reveal my status at work again. December 88 and I took Tracy to Egypt to take advantage of my diving licence and I dived the coral gardens of the Red Sea. What an amazing experience! There's no way I can describe the absolute beauty and the serenity of these underwater gardens in these few lines, you see it on T.V but to experience it, is something else. Yet to know that so much of this beauty that took hundreds of thousands of years to evolve will be lost even before our next generation reaches maturity, is a terrible burden to bear.

October 89 and I was ready for Australia. I'd had an Australian visa in my passport since I had a passport at 17 and now I was ready to use it. I won't go into too much detail about the next two years but the experience of freedom is amazing and my only regret was that I never took the trip sooner in my life. I did everything I wanted and more. Tracy set herself up in Australia before I got there. Which was a little crafty but as I said she seemed to come with the horse, not that we never had some good times. But I did tell Tracy after we brought Searan that I never wanted a relationship and even fell back on my status to put her off. I told her I couldn't love her in the way she wanted and I also told her that my travelling days were for myself and when I travelled on my own, then I was alone as far as I was concerned. I knew she never liked hearing it. But I was being honest and that's how I was these days, which was probably why I spent two great conscience free months in New Zealand, mainly with two other guys who were backpacking and a Norwegian girl that I'd met on the road. It was a great time of my life. My best experience in Australia would come whilst I was crewing a 70-ft. (about 25 metre) Dutch built sailing yacht called Saroja out of Cairns. I'd been told she was a replica of an old fashioned fishing boat of sorts. Lots of varnished wood and very pretty but a good heavy boat with a full twin keel. The owner had used it mainly for drinks on board in the harbour, which I was soon to realise. We were taking his boat to be sold in Brisbane, a voyage of around 700 miles or a little over 1,000 km's. The first clue he gave me was when he asked me to check his navigation, then left it to me to set the course. It seemed my dive boat experience had put me leagues ahead of the complete six-man crew and the skipper. We were doing three-day stints at sea, at a time, when we run into a force eight-nine gale just outside of the Kepples, a group of islands along the southern tip of the barrier reef at about 7.30 one clear June morning. I had the 4-8am watch behind the wheel. It was a good time to be alone and up for the sunrise with the earlier pleasure of watching the twisting phosphorous trail, which could hold me in a trance. I'd always be harnessed on watch and we were under power all the way. When the high winds hit, the skipper appeared from his cabin and quickly hung himself over the side to be sick and immediately declared himself useless, handing over full command of the yacht to myself. This was to be one of the greatest experiences of my life. My first question to the now defunct skipper was. "What was the weather forecast?" the answer was that he never got one, as he was supposed to have before we left our last port of call. I harnessed him to the boat before I went on the radio, which was useless. I would later find out that I was only transmitting, so everyone heard my requests for a weather forecast, but I couldn't hear any response except for a moment I got with Townsville coastguard. I couldn't and wouldn't make an emergency call of any sort. I went up top and took command of the situation. The wind was blowing from the south, south-west and the southern fringes of the barrier reef were about 20 miles west of us. And after having to convince the rest of the crew that I knew what I was doing, as they had only one thought when it came to heavy seas and reefs. It was there that I took her for shelter to a beautiful coral atoll that I'd read about called Lady Musgrave island, where we spent near on a week in the midst of a beautiful tropical garden, whilst we waited for the wind to drop. It's an awesome sight watching the front quarter of a yacht that big disappearing under those big pacific rollers, but I learnt so much about the sea, nature and myself that day. I left the yacht as soon as we hit the mainland, so to speak. I spent the last ten months of my Australia experience living with Tracy in a Central Sydney seventh floor apartment, with a young Japanese fellow by the name of Yasoo. It was a secure luxury apartment in the middle of the red light district and I used to find myself drinking with prostitutes, in one or two of the quiet bars that, few but the locals knew even existed. As for Yasoo words could not speak highly enough of him and I left Australia feeling as much for the Japanese through him as I did the Australians.

I returned to England August 1991 and within five days I was the best man at my brothers wedding. It was a lovely formal affair up in Derbyshire but I was hardly prepared for the fishtail suits and the best mans speech. My cousin told me it was the worst he'd heard. I had to agree. I went straight back to work with the same retail optical company, first at a practice in Slough and I spent that winter living in Eaton near Windsor. It was very picturesque, especially at night in the middle of winter, with the mist and the cobbled streets. I used to pass a lot of time with the flock of swans that live on the river Thames there, I found them far easier to spend time with than the local people.

Searan had gone out on loan for two years whilst I was in Australia to a man called John Owen and I couldn't have hoped for a better horse to return to. He had taken him for his daughter to show jump on and he was now six years old. John had prepared tea and sandwiches for Tracy and myself when we'd gone around to negotiate the return of the horse. I knew an offer might be in the wind, but I knew that I'd reject it and I was offered whatever John could raise after selling what he could for Searan. Which I duly declined, I felt sorry for him though, as I knew he'd built up a strong attachment to the horse. We were then shown three trophies for three jumping championships won and a bag full of first and second place rosettes and this was for his first year in competition. I always had a feeling that there was some form of divine intervention where Searan was concerned. I certainly got a prize gem, that's for sure, but as far as competing went I wasn't feeling competitive about him, I just wanted what I considered a worthy horse to ride and riding Searan now, I would truly learn that nobility was not a birth-right.

Ok, this is going to sound a bit cryptic, but it has to, as it affects another person. Around September that year a woman came up to me with a request, that I should make a promise on and it would be one that I'd keep and would later affect my personal life to a great degree. The following spring that woman had passed on. Three months I waited before I took action on keeping my promise and I went to visit a friend, who had just had a deep personal loss and lost a lover three months previous. I put in front of him an offer and an opportunity. It was in the way of a 250gm bar of cannabis and I was asking him if he wanted to go into business with me, which he did and we both faired well. Now if that causes offence to some people I can understand it, especially on Cyprus where I'll ask people to understand that opinions vary from country to country and this book is as much to the people of the world.

Anyway it wasn't so much for the money, but more to keep a promise and I also knew that it would have a good chance of working and help my friend find a path that would work for him, and it did. I was now working at a retail optical shop in Cambridge where I was also studying at college for my first year in Ophthalmic Optics. My manager there at the time, Mike, was someone that I'd get much inspiration from, him being a worldly sort of man, he is a little over fifteen years older than myself and was from Rhodesia when it was called that, now Zimbabwe. And with his inspiration I would buy a small sailing boat called 'Stealaway' with my friend to set some dreams going. Just before Mike started, I was working under another manager and I got the opportunity to oar a recently constructed replica of an ancient Greek trireme on Mediterranean speed trials. This was something I wanted to do so much. The trireme fleets of the ancient Greeks were the best fighting vessels on the sea in their time and no oarsman was a slave as with the Romans. It was considered a great honour to take an oar on one of these vessels. My upper management said they'd allow it, but my branch manager at the time didn't understand. I don't know if it was anything to do with him being Indian and not having an understanding of how I might feel about it, but he said he couldn't allow me to be so frivolous with company time. I never told him what I thought of him, straight away, but told upper management of his plans to leave the company and go on to college that year. The shops' figures had slumped under him and I found him very dishonest with the staff and patients and I told the management this, right before I told him. It felt like justice to me and he was sacked. The shop would then go on to take its best ever figures and our main private policy within the staff was honesty first to the patients at cost to the company if need be and with our experience it worked. We also went beyond company policy in creating a better work environment for ourselves, which I felt, had a lot to do with it. I was very good at my job by now and working with a good team and I enjoyed dispensing immensely. There is a great feeling as opticians will tell you when someone comes to you after years of having trouble and not being able to see quite right with a difficult prescription, and they walk out with a smile on their face, that tells you you'd got it right. The worlds deceptive enough without having trouble seeing. I saw the greedy side of it working at some practices as well though, which made me sick. In fact in relation to those practices which I watched stealing off old age pensioners, them being the most vulnerable, I considered my other business as very respectable. But in January 1993 I got arrested for possession with intent to supply of one 250gms bar of cannabis. I actually had a couple of others lying around but I was confused as to how the police knew about this one, as I never even knew that it was in my bedroom, when it was. I went to the police station the next day and had an interview. The police switched on the tape and the interview went ahead and they asked me the questions I expected. What is this? And why do you have it? And to cut a long story short I could prove that it was for personal use as I had good savings at the time, bearing in mind I had a good job and I'd made a large withdrawal a week before. Oh, I was lying on tape, but so do they, although I never after it went off. That's when the serious talk starts and I'd use what I learnt. They made me an offer that I knew someone had taken. They said they'd allow me to continue business with a free rein if I turned someone in to them every now and then, just for their own figures. This was a common offer for the police to make in England, offering a dealer a free rein like that and I'm sure many still take full advantage of it to this day. I regard it as being very dishonest on account of the police but perhaps just as important, they open themselves up to being used. I turned them down and walked from court with a small fine for possession of cannabis, as the supplying was never proven. I will never feel embarrassed or ashamed about dealing in cannabis at any time. There are times when the law is simply wrong, as 5,000,000 people in the United Kingdom who are also known to indulge will agree. I failed my first year at college.

That summer I was to meet Gail and love would soon follow and that winter I would find what I'd refer to as my beach, a beautiful secluded place with a very picturesque and remote waterfall an-hours trek up stream, but worth the walk and yes, the climb. The beach was once used as a retreat by Thai kings. Here I smoked my first joint of heroin at the age of 31. I stayed three months and I was faithful to Gail the whole time. I've got quite amusing memories of asking girls to get out of my bed. There's no trick. You just don't get tempted.

January 1994 straight after my return from Thailand and the police came for me again. This time they made a mistake and I knew they were coming. So at 3 am in the morning I tapped on the car window from which they were watching my parents' home and told them not to call in the morning. I also knew who the police informer was and it was a good friend of mine in business in the pub. I'd been sitting in the middle of a playing field, putting together the police's recent actions in their attempt to chase some cannabis they thought I had coming to me on my return from Thailand. I was asking questions to which I already had the answers to and when I walked with tears in my eyes to the policemen on surveillance. Them being there was my confirmation that I never wanted and I learnt a lot about treachery and deceit that night.

Another relevant consideration that took place this year was my blood count had dropped and the hospital told me they would arrange Disability Living Allowance for me. When I enquired as to why I should be on this benefit because of a cell count, it was to discover that the system regarded me as having a possible life expectancy of six months or less. I felt fine, so I took the money and made use of my free time with regards to holidays, supplemented by funds provided by the distribution of cannabis. I enjoyed it and it's innocuous to people and society and my only other option as I saw it was to rot, remembering society tends to outcasts people with the HIV virus, which is sad and not so innocuous to people and society.

April saw Gail and myself on the Algarve in Portugal, with Allen, his wife and two children staying in some sort of mansion that Allen and his wife had paid for. It was on a Friday night early Saturday morning, Allen and Gail had gone to a night-club alone for a drink. Something happened to me that night that I couldn't explain and between 1-2am I was sitting on the edge of a cliff crying my eyes out. I can remember it being a clear moon lit night and I just sat there staring at the ocean a hundred metres below. All I knew for sure was that I'd lost something precious to myself that night and I knew it wasn't anything to do with Gail, although I felt deceit there. It's a night I'll always remember. I just sat on the edge of this cliff not really caring about anything. In terms of grief I can only compare it with the second time I logged on to the Truth site, but this was loss and I never knew what I'd lost. The ocean seemed so powerful against the cliffs, I knew if I slipped I'd be lost, but I cared little about my perch and just cried. When I returned to England two weeks later I was told that Searan had died in agony on his way to surgery, with a twisted gut. He died at around the same time as I was crying on the cliffs. I didn't believe it at first, I couldn't. I went to his stable and then to his large paddock and called for him but it was another horse grazing. Then I knew it was true and I went to his horse-box and curled up on the floor and cried for the dearest friend I'd ever had. By this time I'd lost a lot of friends, some through incidents, but mostly to Aids, one friend I'd been caring for passed at around the same time as Searan, a few never waited and went on overdoses and death was no stranger to me. I've lost and watched a lot of very close and life long friends pass in some terrible ways. But none have I missed more than Searan. Only recently I pondered that statement though, none have I missed more than Searan, and I found myself asking the question if I could have anyone back, who would it be. I already knew before I started the bottle of scotch it wouldn't be Searan, I just had to drink half the bottle to accept that he was still an animal, God given perhaps, but still a beast. I've never drunk alone since.

That summer saw me in Greece and that winter in Thailand with Gail. By summer though I was aware of how much influence Gail had over myself. And well before Thailand and again in Thailand I'd asked her if she was genuine and told her that if she wasn't, it was better she left me. I told her that she could destroy me if she wasn't true. She said she was and I believed her. We spent most of that year in some sort of fantasy world really. We were in love of that I'm sure and we spent much of our time engrossed in each other. After Greece, Gail's mother took her away for a week to Israel. She seemed different after she returned. That winter we went to Thailand where the relationship dissolved and you tend to know when they're dissolving. In all fairness I will only say six of one and half a dozen of the other. I gave Gail a choice between an adventure holiday in Mexico and the beach in Thailand and I told her if we went to the beach, all we'd be doing would be living on a beach, with the waterfall nearby. No night-time entertainment here, except nature and what you made yourself, which some can be happy with and some are not.

After we returned to England Gail went home to her mothers for a week. She lived on the north east coastal town of Scarborough and told me she was leaving me on her return. I put money in the bank for her and had her car repaired and helped pack her bags over the next week. I was actually very pleased for her, as she seemed to know what she wanted and she was doing it cleanly. After all I was 10 years older and HIV+ and I knew we weren't and we couldn't be forever. When the idea of marriage cropped up. So did the thought of telling her mother and I had an idea which way that would go. I used the time to arrange an air ticket to visit a friend in South Africa for a month. But she came back the next day to tell me she wanted to give it a go and the next four weeks was the best month of our relationship. We took time out with long walks on the moors and planned our future out together. A month later Gail just packed up and left whilst I was out, without warning and has never given me a reason for leaving since. But even though she fled 170 miles (about 250kms) she told that she never knew why she went, but at the same time did not want to finish the relationship, which was the main reason for myself getting so deeply involved in her personal affairs.

I would soon find out that she was trapped. Trapped between her mother's bitterness, a selfish friends head games and the influence of both. She told me she left her hometown because she knew that someone was interfering with her mind and she found herself questioning her sanity. I told her I found two people that were doing such things with her. Gail told me she never knew why she left me as she did, she said she was confused and told me that she spoke to no one. But I found out when the phone bill came through that she'd spoken to her mother immediately before. At this point we were still boyfriend and girlfriend.

I went to Scarborough and whilst staying there I opened up to Gail's best friend John, a short and fairly likeable person (at first very likeable) with a hair lip whom I stayed with and told him all about what was going on. Not knowing that he was the one who liked to play with peoples' minds, and he totally messed mine up over the next two weeks. Whilst I, in turn, had turned to smoking heroin and taking temazepam sleeping tablets. Both of which have a hypnotic effect on a person. He was encouraging me by phone to keep confronting Gail over her mothers' bitterness. I knew it wasn't allowing her to have the relationship she wanted with her father. Her parents were divorced when she was 13 and her mother carries a lot of bitterness over it, which she passes on to her daughter. I actually confronted her mother over it and she never even denied it, as Gail was hers and only hers. Gail and I fell out over it and I gave up after two weeks. I told John I was quitting, to which he said I was doing the best thing and he praised me for giving up and walking away, which was totally contrary to what he'd been saying before then. Up to that point in time I trusted him completely. I was under Gail's influence and she introduced him as a tried and trusted friend, whom she loved, it really can work like this. So I too, took him as a tried and trusted friend and thought, as he loved Gail as a friend, so to would he love me and we both had Gail's best interests at heart, so I thought. It's the only reason I can give for totally trusting him in the first place. But that contradiction set my mind off analysing every piece of information that had passed between us in the form of telephone conversations and would find there way to Gail in my letters. He'd been telling me how strong I was for confronting Gail with her problems and how well I was doing, praising me, what a fool I was. He was an ex-boyfriend of hers who lived only 5 minutes from where she was now living with her mother and it was all driving Gail crazy. I just wanted her to be free to choose whatever path she wanted. I couldn't let her go to be trapped in the nightmare I was feeling for her. I told John when I met him that I meet few men that I regard as equal, meaning that I find most men to be selfish and far less than honest. I also told him that I was HIV+ and a heroin user at the time and I think he passed judgement on me and used me accordingly. He was a part time crisis councillor and read a bit of Freud and he knew what to do to push someone. And whether he knew the full extent of what he was doing or not and I can only believe he did, as he knew the implications of what was happening. He pushed me into a crisis.

To get to the truth behind any situation you must abandon your perception of reality towards the subject matter and start afresh, which I did with Gail. I abandoned my personal relationship with her to investigate the truth behind her problems, but at the same time this destroyed the relationship between Gail and myself due to my confronting her. I abandoned my search for the truth, but the reality that I came back to with regards to Gail, wasn't one I could accept. I started realising what games were being played the night I told John of my intentions of giving up, just before a flight that I'd booked to St. Lucia on very short notice. The flight itself was two days later and Gail and I were now not communicating at all and then I was four thousand miles away. The real pain for myself was in the fact that my love for Gail was and always had been of the purest kind, unselfish, honest. John had torn at this love for his own personal selfish reasons and I felt like someone had not only torn at my flesh and my heart with razors, but I was now 4,000 miles away and just realising the extent of it. I regarded him as nothing less than evil. I left two angry messages on his answering machine, one from Gatwick airport and one from St Lucia on arrival.

He lived in a shared house and I knew all would hear the messages, but I didn't care. I was staying in a guesthouse in Castries, the capital of St. Lucia, a dangerous squalid place. I wrote, I was in crisis and I wrote, I wrote like a mad man, but it was to stop me from going mad. Amongst my writing what I was feeling, I was also writing the concepts of reality and truth as I'd been taught them. On my third or fourth night I found myself fully dressed, curled up on the floor of a cold shower searching my heart and soul for whom I was. As now I was questioning my sanity. I found a gem and I'll call her Bronny and what felt for me a week of unquestionable honesty with a lot of affection and some very sweet memories, and through those memories I found myself again.

I told Gail that no matter where I was in the world that if ever she needed me I'd be there. The next day I brought a ticket for the first London bound plane and the following day I was putting my writings through Gail's front door, behind which she was hiding. For in truth it was as much her fault. I told her what had been going on and she'd rather have seen me go under, than confront what was happening around her and with John, he told me the classic before he locked himself in his house.
"I was only trying to help," he never even denied it. I had a taxi waiting for me, whilst I took some personal therapy out on his new car roof, before coming home to restart my life. Only Gail couldn't cut it clean, as I now had to suffer for her mothers' bitterness and she held on to me until that Christmas, another 8 months. With late night and early morning phone calls often pleas' for help and then soon with monthly visits, as I had my own place by now, during which she indicated that she wanted to return. But I knew she wouldn't and that she had to use me and hurt me, as her mother had been hurt and used by her father and I was weak to her. I told her every visit I expected it to be the last time I'd see her and around Christmas of that year it was, she•left telling me to sort out job vacancies for her and she'd be back next month. She never did return though and I'd find out later that year that she'd already met someone else and was, as I already knew, simply perpetuating what her father inflicted and her mother suffered. I don't know if she's in control of herself or not. I was taught that the eyes don't lie but some do, those that do are often those under the influence of others or sometimes insane and her eyes lied but I'd never regarded her as insane. I haven't heard from her since she rang me last April to wish me a happy birthday I guess. I guess because it was midnight and a female friend who was staying over the night answered the phone to which Gail hang up and has never recalled. I suffered much and learnt a lot about people over this period of my life.

By that Christmas though the TB had unknowingly started to wear me down. And a few months later I would be on what many people thought would be my deathbed. I wrote of the experience in my personal notes at the end of chapter eleven. I was in isolation until the tests discovered whether it was contagious or not, it wasn't. It turned out to be a rare M.A.I form of TB, but the tests took three weeks to come back. All in all the experience lasted about five months. Ever since I've felt a strong compassion to those I know, have suffered this painful affliction, it is not a pain that is easily imaginable. It took days after I was admitted to hospital for it to be diagnosed and 36 hours after my consultant had, I was lying in isolation not even able to move my head for the pain. And the cough, the cough would come and the pain would sting, as did the body cramps that preceded it. I'd find myself hanging out of the bed in agony with blood dripping out of my mouth. Not knowing how I got there, just knowing how much pain it would be to get comfortable again. To just lay back and ask God for that five minutes rest and a cigarette of all things and I'd go happily. I got neither, but I wanted to go anyway, so I searched for Searan and I begged him to come. I called him through the mists of my mind and I found him hoofing the ground and panting, before he went off alone, and I knew it wasn't my time. And yes I learnt the only lesson I could learn from such an experience and that if there's one thing worse than living with regret it is surly dying with it. I already knew how to appreciate life and as my personal notes suggest, my serious spiritual passage was just beginning, without me really knowing I was on it.

Summer 1996 I was recovering well but I was never hiding my status and even though I never believed my illness was HIV related, everyone apart from a friend called Sarah wrote me off as the next to go with Aids, family inclusive. I had this confirmed by one of my young nieces, she was taunting me that I was going to die soon, children too can be cruel and I knew then what sort of conversations my family were having. So I started to feel cut off, as I knew they regarded me as dead already and only one person was honest about this, Mandie who wept when she told me. She couldn't help it and I told her I knew, and I understood, and I also thanked her for her honesty, as I knew that it was affecting her actions towards me. I could feel her backing away and that honesty as painful as it was for her meant so much to myself. You know the worst feeling for myself at this time though. I knew that I'd survive. I felt like I had so much more to do with my life yet at the same time I believed that I'd never know love again, in the way that most take it for granted. A life without love, it was a terrible feeling, knowing it existed, but believing that I'd never feel that same sort of love again. Whilst I improved I watched more of my friends pass me by and die. Hence the fatalistic attitude in October 1996. I was recovering though and without the help of the latest HIV drugs, which clashed with my TB medication. I was alone and have been ever since, but for a while back then I felt lonely and through this period I took to the comfort of smoking heroin on and off. More on until February 97. Anyone that's ever-smoked heroin will tell you how comfortable you can feel with it. I used to describe it as feeling like a big fluffy cloud that comes and smothers you and you'll find yourself submersed in it, whilst losing yourself at the same time. Then at some point that cloud becomes a shroud and you find yourself lost. I needed out of it and I thought of a saying by Confucius to help me. 'The way out is through the door, so why don't you use it' and I went to Paphos to clean up, as I wanted my life back. And I decided it wasn't my fault if no one was ever going to love me like that again but I'd compensate for it. I'd decided I'd compensate for it by simply loving all and everything. I spent a week in Paphos drying out returning on a Thursday and I then spent the next three days supporting someone else's habit, before he planned to stop. I smoked a little of what I was buying for him and listened to him lie, to himself and me for three days before that Sunday came, the day he'd set for quitting and I've never touched heroin since that day, but I've learnt a lot about love.

I shouldn't need to tell you that there is a lot of hypocrisy where drugs are concerned. Opium poppies and opium itself actually originated in Greece and made its way to India with the army of Alexander, being used as a painkiller for surgery, although its other properties were being explored as well. It was then taken to China with Arab traders. I heard a funny thing when I was in Thailand trekking in the Golden Triangle. I asked an opium grower where his harvest went and how it went? We had Laos, one side of us and Burma the other and one straight road south. He told me the lorries came. I asked him what lorries and he asked me if I was stupid and told me the Thai Army lorries came twice a year. It was quite an amusing experience. I can understand why they smoke opium in the jungle. It suits their conditions and is less addictive than heroin, which only took off after opium was declared illegal by the same establishments that had for years, been abusing it for their own gain, namely the British government. Now we've got kids doing 25 years in their cells for our hypocrisy, whilst Generals in countries like that get rich. Both the opium and cocaine markets were initially corrupted and manipulated by establishments like the British government in times past and more recently the CIA, for their own selfish gain. I don't touch either of these substances now and nor have I for a long time. But facts are facts and if people demand it, people are going to be supplying it and that is a simple fact of life. I don't drink much at all, but can I pack up smoking? Not yet and what's the biggest killer. But back to a last point on the drug issue, it's a medical fact that drink does far more damage to the brain and body than a clean daily dose of heroin. And if a person wants to live under a shroud for the rest for their lives, who are we to make such an issue of it and create the problems we have. I can say one thing for certain. The only thing that every drug dealer the world over, would fear totally, as far as their business went is an understanding of this concept by the same establishments that totally prohibit it. I'd say it was more about education, but I find that quite amusing. I can't see why we should need educating on substances that have been used by mankind for thousands of years, so what's the difference. Greed and selfishness encouraged by ignorance, in a society that seems to be telling people it's alright to poison us and the planet on an industrial level, but not our own bodies on a personal level. You think your children are going to grow up being able to relate to that sort of hypocrisy, it's a sad thought.

May 1997 and I woke up one morning with a pain in my stomach as if I'd been punched and the fist was still there. The TB had returned now manifesting itself in the form of two swollen glands, one the size of a grapefruit in my abdomen and the other the size of an apple in my chest, behind my left lung. I went on an immediate 2-week course of painful twice-daily Amakacin injections, which I was told would hold it off for a while. It didn't put me off at all though and I carried on in my personal passage for perfection, within myself in every way possible. I didn't care what happened to my body. My soul was simply going for it.

It was around this time last year that I was laying in bed thinking about my life and as much as I regret very little, I was thinking of how different it could have been. I went to take solace in the idea that we are, all where we are in life, through a number of choices that we'd made earlier in our lives. I found that to be far from true in my case. It was a tearful night for myself but it was a new morning. I've never felt resentment about my life regardless of how bad it got at times. I'd always know that there was someone worse off. The last two years have been a time of great reflection for myself, but at the same time a real joy in many ways. Despite everything, I remember writing to a friend before I went to Cyprus in August last year telling them that I'd found the child again. I've always tried to live my life with the spirit of youth, but this was that little part of me that I put on a shelf so many years ago and I promised myself I'd protect from the world, I knew I would be confronting. That treasured warmth I got from the innocence of that child I knew I once was. I felt like I'd kept it safe and I found it again. I took it down from its shelf, felt and embraced that warmth and I promised myself that I'd keep it this time and protect it with the years of experience that I'd gained, and I'd protect it selfishly against a selfish world. In September last year I wrote to another friend telling her the child had to go away again as the man had a duty to perform, but he's coming out again soon.

Christmas 97 and I had to put my Thai beach break back a month for a two week course of daily infusions of Amakacin. The TB was causing some concern again. I was warned against Thailand by my doctor but went anyway and glad I did in some respects and sad in others. I'd taken a friend from England and paid for Bronny to fly out from Australia to meet me. She'd just written and told me she was lost and helpless and needed to find herself again. So I thought I'd at least help her escape the dominating boyfriend who was making her feel like this and it was all for herself. Whilst there I wanted to test myself with regards to my former heroin problem. I went and sat with those that I knew were smoking it on the beach and I made some talk with them, you could hardly call it a conversation. I felt where they were and when I walked away from them, I knew for sure that it was an addiction I was truly free of. It was a year ago last month. It was a sad year for me as far as the condition of the beach went. The road to the bay was nearly completely concrete and much worse my remote and picturesque waterfall had been bulldozed for another road that really wasn't needed, which broke my heart more than falling out with my best Thai friend. Who I'd known for many years for lying to me and being deceitful in his quest to have sex, with my friend Bronny, no less. I told someone I feel like I'd been in preparation for this duty all my life and when I think about it I know by last Christmas, I was fine tuning what I would need. Someone mockingly challenged me at this time, in the resort restaurant, to write all I knew on two small pieces of paper, each about the size of a cigarette box. I walked away at first before returning, and I then took him up on the challenge, and on one of the pieces of paper I wrote.

Is it what is known.
Or what is seen to be known, that is important.
Or what is.
I know nothing.

Is it not from this basis that we should examine the facts. It was also about this time that I regarded with real seriousness the idea of buying a yacht to slip away from civilisation on. I know many people would like to have such an opportunity and for myself the idea of it was just getting more and more appealing and I promised myself that I would regain my full strength to do just that. Whatever the cost as far as longevity went, to die a free man with nature whenever she called sounded like bliss. It was the effect that I could see humanity having on myself. My own soul and I didn't like it. I considered many of our personal faults to be self-inflicted, and in turn we inflict our faults on others. Reflection and perpetuation, I was giving it some serious consideration on the beach one day, whilst watching the tide and thinking no matter what changes befall the planet because of our selfishness, the tide could never be turned. I was thinking of nature again and in turn our nature, but this time reflection and perpetuation. That night I was treating my friends to a firework display on the beach. At around 3 am someone walked a long way up the beach to tell me I woke him up. I could tell by the way he was walking with his blanket wrapped around him that he was very angry, and when he got to us he was furious, stomping about, so I asked him calmly,

"Why the anger my friend?" he flipped and asked me why I thought. Because I woke him up and so forth, but I knew that couldn't have been the whole reason so

I asked him again, but gently trying to soothe him,

"No, I want to know why have you got so much anger in you?" I was actually concerned so I told him,

"I want you to sit and talk with us and get rid of your anger before you go anywhere."

He flipped, he told me how my body could be found in the bay. The sort of things he could do to me with a knife. Of course I knew the place and although it could happen there I wasn't concerned. I just thought him foolish. So I had four-mortar shell display fireworks left and he told me any more and that was it and I told him I had four more left and that was it. At this point I was starting to feel very disheartened with the world in general. I knew this man was being completely unreasonable. So I waited for him to walk some 300 metres down the beach before lighting two of the mortar shells and he came straight back in a fierce rage. I told my friends who were a few metres behind me, to ignore him and to carry on playing their guitars and singing and to let me deal with it. He walked around me whilst I was on my knees. He was still furious. I think the others were quite pleased to be kept out of it. His words were something like,

"Didn't I warn you! Didn't I tell you! I told you that was it!" so I gently replied with.

"And I told you I had four left and that was it, but now I only have two left and that will be it, but it's not the fireworks that concerns me, it's your anger, why have you got so much anger in you?"

I really wanted to know what had filled a man with such anger, as I knew it couldn't have been the fireworks alone, he'd walked way too far and I just wanted to help him if I could. He flipped again and asked why I thought and hadn't he told me once already. So I gave up on his problems, smiled and asked him, as these were the last two fireworks, wouldn't he like to light them and he got even more angry for my arrogance. He came over to me and took my shirt in one hand and indicated he was holding a knife to my throat in the other. I say indicated, I only felt a finger against my throat. If I felt a blade it might have been different, it might, but I doubt it with the way I was feeling at the time. I looked him in the face and firmly told him to take his hand off my shirt, which he did. I never knew for sure whether there was a knife in his other hand or not and I know how easy it is to cut a throat. Having held a couple of suckling pigs whilst they were done a few years earlier. I knew I wouldn't get to his hand in time to stop him so I thought, if he is holding a knife and he is serious, that's it. Because after everything I'd been through in my life no matter what, I refused to show or feel any fear or rise to his anger, I just refused to let him do it to me, knife or not. I thought about the fact that I might, just might die there and then. I took a deep breath and absorbed the beauty of the full moon over the bay and the tide I'd been watching and I thought about how much I loved the place before the changes, and about my life. I thought about how I'd had a good life in all, taking everything into account, it 's been full of experiences. I tell my friends that death is a place I must pass through to get to where I am going. And at that point in time I really didn't mind passing through and it seemed a fitting place and time. I looked him straight in the eye and gently told him.

"The tide will still come in my friend and little will change."

He flipped. He walked around in circles screaming and shouting and told me to light my bloody fireworks and went back to his bed. A few days later I was talking to a local resort owner that I knew well. It was the same resort where the man was staying and she asked me if I was lighting fireworks a few nights previous on the beach and I said yes. She burst out laughing and told me she thought it had to be me. Then she told me straight off that the man thought I was crazy, before she went on to tell me what she'd been told by him. That he was so angry, he confronted me and put a knife to my throat and on my knees with a knife to my throat, and him being as angry as he was. I simply never showed any fear whatsoever and looked him in the eyes and said something silly to him. He said I had to be crazy. She couldn't stop laughing. I never felt a knife but I knew he was serious though. He apologised to my friends for his anger that night as he had an alcohol problem, he was an alcoholic. But he just gave me a fearful look whenever he saw me and he never spoke to me at all, and actually did think I was crazy and might have been justified in doing so. He was very much afraid of me for showing no fear. It was also about this time and perhaps because of it, that I found myself wishing I could free this planet from humanity. I looked around and I despised us for the way we were treating my true mother.

But still I was perfecting myself, through my love and being as honest with the world and myself as I knew how, and I was enjoying it. I tell my friends that my honesty is my shield and it feels like that, this actually scares some people as well though. And it was this man that Cyprus called. Love can be such a strong force, the strongest in the universe and through it I found my destiny. So many times whilst writing the book I asked the question.

"Why me, why me?"

And every time I was given the answer.

"It's the love you feel."

And I tell people I know how to love. I never expected any of this to happen to myself though, especially this last chapter, but who could have imagined it and even I was led through to this. But I'm full of admiration for that that led me, he's been listening. I thought myself unworthy of such a destiny as far as Cyprus went, but my past life has helped me look at civilisation more objectively. I haven't liked what I've found in general, especially our abuse of nature. I know there are so many good people out there but I decided that even though I felt that no one had the right to judge people. I had to reserve the right to judge how people and society would affect me and I decided to act accordingly. My personal plans for the millennium were to be in South Africa buying that decent sized live-aboard yacht to slip away from civilisation on. And I was well on my way. But Cyprus just seemed to have this effect on myself and I've only recently, learnt why, I had to put that child away again. Over a month ago I attacked my cousin by e-mail. After reading my book chapters 1-14, he made a bad mistake for the time and referred to me as an Englishman. I told him that was no Englishman in those final chapters and not to doubt me and that if I had of been in front of him in 1974, in Cyprus and ten years older, then I would have fought him to the death. I then told him that as his mother didn't like talking about my grandfather and my mother was far less than honest with me. I demanded that he told me how far the gas switch was turned. I shortly after sent him one apologising for my anger and asking him to try understand how I felt, not that I imagine he could. I've never received a response from him. Yet I tore at myself recently. I found myself writing an e-mail that I never sent telling someone I resented using Dimitri my given Greek name, even though I confess to preferring it, as I feel used. Not only did I feel like I had to take a lifetime of abuse in preparation to perform the duty that I truly believe was destined to myself. But I knew that I was in the process of slaughtering myself again, for this same duty, here in this final chapter, for a country that as much as I understand now I will never truly feel akin to, now less than ever. We are talking about a country where if you are HIV positive and have a child, it's likely to make national news. And where possession of 14 grams of cannabis could lead to enquiries with Interpol to see if you're related to organised crime. In a sense I just don't fit in. It's funny I come out just as much in defence of the Greek people and that's a language I just don't speak. I know my cousin said it didn't matter but this is something that I'm likely to be victimised for in Cyprus. Greek is a very hard language to learn. It wasn't meant to be easy, as any Greek teacher will tell you, even after the way it was restructured after it had been degraded so much, as it was under Turkish rule. And Cypriot Greek is even harder to learn having its own very distinct dialect. So I'll always be a 'Charlie' the name given to English bred Cypriots so to speak and I don't see why this book should change that. The basic ignorance of humanity that is, which is reflected in people the world over. I am a Charlie and I'm not ashamed of it. It was Cyprus the country and my forefathers that called me and they were all Greek, even though my own personal heritage is as much British. But even that feels as if it got lost somewhere, for Cyprus. I'll never deny that I feel just as much for Britain and the British people whom I love very much, they are part of my heritage, it is part of who I am and one of the reasons I was in so much turmoil whilst writing the book. I found many reasons why it should not be myself writing it, as much as Cyprus called, my mixed heritage and my past were the main reasons I felt I shouldn't be the one. I'd ask. "How can I be so worthy?" or "How could it be me?" but each time I was given an answer. In my hardest moment when I was writing against those that I'd now call my own people, I was lying in bed crying.

My grandfather came to comfort me and he embraced me with his warmth and I felt his sorrow. He was sad because I was in such turmoil and so he wept, and when I felt his sorrow I told him I understood and I really didn't mind. Not really, as hard as it was, I understood why I had to do what I was doing. As the truth sets us free. The 5th of October I was knocking on the door to the embassy of the T.R.N.C. I sent the letter to Harry Scott Gibbons dated the 14th of October with my personal notes. I was always confused by a paragraph in those notes, written in that deeply emotional state. I could never figure it out completely, until now.

I heard your message grandfather I sought out who you were, I heard your message and I believed, and I wonder if you knew that I would be the one, or did you ever wonder I'd do as well.

I'd soon after feel three and a half thousand years of ancestry and then the one other, but it was the knowing eye that kept me going, I would have possibly destroyed the book if it wasn't for her. My urgency up until then was because I wanted to do anything to embarrass the Cypriot government and stop the missiles, because of the flag I pulled off the rock, with what I felt was a life time of deceit and the occasional presence of my grandfather leading me. I wrote a complete book the likes of which I've never read in my life and all in four months. And even though I knew what was expected of myself for Cyprus with this final chapter, I never thought Cyprus or mankind was worth my excusing myself to, not as a whole. I realised then, why this book is my destiny and I had to write it. And of course it was through no fault of my Cypriot heritage, and just as it is for Cyprus, then so to the world.

I feel I've been guided and touched by the infinite through this and the footsteps were the physical confirmation I needed, I need no more physical signs. By the time I'd finished chapter 14 I was convinced my forefathers had joined me for my duty to Cyprus, but they, like my grandfather were leading me to this point. I should at least tell you how I feel towards God, such an abused word, almost as much as love, or perhaps more, it's your life, you abuse them as you wish. I made a deal with God years ago about the religion bit, although I've never denied Christ. God to myself is nature, but not just our nature. It is the nature of all things if you like. The universe the sun, moon, stars and seas. Everything that crawls and everything that breaths. Of time, what was and what is and what's to be. I guess one way of looking at my yacht dream was that I was going to be closer to God whilst alive in a sense. It's how I feel about nature. It was either the yacht or the Canadian wilderness. But if the Great Spirit is in any way as I imagine him to be, then you can imagine he wouldn't be too impressed with humanity in general. Well, as you know I just wanted to drop out of civilisation completely. But God has been listening and watching and I think I've had to come back to tell you, that Humanity as a whole, is the worst thing to have happened to this planet. Which is sad considering that there is so much good in a lot of people. But after everything else that we've done or are doing to our planet where do we think we are going as far as our establishments and their scientists are concerned. Like it or not we've got to a point where we're now as a race playing God in a sense, and whilst doing so we are taking a chance that there is no God to answer to. So I'll ask you here, how strong is your faith?

Many of us buy our spiritual guidance books although it's not so much the bible that many read now but more books of self-enlightenment, which there is little harm in. And I took much comfort in Jonathon Livingston Seagull by Richard Bach. But the end message is the same, Love, Understanding, Honesty and Compassion, Absolute and Total, for one and all. So what of the Great Spirit, if there is one single spirit, then there must be a Great Spirit. Did we really think that God has abandoned us as it may seem and if he hasn't, isn't it time he acted. Zeki told me that humanity is in the mess it is because we're all self centred and the world is full of demagogues. I'm hardly a demagogue. And if I had one single selfish thought whilst writing this book, it was, that it was taking my mind off the two tumours that are carrying the TB infection. I spent most of the year 1998 on a once weekly hour-long drip. I used to sit in the hospital reading my work whilst the infusion was running. I only came off it a week or two before my last visit to Cyprus in November, the TB's incurable. But it's alright I'm feeling very optimistic about my future, now more than ever.

I went to a night-club last week, it's an occasional pleasure of mine. If there's been one place or time that I've been able to put everything out of my mind whilst writing this book, it has been losing myself in rhythm. But I took a step back last week. I stopped and took a step back and realised where some of this was going, but never quite knew then for sure. I, alongside the youth of today were doing little more than our ancestors were doing tens of thousands of years ago, simply losing ourselves in rhythm. If we look at the scale of things and I am talking the universe and everything else, then, If, there is a God out there, as you will all have to decide for yourselves. Then would you, if you were a loving God of any kind, allow humanity to progress any further without a little cutting back, more than a little I think. Do we really think we'll be allowed to go on to destroy other planets even, with our greed and our selfishness? I know there has been much talk about millennium madness, is it that time? All I can say is something happened to me last summer and this book is an end result, and I will be finishing it as honestly as I started. Even before I knew how this was really ending for me, I'd been telling people that I believed that the same force that made those footprints on Pyrgos bay beach. Can move vast amounts of warm water across oceans and drop comets on the earth and strike us down with epidemics. Not too many people are happy about the finish to my book now but I can only believe in my role in this regardless of whether anyone believes me. Mandie came around to visit me today. When I told her where it was leading she saw it could be possible. When I think about it, I am lucky in having a few true and honest friends. But she's been my closest friend these last 17 years, regardless of how painful that truth is and she lives with a high-ranking police officer now, who is planning his retirement. She doesn't want to live with him but she had a child by him, when he was supposed to be infertile. His luck and her joy are also Mandies chains now, as she can't leave her daughter for the love she feels and I feel so sad for her. As he retires from the force he wants more control of Mandie and has planned the rest of their lives out for them. Not a fitting end for one so giving, but I'm sure it will improve for her as I believe it will for many of us.

There have been so many coincidences that have occurred this past year and I've wondered so many times about them and I know now, that they were all for a reason. It's been two years ago today since I've been clean from heroin. I pulled that shroud away because I wanted my life back and I liked myself no matter what I thought of the world we've created. Those last ten days I was in Cyprus and I was reading the Gibbons book for chapter 13 and 14. I'll say here and now that I wasn't smoking anything but tobacco that whole visit. It's those footsteps in the sand that tell me this whole thing is so real and now more than ever are they my anchor.

The day after I'd been night-clubbing I was sitting with a friend and I spoke about how much my life had changed these past six months, and would further because of the book. After he left, I couldn't help but read a book that I'd not read for a long time, knowing where this was going, as I knew when I started this chapter I would leave you with the child. And I felt a great calm. My first thought was wow! But with a great calm, I asked myself, could this be real? Well I have this book that I've written and all that's happened spiritually along the way and those footsteps on Pyrgos beach telling me it is. It was so strange. Some people have nightmares over this book and all I could feel was a great calm and fear has been a stranger ever since. Could I have been so worthy? I had to ask that question so many times, could I have been so worthy? I've just taken a week out as one of the German hitchhikers from chapter five came to visit me at short notice. It was a nice break and very much needed and during it I realised, it really isn't a question for me to concern myself with. I have been as honest as I can and I can only believe and it all fits in so well. That book read like it was written for and to me in parts, the TB's in there and when the angels aren't off doing deeds to the world, I keep reading about myself in places. It even lures me. It never seemed surprising to me though, just amazing. And who is it that gives out destinies if not God himself and I was lead to this point just like a lamb and a slaughtered one at that. The chosen one was born to Cyprus, for this book and now more than ever do I believe my life was in preparation for this duty. I'm truly impressed. I've had months of strange occurrences, this book and a miracle on Pyrgos bay to prepare me for this. And you've had the time it's taken you to read this book. I wrote this for all the right reasons and is it not what we do, but why we do any deed that truly matters. I've been led to this point and what unfolds as a result is not my problem, which is another reason why I'm a lamb I guess. Now I feel so thankful for the life I've been given. As I said I feel very optimistic about the future now. So I'll ask you again, how strong is your faith? No one could have read that book like I did. And when I went back to read it again and again I know that I make my entrance in chapter five and that I've read about myself and the Gibbons book in a prophecy written on the Greek Island of Patmos nearly two thousand years ago. In the Greek language no less. I know I'm not wrong, although I imagine it would be the preference of many of you. I wrote the preface before I read the book and as it was then, so it is now, my destiny. In fact none of the book has been altered since I started this chapter, except for one paragraph about the Ilhan massacre. Three days at least they rotted in that bath and I couldn't believe any race could be so sinister and sick to there own, and now I know why. It's in their nature. But that's been the only alteration. I even wrote the Socrates quote before reading the book, but after knowing that I'd leave you with the child, as I said this has all been so real for myself and it actually makes so much sense now. I'll let the theologians argue it out, which is why I gave my birth time and my placing as much detail as I could in this final chapter, although I know there are many that are expecting me, stand firm the faithful, for the time is at hand. The living God has granted me a gift and a life I could never have expected. We should all give thanks for the events I believe we are about to witness being unleashed on our planet, but few will welcome my words, as they will the day of judgement. Whoever you are and whatever your status in this life, there is a force coming to cast judgement on all, it is near, so the question for you to ask yourself is, what will your future bring now?

Who am I? I am no one, but I've been given a voice. I've got my footsteps in the sand and this book to tell me how real this has been and I know it had to be myself, to bring you the child. I feel I've been used but I've done my part and my destiny I accept graciously, despite my final role. I told Miss Dorak of the T.R.N.C in my first letter to her that I was simply soul searching. Such a deep soul I found I had. Being a Muslim I think she should read The New Testament, last book at least to understand what I am saying. But here I must make a point for all to know and hear, it is, as we all know our faith that matters and that whoever we call our God, there is but one God. Why Cyprus? A faithful Eastern Orthodox country of a half a million people and why Turkey? I think my book's said as much about that, but have a look and see it's written and a mystery is solved, and as we know who we were, so to, do we know who we are, try applying that to humanity.

We forgot something important as a race, although I look around and I know many are ready and will rejoice at what is to come before man. What made us think we could move so fast forward as we are and control what we are doing as a race when we can't even control ourselves. Our own selfishness and our own greed, which few of us are honest about. And whilst we ignore this the innocent suffer and our mother earth is dying, as we race to escape from it. And we lose our feelings for these same things, through our helplessness. I think much of the human race got lost somewhere and now I've been given a reason to believe, even if it's so I never get lost and I can only believe.

I write these final words on the 9th of March 1999, one of my return visits to the book for entries that need to be made. As I wrote, it's not a book the likes of which I've read before. I started packing boxes today. I can see two that might get filled. I'm preparing to vacate what has been my home this last four years. Few can comprehend what I may be feeling. I went to visit my parents today and spoke to my mother about the consequences of my writing this book on her and my father, telling them they might be better off in Cyprus and I have my own path to take. My mother suggested that I change my name for the book, I tried to explain that I wouldn't and couldn't and I tried to tell her the personal importance. But again as an alternative to her and my father taking action it was suggested that I change my name for the book. So I told my mother about the book, not that I hadn't already and how it involved my grandfather and myself and I had to use my own name. I also told her that I knew she'd been less than honest with me about my grandfather and she denied it. Everyone else is less than honest except for my mother according to her, and even when confronted with a case of six of one and half a dozen of another, she is seldom wrong, as in this case. She told me that she doesn't lie to me, as she has told me before, but even then she was lying. It was in relation to my first pet, a faithful dog who it was claimed had run away when I was seven or eight. I found out a few months later it was destroyed for nipping a cousin who approached it whilst eating. Such lies were I brought up with and only now do I know why I'm so different. I feel some sorrow at saying goodbye to my parents, but I stand alone before God. We spoke of my grandfather and I found out I was wrong about the year of his death. It was 1966. Why I so strongly believed that it was 1968 I don't know, but when it was confirmed by my father my heart sunk further and my anger rose, the Akritas plan. I couldn't work out why if my grandfather and I were so close it took me until I was six to learn up to Ipsilon, but I wasn't six, I was four and my grandfather was my only tutor. I thought I'd finished this book, I thought, but I wasn't certain as I've been getting signs right through writing this. Why this final twist if not to leave me with anger in my heart for the lies that were told. The twisted lies that my grandfather would have believed. The one other was

Archbishop Makarios the third. But they all want justice as do many others, and the day has come. I'm amazed at how this has turned out for myself and I give thanks to God from the child before man, for the power he has given me, and I in turn, stand his servant to command, but it's the child that I'll leave you with.

He was a solitary child. But he loved to read. He always had a very high reading age and would make the most of it and considered the full set of The Encyclopaedia Britannica his parents had acquired as much of a blessing as the bible that was always lying around. And with his thirst for knowledge he would often lose himself in these books. He was a wise child in other ways as well. During this time there was another man that showed the child kindness, Uncle Tom. Uncle Tom was a warm and playful man, he had married a local woman with four children of her own, that the child used to play with. He was a Colonel in the U.S. Air Force. A navigator on Phantoms at the nearby U.S. air force base. And he would take the child to sit and play with the pilots and the airmen in the officers' mess. They knew how to make a child happy. Uncle Tom would always bring the child back some piece of kit or a souvenir from Vietnam whenever he'd return from there. It was the gift factor that mattered. The child knew of the conflict in Vietnam. And he knew that it wasn't evil men dropping the napalm and the cluster bombs that he'd watch being unleashed on the television, but the machine, and he'd just wonder at the ways of the world. After his grandfather passed on the child turned to the bible and for a long time took pleasure in the scriptures of Jesus Christ. Then one day he realised the book of Revelations was different, a day of judgement. The child read the book and liked what he read, and when he looked at the world around him, he asked.

"How long?"

He was sitting on the stairs one afternoon. The house was empty and the lights were off. And on the darkened staircase the child sat with his knees up and his head resting on his folded arms, as he thought about the day of judgement of which he'd read and he knew that he'd want to be a part of it. He looked up to God and he knew that if God listened to anyone, he listened to children. So he asked God, not earnestly as some may ask of God, but as a grandchild to his grandfather, he asked,

"Please, please let me return as one of the four horsemen of the Apocalypse,
                                        Let me return! And call me War!"

Final Note:

One day after my return from Cyprus on the 19th of April 1999 and one week before the book went to print I was arrested at Peterborough Passport office on charges of attempting to obtain property by deceit Namely one British Passport in another name. I will appear before Peterborough Magistrates Court on the 19th of May 1999 and my mitigating circumstances will be that I was acting under the command of the Highest. As I wrote. I can only believe.